THOMAS WOOLNER, R.A.

THOMAS WOOLNER
From a drawing by D. G. Rossetti, 1852, in the possession of Miss Orme.

THOMAS WOOLNER, R.A.

SCULPTOR AND POET

HIS LIFE IN LETTERS

WRITTEN BY HIS DAUGHTER
AMY WOOLNER

AMS PRESS
NEW YORK

Reprinted from the edition of 1917, London

First AMS EDITION published 1971

Manufactured in the United States of America

International Standard Book Number: 0-404-07030-2

Library of Congress Number: 70-158614

AMS PRESS INC.

NEW YORK, N.Y. 10003

TO

MY SISTERS

I DEDICATE

THIS LIFE OF THEIR FATHER

WORK

Why has no religion this command before all others:
Thou shalt work?

.   .   .   .

See, my hands are rough with work—I have not
merely raised them in prayer.

It is well for me that I can work.

It is not joy nor repose which is the aim of life. It
is work, or there is no aim at all.

.   .   .   .

T. Woolner.

PREFACE

A LIFE of Thomas Woolner has been long in contemplation and preparation, but many reasons and difficulties
have come in the way of its realization. First and fore-
most is the desire to plainly and truthfully demonstrate
the great industry, thoroughness and pure ideals of the
Sculptor—and to show the admiration in which he was
held by so large a number of eminent men of his day.

This record of a life's work has been compiled from
personal knowledge, autograph letters, MSS. and diaries,
most of which are in my keeping. I have received the
greatest courtesy and kindest response from almost every
one written to for permission to publish letters. And my
special thanks are due to Hallam Lord Tennyson for
permission to publish and for kindly help; to Mrs. Coventry
Patmore and Mrs. Allingham for advice and suggestions;
and to Mr. H. N. Gladstone, Mr. William M. Rossetti,
Mr. Alexander Carlyle, Miss Froude, Miss Boyd, to my
sisters for their help, and many others for permission to
publish.

Besides these my thanks are tendered to Messrs. Smith,
Elder & Co., for permission to print the letters of Robert
Browning; to Messrs. Macmillan for the permit to include
in this memoir " A Sea Story "; and to the Proprietors
of *Punch* for special permission to reprint the verses of
November 12, 1859.

AMY WOOLNER.

INTRODUCTION

It may interest some who have not had the opportunity
of studying the sculptor's art and methods to learn how
he proceeds. Woolner—and probably this is the way with
most sculptors—made a rough pencil sketch of his subject.
If an imaginative work or a statue, a small clay model-
sketch was made and cast in plaster of Paris, and when
approved of by those who gave the commission, he set
to work on the large clay model. For a statue a rough
frame was erected and the clay stuck on in large masses
by one of the studio men, roughly indicating the form :
when the sculptor had worked on it himself, and it was
finished up to the point of perfection he considered necessary,
the model was cast in plaster, an intricate business, the
plaster cast was cleaned up, the seams removed, and any
little blemishes caused by air-holes filled up—and the
work would be ready to be sent to the foundry to be cast
in bronze or to be carved in marble. The block was first
hewn into a rough shape, then " pointed " (a mechanical
process) by a skilled mason, who brought the work to a
close resemblance to the original, when Woolner would
begin to carve it himself, so that the surfaces of all his
marble sculptures show the work of his own hand.

CONTENTS

CHAPTER I

PAGE

Birth—Youth—Early works—Association with the P.R.B.—First medallions of Tennyson and Carlyle—" The Germ "—Wordsworth medallion in Grasmere Church—Tennyson's letter on its epitaph—Wordsworth Memorial competition—Sails for Australian gold-fields 1852   1

CHAPTER II

Letter to his father on board *The Windsor*—Arrival at Port Phillip —Goes to Melbourne—Dr. Godfrey Howitt—Journal of the gold-fields—Letters to and from England—D. G. Rossetti— F. G. Stephens   15

CHAPTER III

Sea Story—Returns to England—Log on *Queen of the South*— Arrival in England, 1854—The Australian medallions—His early friends   74

CHAPTER IV

Letters to and from Mrs. Tennyson from October, 1854, to August, 1856   104

CHAPTER V

Letters from Sir John Simeon, James Spedding, William Allingham, Vernon Lushington, Robert Browning, W. B. Scott, D. G. Rossetti and Mrs. Tennyson—Woolner's letters to Mrs. Tennyson, W. M. Rossetti and Mrs. Patmore   117

CHAPTER VI

Letters from Vernon Lushington, W. B. Scott, Mrs. Tennyson, Hallam Tennyson, Mrs. Carlyle and T. Palgrave—James Spedding—Woolner's letters to Mrs. Tennyson, 1858–59 .   140

CHAPTER VII

Letter from T. Carlyle—Hogarth Club—Dr. Hooker—Letters to and from Mrs. Tennyson   164

CHAPTER VIII

Letters from Vernon Lushington, Mrs. Tennyson, Edmund W. Lushington—Correspondence about Tennyson Bust for Trinity Cambridge—Letters to Mrs. Tennyson—*Punch* poem on Bust at Trinity, 1859   173

CONTENTS

CHAPTER IX

PAGE

Letters to and from Mrs. Tennyson—Professor Sedgwick—Edward
Lear and Mrs. Combe—Sedgwick and Hooker Busts . . . 181

CHAPTER X

Letters to and from Mrs. Tennyson—Letters from Browning, Lear,
Dr. Montagu Butler, Mrs. Carlyle's letter on her cat—J. A.
Froude—Letters to Coventry Patmore and F. T. Palgrave . 193

CHAPTER XI

"Enoch Arden" 208

CHAPTER XII

Letters to and from Mrs. Tennyson—Browning writes stanza on
Woolner's group "Constance and Arthur"—Letters from
Mrs. Carlyle, Professor Sedgwick, Thomas Carlyle, Sir John
Simeon (Godley Statue) and Dr. Montagu Butler—"Aylmer's
Field" or "The Sermon," 1862—Letter to F. T. Palgrave . 215

CHAPTER XIII

Thomas Carlyle and Woolner hear Dickens read—The decorations
for New Assize Courts, Manchester—Letters to and from C.
Patmore ("My Beautiful Lady")—Letters from Allingham,
Browning, Mr. and Mrs. Combe—First Gladstone Bust—
Letters to and from W. E. Gladstone—Visit to Hawarden—
Letters to and from Mrs. Tennyson—Haehnel's Wild Boar . 232

CHAPTER XIV

Letters from H. N. Gladstone and Carlyle—Engagement—Congratulations—Marriage, 1864—Letters to and from Mrs. Tennyson
—Letter from Mrs. Carlyle 246

CHAPTER XV

Woolner and his studio men: Jimmy Holland, Woodington and
the "Old Temeraire"—Letters to W. E. Gladstone, Allingham, F. T. Palgrave and Mrs. Tennyson—Letters from Mrs.
Carlyle, Thomas Combe, W. E. Gladstone, Allingham, J. H.
Newman and F. T. Palgrave 260

CHAPTER XVI

Letters from Gifford Palgrave, Edward Fitzgerald, Mrs. Combe,
F. T. Palgrave, Dr. Hooker—His picture-collecting—Letters
from Charles Darwin ("Woolnerian tip"), Edward Lear,
Edward Fitzgerald—Letters to and from Mrs. Tennyson . . 277

CHAPTER XVII

Elected Associate of the Royal Academy, 1871—Lord Lawrence
statue—His works at the Royal Academy—Letter from
Mrs. Tennyson, 1872—Cranesden—Letter to V. Lushington on
the death of his father—Letter from J. A. Froude—Letters to
and from John Frederick Lewis, R.A.—Captain Cook statue
and correspondence thereon 289

CONTENTS

CHAPTER XVIII

PAGE

Letters to and from J. F. Lewis, R.A.—Bluecoat Boy Group—
Portrait by Alphonse Legros—Visit to Italy—Elected a Royal
Academician, 1874—Letter from J. A. Froude (Reredos)—
Kingsley bust for Westminster Abbey—Letters from Mrs.
Kingsley—Letter to F. T. Palgrave (Flaxman drawings)—
The bearded marble bust of Tennyson—Elected Professor of
Sculpture—"Godiva"—Letters from William Allingham and
his Sonnet on Captain Cook 299

CHAPTER XIX

W Aldis Wright, visit to Cranesden—Letters about the poem
"Pygmalion" from W. A. Wright, Cardinal Newman and
W. E. Gladstone—Urban Club—Speech on Shakespeare—
"Our Club"—and other clubs—Anecdotes 309

CHAPTER XX

Letters to and from W. E. Gladstone—Busts of English Premiers
for Sydney—Death of his son Geoffrey, 1882—Letter from
W. M. Rossetti—Drawing of his brother—Letters to and from
W. E. Gladstone—Guildhall bust—Letters to and from C.
Patmore—Cruise around Irish coast, 1884—Cruise to the
North Cape with Sir Donald Currie—Letter from Cardinal
Newman on "Silenus"—Sir Frederick Weld and the statue
of Sir Stamford Raffles—House in Sussex—Letters from W. B.
Scott, W. Aldis Wright, Dr. Montagu Butler—Honorary Free-
dom of the Salters' Company, 1891—Last work, "The House-
maid"—Illness—Death, 1892—His family life—Appreciation by
J. Callander Ross 320

List of Works 336

List of Writings 346

Index 347

LIST OF ILLUSTRATIONS

PORTRAIT OF THOMAS WOOLNER, BY D. G. ROSSETTI, 1852   *Frontispiece*

To face page

PORTRAIT OF FATHER OF T. WOOLNER, 1842 7

T. WOOLNER AS MR. B——'S TYGER 14

" PUCK " 21

DESIGN FOR WORDSWORTH MONUMENT, 1852 28

MEDALLION OF W. C. WENTWORTH, 1854 35

MEDALLION OF ALFRED TENNYSON, 1856 42

MEDALLION OF ROBERT BROWNING, 1856 49

STATUE OF BACON, 1857 56

ST. JOHN : MOSES. (Designs for pulpit of Llandaff Cathedral) . 63

BUST OF ALFRED TENNYSON, 1857 (Collotype) 70

BUST OF PROFESSOR SEDGWICK 77

MODEL SKETCH FOR CAWNPORE MEMORIAL 84

DRAWING OF PIPING SHEPHERD. (Frontispiece to " Golden Treasury ") 90

CONSTANCE AND ARTHUR, OR DEAF AND DUMB, 1862 . . . 95

SPECIMEN OF WOOLNER'S HANDWRITING 100

TASSIE MEDALLION OF DR. ALEXANDER WAUGH 107

PORTRAIT OF ALICE GERTRUDE WOOLNER, BY ARTHUR HUGHES . 113

THE SCULPTOR AMONG HIS MEN 119

HEAVENLY WELCOME, PEEL MONUMENT (Collotype,) . . . 126

BUST OF DR. JOHN HENRY NEWMAN 134

THE LORD'S PRAYER, TREVELYAN GROUP (Collotype,) . . . 142

VIRGILIA (Alto-relief) 150

" ACHILLES SHOUTING FROM THE TRENCHES " (Bas-relief in Bodleian) 157

IN MEMORIAM, 1870 164

IN MEMORIAM G. B. 171

GUINIVERE 178

CRANESDEN 185

FEEDING THE HUNGRY (Bas-relief on Wigton Fountain) . . 193

HEAD OF OPHELIA 200

MONUMENT TO MRS. ANTHONY FROUDE 207

THE LISTENING BOY 213

To face page

The Bluecoat Boy Group 219

Statue of Lord Lawrence 229

Bearded Bust of Alfred Tennyson, 1876 237

The Crucifixion—Reredos 244

Bust of Charles Kingsley 252

Sir Cowasjee Jehanghir Readymoney (Marble Statue, Bombay, 1876) 259

Portrait of Thomas Woolner, 1877 266

Godiva. Marble Statue (Collotype) 273

Captain Cook (Colossal Statue, 1878) 280

Bust of Right Hon. W. E. Gladstone, 1883 287

Dorothy (Marble Medallion, 1883) 292

Alice Gertrude Woolner (Medallion, 1883) 299

The Water Lily (Alto-relief, 1884) 306

Sir Stamford Raffles (Colossal Statue, Bronze, 1887) . . . 313

T. Woolner in his Studio 325

The Housemaid (Life-size Bronze Statue, 1892) 332

THOMAS WOOLNER, R.A.

CHAPTER I

THOMAS WOOLNER [1] the sculptor was born at Hadleigh
in Suffolk on December 17, in the year 1825. There is
little to say of his early childhood and youth, but a few
anecdotes are told of him. When a very small boy he
slept in a little bed in the room of his grandfather and
grandmother. He remembered distinctly the flowered
nightshirt he wore, and how he used to collect beetles and
grasshoppers in the daytime and fill his jacket pockets
with them, and at night they would escape and make
strange noises and clickings in the room and rouse the old
grandparents, who with much trouble would light a candle

---

[1] The name Woolner is of Anglo-Saxon origin from Ulnod, Woolnough
being the modern way of spelling the name. Ulnod or Woolnough was a
freeman in the time of Edward the Confessor—indeed, there were several
freemen of that name holding lands in Suffolk, mentioned in the Suffolk
Domesday. Ulnod or Ulnoth, Wulfnoth, Woolnoth are the same name
becoming in later times Woolnough, changed into Woolner by the great-
grandfather of Thomas Woolner, the sculptor. His great-grandfather
went to India in the service of the East India Company; when he returned,
after some years, he found his brother had treated him badly with regard
to some land he had; he was so indignant that he altered the spelling of
his name from " nough " to "ner," to be different from his brother. This
man's son, the sculptor's grandfather, fought in the Peninsular War; he
held a breach for a short time against a number of the enemy; his bravery
was noticed by the Duke of Richmond, who said : " A Woolner shall
never ask a favour of a Lennox and be refused ! " This promise was
redeemed later on when Thomas Woolner's father asked the then Duke
of Richmond for an appointment, which was given him. The sculptor's
father was a very handsome man, and his brilliant dark eyes bore evidence
of the Spanish blood in the family, through the marriage, some generations
back, of a Woolner to a lovely Irish girl, Mary Castlereagh, whose far-
away ancestor was a Spaniard, from the Spanish Armada, washed ashore
after the vessels had been wrecked on the Irish coast. And, oddly enough,
from that day to this there has always been, with one small break, a
Mary in the family.

B

by aid of a tinder-box, and he recollected the sound of
the tinder striking and the old folk saying : " It's that
Tom again with his grasshoppers and insects ! "

He was also very fond of catching butterflies of all
kinds, nipping a tiny bit out of their wings and letting
them fly away again, and he used to recognize with pride
his butterflies all around the country-side. From his earliest
youth upwards Woolner was a great lover and observer
of nature, as are most true artists and poets.

Of his childhood there is little more to tell, but if one
may judge by the exquisitely neatly written school copy-
books, still preserved, he must have been a promising
scholar. He was very dainty in his care of things, and
disliked to see furniture scratched or china cracked. He
made a collection of china in later days, and would never
knowingly buy a specimen if cracked or mended.

Woolner received his first education near Ipswich, up
to the age of ten, and afterwards at a boarding school at
Brixton; but when his father and the family settled in
London he was taken from Brixton and used to go to a
day school near Stanhope Street, afterwards called Mary
Street. When he was about thirteen years old he was
sent to Behnes the painter to study; his father was not
very sympathetic about his son's artistic aspirations, and
it was his stepmother who really helped him to attain
his object and herself paid the initial expenses.

The painter unfortunately soon died, but young Woolner
showed such decided talent that the well-known sculptor
William Behnes, brother of the painter, took him as a
pupil. He became a favourite with his master, who
showed great interest in him and thoroughly taught him
all the technical part of a sculptor's education. Woolner
stayed with Behnes for six years and carved for him
later on.

During his apprenticeship he had an amusing experience.
One day when left in charge by Behnes, who was then at
work on his statue of " Godiva " (a nude figure on a horse
with a piece of drapery falling over one foot), a city magnate
came to see the statue—and walked round it several times

and began counting the fingers on each hand thus :
" One, two, three, four, five, right ! One, two, three,
four, five, right ! " And then the toes were likewise counted ;
but one foot having the drapery over it, he said : " One,
two, three, but where are the others ? " Upon being
shown they were hidden by a fold in the drapery he was
satisfied, and turning to young Woolner said : " Tell him
it's perfect ! "

The young student was so devoted to his teacher that
an artist as a joke made a caricature of him as Mr. B——'s
Tyger.

Woolner carved for the master Behnes for some years,
and it was at his suggestion he became a student at the
Royal Academy Schools, which he entered on December 16,
1842, the day before his seventeenth birthday. He worked
so well and diligently he was able to send the next year,
1843, a model group of " Eleanor sucking the poison from
Prince Edward's wound " to the Royal Academy, where
it was exhibited.

In 1844, he exhibited in Westminster Hall an ambitious
life-sized group of the " Death of Boadicea," a dramatic
piece of sculpture mentioned in the *Athenæum* of the time,
from which paper the following extract is taken :—

" Exhibition at Westminster Hall. — In mentioning
Mr. Henning's ' Boadicea ' we should not have forgotten
the good word due to Mr. Thomas Woolner's ' Death
of Boadicea ' (154). This, like Mr. Henning's, is a fine
group. The dying queen, mastered by the anguish of
the hour, lies like a royal martyr in the arms that
sustain her. There is great force of hand here ; suffering,
moral and physical, are powerfully expressed. The
treatment is highly dramatic and the language of its
drama is pure sculpture."

Woolner was hardly nineteen at the time. This group
was on show at the Coliseum, Regent's Park. Woolner
wished to break it up, but a man begged leave to take it
away, and what afterwards became of it is not known.
There is no photograph of it nor any model sketch. In
1845, Woolner won the silver medal of the Society of Arts

for an original design, a bas-relief entitled " Affection."
This medal is still preserved.

When nineteen Woolner began his figure of " Puck,"
but it was not exhibited in the British Institution until
1847.

This little figure (twice cast in bronze—once for Louisa
Lady Ashburton in 1866 and exhibited at the Royal
Academy, and once again for Sir John Bland-Sutton in
1908) is one of Woolner's most admired and attractive
earlier works.

The following short description of it cannot be improved
on : " The sprite stands on a toadstool. A snake is
stealthily creeping towards an unconscious toad. Puck is
about to touch the toad with his foot, that thus warned
it may escape the jaws of the enemy. A smile of half
mischievous satisfaction is on his face."

Between the time of beginning his " Puck " and its
completion in 1847, Woolner modelled a bas-relief
" Alastor," and also sent a medallion portrait to the Royal
Academy in 1846. In 1847 his " Puck " was exhibited
at the British Institution ; and he modelled a little group,
" Feeding the Hungry," a pretty design of a small child
and chickens. The little fellow seated has his hand raised
dropping grain to the expectant chicks below; this was
exhibited at the Royal Academy the same year.

His first introduction to the Pre-Raphaelite Brotherhood
took place about this time : most of whose members sooner
or later became his friends, some remained so till his
death. Dante Gabriel Rossetti was the first of these, and
Woolner and he soon struck up a friendship; the sculptor
shortly after becoming acquainted with him joined the
Brotherhood and was one of the original seven, the others
being D. G. Rossetti, W. Holman-Hunt, F. G. Stephens,
J. E. Millais, J. Collinson, and W. M. Rossetti, the
Secretary to the Brotherhood of the little group of earnest
young men bent on regenerating Art. They were full of
the most honest enthusiasm, and their real affection for
each other and the active steps they took to advance one
another's fortunes will ever remain a pleasant record of

the early feelings and actions of these young artists. In those days men had time to write long affectionate letters from the heart, entering with genuine and lively interest into the affairs of business and pleasure of their artistic brethren. The letters that follow later will speak for themselves. In 1848 Woolner exhibited his " Eros and Euphrosyne," a graceful group, the little Eros perched on the nymph's shoulder is tenderly kissing her upturned face. It was reproduced by Wedgwood in black jasper, and from the unusual length of the limbs was called by the workmen at Etruria " Lanky Nan ! " He also modelled and exhibited at the Royal Academy a bas-relief, " The Rainbow." This design was afterwards reduced and carved as a cameo, but was never executed in marble or cast in bronze.

Woolner sent to the British Institution, 1848, another ideal group: " Titania caressing the Indian Boy "; all these works being designed and modelled before he came in touch with the Pre-Raphaelites, and while still working more or less for Behnes. His first studio, during the latter years of his apprenticeship, was a very modest place, little more than a barn : a shed, in fact, at the end of a yard in which grew two lilacs and a laburnum tree ; in the wall was a mountain ash. Laburnum and lilac were ever favourites of his. The studio had shelves all round and big tables and benches, and an old man used to come in to beat up the clay for the young sculptor.

He next took the Stanhope Street Studio, where the Pre-Raphaelites used to meet, smoke and have tea, discussing the Art and Poetry of the day. They were great admirers of Tennyson, Browning and Patmore; and the following letter from Rossetti shows the keenness of his interest in Browning.

Sunday night,
November 1848.

DEAR WOOLNER,
    I have just heard of something which will probably take me from the study to-morrow night, but which nevertheless, I hope, will not deprive me of your company. As

thus. I am told that to-morrow is to be the first night at
Sadler's Wells Theatre, of Browning's "Blot in the
'Scutcheon." I think you do not know this play. It is a
most wonderful production, and possessed moreover of
that real, intrinsic, and unconventional purity which
never fails to excite the moral execration of the enlightened
Briton. It was acted for 3 or 4 nights at Covent Garden,
under Macready's management, amidst a shower of hisses
and puritanical anathemas. Its reception this time, however, will not probably be so violent, as I suspect that
virtue is less sensitive at Islington. I suppose the less
said of the acting will prove to be the soonest mended;
but of course I must be there, as the great author may
be visible. Of course William will go [if back by then]
and I believe Hunt also. We will therefore call on you
at ½ past 5 or a little before 6 o'clk in the hope that
you will accompany us. You need not trouble yourself
to let us know before hand, as it is almost in our way to
the theatre. . . .

> Your sincere friend,
> GABRIEL DANTE ROSSETTI.

To-day being Sunday, I presume that Prometheus &
Orpheus (persons I fear not much addicted to the established church) have proceeded with the instruction of
their respective classes in reading and music. St. Ann
put on a red hood to-day, and Rienzi indulged in a white
stocking.

In the year 1848 Woolner went for a short time to Paris;
this was his first visit to the Continent. While in Paris he
saw the painter Ingles, for whose art he had then and
always the greatest admiration. The passport for this
journey is still preserved and gives a strangely inaccurate
description of his personal appearance, stating his eyes
were blue : they were dark brown, his eyebrows and eye-
lashes were dark—his hair a beautiful chestnut colour.

During the next years—1849, 1850 and 1851—Woolner
worked hard for a livelihood at portrait medallions. One
of these was of the poet Coventry Patmore, who was introduced to the Brotherhood by Woolner. He greatly admired Patmore's poetry, and sent him a cast of his " Puck "

[*Photograph by H. Dixon.*

THOMAS WOOLNER, FATHER OF THE SCULPTOR
From a drawing by T. Woolner, 1842, in the possession of Mrs. Meadows.

[*To face page* 7.

as an expression of his admiration. The following letter is the poet's acknowledgment—

Coventry Patmore to Thomas Woolner

19, *Randolph Street,*
April 20 [1849.]

MY DEAR SIR,

Pray receive my best thanks for your " Puck." I know that I am not a competent judge of its merits, but I know also that it gives me very true pleasure, entirely apart from the pleasure it gives me as the gift of so sincere an admirer of my own efforts in art. I will not run the risk of making you doubt the satisfaction I take in contemplating your work by endeavouring to analyse my enjoyment. I was charmed, when the man uncovered your present, to find that it was the product of a grotesque fancy in harmony with the modern mind, instead of being an attempt at that kind of beauty in which it seems to me, we can scarcely hope to compare with the Greeks. Being constantly haunted with the idea of Greek sculpture whenever I visit an exhibition of modern art in the same kind, you cannot think what a strange impression of vapidness and impotence I receive on such occasions. But your little production quite satisfies and pleases me, for it is the best in its kind that I have seen—at least, such is my uneducated judgment of it. I feel confident that your work will grow upon me : I write late at night, and I like it now three times as much as I did at the beginning of the evening—and I liked it then.

Be so kind as to drop me a line a day or two before you are coming, as I am just now often engaged out of an evening, and I should not like you to call and find me away.

Believe, my dear Sir,
Very truly yours
Coventry K. Patmore.

T. Woolner, Esq.

Woolner spent part of the autumn of 1849 down at Great Marlow, and revelled in the beauty of the country after being shut up in London.

LETTER FROM T. WOOLNER TO WILLIAM ROSSETTI AT VENTNOR

> *Mr. Hobbes,*
> *" George & Dragon,"*
> *near Suspension Bridge,*
> *Gt. Marlow,*
> *October 2, 1849.*

MY DEAR POET,

I am in the country at last and a most glorious country it is; I took a walk this morning amidst the most delightful scene I ever witnessed. Gigantic juniper trees with most quaint aspects, grand old white thorns clambered over with woodbine & deadly nightshade,[1] fern red and green, forests thick with trees & underwood extending for many miles, and as solemn as even a poet could wish. I should like you to be here and see all this beauty. . . . Remember this is the country of the divine Shelley : I met an old gentleman yesterday who knew him, he says he once met Shelley coming from an adjacent wood with his hat surrounded by some sort of weed resembling ivy; I dare say Shelley thought if no one else would crown him he would crown himself. I will not say a word about business. . . . I am down here for pleasure.

THOMAS WOOLNER.

W. M. ROSSETTI ℞

The extract from the next letter to W. Rossetti, written the same autumn, is evidenttly in answer to requests for more information about the poet Shelley—

> *Gt. Marlow.*
> *[Autumn, 1849.]*

I am sorry to say I can get no information about the Divine [Shelley]. I only hear he was always reading large books, and walking in a large wood near here, in which I often walk on purpose to think about Shelley. Such a wood, Mon Dieu ! without exception the finest wood I was ever in, filled with the most delightful breaks, thro' which you see the placid river gliding along " like a sweet thought in a dream." This is as true as possible & not mere poetry (the quotation I mean). The leaves are as tender

---

[1] This is an error. Probably what he meant was the woody nightshade (*Solanum dulcamara*).

as the first flush of spring shows them, in consequence of the thickness of foliage.

THOMAS WOOLNER.

Woolner was not quite twenty-four at this time—his love of the country was always great, and he is continually regretting in later days being obliged to live in London,[1] although he realized it was necessary for a Sculptor. Two lines from his own poem express his feeling—

> " It makes them quit a happy sylvan life
> For contest in the roaring capital."
> *My Beautiful Lady.*

Woolner modelled a medallion of the wife of Coventry Patmore (" The Angel ") in 1850, and the poet wrote : " The more I look at your medallion of my wife the more I admire it and the more I feel the great obligation you have put me under in doing it."

In January, 1850, was published the first number of a magazine of high ideals called *The Germ*, brought out by the members of the P.R.B. It had but a brief career—only four numbers being issued. In the first number some of the chief contributions were " My Beautiful Lady," " My Lady in Death," by Woolner, with a very remarkable frontispiece to illustrate the poem by W. Holman Hunt. Woolner also wrote two short poems for the magazine.

Another poet introduced by Woolner to his P.R.B. friends was William Allingham, and in a letter to him dated November 8, 1850, he writes—

Most of the P.R.Bs. have been at 7 oakes painting backgrounds to their next year's pictures. Hunt has succeeded in a remarkable manner with his, he has given the effect of a large rough forest on a small space better than ever I remember to have seen it done before. I am glad to hear from W. Rossetti that you liked his review on your poems; he bids fair to be one of our best in the review line—he takes more pains to discover the author's intention and less to display his own learning than most journalists.

[1] " The Voice of Duty."

Woolner was expected to join the forest painters and was censured for his non-appearance in the following amusing note sent by D. G. Rossetti and addressed to—

THOMAS WOOLNER,
101 Stanhope Street.

P. R. B.

At the town of Sevenoakes : County of Kent)

This 27th day of October 1850

RESOLVED

by us the undersigned :

1st.   That the conduct of Thomas Woolner P.R.B. in failing to come hither on Thursday was ill-advised.

2nd.   That the conduct of Thomas Woolner P.R.B. in failing to come hither on this present Saturday calls for explanation, if not for apology.

3rd.   That the conduct of Thomas Woolner P.R.B. should he fail to come hither on the Thursday or Saturday next ensuing will be wholly unjustifiable.

(Signed) W. HOLMAN HUNT,
FREDERIC G. STEPHENS,
DANTE G. ROSSETTI.

FURTHER RESOLUTIONS

1st.   That the sonnet has thirteen lines.

2nd.   That sensuality is a meanness repugnant to youth and disgusting in age, a degradation at all times.

3rd.   That who will may hear Sordello's story told.

This little note in 1850 confirms the position of F. G. Stephens as one of the early members of the Brotherhood, about which fact there has been some discussion.

It was in the autumn of this year Woolner had the pleasure of visiting Tennyson, whose acquaintance he made as early as 1848.

The Tennysons were staying at Coniston, and there Woolner during his visit modelled a medallion of the Laureate—with which later on he became dissatisfied; and after his return from Australia he modelled another, the well-known one, 1856, which decorates as frontispiece the volume of Tennyson's poems illustrated by the P.R.B. and others, and published in 1857.

In a letter from Devonshire to Mrs. Tennyson in January 1851 he says, referring to this first medallion :—

" You quite mistake in supposing that I have gone to any expense and trouble on your account; it would be unjust on my part to allow you to think so, for I have been gratifying my own feelings of admiration entirely in whatever I have done with regard to the medallion, and I am wholly indebted to your gracious kindness in permitting me to visit you at Coniston and doing so. Tell Mr. Tennyson that I sent a cast to Mrs. Fletcher as he desired—pray remember me in the kindest way to the divine man."

In a letter from Mrs. Fletcher from Ambleside, dated January 6, 1851, she writes : " A few days ago I had the very great pleasure to receive your excellent medallion of Alfred Tennyson, and I beg you to accept my best thanks for this noble specimen of your beautiful art. It is considered by all who have seen it an admirable likeness. You have happily caught the expression of your subject. It was a remark of Samuel Coleridge, which I once heard repeated by Dr. Chalmers, that ' all men of genius had a feminine expression of countenance.' I was reminded of this observation by your medallion, for though the forehead is pre-eminently masculine, the lower part of the face is full of tenderness and pity."

Woolner had immense admiration for Thomas Carlyle and Mrs. Carlyle, and was anxious to do a medallion of the great writer; and through the kindness of Coventry Patmore, who persuaded Carlyle to sit, he was able to satisfy his desire. In a letter of January, 1851, Patmore tells Woolner the good results of his efforts on his behalf.

Coventry Patmore to T. Woolner

January 11, 1851

My dear Woolner,

I went to Mr. Carlyle's on Wednesday about the medallion : and I am glad to say succeeded in my mission. He seemed a little doubtful as to whether it would take too much of his time, but I told him I thought you could do it in about four sittings of a couple of hours—about the time mine took. Mrs. Carlyle wishes to have a cast of Tennyson. If you like, I will send her mine, as it may be a good while before you can get another finished up. Write and say.

Yours faithfully,

C. K. Patmore.

The following May Carlyle wrote from Chelsea to the sculptor.

Thomas Carlyle to T. Woolner

Chelsea,
May 21, 1851.

Dear Sir,

If you will come to us, to tea, on Monday night (the old hour) I have good hopes of producing Mr. Ruskin for you. Unluckily, however, it is not quite positive. Mr. R. is out of town and not absolutely certain to be back before Monday; but my Wife will write to you early that day if things turn in the negative, so if you hear nothing farther, come along : If you do hear, I expect it will be the proposal of some new evening for the object in question. The Medallion is favourably hung up; and excites the approbation of a discerning public—as it deserves to do.

Yours always truly,

T. Carlyle.

During a great part of the spring of 1851 Woolner had much correspondence with Dr. Davy about the medallion of Wordsworth modelled for Grasmere Church. Dr. Davy was in charge of the funds for the memorial subscribed to by friends and admirers, and much consideration was given and many letters written, as to the best and most suitable epitaph for the medallion tablet. Tennyson was asked for his opinion, which he sent in a letter to Woolner dated March 10, 1851.

March 10 [1851].

MY DEAR WOOLNER,

I had rather let Dr. Davy have his own way but since he & you require an opinion, look here is an epitaph on the Duke of Wellington.

To the memory
of the Duke of
Wellington

who by a singular calling & thro' the special foresight of Alm. God was [raised] up to be the safeguard of the greatest people in the world—who possessing the greatest military genius wh. the world &c. won the battles of Waterloo &c. &c. &c. &c.—who was equally great in statesmanship as he was &c. Now look here, do not the very words

Duke of Wellington

involve all this?

Is Wordsworth a great poet? Well then don't let us talk of him as if he were half known.

To the Memory
of
WILLIAM WORDSWORTH
The Great Poet.

Even that seems too much but certainly is much better than the other, far nobler in its simplicity.

My dear Woolner, I wd. have answered you sooner but your letter did not know where to find me.

Ever yours
A. TENNYSON.

I am leaving this place [Park House, Maidstone] to-day & going if I can to a house in Twickenham.

I am very glad to hear that you have got work to do. My wife desires her kindest regards.

But the grand simplicity of the suggestion was not adopted, it was considered too severe, and a somewhat lengthy inscription was decided upon, and this was cut into the marble above the medallion, and in August, 1851, the monument was in its place in Grasmere Church. Next year besides the medal " England rewards Agriculture," exhibited at the Royal Academy, Woolner made his design competing for the Wordsworth Monument—a seated figure of the poet, with a bas-relief of Peter Bell and the Ass set in the pedestal, and a group of two figures on either side : The Father admonishing his son; the Mother guiding her daughter to observe the beauties of nature. And although this design was very highly praised Woolner failed to gain the commission, and he was so disappointed he determined to leave England; like so many at that time, he felt a desire to try his luck at the Australian gold-fields, in order, as he hoped, to get money to carry out his ideas in sculpture and do ideal works.

Several of his friends went to see him off in July at Gravesend; amongst them was Ford Madox Brown, whose picture, " The Last of England," was inspired by the sight of seeing his friend Thomas Woolner leave for Australia. The sculptor went well equipped for digging with two friends, Bernhard Smith and Edward Latrobe Bateman, nephew of the Governor of Victoria, both being bent on the same adventure.

They sailed from Plymouth on July 24, 1852, by the ship *Windsor*, and reached Port Phillip, Victoria, on October 27 of the same year.

CARICATURE OF THOMAS WOOLNER WHEN A YOUTH IN BEHNE'S
STUDIO

[To face page 14.

CHAPTER II

DURING the voyage to Australia Woolner kept a log,[1] and this was sent on his arrival in Australia to his P.R.B. friends and his relations in London to read. It was very interesting and gave entertaining accounts of his ship companions and beautiful descriptions of sunsets and sea effects.

A letter to his father, dated August 21, 1852, ship *Windsor*, gives a good idea of a sea journey in a sailing vessel in the 'fifties and how he spent his time on board.

T. WOOLNER TO HIS FATHER T. WOOLNER

1.54 N. Latitude.   *Ship " Windsor,"*
                                              August 21, 1852.

MY DEAR FATHER,

As you will perceive by the latitude above, we are now very near the line, and as that or near there is the place where ships are most frequently fallen in with, I take the opportunity if it should occur of letting you know I am in, not the land of the living, but still alive and I may say kicking, for there is scarcely any rest to be had on deck for moving here and there out of the way of sailors, who are continually tugging at the ropes or scrubbing or sweeping, etc. We have had a delightful voyage hitherto, and have been becalmed not more than 2 or 3 days altogether : this is where calms and oppressive heat are usually expected, but we have had a strong breeze for more than a week tho' part contrary, and the sailors say they never knew such a wind before.

. . . .

If we progress as well as we have done we shall make the journey in less than 90 days : the *Windsor* did the voyage in that time the last she made. We have plenty to do in the way of work and amusement. I rise at 6 a.m., bathe,

[1] This log has been destroyed.

15

fetch our day's allowance of water, walk till breakfast, 8, then we wash our cups, plates and traps, go on deck, read or look at the sea till dinner, which with me is generally rice or preserved potatoes or pudding : they have capital soups and fish and very good meat tho' I seldom touch either; after dinner the plates have to be washed again. This washing is one of the greatest nuisances we have. I then write some to my journal and read till tea. Then the washing. Go on deck to watch the sunset and smoke a pipe, then chatting and lounging about till 10 p.m., then turn in. The sunsets are splendid, larger and grander than are seen on land because there is nothing to interfere with the colors. We see shoals of flying fish, they resemble flocks of sparrows in the distance. Two came on board about a fortnight ago.

. . . . . .

On a dull day the sea looks like molten lead, but when the sky is clear it is the deepest and most beautiful blue can possibly be imagined; sometimes in the evening it is like copper coated with verdigris, with occasional touches of the bright metal. At night as the prow of the vessel drives the foam forward it shines with phosphorescent fire and looks as if the ocean itself would soon be ablaze. It is very amusing to hear the different conjectures upon it; whales, dolphins, porpoises and grampuses have been seen, but only one shark, which the sailors nearly caught, the beast slipt off the hook as they were drawing him up. I did not see the fun for it happened in the night and I was in my berth.

The men make as much fuss dressing on Sundays as if they were going to strut about the streets to show themselves off or going to see their sweethearts; the captain reads prayers in state, a flag is spread over the capstan and he stands there and fires away. I have the greatest respect for prayer time because the people go on the upper deck and leave our place pleasantly quiet : this is the only time I can write with any comfort & a few others feel the same for they generally begin also.

We have the queerest set of fellows on board imaginable, many seem about as fit for digging as they are to be Prime Ministers : some have spent their time hitherto in doing scarcely anything but drinking, the consequence has been innumerable rows disturbing every one else. They are stopped for several days for the steward is not permitted to sell spirits till we are some distance from the line, as the sailors might get drunk and endanger the ship's safety.

I wish I had known before starting what I do now—instead of preserved meats nothing should have been put into my hampers but marmalades and other fruits. The few jams I brought from home have been a godsend to me.

.   .   .   .

I find those hot peppers come in well you gave me, the vinegar they give us plentifully, we put it in the pea soup. The lime juice is one of the best things we have, I drink nothing but that mixed with water and sugar, and my tea. . . . We found the steward cheated us of about one third of our flour, now we insist on having it weighed every Tuesday, and everything else we care for we weigh.

.   .   .   .

The steward is a thorough humbug. He charges 1/6 per pound for common cheese, ditto for ham and other things in the same proportion; he is an ugly little brute and looks like a baboon grinning. The sailors did not tar and feather anybody, for they all became so drunk the night before the ceremony was to come off the captain put a stop to it. One Mr. Fox had a scolding for giving grog to the men. We have lost the fun.

.   .   .   .

Monday, October 4.—Long. 82° 35′ E.; Lat. 39° 1′15″.

We are within a fortnight or a little more sail of Port Phillip and have fallen in with no homeward bound vessel : as far as we have come the voyage has been delightful. Sailors say they never knew anything like it during their experience; it has been neither very hot nor cold but much about the temperature of England in different seasons. I will say nothing of particulars or people here for I have kept a careful journal of everything I thought worth noting. The characters of some of our neighbours I think will amuse you. I have given short descriptions of the sea when it was more beautiful or threatening than usual, and all the glorious sunsets there have been, effects of moonlight, etc., so you will be able to gather an exact idea of what our journey has been by reading it. Bateman will be sending a packet to Mrs. Howitt and you will receive it through her I believe. He intends making a copy of it himself for to be sent to London and lent to the P.R.B.'s and others of my friends ; yet you had better not lend it to any one when you get it or else it will be lost to a dead certainty. Bernhard wants his brother to see it. Let him have it for a fixed time, say a week or fortnight.

c

I will wait till I arrive at Port Phillip, then say if anything has occurred and post this.

.   .   .   .   .

Dr. Godfrey Howitt,
Melbourne, October 28.

I am here, safe at last. We left the *Windsor* by steamboat on Monday, 25th inst. I am staying at the above address and receive every kindness possible for a human being to have from another. The Howitts are delightful people and live exactly like rich people do in England. Bateman sleeps at his Excellency's, Mr. Latrobe's, to give more convenience to us. We have to dine with that great man to-day : he wants to know me because Bateman found that my little figure of Red Riding Hood was one of his favorite ornaments & told him that I did it : he says I must not leave the Colony without doing something in the fine arts first : we hope to get much valuable information from him, but the diggings by all I learn is by no means a certain affair as to realizing a fortune, tho' many do : numbers return without paying their expenses and those who are successful squander it in most disgraceful manner. Everything is very dear, the luxuries none but triumphant diggers can purchase—fancy an ordinary cauliflower 3/6 and all suchlike things in proportion !

.   .   .   .   .

The commonest labourers get 4 pounds per week; others 1 pound per day : but living is terrifically expensive. Dr. Howitt's household expenses are 4 times what they were before the discovery of the gold and any man who has strong shoulders will get employment that will pay them well. I have no time to give you a full account of the country, the people or anything in detail but merely scrawl this down hastily to say I am here : when I have been a short time at the diggings you shall have a more lengthened account of things there, for they are the only objects of interest just now and what most concern me. One can scarcely tell without looking closely he is not in England. Everything seems arranged much in the same way : the people are the chief difference. They mostly wear beards, carry firearms and are immensely independent : they dress something like the prints you have seen of red French Republicans, much of that loose air and swagger. Bernhard desires his kind regards to you, he is wonderfully well and feels quite up for the diggings. We are now going to have our hair cut, it has grown to such a length that with our beards we look just like savages. Our friends in England would not know us I think in our rough garb. Do write to me as soon as you can directed to Dr. Godfrey Howitt, Melbourne.

Give my kindest love to Mother, Helen and all of them and say how delighted I shall be to hear news of them. . . .

Your affectionate son,

THOMAS WOOLNER.

As Woolner was anxious to begin digging at once he did not remain long in civilization. He stayed at the hospitable house of Dr. Godfrey Howitt in Melbourne, whence he writes October 31, beginning his journal of the gold-fields.

[1852] *Sunday, October* 31.—I am in Melbourne at the house of Dr. Godfrey Howitt waiting for Tuesday next when I expect to start for the Ovens Diggings. . . . We have been busy making arrangements since we landed, a week to-morrow, and have had little time to study the aspect of things here. This morning I did a little to a sketch of Charley Howitt. . . . I fear my journal will not be so regularly attended to in my journey up the country as it was on board the *Windsor*, after a hard day's march a mug of tea and a rest will have more seduction than pens and paper. . . .

. . . The price of things here would seem fabulous if not true. Nature and Custom are topsy-turvy in this country, the reverse of England : day and springtime here when night and winter there : here the trees shed their bark instead of leaves, vegetation stops in mid summer and cherries grow with their stones outside. The man of labor only buys the luxuries of life, and servants rule their masters who bow down and flatter them : such is the power of Gold. . . .

Monday, November 1.—After breakfast I went into the cottage to arrange my traps : my bed will consist of a piece of green baise, one blanket and a waterproof coat to place on the ground as a protection against damp. . . .

I finished a letter to Rossetti which Mrs. Howitt has kindly enclosed in a parcel she intends sending to her son in England. . . .

Tuesday, November 2.—After a hard day's work we have left Melbourne and are encamped at a village 3 miles distant; our first night of a wandering life, and it is beautiful, surrounded by a gorgeous sky and on one side by mountains rich in color : the village people and quiet oxen move about peacefully. . . . The Howitts took a most affectionate leave; blessed souls those. The Australians are romantic in hospitality. . . .

Wednesday, November 3.—We passed thro' a splendid country that looked like an immense park left to decay and run wild : the trees stretch and shoot in sinuous, fantastic growth, some felled, others tumbling to ruin; the ground was spangled with serene little wild flowers and graceful grasses. Mr. Overman shot a lizard. The skill in managing the oxen by the driver was extraordinary. This will be my second night of sleeping in the open air. . . .

Friday, November 5.—How new and wild the sensation is of bathing in the moist air at sunrise : then walking and looking at the quaintly grown gumtrees, then a simple breakfast on the grass, our arms lying near; then packing up and loading the dray; then harnessing or yoking the oxen, then the cheerful move forward. However well one feels before this adds to his pleasure tenfold : the whips snapping like rifle-shots, the energetic cries of the drivers the patient, enduring and hard-pulling oxen; the new sights rising or opening before us, all together give a feeling that town-dwelling people cannot suppose. . . . We see numbers of exquisite parrots, they seem as if the green beauty of the trees were condensed into winged oval shapes and painted with sunset colors. The sun has been so bright the trees' shadows were not only very dark but literally seemed to soak darkness into the earth. The ants are almost I think quite as numerous as the grassblades one cannot sit on any place in the country without sitting on them, and some have a great faculty for stinging. . . .

Wednesday, November 10.—We fell in with Mr. Howitt's sons and Edward, Dr. Howitt's son : he is a calm-minded youth, with a great amount of knowledge pertaining to the colony, sound reflection and gentleness; a son well worthy

"PUCK," 1847

From the plaster model.

[*To face page* 21.

of such noble parents. . . . I gathered a handful of native cherries, stones outside; not bad : saw a tree on fire inside; wind roared up it like what it was, a furnace; it fell with a big crash and shattering in unison with this wild scene : everything is done on a large scale here, a man chops down a tree to boil a can of tea; chops down a young tree for the top which we may condescend to look at to see if it will do for a whipstick : a butcher wonders if he is asked for less than half a sheep each time. I and the Bs. went up a creek with a man for some milk; the man asked Bernhard if he would sell the breeches he had on. . . .

Friday, November 12.—We camped early to-day at Honeysuckle Creek : there is a large tavern where enormous prices are charged, 1/6 for a glass of bad ale, 3/6 lb. for common cheese. I have not felt well since I caught my cold, but weak and oppressed : the bush-life does not agree with me yet, the food particularly, no vegetables or fruit of any kind, not even bread only bad rice peppered with flies and hard biscuit permeated with road-dust : not good fare. We meet many people returning from the Ovens who nearly all give ill news. . . .

Saturday, November 13.—The day has been very warm and of course chokingly dusty : this is bad, but the greatest pest we have to withstand is the common domestic fly : these pernicious wretches torment the day from dawn to sundown and make it essential to wear a veil, but that afflicts me more than the pesty brutes themselves, rendering the senses smothered with closeness. . . . Our marksmen often shoot parrots of lovely plumage, principally of the rosella kind, young Pinchin shot a white cockatoo last night and he is now cooking it for supper. It is growing dark. I was resting under a gumtree to-day when a set of rough fellows sat beside, and after jabbering to each other some time one began to quote Tennyson, mocking some person he heard quote " The May Queen."

Monday, November 15.—We started this morning after our sabbath rest and passed the Broken River : we halted at a tavern called the Black Swan, the drivers wanted their nobblers I suppose : I saw there a black man attiring himself, performing toilet duties with grimaces of fastidious self-admiration : he combed his thick shock of wool with some pain to himself, then (smeared) it with grease and rubbed some fat over his visage, then combed again twisting his delight into hideous leers; after he had finished I told him he had made himself look very pretty, he grinned at me in ecstasy and asked if I wanted a light for my pipe. At the township of Broken River I obtained a pint of milk just warm from the cow; it was a soothing draught to thirsting fatigue. At our midday halt I yarned with an Adelaide man, found he knew Mrs. Orme's brothers settled there, at least he knew one. . . .

Tuesday, November 16.—I have enjoyed the walk more than heretofore which has been thro' country where the flat is considerably broken by variety of broken ground : it is tedious travelling, a dead level, trees everywhere, trees right and left, trees before and trees behind, boxed in with trees; I feel as if I were travelling shut up in a basket. A camp scene has a busy and wild effect, the fires blazing, meat frying, bullocks being unyoked, snapping of whips, people getting their traps from the drays, dogs barking, guns banging away in all directions etc. . . .

Thursday, November 18.—We are at noon-halt in a pretty spot beside a river, still the Wangaratta I believe : I walked a few minutes ago along the dried bed of a swamp and a delicious odor rose up from minute lilac star-flowers; this I thought extraordinary for such an unpoetic country : a land where the birds cannot sing, nor flowers give perfume, scarcely : a land without fruit or vegetable. . . .

. . . We are encamped beside a little creek seven miles from the diggings : there is the battle-field close to us and we shall see it to-morrow; soon after discover if it be worth leaving civilization for and coming 16,000 m. for, and enduring every kind of annoyance for and, in short, if it be a good speculation we have made. The road is well filled with people going and returning from the diggings, most give bad accounts, some middling and a few quite good news : I take but small notice of either, knowing what a vague and dishonest thing rumor is. We shall soon know what gold seeking is, and will need no tongues upon the matter. . . .

Friday, November 19.—We started late this morning, it rained hard. I saw the diggings this afternoon, a vigorous scene, bustle among men, the earth looks as if an earthquake had torn it up. . . .

Sunday, November 21.—The numerous tents scattered everywhere give me the notion of this place being the grand meeting place of all the gipsies on the earth, all the men look like gipsies. I am obliged to leave off writing to fetch a sheep's liver for the dogs.

We went this afternoon and selected two spots for digging to commence upon to-morrow : there will be plenty of water to take out as they are just beside the creek. The country round here is magnificent in scenery much the best I have seen. . . . Nearly all diggers smoke, they go to any one's fire to light the pipe : they seem a tolerably friendly set, rough enough, coarse as brickdust, but nothing more. . . . This digging will be anything but dreaming on a couch of down : standing up to and over our knees in water, and aching with labor in each joint; the strongest and most accustomed are thus, so that beginners need not expect it will be better with them. . . .

Monday, November 22.—Digging for gold is not play. My hand trembles so much I can scarcely write. I have been digging, felling trees, barking and carrying bark, baling water the whole day. We have sunk our hole 5ft. deep; the water comes in fast upon us. The Pinchins are admirable workers, first-rate fellows. This has been the hardest day's mere labor I ever did. The creek fills with people fast.

Wednesday, November 24.—I wrote nothing yesterday, I was too tired, for we were baling out water and barking or digging till after washing several dishfuls, the holes proved of no worth, only two or three specks in a dishful. We gave them up. . . .

Thursday, November 25.—I have been fossicking and prospecting all day. . . .

Friday, November 26.—We have been working hard at our

hole all day, and I think it contains promise; it has one
advantage, dryness : the wet is making many ill with violent colds. Our hole is a round one, and some old miners
were looking at it just before we knocked off work and
praised it : if the result equal the striving for it we shall
be satisfied. The two Pinchins are our bulwarks and contain our chief strength : famous workmen. . . .

Saturday, November 27.—We have been hard at work all
day; some washed clay and gravel stuff mixed with quartz :
we got as much gold as would half fill the shell of a small
hazel nut : a minute quantity to satisfy six greedy fellows as
we are. We are more than 12 ft. down, much lower than any
around us : experienced diggers think it a likely hole : we
intend following it to the bare rock if possible. I begin to
use the pick with some freedom and not so much labor to
myself as at first, the spade and shovel are easy to me,
comparatively. . . .

Monday, November 29.—We have been hard at work
among the rocks, we must have moved tons of them : our
fellows are short-seers and expect every day if they work
a few hours to clutch reward,—expect a harvest in the
evening if they sow in the morning. I could only give half
my attention to work for the other half was employed in sustaining the drooping spirits of the mopers. Nonentities. . . .

Tuesday, November 30.—My anticipations are considera-
ably moderated since I began digging, now I see no very
sparkling fortune in the future : soon as ever I get a little,
enough to give me a start in London, I am off to a certainty.
The chief good I have gained at present is a keen appreciation of civilized comforts, things unknown in these parts...

Wednesday, December 1.—Worked all the morning; after
dinner went to the Ovens for our licences; found that
Howitts had arrived, could not find them. Dark.

Thursday, December 2.—Found that our 3 holes would not
pay for washing; struck out another claim in a line with
others that we know are doing tolerably, and another near
the most successful spot in the creek. . . .

Friday, December 3.—I have been hard at work all day,
picking, digging, baling and prospecting. Pinchin and I

went down with a hole this morning and hit the rock : we have not yet given it up; next we struck into the flat opposite our tent but found the water came in at about 4½ ft. and have given it up for a time; soon after we began a great number of folks came to see and talk with us upon the subject. . . .

Tuesday, December 7.—I was hard at washing and rocking yesterday : we did pretty well, nothing to fall into rapture about. To-day I have been sinking next our old claim which we have now worked out. . . .

Thursday, December 9.—This day I have been sinking by myself; I find it much more pleasant to work alone. . . .

. . . Gold digging is the hardest work done in the world; all classes of men have tried it, and all join in this opinion. Every one works for the golden key wherewith to unlock the prison gates that shut them from freedom, light and human growth, and strives his utmost : many work for these harder than they would to save life itself, if life would want these. A gold-digger considers his wages a pound of gold per week, and nothing less.

Friday, December 10.—We were washing in the morning and got about 10 or 11 oz. After dinner the party broke up, Pierce & Brown together, the others as they felt inclined. I went into my own claim and have been picking thro' cemented granite so hard it breaks and bends the pickaxe : I have hope of it.

Murder is growing frequent in this district; one poor murdered man was buried here this morning. I heard of two others to-day.

Saturday, December 11.—H. Pinchin and I have been working in a claim like a steam-engine all day and found the stuff not worth washing; we must look for another place to strike in now. . . .

Four of the rascals connected with the recent murders in this district were taken on the digging this afternoon by the police. . . . A man was murdered in his tent last night, about 300 yds. from our place : the dogs made an extraordinary noise which was remarked by many people : I said this morning most probably it was caused by the prowling of some villain among the tents groping for gain. . . .

Tuesday, December 14.—We are on the march again, bound for the Devil's River diggings; we have just camped where we made the mid-day halt Nov. 17 about 16 miles from the Ovens diggings. Yesterday at noon Mr. Graves came in our tent and said whoever wanted to accompany him to the Devil's River must pack up and be ready in 2 or 3 hours; I was sorry to start so suddenly but there was no help. . . .

Wednesday, December 15.—We came 10 m. to-day and found Bateman and party at last : we learned that Mr. Howitt had been dangerously ill but he is well now : they are off to the Spring Creek diggings partly to see them and to obtain their parcel of letters from Mr. Smythe which contains two for me. I am burningly anxious for these letters, I want to know how my friends in England are. Bateman looks pretty well, rather worn I fancied. We have lost half a day thro' rain : most of our party are fishing in the Wangaratta river, about a mile from the township. Last night there was a gorgeous lightning storm, thunder rolled round the night in hard, metallic crashes and rain fell and cooled the air. . . Sometimes the thought comes in me like a death-chill, that I shall never see England again.

Thursday, December 16.—We are encamped for the night in a swampy place 15 m. from Wangaratta : a very decent day's march. . . . It has been a very pleasant tramp all day; we crossed the Ovens in a punt at about 8 a.m. and halted 2 hours at noon, one of the most azure noons I ever gazed on, the leaves shook and shone against the sky, and the forest glowed, soaked with sun throughout every fibre. . . .

Saturday, December 18.—Yesterday was my birthday and I intended to have written it an azure day, for it had been a long and delightful journey from our last camping place to the Broken River where we are staying, till the evening brought horror and grief to all of us : several of us went to bathe in the river, the Pinchins were the first who entered and after sporting awhile Henry went out of his depth and lost balance. Bernhard swam towards him but could not support him against the strong current and to save himself he was obliged to let go : I saw Pinchin's face rise to the surface for a second after this and saw it no more : Bernhard's face as he swam to the bank was quite white : Mr. Graves hovered about the spot some time in hopes he would rise again, but it was not to be. His death sent a stun thro' our party, it seemed as if some hand had reached and snatched him from us. Two men dived for half an hour in search of the body but could find nothing of him. Poor Joseph is crushed down by this great affliction; they were most loving brothers, no two could love each other more. We have been dragging the river all the morning but to no purpose : a black woman was diving for a long time but could not find him. Now we are in a very unsettled state and know not what to do.

Sunday, December 19.—We left Benalla on the Broken River this morning after having arranged with the authorities of the place for the burial of poor Henry : the Broken River is a place few of us will forget. We passed thro' country to-day that was like a continuous pleasure-ground, so beautifully patched with shrubs and trees and broken with hills and creeks; we came to a shepherd's hut that was in a spot which might by labor be turned into a paradise : the man's wife and family were there, it had something wild and comfortable in aspect, one little girl was swinging, a graceful little creature. I will make a bas-relief of her when I get back to England and the fine arts. The place we are camped in is the most beautiful we have seen and the wildest : the big white gumtrees are dropping their manna now, luscious morsels with the flavor of almonds, and the great white cockatoos and rosellas screech and scream about. . . .

Monday, December 20.—The colors of sunset are sober but infinitely varied; wild cranes are showing their grey bodies to the light, a little quail has now passed by me on the grass by the creek, so near I could almost reach it. . . .

Tuesday, December 21.—We are at noon-halt in a hollow between immense mountain ranges and where creeks and gullies join : we started in fair time this morning : the journey has been thro' country more and more wild, sometimes mystic shadows and vapors hung over the hollows. Our folks are busy plucking ducks and doves which they succeeded in slaying to-day, intending to make a meal : these doves are lovely creatures, their legs and feet crimson, on the wings are some of the most splendid touches of richness I ever saw; the colors literally seem to burn as if they had been plated by fire; underneath the wings it is a warm, soft fawn color.

We are encamped for the night, which we had to do rather prematurely thro' the dray getting stuck in a creek : the dray was unloaded before it could be freed; this was the second day we had to unload and the second time of being stuck to-day : we have had to pass innumerable creeks and gullies in this short journey. It is a beautiful spot we are at; a creek runs three parts round big as a young river, a line of grand purple mountains surround it; its waters are haunted by wildfowl, the marshes are dangerous with waterholes : the ground is clearer than I have seen before for any space in this great wood country. Men of sport would run crazy to be in such a place as this, for there is no end of objects to practise on, pigeons, plovers, quails, curlews and all kinds of suchlike : not many of our gang are good at shooting, indeed I may say none, or we might live as far as game goes most voluptuously. Two ugly blacks paid us a visit to-night, they came in a most stealthy way, which is natural to the animal I suppose.

Wednesday, December 22.—We are making halt by a large lagoon covered with rushes and filled with wildfowl : our sportsmen have just shot two teal and great preparations are going forward for a grand attack. Plummer is the most inveterate gunner but somehow he succeeds not altogether well : just now it was sport to see Overman rush madly in the water after a creature he had winged. Our journey is still accompanied by the purple ranges, one near us rises abruptly rather conical, covered as most of them are by trees. We have been stuck again, and it took a great

DESIGN FOR THE WORDSWORTH MONUMENT, 1852

[To face page 28.

deal of digging, lever-using, bullock-thrashing and swearing to get us out. We were stuck 3 times yesterday, not twice only as I said. We must be within 8 or 9 m. of our destination : the place where the diggers have worked on the Devil's River is called " Hell's Hole," a curious name, and unusual to say the least : the names of places in Australia often are peculiar, such as " Jackass Flat," " Pigleg Gulley," " Bacon-face Flat," and others stranger still which I forget for the moment.

Thursday, December 23.—We are still where we halted . yesterday, imprisoned by rain which falls in fierce and sudden showers. Plummer and I made an excursion round the lagoon early this morning in search of wildfowl, but met no success, instead thereof a sound drenching or two by rain and water below feet. . . .

. . . . We hear that Henry Pinchin was found and buried the day after we left the Broken River on Monday. I am glad. . . .

Plummer and I went up the high sugar-loaf mountain opposite our tent yesterday afternoon and lit a fire on the top, smoked a pipe and made ourselves comfortable. The scene from the height was as magnificent as ever surprised and blessed the sight of humanity : endless ranges of mountains winding round and beyond each other, of all forms and colours and covered with a pale celestial light and mist : great trees were like smallest shrubs and creeks and rivers could not be seen. We found a party of gold-seekers had been up there and left a ticket fixed in a bit of stick giving their names and date—Dec. 10—and country —New Zealand—we added ours, names, date and country. The descent was difficult and dangerous, a slip of the foot —good-bye ! it was dark when we arrived at the foot of the mountain and had the most awkward places to wade before we found the tent.

Friday, December 24.—We started in good time this morning . . . came to Lock's Station near which we have camped for the night. It is a lovely place, a swamp and mountains before, with wattle, honeysuckle and gumtrees behind : the sun shines cleanly now and everything looks

bright, fair and tranquil, but the day has been blurred
with plentiful showers. A lovely place, filled with the
noises and flight of strange birds : I saw one tree as thick
with white cockatoos as the balls of bloom on the guelder-
rose : the rosellas dart and flutter their rich hues thro'
the air. How happy a man might be here if his friends
were with him. Mr. Lock told us gold was found 7 m.
from here in Blanket creek. I believe we are going there
to-morrow prospecting, and if it turns out favourably we
will strike in manfully and do our best.

Saturday, December 25.—Christmas ! . . . Mr. Graves
went on his mare to examine the road to Blanket creek
and found it very good : I believe we start for that place
to-morrow. Some of our fellows are cleaning the gold
we got at Reid's creek before we divide it : I shall be glad
when everything of this sort is settled to be quite free of
some. . . .

. . . I am lying along the grass behind the dead honeysuckle's branches ; it is near evening and the sun sends
long shadows.   . . . .

. . . If one thing in nature could send me suddenly mad
it would be a clear and settled conviction that I should
never see England again.   Sometimes in moments most
pleasant to me the possibility sends a shiver thro' me more
foully horrible than anything I ever felt—almost like a
brief gap giving a glimpse of hell. I fear dwelling on the
notion much. Death I should care but little for : it is
the dread of becoming so reconciled to here, or thro' other
circumstances as not to reach England—to yield what I
have hoped and striven for—to step down a little lower in
creation, not society. I heed but little the steps and grades
there : to begin for a high mountain top and willingly
turn back and descend at leisure, that is what I loathe :
if he faint and die on the road bravely toiling, I clothe the
fallen hero with my honour, as sincerely as if he had been
victorious, but detest the craven who for bodily comfort
would slink from his object—the purer atmosphere—the
wider world-range, and being nearer the sun.

Sunday, December 26.—We left our beautiful camping

ground this morning and we pitched in and about the Blanket hut by Blanket creek : we intend to try this place and until this be done we can come to no resolution : most of our party seem more for Melbourne than any other thing. . . . Two parrots flew past me just now with slate bodies and crimson heads.

Monday, December 27.—Our gold-digging must be postponed for a few weeks for we go on the tramp again to-night or to-morrow morning : we have sunk a few holes to no purpose and Graves chooses to start for Melbourne; as we have no other chance at present for a conveyance to other diggings we must go too. This has been an unfortunate expedition and all we get by it is experience purchased rather dearly. . . . I have not had time to complete the hole I began even and shall leave this place filled with disappointment. I expect Bernhard and I shall leave Melbourne for Forest Creek or Bendigo ; one thing, when we start again it will be with a better knowledge of what we are going about, and for the future will place less trust in report.

The sun has just set and left a few rich spots upon the sky. We have left the Blanket hut and are camped in the flat opposite Lock's station near the place where our Christmas passed. This ends in earnest our expedition to the Devil's River. . . .

Wednesday, December 29.—We went or came in good time to-day and reached a place called the Big Hill, we reached the middle of it about noon. The scenery to-day has been very simple and large, not unlike the Ovens hills. I saw an ant seize the tail of an opossum-mouse. The small creature could scarcely run for it : Bernhard freed him. It was something like our mouse, only its head and shoulders were much larger in proportion. I have just had a delicious bath in the creek opposite our camping place : a bath and pipe after are the only luxuries I can indulge in : one is healthy the other injurious. I must now write to Bateman asking him to return my letters to Melbourne. We made 18 m. this day. . . .

Friday, December 31.—This day concludes 1852, an

important year to me.   I have left nearly all I love to seek
nearly all I want.   We started in pretty good time, but
the mid-day halt was rather prolonged thro' a hot wind that
blew :   when we advanced some distance on the road the
cause was obvious;   first an odour of burning, then a dense
volume of smoke, lastly fierce serpent belchings of flame
from the smoke licking the great trees and swallowing up
the hay dry grass;   a kind of consternation came over
some but fortunately it turned from us and the air became
suddenly cooler; a great boon ! . . .

[1853] *Saturday, January* 1.—We are camped beside the
Goulbourne river and shall remain so to-morrow and
perhaps the day following. The country is tame and
monotonous again tho' the part just passed contained
pretty spots : much drier than when we went up, swiftly
running creeks have stagnated to chains of waterholes.
I went down to the river for water, a short while ago, and
had scarcely parted from the place when the huge limb
of a tree fell into the very spot I was upon : had it struck,
it would have crushed me, as a man's foot would a beetle.
This country has most dark and dangerous rivers, they
contain holes of fearful depth, their bottoms covered with
nets of snags and logs—trees fallen from the side and
washed down the stream, rushes and tangles of strong
weeds.   An ugly country surely where a man is half
roasted on the Friday and scarcely escapes a broken back
and drowning the following Saturday : a pretty way to
begin the new year.   I saw what might be fairly called
a pretty girl to-day, at a place where Bernhard, Pinchin
and I went for milk; the girl's mother gave us currant
cake with our milk, old English custom, which was pleasant.

I mentioned on Friday Nov. 26, that a set of fellows
whose aspects I disliked came to the diggings; these
fellows have proved to be notorious bushrangers and have
kept the country in terror by villainous tricks, the man
who keeps the punt here has been giving me an account
of their robberies at Goulbourne township : impudent
scoundrels.

Sunday, January 2.—In the same place, uncomfortable

thro' delay. I had a delightful bathe in the river this morning, and a walk along its banks chiefly under the shade of wattle trees. About 8 days more and good-bye to this bullock team; I shall feel as if released from prison. The Goulbourne banks are steep, sandy, loose and dangerous, but in parts most lovely to gaze upon : vigorous rushes, brilliant grasses, so bright it seems the earth sheds light, the dark, rich green of the wattle flossed with bloom : the gaunt, fantastic boles and branches of the white gum, the bare complicated nets of root-work, water-worn, dry and dirty; the birds of strange note and romantic hues, the insects burning with emblazonment that dart or flutter amidst all this; the many flowers and shrubs nameless to me, but beautiful, all assisted to give me as much pleasure as I could feel in such circumstances; being away from my chance of advancing in life and attaining that for which I strive. When I once get to work again it will be something more than a little that will seduce me from it.

Monday, January 3.—A decent stage to-day, we are near where we were Nov. 7 encamped beside some waterholes. I have been cutting Pinchin's hair : a barber, what shall I be next ? I had thoughts of turning sheepshearer and reaper till fresh diggings broke out. The numbers of folks we meet bound for the Ovens is extraordinary, almost as many old hands as new chums. It seems great nonsense writing such trifles down : of course, they would be quite uninteresting to any other person, but will serve to call up pictures and events to me at some future period—perhaps. How vague the fact; every little section added to this book is the record of a day taken from my life.

Tuesday, January 4.—Four days melted from the new year. We are about 1 m. from Kilmore, that charming town of shabbiness and filth, encamped on where there is no water; a great oversight; two hands have been full an hour searching for some and found it not. Pinchin and Jack have now set out in quest. About 3 more days and we are free again. The weather has been very cold during

D

the greater part of the day. I frequently wished for
something more than my Jersey or Jumper, as it is called
occasionally.

Wednesday, January 5. . . . The road to-day has been
even fuller than usual with drays; the accounts from
the Ovens seem to grow in promise as we recede from
them, most other diggings seem flat and uninviting:
we are not more than 28 m. from Melbourne, how I hope
there will be letters for me. My anxiety to hear from
England in a measure interrupts my thoughts and resolves
and injures my worldly interest; I wonder if they, my
friends, think of me as often as I think of them; I expect
not, for their lives progress in the usual way, surrounded
by numerous friends, and one absent is no more than a
bead from a necklace; whereas everything is new to me
here and contrasts are ever striking me. I compare the
people about to those I left behind and sometimes feel
strangely isolated.

Saturday, January 8.—We reached Melbourne Jan. 6,
in the evening and had to search half thro' the town for
a night's lodging, it was procured at last with some difficulty
for the landlord of the Imperial Inn did not seem much to
relish our uncouth aspects, rough from bush-life : the bed
notwithstanding my fatigue suited me badly; mosquitoes
tormented for more than half the night; I felt something
heavy walking over me and on giving a kick a great rat
fell lump on the floor, whirled about, squeaked and scam-
pered off with another wretch. . . . I and Bernhard paid
a visit to Dr. Howitt's whose family were as kind as when
we landed from the *Windsor,* the utmost that can be
said; they wished us to come and stay with them; Bernhard remained at the Inn with Pinchin. I am at Dr.
Howitt's where B. will probably soon come. We both
dined here yesterday, in the afternoon Mrs. and Mr. La
Trobe called with Mrs. Lonsdale, wife of the colonial
secretary. Last night was the first I have enjoyed since
I left Melbourne for the diggings; I rose without my
shoulders aching from the hard ground. We are waiting
now for news of the Ovens from Bateman, if his news be

W. C. WENTWORTH, 1854

[To face page 35.

good we shall return there, as we hear no promising accounts from other diggings.

Safe from the bush, for a short while comfortably reposing, thus ends what I call our " Expedition of Experience." We may consider ourselves fairly initiated into the peculiarities of colonial jobbing or swindling or gadding or any name one may please to call it; at all hazards a something to be wary in trusting.

Sunday, January 9.—Nothing occurs to note, things in civilized life go so regularly onwards : the chief occupation of my mind is " Where shall we go next ?" until we hear from Bateman this cannot be decided. I feel this a large comfort to be able to write on a table. . . . Dr. Howitt's collection of plants and flowers are most choice and beautiful, his gardener told me it was the best in all Victoria. I look upon a good garden as the essence of a country's beauty; the loveliness scattered over wastes and loose patches of earth is here compressed into a set space that may be refined and enriched at will; in this matter-of-gross-fact country it is almost the only region wherein the beauty-loving soul can enjoy itself and forget that most of its fellows heed nothing but corn, sheep and the accumulation of gold. . . .

Tuesday, January 11.—I went this morning to meet the dray which came in town at 11 a.m. We got our goods and paid for their carriage. . . . We expect to start for Fryers Creek in 2 or 3 days with Pinchin and a friend of his, Mr. Vesey.

I heard from Bateman yesterday, he gives no promise of the Ovens, but expects good from a quarter yet unknown : he sent my letters, one from my father. . . . No one who has never tried or known it can tell the delight in receiving a little gossip from home when 16,000 miles away. I expected a letter from Mrs. Orme and one from Wm. Rossetti—did not get them. It is raining hard this day : everything looks fresh and beautiful but wonderfully sad to me ; looking from the window I see a fine pomegranate tree. It is a body of sparkling and deep green with such outbreakings of scarlet splendours that my soul feels sick for love of it, yet I am sad; it sprung from darkness, aspires thro' light, seemingly towards gloom again, this vainly beautiful pomegranate tree.

Wednesday, January 12. . . . I hope greatly to make a start the day after to-morrow, partly that I am anxious to develop swiftly as possible the little destiny of mine in this poor state, and also I fear the comfort I enjoy at present may tend to unfit me for the rough life to come, by refining my sensations too much and rendering me weak for lack of exercise. . . .

Sunday Evening, January 16.—We did not start yesterday thro' some business of Mr. Vesey's : B and I slept at the Port Phillip Club Hotel, for I disliked returning to Dr. Howitt's after wishing them all good-bye. We left Melbourne at noon to-day and are now camped at Keillor, a place 10 m. from town. I am rather tired : a delightful rest such as mine has been, among the most refined of human beings, does my soul more favor than my body, for it rather unfits me for common labor and makes me half yearn to go to my Art again. The country we passed thro' to-day is almost bare and undulates. The sky is gloomy.

Monday, January 17.—We left Keillor this morning in fair time; passed over a large plain, of a uniform whitish, yellow, in the distance were forms of delicate blue mountains : a sublime reach of even distance. We are halted by a creek with but little water, but that very good. Nice water is verily a blessing to the traveller. . . .

Tuesday, January 18.—We started early and halted near the Bush Inn, are now camping, about a mile farther on the road. We came to a steep hill our old horse would not ascend, and an owner of some bullock teams let us fasten on to one of his drays when we came up neatly enough. The country here is beautiful, we are beside a large swamp and the trees, grass, etceteras of vegetation are consequently green : there are many camped round. Bernhard is going to bake a damper, the first during this expedition. We go on much more comfortably than hitherto; Mr. Vesey is a very nice fellow, fond of reading poets and good-hearted. Burns is a favorite of his.

Wednesday, January 19.—We came thro' the Black Forest to-day; I saw nothing but the trees' trunks that struck me as being particularly black—many white gums were quite shining. The old horse did well, he tried to jib a bit but Pinchin soon convinced him such tricks were of no avail. We are near the 5 m. Creek, about 35 m. from Forest Creek. We have had hills and hollows all day. . . .

Friday, January 21.—Reached Fryer's Creek late, went 10 m. out of our road. I never saw anything more desolate than the first sight of Mt. Alexander was to me : it was what one might suppose the earth would appear after the day of judgment has emptied all the graves. I saw holes with grass and wild flowers growing on their borders. The whole thing gave me one of the saddest impressions I ever felt—the carcasses of labor—the earthy shells of hard endeavour, often fruitlessly, and sometimes success proved a curse.

Saturday, January 22.—Went and saw Mr. Gilbert the commissioner; he is a most kind and courteous man, treated us with all attention, introduced Mr. Herring, com-missioner of Fryers Creek, to us who is to show good ground on Monday. This is anything but a lovely spot where we are camped; surrounded by hills it looks like an old tin oval dish, at this time covered with smoke and dust. Dust is a nuisance.

Friday, January 28.—We are sinking two holes now, one up a dry gulley is a miracle of toughness, the other is not hard but must be worked to a great depth and there will be plenty of water, but it is in a promising place near where something has been done. I have done nothing scarcely for two days, my hands have been too sore. . . .

Tuesday, February 1.—Been working hard all day at the deep hole, are near the bottom and shall know by to-morrow noon if it be of any value; the two holes near ours are, I believe, paying tolerably well, so our chance is fair. My hands are better, one is nearly right, the other

shows and feels rather badly yet : I think myself improving
in health for I feel in better spirits. I should like letters
from my friends in England at least once a month.

Wednesday, February 2.—Am rather tired, been working
all day at the windlass : we are at the bottom of our hole
and it bids fair to pay, not well, but up and even above the
average. My hand still keeps me from putting that
spirit in the work I would : I must hope that perseverance
will conquer. . . .

Friday, February 11.—I have been hard at work under-
mining in the hole which made a better show to-day. The
Creek begins to look thin, people are off to Bendigo,
Ballarat or elsewhere.

Saturday, February 12.—Been at work in the hole all
day, found a nice little pocket of gold. In the afternoon
a heavy rain and thunder storm came down upon us, we
were obliged to knock off work. An immense number of
people get drunk, in this part : there are numerous sly
grog-shops. We began to cart our washing stuff.

Monday, February 14.—I did nothing of any account
yesterday but a little domesticity and a walk towards the
junction of Fryer's Creek and the Loddon : it was raining
all day and has been this day also : I have been working
at the hole a little, but the wet makes it very difficult and
disagreeable. This is like the weather they have in England
during February, very unusual, they say, here. My cold
has turned to a cough which annoys me sadly at times.
. . . I think this country never will agree with me and I
half suspect this gold-digging life will finish me off before
I can make a fortune at it ; however I will keep at it as long
as I can. Mr. Vesey lost his horse yesterday and cannot
find him to-day. Many drunken squalls here.

Tuesday, February 15.—How time passes with me.
Been at work in the hole all day driving : I fear it begins
to be dangerous but there is no help for it in this work,
where there is gold there we must drive. I found a neat
pocket of 4 oz. or more this morning. . . .

Thursday February 17.—We have been cradling all
day and have worked a great quantity of our stuff which

is not so good as we expected. . . . In the afternoon I went to Castlemaine for letters : received one from dear old Hunt who is in Syria now, by his own account; one from Mrs. Dr. Howitt : what a pleasure it is communicating with refinement, to a person dwelling in this half savage state : I also heard of Bateman who may be here at Fryer's Creek before long. . . .

Friday, February 18.—Been cradling all day and finished all our washing-stuff, the gold is not weighed but I think it will not be much short of four pounds. Probably Bernhard and self will part from Vesey and Pinchin; we none of us pull the same way comfortably. . . .

Saturday, February 19.—This morning we cleaned, dried and washed our gold : each share was ten ounces 40 oz. in all. We also had a general settling of accounts : Mr. Vesey wanted us to bear part of his expense thro' loss of his horse which we flatter ourselves we did not accede to, considering we had no concern in the affair : the small man says he will go to Melbourne and try to get money by other means than gold-digging, an occupation he is as fit for as I should be at his business—a tallow-melter for candles. . . .

Tuesday, March 1.—Been driving in the hole all day ditto yesterday, the two days' work come to less than an ounce; we intend giving to-morrow and if the stuff betters not give it up. We have joined Pinchin's Corsham friends in going down with a wet claim.

Wednesday, March 2.—I was at the windlass all morning and part of afternoon : the hole grows backwards or worse not better; I will begin a new drift to-morrow and that will be testing enough. . . .

Friday, March 4.—Worked at the hole all yesterday, to-day also till noon then gave it up : we have got about 1 oz. from it. This day after noon I went to Castlemaine for letters, received one from Mrs. Orme : how truly faithful to her promise she is : her letter is dated Sep. 20, 1852. . . .

Sunday, March 6.—The sun is down behind the hills and another day has passed from me. We got our

tarpaulin over the tent in the morning and feel the benefit
of so doing, for we have been able to remain within tent
without being quite roasted; we are chiefly indebted to
Bernhard for his exertions in this affair. I want to write
home and to Mrs. Orme greatly but can get no opportunity :
I have not one quarter of an hour during the week, and
Sunday is half employed washing wearing apparel and
getting my bed traps in order. We have no table and there
never is any quietness in the tent, so that I am obliged to
keep postponing it till I fear they will think I slight them
or some other incorrect thing. I have just come down
from the hill behind us, having enjoyed a quiet time reading
the packet of letters sent me by Mrs. Orme. . . .

Tuesday, March 8.—Washed a tubful of stuff from
our wet claim and found but a few fine specks : have
given it up for the present. We are now, at least I, engaged
sinking a hole on Dead Man's Hill. . . .

Sunday, March 20.—I did not note the 3 last days
chiefly thro' want of time; Thursday we worked all
day sinking; Friday we could not stop to have dinner
because water made upon our work so fast, we bottomed
the hole notwithstanding; yesterday we washed all day
and the result for the week's hard work was half or little
more than half an ounce; this for four men is not an
extravagantly rich return. We have been doing very
badly of late, and if it keep much longer thus I fear my
Gold-digging days must come to a conclusion; we do not
nearly earn our food. . . . The years sliding from me and
no real work done—the road uncut that I must pass thro'.
I begin to have grim, heavy doubts if I did well in leaving
England : I am away most effectually now and must make
the best of it and crawl along if I cannot run. This day is
full of sunshine and cheerful air; this will be a beautiful
land when brought properly under man's sway; it is
beautiful and grand now, but man wants cultivated spots
wherefrom to enjoy it all. . . .

Tuesday, March 22.—Been prospecting but have found
no ground to suit; we went into a hole and bottomed it
this afternoon but found nothing. . . .

Friday, April 1.—Been sinking near Spring Flat all day : yesterday ditto. Andrews is not well; last night he shot an opossum, to-night he skinned the creature, prepared the skin with alum for me; I want to make a tobacco-pouch with it.

Saturday, April 2. . . . I am growing weary of gold digging, the labor is too great for the return; a poorest menial could make more at his work in Australia than we have since ours began here. . . .

Wednesday, April 6.—We are unfortunate gold diggers for we get nothing by working hard. There was a funeral at Castlemaine to-day of Cap^n Blake who was killed by falling from his horse : a man well beloved. . . .

Friday, April 22.—Started in good time, passed the Porcupine, halted for dinner a little before the Bullock Creek, crossed it, then passed over the Big Hill at the foot of which we have camped for the night. The scenery has been similar to parts of the Ovens and Broken River, the mountains granite : this side of the Big Hill we find sandstone rock and quartz. We are two miles from the diggings where they commence. The road has been all day thronged with drays, most of them returning from Bendigo empty, others going up with stores.

Sunday, April 24. . . . The Bendigo is an enormous stretch of diggings; there is something sad in the sight : the immense amount of human life used in lifting up these rings and mounds of earth, gradually settling to the common level of the flat again : the tons of gold eagerly snatched and riotously wasted, the tremendous labour done by Ignorance, the tremendous gains made by Cunning —the little real value affected by all this, the almost infinite harm to many. Everything looks old and established here, a matter-of-course straightforwardness in doing business, the Storekeepers charge as much as they think they can get without the smallest reference to decency; for instance, Andrews went last night to a Store for an axe handle, they wanted the moderate sum of 18*s.* He went this morning to another Store where they charged him 3 shillings, the ordinary price. . . .

Wednesday, April 27.—The rain has baulked our work several times to-day. We have been sinking in our claims : come on to the crust, stuff so hard the pick will not touch it, obliged to use gads and a sledge hammer. There is hard work going on about us, people are all day damming the waters and blasting the rocks : I hear no grumbling even, the men are so busy one way or another. I found and caught an oppossum in a tree. Bernhard caught a scorpion in our tent.

Thursday, April 28.—Been sinking all day : our holes are harder than anything I ever attempted to cut thro', the gads will scarcely touch one of them. I received a letter from Mrs. Orme : it was posted in London February 9. A letter from Bateman who says he will soon be up at the Bendigo. I am anxious to write home but this laborious life gives me no opportunity; if I tell them this it will be difficult to make them understand, as they can have no conception of living in the Bush. . . .

Friday, April 29.—The number of tents is astonishing and they increase daily. Bendigo is a busy place and certainly worth seeing. I always feel better spirits after having news from England. . . .

Sunday, May 1. . . . I have been washing, heaving logs and attending to dinner duties, my day's work. I was sorry it was Sunday because I was anxious to get to the bottom of our claim now we are thro' the crust. Andrews cut my hair to-day, and did it as well as any barber could do it. . . .

Thursday, May 5.—We have not bottomed our hard hole yet, there is a quantity of cemented iron-stone slag that is extraordinarily tough to get thro'; we broke another pick to-day and think of going the extent of a sledge or an 8 lb. driving pick : the hole next ours is slightly improving and dipping to a gutter. . . .

Friday, May 6.—We have reached the bottom of our hard hole at last, and are going to wash a tubful to-morrow to see what it is worth. . . .

Saturday, May 7.—We washed two tubfuls and got about half a pennyweight : we intend driving it a little ere

ALFRED TENNYSON, 1856

[*To face page* 42.

giving it the ding. Smith and Pinchin bottomed theirs but the prospect is of no account. The spirits of our party are low and well they may be. I spent a miserable last night, am a little better to-day tho' very weak. I could scarcely lift a bucket of stuff off the hook at the windlass. Bendigo is to be another Fryer's Creek, I fear.

Sunday, May 8.—The day has been remarkably fine : I went in the morning for a long walk and noticed one peculiarity belonging to the birds of this country which in part compensates for their want of song, it is the exquisite gracefulness of their flight; they strike wildly and catch up in sudden check, whirl lightly round darting their heads nervously a few times at something, then float calmly away : after my walk I fetched water, made some dumplings for dinner, spent the rest of the day doing nothing in particular. Smith went to Sandhurst. . . .

Thursday, May 12.—Washed the remainder of our stuff, got about 3 pennyweight, not worth the washing by any means. Sold the tubs and one cradle, expect to sell all shortly. Bernhard is gone to Sandhurst in hopes of meeting his brother and to dine with a Captain Herriot. This great Mt. Ivor rush has thrown many storekeepers out of their latitude fearfully : diggers grieve not at their mishaps, but slightly chuckle. Weather is agreeable. . . .

Monday, May 16.—Still on the Bendigo, the dray starts to-morrow morning 8 for Forest Creek that we go by. Bernhard starts for Lookers Station near the Mt. Ivor ranges till he gets his commission. Everything is getting flat at Bendigo, storekeepers wail, diggers flit about, the doctors stick fast, for many are ill and die here— poor diggers. We finished selling off our things, and allowing for the place, very well. To-morrow good-bye to Bendigo and the gold fields generally. We have given them a trial sufficiently long I think, and if I do not succeed better in my next effort I do not think it likely the gold fields will tempt me again as a digger : my fortune is not to be this way.

Wednesday, May 18.—At Castlemaine, Forest Creek,

last night reached Barker's Creek after dark, we made about 28 m., came here early in morning : I went to the camp, saw Alex. Smith, had luncheon at the mess, spoke to him for Andrews concerning work, etc. I expect to start for Melbourne to-morrow, if so this is my last night on the diggings. Try life in other shapes. Bernhard started yesterday for Lookers Station, knapsack on shoulder.

[Between these two entries Woolner received and wrote several letters (between May 18, 1853 and May 26, 1854), and these letters will take the place of the unwritten journal.]

[1854] *Friday, May* 26.—More than a year has passed since I wrote in this book. Now I am in Sydney modelling likenesses of some of its inhabitants. It certainly must be indolence that I have not continued my journal for certainly I have had more leisure and opportunity than when I was on the diggings, and I think my changes and adventures have since then been equally interesting to myself. I have on the whole enjoyed my last 12 months more than any other during my life. I hope within a month to be in Melbourne, thence to start for London.

> 14, *Chatham Place,*
> *Blackfriars Bridge,*
> *Saturday, January* 1, 1853.

MY DEAR WOOLNER,

Among the many sins of omission for which I am hoping that this New Year is to witness some atonement, as I have hoped in other new years, I have at least sat down to make sure of one—perhaps the heaviest—the letter which I have so long owed you. If, when we were together on the steamer upon that 16th of July which I assure you, my dear friend, is not and cannot be forgotten, any one had then told me that I should not write to you till next New Year's Day, it not only would not, but could not have been believed by me. And what is most on my conscience, is the knowledge that, well as you know my nature, you would not have believed it either. The fact is, that my other many remissnesses have been the cause of this one; for often, when I have been on the point of writing, I have again deferred it, finding that I had nothing to say except to hover round the old desperate desultory story. However, I will now try to believe that the spell may act both ways, so that after writing to you, I may find other duties getting fulfilled in their kind, and go on my way rejoicing. One thing, however, I know you have not doubted, for all my long silence; and that is, that every night, in lying down, I have thought of you and of our friends who are with you, and that the thought

of you has been brought to me constantly from all sides, in all manner of sudden ways. I know none of you have doubted this, and you have been right.

I date this from my new rooms at Blackfriars, but it is written at Arlington Street, where Hunt and Stephens have just left, having dined with us, and spent the New Year's evening. Hunt has just returned from a Christmas at Oxford, jollier than ever, with a laugh which answers one's own like a grotto full of echoes. Stephens smiles as of old, as cordially as the best but with a shade of nicety—the philosopher of reluctance. We have been amusing ourselves since dinner with trying to sketch heads from memory. They are lying about the table—all more or less mulls. Here is one of yourself which looks like a fire-fiend. Of course I do not mean this marginal one, which is William fallen asleep, while I write, in one of his usual anti-anatomical actions. The candle has just been gulped into its socket, and I wake him unrelentingly to ask him if there is another in the room. He says " no " with benevolent self-possession, and falls asleep again. But he is wrong, for I have found one. These are my environments at the present writing—as familiar to you as the scrawl you are reading. Let me hear, when you write, exactly how you are occupied and surrounded at the moment of receiving this, and I shall get as clear a glimpse of you, I suppose, as possible, and let me know, too, all about your voyage, and the time of your arrival, and about your present work, and your plans, and about everything and everybody.

Meanwhile I will turn over these scratches and carica-tures that lie on the table, and tell you something of the originals.

Here is Millais. But all the letters you have must speak of him—conquering and to conquer. And here is William Millais, who has just done some landscapes worthy of almost any one except his brother. Here is Hunt. It is one of William's queer portraits, but it has something of him. It looks like a fellow who would have a try at anything, even to making the sun stand still—and indeed he has done that, on his canvasses which are more vivid than ever. You have heard from him, and will know that he is at last coming into his rights, and, as Tennyson says, in his ode on the Wellington fever,

> " has found the stubborn thistle bursting
> Into glossy purples that outredden
> All voluptuous garden roses."

Here is Brown—at least something meant for Brown. He is still at Hampstead, and painting, I believe, a small modern picture about emigration.[1] From his description, I should think it would turn out first-rate, but I have not found my way to Hampstead lately. I have seen him

[1] "The Last of England," by Ford Madox Brown.

sometimes at the Camden Town School here, where he has
taken a mastership, and where I have several times seen
your young brother, who gives, I assure you, great promise
in modelling. My sister goes there too, and I believe Miss
Orme is likely to join shortly, they being now known to
each other. Here is a portrait of the latter, among the
rest, but perhaps it is not quite equal to yours. I have
spent various evenings with the Ormes since you left, in
company with William and sometimes Christina, and
indeed, I think we may now consider ourselves in the circle
of family friends. William and I were there on Christmas
night, but I was taken unwell and forced to leave. You
may guess how many conjectures about your doings have
passed there among us at different times. I gave Mrs.
Orme my sketch of you, and she has had it framed and
hung up.

Here is an abortive attempt at Hannay. . . . His intended is a most lovely and charming creature; . . . he
introduced her one night here to my family, who were
delighted with her.

And here is another, which ought to be familiar. It is
very hirsute, but perhaps not exceedingly like—yet may
be, a better bodily resemblance than that spiritual image
of himself which this unlucky devil has been setting before
himself any time these four and twenty years— . . . .

But it is striking three while I write, so I will put off
the finish till to-morrow.

Blackfriars,
Saturday night, January 8.

Here of course has been another delay of a week, and
perhaps with some ingenuity I might manage to prove
that I have been less to blame than usual. *Mais a quoi
bon ?* I wonder again as I write, under what extraordinary
conditions of being you may read this, and whether Bateman and Bernhard are present *now* (i. e. *your now*), and
how they are occupied. O for a state of coma !

I had a gathering here last night, at which almost every
one was present—neither was Woolnerius utterly absent :
the daguerreotype being set open over the mantelpiece.
You cannot imagine what delightful rooms these are for a
party, regularly built out into the river, and with windows
on all sides—also a large balcony over the water, large
enough to sit there with a model and paint—a feat which

I actually accomplished the other day for several hours in the teeth of the elements. I have got those four sketches of yours framed and hung up, with the inscription you wrote on board : other Woolnerian relics are also about —Bateman's geometrical eye, however, would suffer acutely in this crib, as it has settled into the river and put all the lines awry. I remember his sufferings at the Hermitage from similar causes. Hug that dear old fellow for me, and tell him that the time I spent with him this summer was one of the jolliest of my life. To him and to Bernhard the Stunner, I shall lay in energy to redeem very soon my epistolary promise. Meanwhile this letter is, of course, as much to them as to you. I have not seen Mrs. & Miss Howitt for some time, purely, I confess, from absolute shame lest they should ask me whether I had yet written to any of you. Now, however, being strong in the consciousness of comparative rectitude, I shall post a letter to Miss Howitt at the same time with this one, to ask her to fix an evening when I can take my sisters to the Hermitage, a subject long in debate between us.

Pray remember me most kindly to Mr. Howitt and his son. . . . Hug Bernhard and tell him I called on his brother one day at Brixton, but finding him out could only leave my card, a proceeding by the bye, which no doubt appears to you now, in your abnormal dignity, extremely contemptible. I shall try my luck again some day. Has North yet found his way to the diggins ? Bliss has, for I met him about a month after you left, and he was just going to start by steamer. So you may expect him ! ! !

Last night at my party, it was agreed that all your intimates here should meet at a certain day and hour, the equivalent of which was to be found by you Australians (as in the case of the Christmas pipe), for some act of communication, the nature of which was left for me to decide. I therefore fix that on the 12th of April (which will keep us clear of the Exhibition burners) at 12 o'clock in the day, we shall each of us, wheresoever we be, make a sketch of some kind (mutual portraits preferable)—or for any who do not draw, some verses or a letter—and immediately exchange them by post, between London and Melbourne (or whatever other address you may send us by that time). I think this will be as good as anything.

And by the bye, this brings me to art—the last thing

ROBERT BROWNING, 1856

[*To face page* 49.

with me as usual—you have heard, I believe, that I have
got rid of my white picture to an Irish maniac. There
are two Dantesque sketches of mine at a Winter Exhibition
in Pall Mall—one which you remember my making at
Highgate, and another which I hope to paint some day or
other, to be called " The Youth of Dante." The main
incident is that old one of mine, of Giotto painting Dante,
but treated quite differently from anything you have seen,
and with the figures of Cimabue, Cavalcante, Beatrice,
and some other ladies. It illustrates a passage in the
Purgatory which perhaps you know, where Dante speaks
of Cimabue, Giotto, the two Guidos (Guinicelli and Cavalcante, the latter of whom I have made reading aloud the
poems of the former who was then dead) and, by implica-
tion, of himself. For the introduction of Beatrice, who
with the other women (their heads only being seen below
the scaffolding) are making a procession through the
church. I quote a passage from the Vita Nuova. I have
thus all the influences of Dante's youth—Art, Friendship
and Love—with a real incident embodying them. The
combination is, I think, the best which has yet occurred
to me in illustration of this period of the poet's life, and
the design is certainly about the best I have made. I have
done many other designs lately, but have bored you so
long about this one that the rest can wait. I find I am
pretty certain of selling any water colour drawings I make,
and advantageously, the two exhibited having excited a
good deal of attention and (unpalateable) praise. I am
now working with a vague reference to the Exhibition
of this year, but on that vexatious subject shall defer
speaking till my next. Every one who writes will of course
tell you about his own performances, so that I may confine
myself to mine. To-day I saw the new frescoes in the
House of Commons. Herbert is rigid, Cope frigid, . . .
Watts truculent, . . . This I think is all the Art News
afloat just at present.

And now, dear Woolner, with a strong present recollection of the many days and nights we have been jolly or
sulky together, and a warm anticipation of those which I
hope we shall yet live to see,

I remain always,
Your affectionate friend,
D. G. ROSSETTI.

THOMAS WOOLNER P.R.B.

E

14, *Chatham Place,*
Blackfriars Bridge,
London,
April 16, 1853.

MY DEAR WOOLNER,

This letter is accompanied by, or rather accompanies, the sketches made by the P.R.B.'s now in London, on the 12th, according to the appointment which I made in my last letter to you. This however, I now fear, may not have reached in time for yourself, Bernhard and Bateman to have reciprocated as they are proposed. And indeed it even seems by the last news I have of you, that you are no longer all together. I trust that you are now doing better than your £20 apiece in 3 weeks at the Ovens, though indeed I suppose even that is rather beyond the average, is it not? I last night saw your Father, who had not yet received this news of you which reached me through the Howitts; and to-day I have written to the same to Mr. Edward Smith, as your father felt sure that he also must be ignorant of it. Your "Sea-Log" gave me the greatest pleasure I have had for a very long while. I am glad and surprised to find how well you managed as a sailor, though many of your fellow-passengers seem by your account to have been fiendish enough for the pit of Achevon, or for that voyage, unaccompanied by cares of outfit, across the River Styx. However, I hope something is to be allowed for a Carlylian kaleidoscope (or rather Kakeidoscope) and for those peculiar Woolnerian idiosyncrasies which set me roaring many times before I had got through the little book. The descriptions of sunsets, etc., are really glorious and altogether the thing gives one as intimate a knowledge of your sea-life as if one had made the voyage with you. By the by, though, I was quite angry at hearing no more of Bateman towards the close—it almost looks as if you had quarrelled, though of course this was not the case.

. . . . . .

Your letter was read aloud on Tuesday morning (the day the sketches were made and the day after I got it) at breakfast at Millais', where we met to draw, and afterwards spent the evening together here. I could not and need not say all that we said and conjectured about you. Are not Hunt's sketches wonderful? They are made with "Swiss chalks" not Creta Levis. The "Swiss" are softer than the Creta, but I think much more beautiful in colour. Hunt will send you out some of both. Some of William's sketches are very rich. My Hunt is universally pronounced to resemble Rush on his trial. I am therefore bound to say, that, while it was made I distinctly remember Hunt's wishing that he could hang Rowland Hill, for increasing the burden of his correspondence through the penny postage. This may probably account for the murderous expression. But by the by, I ought only to write on one side of this thin paper, or I fear it will be illegible by the time it reaches Australia. I have seen Mrs. & Miss Howitt frequently since you left. They have made the Hermitage—especially the " nest "— a perfect fairy palace. I was there on the evening of the 13th to show them the sketches, and they read me long passages from Mr. Howitt's letters, among others the one describing your coming up with him on the road. What a wonderful life.' When you write again, make sketches in the margin of yourself Bernhard & Bateman (if then with you) in your present disguises. But perhaps after all my letter may have reached and we shall get portraits in return for ours. I fear this letter must be a short one, as I have got to take it and the sketches to Mrs. Howitt to-day, that they may go in a parcel of hers. But I will write again soon.

I have been going very often to the Ormes, though not now for nearly a month. I shall probably go again in a night or two. Mrs. Orme gave me this foreign paper to write to you on, and we were to have written a joint letter. But this must be for the next time, as I am so hurried to-day. What friendly hospitable people they all are ! Miss Orme and Miss Andrews spent an evening at Arlington Street with my family, and seemed to be struck with wonderment by the cuneiform character of the Governor, with whom they played some games of Chess,—regarding him apparently in as mysterious a light as the *Rosetta* stone itself. (This pun is almost punishment enough for the swarm with which you used to afflict me.) He (the G.) wrote some Italian verses in Miss Orme's album lately at her request. William also wrote something inscrutably metaphysical—Christina something rather intense—and I, the sonnet on the next page, addressed to yourself in imagination some time before, on the 9th February, which was the first evening of snow in London this past winter, and by Primrose Hill.

" Woolner, to-night it snows for the first time.
Our feet knew well the path, wherein the snow
Mine leave one track.   How all the ways we know
Are hoary in the long unwonted rime !
Grey as their ghosts, which now in your new clime
Must haunt you, while those singing spirits reap
All night the fields of hospitable sleep,
Whose song, pass'd the whole sea—finds counter-chime.
Can the year change, and I not think of thee,
With whom so many changes of the year,
So many years were watched; our love's degree
Alone the same ?   Ah ! still, for thee and me,
Winter or Summer, Woolner, here or there,
One grief, one joy, one loss, one victory."

This is the only verse I think, (or almost) that I have
written since you left,—except something *de rigueur* on
the Duke of Wellington, which I keep as a monument of
the universal influence of public frenzy even on the most
apathetic.   I told you in my last that I had sold my old,
old white picture [1] at last to a man in Ireland—a certain
M‘Cracken who bought Hunt's " Gentleman and a half
of Verona."   Said M‘C. afterwards sent said white daub to
Ruskin, to whom he had wanted me to submit it as a
preliminary to the purchase which I had sternly refused.
Ruskin's opinion (I suppose) has induced him to give me
a commission for £150, and I have chosen a subject of the
" Virgin in the house of St. John " which I am now about.
There is another man at Liverpool who has seen the white
abomination & wants a picture of mine, but I have said
his best plan will be to wait till I have something ready
for him, as I find already with M‘C's picture that I shall
be making it worth more than the stipulated sum.   M‘C.
sent me a passage from a letter of Ruskin's about my
Dantesque sketches exhibited this year at the Winter
Gallery of which I spoke to you in my last.   R. goes into
raptures about the color and grouping which he says
are superior to anything in modern art—which I believe
is almost as absurd as certain absurd objections which he
makes to them.   However, as he is only half informed
about Art anything he says in favor of one's work is of
course sure to prove invaluable in a professional way,
and I only hope, for the sake of my rubbish, that he may
have the honesty to say publicly in his new book what he
has said privately, but I doubt this, Oh ! Woolner, if

[1] " The Annunciation."   The angel in the picture was painted from
Woolner—the head, hair and poise of the head being characteristic.

one could only find the " supreme " Carlylian Ignoramus, him who knows positively the least about Art of any living creature—and get *him* to write a pamphlet about one—what a fortune one might make. It now seems that Ruskin had never seen any work of mine before, though he never thought it necessary to say this in writing about the P.R.B.

I have said all this to you about my " professional prospects " (ahem !)—a subject on which I am always profoundly speechless—because I know your friendship is really interested to know that there is a prospect of my getting on all right if I can make myself work.

How queer that Mr. Latrobe should have your "Red Riding Hood." I remember you were working at that the first time I ever saw you. I feel quite confident as to portraiture in Australia, in case digging fails.

Hermitage,
Highgate,
Half past 3.

I have just been taken with an idea that Mrs. Howitt's Australian packet would start without this missive, and have therefore hurried down here, and finish this letter in Miss Howitt's nest. She is engaged copying a portrait of Mr. Howitt on the wood, to be engraved in the *Exhibitor*, and has just been saying that she misses Bateman's correct eye for corrections. You could scarcely imagine how elegant and habitable this room has been made since the days of my savage bivouac in it.

You will be quite surprised to hear that my family are going to settle in Somersetshire. My mother & Christina are already gone, and my father, whose health I hope will benefit by the change, is to follow as soon as ever they are a little comfortable. Maria and William remain in London. I shall then have a *pied à terre* whenever I am able to get into the country, which will be very jolly, but I shall miss them here, as I have been getting more domesticated of late.

Let me think now about news of friends. Hunt has sent three pictures into the R.A.—" Strayed Sheep," " Measure for Measure," and " Portrait of a Parson "— all glorious. His figure of Christ in the moonlight he was after all unable to get finished—this is the best thing he has yet done. He starts for the East, he at present believes, about August, and Seddon goes with him. Millais has sent in two pictures—" The Release," an episode from the

Jacobite period, and " The Proscribed Royalist "—a
subject of the Commonwealth, both very remarkable
works indeed. Brown, who has become a Hampstead
hermit, and who would not attend our meeting on the
twelfth, has only sent one which I think you saw, called
" The English Fireside." Collins has sent one little figure,
but was baulked with his chief work. Collinson has gone
into a Jesuit college somewhere in the country (!) and I
suppose will never paint more. Deverell sent in, I think,
five pictures, of various merit, but some really excellent.
Cross has, I know, sent his " Becket," though I was unable
to the last to call and see it. Stephens has sent a portrait
of his father. Munro has got several groups and sketches
the chief one—portraits of some children—very beautiful
I think. He came in at Millais' while we were making
the sketches the other day, and did a profile of William,
which accompanies his best remembrances to you.
Hughes, always behindhand like myself, began something
at the last moment, and did not finish. I of course do not
send at all, though I have several things still in hand. . . .
Anthony has sent a picture 16 ft. high, of a part of Windsor
forest, and another smaller one, both full of beauties. He
has cut Suffolk St. Hannay is married and (I really
believe) settled. He does not come to one's parties when
one asks him !—though perhaps this may be owing to his
having been very ill with rheumatism both before and
since his marriage—a lamentable infliction. He was
obliged to marry in a great hurry at the last, owing to his
wife's family starting for your Australia, where they now
are. Her father, Mr. Thompson, is director of a branch
of the Oriental bank now established at Melbourne. She
is I think one of the most beautiful and charming girls I
ever met with.

You see I have adopted writing on both sides as I have
no more of this paper here, but I hope this will be legible.
I find there will be a week's delay in the sending of Mrs.
Howitt's parcel, so that I have no doubt a good many
other letters from our circle will accompany this. I shall
myself try to write also to Bernhard and Bateman.

Arlington Street,
April 17.

Yesterday finding I had so much time, I relinquished this
letter for a walk with Miss Howitt and her little sister.

I suppose there is more news to tell you if one could only think of it. The R.A. will be a thin exhibition it seems this year, but I shall be able to speak more on this world important matter when it has opened. Coventry Patmore has published his poems at last. "Tamerton Church Tower" is the name by which he now calls the "Storm." I believe there has been as yet but one review of them (*Athenæum*) favorable but rather supercilious. I have not seen the volume. Its author does not intend to give any copies at all—a piece of news which he told Millais. . . . I see to-day William has got another invite from his lady, saying at length that she supposes it is no use asking me. She has done so without effect several times between this and your departure. I almost think I shall go down this time for a lark. . . . Nothing is talked of just now but Alexander Smith. You will remember this genius appearing in a fragmentary state in the *Critic*. Do you know I rather fancy we did not then quite do him justice, full of faults as he certainly is. I looked slightly over a copy of his vol. which Mrs. Orme asked me to get for her, and I see he is quite marvellously redundant of some qualities, at any rate I shall read him. It seems he is coming to London to divide the honors with Mrs. Beecher Stowe. Hannay knows someone who knows him and I have no doubt I shall turn him up somehow. It seems he is some Glasgow nobody of about 23 or 24, who has been in the habit of existing by drawing patterns for linen drapers, so I suppose he is an artist of a sort.

> "Within a city one was born to toil
> Whose heart might not mate with the common doom
> To fall like a spent arrow in the grave."

This is very fine I think, and seems to have been quite his own case. It seems he has actually got £100 from Boque for his poems!—owing to the puffing that has gone on during the past year. Allingham is heard of by nobody. I am sure he must be masticating his identity in a frightful way out at Ballyshannon about the news of Alex. Smith. I should think that nothing were more likely than its bringing him up to London to do battle with tooth and nail: I have read nothing I think since you went, except, I must not forget to say, *St. Augustine's Confessions,* a delightful book. I am just going to try to read Carlyle's Goethe's *Wilhelm Meister*, which Hannay has lent me.

Good-bye, dear Tommaso. Write as soon as you can,

101 Stanhope Street

THOMAS WOOLNER AS "FIRE FIEND."
Sketch by D. G. Rossetti in letter of April 16, 1853.

and tell me all news, over which I wonder and puzzle as to what it will really be. Give my love to Bernhard and Bateman, but I hope energy will aid me to write to them before the parcel starts, and that news will serve which is another necessary. Brown wrote to me yesterday

STONE STATUE OF BACON IN POSITION, OXFORD MUSEUM

[*To face page* 56.

to say how heartily he wanted to be remembered to you, though he did not attend the sketching reunion.

Your D. G. R.

April 22.

P.S.—I have forgotten to give you news of Scott.[1] He has been in town once since July last, and then made his stay with us at Camden Town for a week or two. Part of this time the poor stunner was laid up, and I hear has continued more or less unwell ever since. He has not yet published his poems though I believe he is getting them under way. He has sent a picture of " Fair Rosamond " in 3 compartments to the Academy. Hunt and I the other evening amused ourselves at the old game of sketching friends from memory. Here is a historical portrait of you which I did. Send me in return one of yourself under your present metamorphosis. In mine you will see that the accessory alligator is on the epic scale.

I should not forget to say how much Scott always talks of you and wishes to be remembered to you. No one I know will enjoy your journal more than he. By the bye, you must understand that people are always sending their affections to you against I write, but you know my sad memory in these matters. I met Cox one day in an omnibus, and he talked much of your affairs. I must manage to let him see your journal as he seemed most friendly.

P.P.S.—As Bateman is probably I suppose still away from you, I write to him; but not having news for three, must put off writing to Bernhard till I have. Give him my love.

F. G. Stephens to T. Woolner

59, *Walcot Place,*
Kensington Road, London,
April 21, 1853.

Dear Woolner,
I have short notice to write to you and shall not be able to send quite such a lengthy epistle as my last in December. However here goes to make the best of it.

---

[1] W. B. Scott, the poet and painter.

We had a meeting the other day according to agreement made by Gabriel Rossetti with yourself by letter, it was held at his chambers whence we adjourned to Rochester or rather to correct an Irishism, we intended to get there but the weather was so bad that it was resolved to stop at Blackwall, where we had dinner, most of us over-eating ourselves, excepting Gabriel.

.   .   .   .   .   .

We agreed then to meet at Millais' house on the Friday and make the sketches, which was done, and I understand you are to receive them with this. You will recognize doubtless the ghastly countenance of one of your Friends, which J. E. M. drew.—I made an attempt at his most splendid head, but the failure was utter and in spite of all the tauntings he could pronounce, with proddings from Hunt, I viciously refused to proceed. You will I hope forgive me, when I add that I was very ill or so sick at heart from some bad news I had just received that any noise was welcome, but actual thought seemed almost madness. I am giddy still at times.—However, Hunt, with his indefatigable affection for me leaned over my shoulder and altered it, so that it may be just recognizable for the handsome Johnny's head. He blew up furiously and has not forgiven the slander yet.

I must mass all the news together anyhow, and hope to hit upon something which others may forget. Jack Tupper has gone to Oxford to see about an appointment, which was offered to Hunt; on his rejection and passing it on to me, it was again declined, when Jack accepted the berth and since Xmas has had it in negociation.

.   .   .   .   .   .

I am writing in my own room at Walcot Place.

.   .   .   .   .   .

I shall not say anything of the Rossettis, or Hunt, because I know they are writing to you. G. Patmore is still at Fairlight and is, I understand, undecided about going to the Church or going to Australia. I had a note from him on Monday : with which he sends a copy of his Brother's Poems, the new edition, for me.

.   .   .   .   .   .

Lear has a picture at the B.I. which is capital, he delights to acknowledge his obligations to Hunt for instruction while they were staying at Fairlight together. He goes everywhere saying that Hunt taught him all he knows and he has improved wonderfully. Millais has obtained £500 for the copyright of one of his pictures he sends to R.A. this year. Deverell sends five pictures to R.A. small and large. He, I hear from Gabriel, contemplates to take a part in some Comedy which is to be acted at Richmond shortly, with, I fancy, a view to going on to the stage.

.   .   .   .   .

I was dining in Arlington St. the other day when your Father brought the journal you sent him. William Rossetti brings it here to-morrow evening when I shall have an opportunity of reading it. I saw your letter to Gabriel and am glad you appear to have had so pleasant a voyage.

.   .   .   .   .

Hunt is becoming more established and acknowledged every day. People begin to see more in the old stunner than they were willing to do at first. He will get his right place at last I know.

Gabriel has looked very unwell for some time, seems in a curious state of mind, the old moodiness. . . . He will doubtless tell you of the Commissions he has received. " The Annunciation " picture you will remember, he has sold to McCracken of Belfast, and has been working on it with great success, is quite another thing, well worth three times £50 which he gets for it.

.   .   .   .   .

I have nothing to add but good wishes,
Dear Tommy.
Yours very truly,
FREDERIC G. STEPHENS.

Direct me to care of
Dr. Godfrey Howitt,
Collins Street,
Melbourne, Victoria,
July 10, 1853.

MY DEAR FATHER,
I received your parcel of letters on Friday evening, July 8, and a great delight it was to me hearing you were all so well.

.   .   .   .   .

I had just returned from the Ovens Diggings after a very unsuccessful expedition there and the Devil's River and felt a great disinclination to send you such bad accounts as I must have done had I written at all. I stayed a few days in Melbourne and started with Bernhard and two others for Fryer's Creek : we were a little more successful there for a time but that soon failed : on April 20, we started for Bendigo but there got scarcely a speck of gold, and after sinking hole after hole in vain we determined to sell off tent, tools, etc., break up the party and seek our fortunes by other means.

Pinchin, his name is mentioned in my journal, and a friend of his, W. Andrews, have taken to carting. Bernhard has gone up the country to stay with a friend of his. I have come to Melbourne to work at my art. There is every prospect of my doing well, as I have powerful friends who are anxious to aid me in every way. I am staying at Dr. Howitt's and the kindness of his family to me is wonderful. I have executed a medallion of the Doctor, one of his Excellency and another of little Charles Howitt. They all give great satisfaction here and you will see what the newspaper says which I send you. Will you be good enough to send it to Mrs. Howitt at the Hermitage when you have done with it ? If I get some commissions which I have fair hopes of I shall return to England about the middle of next summer to execute them. . . . Now I am fixed in town I can write, but at the diggings it is a thing next to impossible.

Tell Henry to give up the notion of gold-digging at once, henceforth and for ever, for in this Colony it is on the average the poorest occupation going. I have had as much experience as most people and speak from certain knowledge. All the glorious accounts we read in the beginning of 1852 were quite true. I know numerous cases more wonderful than any printed in newspapers, but they are useless to give any details of : we were just 8 months too late, the numbers had multiplied vastly, the richest places were exhausted or so loosened by half worked holes that they could not be worked any more by private parties and now altho' occasionally prizes are found the greater number do not make wages; all sensible people give it up and take to their businesses whatever they may be and do well. If you are asked my opinion upon the desirability of any person coming here, say, if he be a mechanic or a labouring man, to come by all means. Carpenters in town get 30/- per day, other trades more or less according to demand. No labourer gets less than 30/- per week and food. Contrast this with England ! A tradesman with common sense and a capital is sure of making a great deal of money, but no professional man would I advise to come here to practise be it what it may; he might succeed but I see no certainty. This is the country for a poor hard working man. Men owning a dray and 2 horses can clear £20 per week.

I should be able to make some money quickly if it were not for the difficulty I have with plaster of Paris, that which is sent from England gets damp with sea air and is spoilt for artistic purposes. I had a piece of gypsum given me which was a godsend, and have to break it to small pieces, then bake it in an oven, then pound it finely in a mortar, after that sift it thro' fine muslin : all this before one cast can be taken. I had to make some modelling tools ere I began and dig in the earth for some clay— this I could do to perfection after my 8 months' digging-experience—which was the color of that I modelled " Boadicea " in. I have my tools a little in order now and mean to work hard. I get 25 pounds for a medallion here. In England they would not give me 25 pence. I should ask you to send some clay and tools but I am quite uncertain when I shall return. . . . I lost a little over 30 pounds by my gold digging in actual outlay, in time and chances of making money I cannot calculate, for several people have returned home whose heads I might have done. I got gold to the value of £50 and the expenses came to something over £80. By travelling about I had the best opportunity of seeing the country : and such a country and air ! The winds of paradise could not be more pure and filled with living brilliancy. The big white cockatoos fly in troops against a sky that remains blue, perfectly, for months and some of the gum-trees drop manna more delicious than any confectionery in a Regent Street shop. Bateman and Mr. Howitt's party have been more unfortunate than we.

Although I was so unsuccessful pecuniarily, yet I do not regret going to the gold-fields, it has made me strong and more vigorous than I ever felt before, and given me an appreciation of home comforts that makes civilization more delightful than it was till now; and above all things it let me know how dearly I loved my friends at home, and what immense delight it will be to see you all again.

.   .   .   .

I have just paid nearly 6 pounds for two frames. Most of the things I have bought have been 6 and 12 times the price I paid in England.

.   .   .   .

July 15.

This is the day I left England and this year has given me a considerably varied experience : the chief lesson I have learned is, that it is best to work at that business you have learned. The *Morning Herald* gave me a leader the other day, this is thought a great honour. I send you the paper so that you can judge. I hope earnestly for the statue there mentioned. . . . When I hear anything definite I will write immediately; do you write me news of home directly you receive this. . . . The *Eagle* starts with the mail to-morrow and I must write a note to Helen [1] with this.

.   .   .   .

Tell Rossetti I will write shortly but cannot by the present post.

Hoping soon to see you, my dear father, believe me
Your loving and affectionate son,
THOMAS WOOLNER.

T. WOOLNER TO W. M. ROSSETTI

Extract from letter of September 16, 1853, to William Rossetti, after receiving the portraits [2] by the members of the P.R.B.

" Your brother's drawing of you is a very great boon to me : It looks as calmly upon me as your own face was wont, and as I contemplate it my own soul in some unknown way holds communion with yours : in your brother's

---

[1] Sister of T. Woolner.
[2] Woolner had these drawings for many years in his possession, he did not sell any of them : he gave some to his friend, Mr. H. W. Cosens, who wrote in 1876 to thank him for his " splendid gift," and how he will be his " debtor for ever and ever." The portrait of D. G. Rossetti, by W. Holman Hunt, Woolner exchanged with W. M. Rossetti in 1882 for a drawing of a tree. The portrait of William M. Rossetti by his brother D. G. Rossetti was sold at Sotheby's when the family left Welbeck Street, after the death of the sculptor's wife, 1912.

[*Photograph by W. Jeffrey*

ST. JOHN   MOSES

Two of the bas-reliefs on the pulpit of Llandaff Cathedral.

[*To face page 63.*

first letter there is a little sketch [1] of you fallen asleep
which I treasure as it is admirably characteristic in two
ways."

Dr. Howitt's,
Collins Street,
Melbourne, Victoria,
December 13, 1853.

MY DEAR FATHER,
        Mr. Duerdin a friend of Dr. Howitt's leaves Mel-
bourne in a few days for England and offers to take any
little parcels, therefore I take this opportunity of sending
some daguerreotypes and little nuggets in a myall box—the
wood is a native of this country. Will you let Hunt have
one of my likenesses? And give the Bashaw one of the
nuggets. I leave this place very shortly for Sydney wherefrom I will write and tell what I am doing at more length.
I did not get the Queen's statue to do as I hoped for it was
allowed to drop and no one took any more interest in it.

Did you get the newspapers I sent referring to it?
There was talk of getting up a statue of Mr. La Trobe as
a testimonial, but that is now changed into a gold cup
and plate service—several other things I hoped to get
have died away, so that I think there is very little to be
done here : however, by all accounts Sydney is likely to
prove better, if it do not I shall pack up traps and start
for home sharply or I shall be forgotten entirely by the
public and my friends.

        .   .   .   .   .   .

Bateman is gone back to the Ovens diggings much
against the wishes of his friends here and his own interest.

        .   .   .   .   .   .

We have some fearfully dusty days thro' not having
had rain for many weeks; it is a perfect misery to be in
the town, eyes and nose smarting and throat aching with
the dust. . . .
These are fine times for mechanics, some of whom get
upwards of two pounds a day for their labour.

        .   .   .   .   .   .

I often wonder if Mr. Haehnel [2] has called upon you
since; if you do see him give him my kind remembrances.
        .   .   .   .   .   .

[1] The sketch of William Rossetti fallen asleep—in the letter of
January 1, 1853, from D. G. R. to T. Woolner.
[2] Julius Haehnel, the German animal sculptor, whose acquaintance
Woolner made in 1849. They remained always the best of friends.

I begin to grow uncommonly anxious to get back for I feel the want of an artistic atmosphere. I saw by the papers what a great stir the P.R.B.'s made this year. I am glad Hunt and Rossetti are getting on at last and do really sell their works. I wish I had known how to paint portraits in oil. I might have made plenty of money in no very great time, but sculpture requires a very hard push indeed to make it go down with the public.

I hear very little of the gold fields now, tho' I believe they are in much the same state as when you heard from me last.

.   .   .   .   .   .

How often I wish for a few of my modelling tools for I cannot work so comfortably with the tools I have here as with those at home.

.   .   .   .   .   .

I often wonder how the children will look when I see them again. Give my hearty love to them all. . . . I will tell you all about Sydney when I get there, it and its vicinity are remarkably beautiful from the accounts I hear. . . .

Your most affectionate son,
THOMAS WOOLNER.

Direct to
Dr. Howitt,
Collins Street,
Melbourne, Victoria (as before).
Sydney, January 24, 1854.

MY DEAR FATHER,

You see I have changed quarters since my last letter. I worked out all the good folks I could get to sit to me at Melbourne and came here chiefly to try to get a statue of Wentworth, the Sydney folks have been subscribing towards : they have already raised nearly 3000 pounds. I fear I have but little chance, tho' I am the only sculptor, they are afraid to give it to any one whose name they are not familiar with. The bright old boy Bailey seems to stand the best chance for there is here already a statue of Sir Richard Bourke by him, a monstrously ugly thing but that is no matter. The people here are very well satisfied with it and so they would have been if it had been the figure head of an old ship !

That statue of the Queen I hoped to get at Melbourne dropt to the ground because they could not raise funds sufficient, or I stood a very good chance. If this Wentworth statue were in Melbourne instead of Sydney I could make almost certain of it; but here I have no friends particularly interested in my success. Of course I could not expect to find such friends as the Howitts. I might wait a long time for that. Sir Charles Nicholson, Speaker of the Legislative Council, is remarkably civil to me in introducing me about and inviting me to his house etc., etc., but what good is all this to me, unless I obtain work thro' it?

. . . . . .

I mean to give 2 or 3 weeks more and if I fail in obtaining work will go back to Melbourne where I expect to do a few more medallions, after which I will pack up traps and return to England. I can say nothing certain as yet.

. . . . . .

Did you get some newspapers with long notices of me in them? It is so long since I heard any news of you I think either my communications or yours or possibly both may have been lost.

. . . . . .

I saw by the papers the P.R.B.'s did great things at the R.A.Ex. Millais seems to be looked on as one of the great London Lions. I should wonder but little if the Queer knighted him soon.

. . . . . .

It is a great pity I did not bring a few specimens of my own work with me. They would have been of infinite assistance. The medallions of Carlyle and Tennyson people are constantly asking for. If I had little " Puck " here I know I could get some commissions for him in bronze at a good price. I wish I had taken more pains to hunt up reviews of my works, for the few I have been able to get are of great assistance. Those from the *Spectator* particularly as it is celebrated as a first-rate critic on Art. I wish you could see Sydney. It is a most lovely place. I believe from what celebrated travellers say there is scarcely a more beautiful harbor in the world. Trees are close down to the water except where the hills are broken by abrupt picturesque rocks. The Botanic Gardens are most wonderfully fertile, not a tree, plant, flower or shrub can be mentioned that does not grow here in glorious perfection. English and Indian plants grow side by side

F

European and American. In fact they, any of them, grow just as well as the native grasses and shrubs. I hope you will write to me as soon as you receive this. . . . It may be a month before the Wentworth Statue is decided on.

．　　．　　．　　．　　．　　．

People who are acquainted with useful trades here make almost as good wages as they do in Melbourne, tho' there some of the prices given for labor are preposterous. What think you of plasterers being advertised for at £3 per day? In London a good one gets but 30s. per *week*, a considerable difference this : stonemasons, carpenters, blacksmiths and such kind of workmen can make a very great deal of money. The people who suffer most hardships are clerks and highly educated young men who are unacquainted with any useful business or profession : they are longer than any kind of persons in obtaining employment at all fitting them; but notwithstanding, any fellow determined to get on may if he will but throw overboard any nonsensical notion of dignity he may be troubled with. Living in the same room with me is the son of a foreign nobleman, who wasted what money he had, and finding there was nothing left but to buckle to, as he knew no friends, he got employment in a merchant's office and he is now doing very well : and this is a fellow accustomed to all kinds of luxury and with the best possible education.

Give my best love to Mother and tell her I long greatly to be back and see her and the children.

．　　．　　．　　．　　．　　．

I wonder if you have heard or seen anything of the Rossettis; it seems an age since I heard of them.

．　　．　　．　　．　　．　　．

Hoping ere long to see you, my dear father,
Your affectionate son,
Thomas Woolner.

D. G. Rossetti to T. Woolner

14, *Chatham Place,*
Blackfriars Bridge, London.
Sunday, February 5, 1854.

My dear Woolner,
I began a letter to you on New Year's night, but when I took it up next day it seemed pitched in a dreary

and artificial key, though true I believe then to the train of thought that night generally brings to one. I tore it up, and a month has passed since then, during which nothing certainly has happened to make my letter now less melancholy. I ought to have written before, but have had much to distract me.

You will grieve, with all of us, to hear that our friend Walter Deverell died on the 2nd of this month—three days ago. I suppose my last letter to you was scarcely late enough to have contained the news that he was very seriously ill, which had been the case for some time past. . . . The last time I saw him was less than a fortnight ago, but it was only for a few minutes, and even that against his doctor's injunction. . . . He said to me, "however I must not holloa before I am out of the wood." I do not think though that then he at all believed himself in imminent danger. Last Thursday morning he was told he could not live through the day, and I understand showed no emotion, saying he supposed he was man enough to die. At 4 o'clock he died, retaining perfect consciousness to the last, and without particular pain. During several months' illness he had suffered much at times, but had not taken to his bed till very lately. He continued painting almost to the last, and his last picture, which remains unfinished, was, strangely and sadly, one to be called " The Doctor's Last Visit," in which a doctor was endeavouring to break the news to a family that there was no hope for the patient. This was a design which I remember his making at the time we lived together, and I am sure he took it up lately from no morbid feeling, such being quite foreign from his nature; neither, I am sure from what he often said, and wrote to me, was he at all persuaded then of his great danger. At the time of his death, he and his brothers and sisters were at Chelsea, whither they had removed from Kew when their father died last summer. I believe Deverell's last illness had been in great measure contracted in going backwards and forwards between Kew and the School of Design, returning often late at nights in railway coaches full of draughts, and sometimes even walking all the way, most likely on wet nights when the conveyances were least attainable. Sitting out in all weathers to paint, too, was no doubt one cause, and you know how reckless he was in all things of that sort. He was the eldest left of what one might almost think a doomed family,

so thickly have misfortunes fallen upon it within the last
few years. What the others will now do without him is
difficult to say. . . . I shall accompany poor Deverell to
the grave, if the presence of a stranger will not give pain
to the family. His was the happiest face when our circle
sat together, and it is the first gone that may not return.
None of us had known him so long or perhaps so intimately
as I had; and these very lines of writing seem almost cold
and shocking to me, when I think that they relate to him
whose heart has so often beat with mine in the longing which
death only could end for either; and in so many days of so
many hopes already forgotten. Our friendship has been
long enough to make me now feel old in looking back to its
source : and yet if I live even to middle age, his death will
seem to me a grief of my youth. May God have blessed
him, and bless you and me.

This past year, too, has been the first year of death that
I remember in my own family. In its spring, we lost
my grandmother; and at its close, my grandfather also.
The death of the former had long been looked for, nor had
I seen her for many years, as she was confined to her room
and saw no one but her own children, and my sisters. My
grandfather was past 90 years of age, but a wonderful old
man, and died at last almost suddenly through congestion
of the brain; suffering to the last no decay of intellect, nor
indeed of body in any degree commensurate with his age.
. . . He had the warmest affection for me and all his grandchildren, and his loss is a great loss to all of us.

A subject of the greatest anxiety to us at present is
my father's health. I think you know that for about a
year now, he has been living in Somersetshire with my
mother and youngest sister. During that time he has
become much reduced in every way, and lately we received
such an alarming account of him, that my sister Maria,
William and I, went down together at once. Since then
I am thankful to say he has got rather better, and next
month are all coming to settle in London again. You are
right in supposing that I have missed them greatly. Probably there is scarcely a man who at his outset in life does
not turn wanderer in one way or other, but a very few years
are enough to bring one to wonder at the peace within one's
father's house, and to cherish it as a chief blessing. Shortly
before my father left London, I made a full-length drawing
of him, seated at his writing-table, which every one declares

to be a striking likeness. I should like to paint a portrait now, but he could not bear the fatigue of sitting : I did paint one some years ago, of a large size, which I think you never saw, and which was sent to Scotland. I should like to have it now, as I believe it was a fair resemblance, though not a very first rate piece of painting.

Tuesday, February 7.

To-day I attended Deverell's funeral. Stephens, Munro, and Madox Brown were present also. Millais, who had been most attentive to Deverell during his illness, did not come; you know his excitable nature, and I fancy he would not trust himself.

I have referred as yet so entirely to melancholy subjects that I feel as if I still owed you a whole letter; nor have I yet spoken of the matters so important to our dear friend Bateman, to which your last letter related. On getting that letter (the duplicate copy reached first) I went the same evening to Miss Howitt, and showed her a copy of the letter which I made . . . she has relieved me from even the suspicion of seeming, by being the reporter of her words, to have acted any but a friend's part towards Bateman.

.   .   .   .   .   .

I have been to the Hermitage many times, and many long conversations have we had there about you all. I suppose you know that Miss Howitt's book, *The Art Student in Munich,* has been very successful. I am sorry to say she has not been equally so with a picture of " Faust's Margaret " which she finished lately and sent to the *British Institution.* The wretches have not hung it. It was an open air picture, in sunlight, a most difficult task, and a very good picture. I have not seen her since they sent it back, and hope she will not let it discourage her. But I do not think this, for I never knew any artist with more genuine hopefulness and enthusiasm. The institution snobs have also rejected a picture by W. B. Scott, of the lovely beloved old market place at Hexham, between Newcastle and Carlisle. He and I were there this last summer. We sat and looked at the market place from the deep window of an inn some centuries old, and talked of friends for one pleasant hour, while sun and air seemed whispering together, and the " hovering pigeons " touched the street. It was then that Scott determined to paint the scene, and now these

wretches have given even that hour its unpleasant side.
I have not seen the picture, but am sure it must be good,
from Scott's present ideas and later doings. His poems
are not out yet, but I write to him what you said about *your*
copy that is to be; and he will take care you get it as soon
as published :—but perhaps after all it may not find you
and you may be in England again by that time. Few of
your friends will be gladder to see you than its author.
Besides visiting the North last summer, I walked through
some part of Warwickshire for a week or so, seeing Stratford
on Avon, Coventry, Kenilworth, etc., etc., and having great
glory. Stratford, and still more perhaps the old villages
round about, are perfectly delicious. I shall try and get
that way again for further researches this summer. I was
there when the heavy floods came on, which we have had
this past year; and I saw some wonderful things, sad as the
prospect was to think of. One thing I remember was an
extremely ancient disused chapel and churchyard at
Alveston near Charlcote, which standing rather high had
become islanded by the floods, so that going to pay them a
second visit I could not get to them. All round the fields
were full of water in which the trees and hurdles and hedges
stood reflected. The chapel and ancient graves standing
alone in the midst under the sky, whose heavy clouds even
offered more variety than the features of the desolate
landscape, would have made a most solemn picture. I will
append [1] a sonnet which I wrote at Stratford (almost the
only " poetry " I have done for a year or more) on the site
of Shakespeare's mulberry tree, which was cut down many
years back. . . .
   Your father and eldest sister were here the other day.
The latter, who had not been before, was much struck
by your daguerreotype. Your brother Henry spent one
evening with William and me some time back. . . . Letters
from all of your family will I believe reach you with this,
as they are all to go by the friend of Stephens, who is about
to leave for Melbourne.
   William's letter, accompanying this, is to contain news
of all friends whom I have on that account not mentioned :
it will tell you how Hunt—the world's great man at last
—is off " for the East indeed,"—and of what pictures he
has painted, celebrated already before the town has even
seen them,—and how during his last months here he had

---

[1] This sonnet has been omitted owing to its rather pungent quality.

BUST OF ALFRED TENNYSON, 1857

[*To face page* 70.

become such a swell that he regarded the great Millais as a mere tyro in that particular, and used to be severe on his imperfections. I had a long letter yesterday dated *Malta,* from the glorious old boy; it is full of travelling matters, but nothing transcribable. You will hear how the pinions of the great Millais have grown, till now he takes even the great Ruskin under them, as a poor well-meaning fellow, who must not quite be bullied down :—and of all our friends, less friends with Fame than these :—how Allingham has brought out *Day and Night Songs* in a sixpenny pamphlet : how Brown is married—you guess to whom . . . how Hannay has a babe to perpetuate the family shield and let us hope to care less about it; how Stephens is Stephens still; how North writes now and then, with details of a life precious now to science and literature, but which each letter announces to be within 3 or 4 days of dissolution, in the event of the non-arrival on these shores of a certain amiable being; and how he sends poems " to be taken to Moxon," which it is thought, as that publisher is not resident in Holywell Street, might be reserved against his removal thither :—etc. etc. etc. Of the Ormes, no doubt, you hear from themselves. I spent an evening some time back with our fine old Bernhard's family at Brixton, and heard his letters read there, giving capitally complete notions of everything Australian. I shall write to that first-rate old stunner very soon, as I ought to have done long ago but have always somehow managed to exhaust all news in writing to you. I shall send you my letter for him, as I do not know his address. I suppose you do not see him ever, but if you do, give him my best affection, as also to the best of Batemans.

And now I have really said hardly anything of myself—at least of that sort of news which my true friend Woolner wishes, and ought, to hear of me. Really there is little to tell him. I have begun a picture of which I shall speak in my next, as I am tired of speaking about things begun. And I fear positively that the only thing I have *finished* since writing to you, is a water-colour from the Vita Nuova (as usual you will say !) where Dante is interrupted while drawing an angel on the anniversary of the death of Beatrice. It is quite a different design from one of the same subject in pen and ink which I gave to Millais some years ago; and is far more complete than any water colour I have yet done. It is sold to MacCracken of Belfast, but I overreached myself, after my fashion, by fixing a price on it before I knew how long it would take me. I fancy however he will have the decency eventually to stump up something additional. In poetry, I have done absolutely nothing worthy of mention.

I need not say how happy it made me to hear that there was a chance after all for you at Melbourne, in spite of the failure of gold digging. May the increase and not any decline of success, be eventually the cause of your return to England, though indeed I could almost be selfish enough to wish the latter rather than that you should not return at all. God speed you, dear Woolner. This has been indeed a strange experience for you; and I have full trust that your genius will profit by it in the end, as your health and peace of mind have already. It is a great thing too that you have fallen, in your new country, among such sure and excellent friends. You are one on whose account, even in the roughest path of life, those who love you ought to feel no dejection; nevertheless it is always a pleasure to think that your journey should have brought you, as well as much moral gain, those kind of enjoyments in life which you could least have looked for from it.

Your affectionate friend,
D. G. ROSSETTI.

By the bye, I forgot to say that, at the time you wrote up for coloured chalks, etc., Hunt got them immediately and they were forwarded to Dr. Sibson at the address you gave me. He answered " he should be happy to keep the parcel till Mr. Woolner sent for it." This seemed to me a mistake of some kind, and I am now sending again for it, that in case it has not reached you yet, it may go with this letter.

T. WOOLNER TO HIS FATHER, THOMAS WOOLNER

Address :
Dr. Howitt's,
Collins Street,
Melbourne, Victoria.
March 19, 1854.

MY DEAR FATHER,

I promised to send you word how I proceeded with regard to Wentworth's statue, and now I do so the news is not so satisfactory as I could wish. A few days ago I felt certain of it, as much so as possible without having received the commission, for many of the committee have the strongest wish I should be the sculptor and I was spoken of as such as if it were a thing settled. You will have seen by the newspapers I sent how highly a medallion of Wentworth I did is spoken of. There has been the greatest praise bestowed upon it but as was the case in England with me the matter seems to end there. I should have been quite sure of the statue but one sharp and wise gentleman suggested that it was no reason I could do a statue because I had done a medallion no matter how admirable; this notion frightened most of them and the few who fought for me were beaten : the consequence is they are going to appoint judges in London to decide upon the sculptor; and Wentworth told me last night that if I could show them any works which proved my capability of executing a statue the committee would rather give it to me than to any other. The consequence of this decision is I must return to England quickly as possible, this course being my only chance.

I make a great sacrifice in doing this as I have just become known in Sydney and can obtain as much work as I can do modelling people's heads, but the statue is £2000 commission and too good an opportunity to allow any chance to escape.

. . . . . .

I expect in about 3 months to leave Australia so that I think within 6 or 7 months to be in England. It is an immensely long time since I heard anything of you, quite 9 months, if not more.

. . . . . .

I hear the sculptors in London are very busy; this Wellington death seems to have made them plenty to do. I long to get among artistic affairs again.

. . . . . .

I have had to write a long letter to W. Rossetti concerning this statue business. I am my dear Father,
Your affectionate son,
THOMAS WOOLNER.

CHAPTER III

BEFORE Woolner left Australia by the steamer *Queen of the South*, he went on board the sailing vessel the *Windsor*, which had brought him to Port Phillip nearly two years ago, and renewed acquaintance with his shipmates while the ship was in harbor. The following story (reprinted by kind permission of Messrs. Macmillan & Co.) will take the reader back to the beginning of the voyage out to Australia.

A SEA STORY

I know of no greater pleasure than to chat with good-tempered, intelligent sailors who, enriched by experience in their perilous duties, show in their observations the fresh stamp of individuality. To enjoy this was my good fortune from July 24 to October 27 in the year 1852.

Tired of what then seemed to me the monotony of civilization, and pricked by a spirit of adventure, I joined two artist friends and took passage in the good ship *Windsor*, bound for Port Phillip, in Victoria, our intention being to try our fortune in the gold-fields there. Soon after leaving Plymouth we ran into what the sailors called " a nasty cross swell," in which the vessel pitched and shook so violently, that nearly all the passengers on board, for imperative reasons, sought their cabins, where, the scuttles being fastened close, the confined atmosphere made them worse than they were in the open air. We who remained on deck were continually washed with heavy spray that dashed over the bulwarks; but the appearance of the sea being wild and exhilarating we only took heed of our wetting as a necessary part of the entertainment.

In a few days, having arranged our cabin comfortably, we had plenty of leisure to read, watch the waves and the clouds, discuss our prospects with other passengers, and, as occasion offered, chat with the sailors, with whom I soon became on very friendly terms. On days when the vessel was moderately steady, I used often to sketch likenesses of the officers and others, and these sketches gave considerable amusement on board.

Charley Webb, who had by irregularities been reduced from the dignity of skipper to an able-bodied seaman, came to me one day with a mysterious air and mumbled out that he had a great favour to ask, and if I would be so good he should be very much obliged. The truth was, at Demerara was an old black gal who was very partial to him; and he knew nothing in the world would please her so much as a bit of a likeness of her Charley. Would I just take his figurehead off a bit for her? When he got to Sydney he should be sure to find some old shipmate who would be going to Demerara, and he could get him to take his likeness to the old gal.

Charley was a favourite of mine and I took unusual pains with his portrait, finishing it more carefully than I had done any of the others. The result was a likeness as exact as I was able to make it. One of my friends mounted it on tinted paper with gilded lines and secured it under glass so that it looked presentable and compact. Old Charley was the idol of all the other sailors, and their verdict was unanimous in praise of his likeness, and by this I became so especially popular with them that everything I said or did was sure to be right. Indeed, they carried their admiration so far that on rainy nights when I joined them in the forecastle to smoke and yarn, they told me I ought to have been a sailor. It was a pity I wasn't. I was in fact a good sailor spoiled.

Among my sailor friends was one I name Lee. He had singularly small, white hands, and though doing his work as well as the rest, I rather wondered at there being so much power in those delicate proportions.

One Sunday Lee appeared at the capstan in his daily costume to attend morning service, and was reprimanded by the Captain for " coming dirtily dressed to prayers."

In this the Captain was mistaken, for although Lee was in an ordinary working blouse, it was as clean as it could be; and to my picture-loving eyes he looked as natural and as proper as a man could look.

On the Sunday following my friend appeared in magnificent attire. White duck trousers, a handsome blue frock coat, black waistcoat, silk necktie, black kid gloves, black beaver hat, fine boots, and a handsome cane. After service Lee received a lecture from the Captain " for making a buffoon of himself "; whereat he was, or affected to be, indignant, having taken so much trouble to appear smart.

One day, having Lee to myself, and wanting to understand the secret of those neatly made hands and superior manners, I asked for an account of his life. He told me that he was the son of a clergyman in Devonshire; and being of an unruly disposition, when a boy he ran away to sea, where he had remained ever since; for, being ashamed of what he had done, he had never returned home.

At that time I was given to phrenology and studying the formation of heads with reference to character; and often during fine evenings upon deck I would examine the heads of sailors and of passengers to tell them their ruling tendencies and dispositions.

Once when it was Lee's turn to have his nature unfolded, I told him that he had ideality in larger proportion than any other faculty, and that, above all things, he was fond of anything charming and beautiful. He owned, in an awkward kind of way, that he was rather fond of pretty things.

" ' Rather,' " said I; " your love of beauty has nothing to do with rather. You love pretty things so well you would sooner lose your dinner than miss seeing any beautiful sight."

" No, no," he retorted; " I am not so bad as that. I am fond of such things, but I would not lose my dinner for them. No, no."

He, of course, imagined this disclaimer supported his dignity for rough manliness, and that I should be satisfied with his faint admission. But he had, in this instance,

PROFESSOR ADAM SEDGWICK, 1860

[*To face page 77.*

reckoned without his host; for I began to talk of general subjects, and, after a while, gradually veered towards the beauties of Devonshire scenery; describing the huge forest trees I had seen there; their broad shadows on the grass; undulating glades, barred and mottled with sunshine, tempting onwards to the blue ethereal distance, unless some bright pool, half smothered in flowers, and haunted by innumerable wings, carried attention some other beauty-bewildered way.

" And think of all this scenery," said I, " after a summer shower, when every petal, grass-blade and twig is hung with waterdrops; and, as the sun breaks forth again, every drop, smitten to a little sun, twinkles and burns, and glistens like the great original. Think of all these, and a thousand other delightful things, and then tell me if there is anything else in life to rival them, unless it be a taut ship going, with a spanking breeze, fourteen or sixteen knots an hour."

" You are right," cried Lee. " Many and many a time have I wandered in just such a place when a boy; and many a time have I been wetted through, and walked on till I was dry again; and often have I been scolded for coming in long after dinner-time by my mother, who used to threaten that the next time I was late I should go without any. One day—how well I remember it !—it was so bright and beautiful, I went on from one place to another, farther and farther, till at last it began to be dusk before I thought of turning to go home. And when I did reach home it was so late all there had begun to be alarmed, and were wondering if anything had happened to me. My mother was very angry, and said my conduct was beyond endurance; and, as she had often threatened, now I really should suffer punishment, and have no dinner for my disobedience; and I was actually sent dinnerless to bed."

" So that you really did prefer to lose your dinner than to miss seeing the beautiful sights. That is just what I told you that you would do."

The roars of laughter and merry banter that followed threw poor Lee into sad confusion. His face became red as the wattles of a turkey cock, and he walked away, shaking his head, but saying nothing.

About the middle of October we reached Port Phillip, where the multitude of masts appeared to stretch to an infinite distance. All the vessels of the world seemed there lying peacefully at anchor.

On board our ship nothing could exceed the confusion; packing and unpacking, boxes passing to and fro from the hold, and the universal restlessness of passengers and crew. We had to wait many weary days before we could get a steamer to carry us ashore, so busy were they all in those days of the golden age.

One evening the Captain had all the sailors upon the quarter-deck, and made them a speech promising good wages and a bonus if they would remain with the ship, and that everything should be done to make them comfortable. There was not much response to these good offers, the men being most of them bitten with the gold fever.

Some time after the Captain had finished his harangue, as the sun was setting, Lee came and said that he wanted to have a talk with me, and I went with him on to the forecastle.

He then in a low voice, not much above a whisper, told me he meant to leave the ship, get a berth in Melbourne for a time, save money, go to the diggings, and get a lot of gold. He should then send for his wife and daughter and regularly settle in the country, and he asked me what I thought of his plan? I demanded what possible good could come of my giving him an opinion if he had already made up his mind what he was going to do?

"But I want to hear what you think," he said.

"Oh, very well. Then if you must know what I think, I consider yours a very bad plan. You engaged to sail to Australia, India and China, and to return to the Thames in the same ship, and in common honesty you are bound to perform your contract. If every man broke his engagement whenever it suited him to do so there would be an end to every enterprise in the world, and we should none of us be able to exist as civilized beings."

He moodily replied that a man was bound to do the best for himself and his family.

" Yes," I said, " that is perfectly true; a man should always do the best for himself and his family; but the question is whether behaving dishonestly is ever doing the best. I think not."

He urged that a man did not often find a chance of making his fortune, and must be a fool to miss one when within his reach. Did I not think so? I told him that I would describe two pictures, and he might select which of them he liked best as an example.

" We will suppose that you get safely away from the ship. You then easily obtain a berth in Melbourne, and receive high wages. After awhile you have saved enough to venture an expedition to the gold-fields, where by hard work, aided by sailor skill and dexterity, you succeed in obtaining a handsome amount of gold. You then send to England for your wife and daughter, enter into some business, and become very prosperous; buy land amidst beautiful scenery, build your house; and, as this is a great country for vines, you may have them trailing over your own doorway, and enjoy the rest of your life surrounded by your own flocks and herds in old-fashioned patriarchal grandeur."

Lee was in high rapture, and said that I had hit off his own thoughts to a T, and that it was exactly what he had been looking forward to. Nothing could please him more.

" Yes," I said, " the picture is pleasant enough so far; but wait until I have finished before taking it entirely to heart. In the evening of life, resting in the shadow of your patriarchal vine, you may be gladdened with many stalwart sons and graceful daughters; and do you think that, considering the circumstances you can never fail to remember, you will be able to look them in the face and discourse upon the dignity of truth and virtue and the evil consequences of any deviation from either in the way a father ought to talk to his children? Will not the thought that all your prosperity was based upon a great wrong to your employer check and paralyse all you would say to them? And could a man feel a deeper degradation than in knowing that he dares not speak worthily to his own children?

" This is one picture. I will now give you the other.

" You keep to your engagement and stand by the ship; you go to India and China; you return to England and receive your high wages with likewise the promised bonus. Your diligence has recommended you to the favour of the Captain and officers, who allow you on their next voyage to work your passage out as passenger seaman. You bring with you your wife and child as passengers, and you all arrive safely at Melbourne, where you are soon employed at a salary better than you could ever have reasonably expected. Whether you go to the gold-fields or stay in the town you are sure to be prosperous; and whatever wealth you may then make you can always feel that it is really and truly your own; and at the close of your days you will feel that throughout life you had always done your duty as an honest man."

My friend Lee seemed nervous and jerky, and did not regard the last picture with much complacency; for I suppose it seemed somewhat dull and jog-trot, wholly unlike the visions that had crowded his mind for some time past; and he again asserted that a man should do the best for himself when the chance offered.

I told him that he must please himself; I had put the two ways before him : the wrong way, and the right way. The first seemed pleasant enough, but unfortunately it led to evil; whereas the other was the path of virtue and led to peace and happiness. If he preferred the evil, he knew the way to it. It was no concern of mine which way he went; he had asked for my views, and I had given them; but it rested with himself whether he would take advantage of what he had been told.

I then relit my pipe, which had gone out during our conversation, and left the sailor to think matters over; and should probably, but for the following incident, never have remembered the subject again.

Two days later, about five o'clock in the afternoon, the

steamer which was to take us ashore lay alongside, and we
were all crowding at the gangway to get on board as soon
as we could. While I was awaiting my turn, I felt my
coat twitched several times, and on looking round I saw
Lee with an agitated countenance, who said he wanted
to speak to me. I went with him to the port side of the
ship, behind a huge pile of packages, boxes and trunks,
where he gripped my hand and said he should follow my
advice. I asked him what advice I had given. He told
me it was about not leaving the ship; he meant to stick
to her; and he should never forget my words. Poor
fellow! his eyes were full of tears. He hung down his
head, and giving my hand another hard grip, said : " God
bless you; I shall never forget you," and went hurriedly
away. I never saw him after.

This occurred in October, 1852.

In January, 1854, I went to New South Wales, having
spent the interval mining in the various fields of Victoria,
travelling about the wild, strange country there, and
modelling small medallion likenesses in Melbourne.

After I had been some weeks in Sydney, modelling likenesses by day, and in the evenings enjoying the beauties
of its matchless harbour, within whose waters the blues
of the forget-me-not and the sapphire hold the field in
ever-interchanging rivalry, I heard that the *Windsor* was
lying in harbour.

I was not long in discovering where she lay, when I took
a boat, went on board, and had the gratification of again
seeing my friends : the officers and some of the sailors
with whom I had spent so much pleasant time. They
made numerous inquiries of our shipmates, who were also
gold-digging companions, and of our expeditions, our
success and prospects, and of all that friends would know
who, endeared by close association, meet after a long
absence. I made abundant inquiry concerning the sailors
and officers who were not then with the vessel. At length
I asked one of the mates if he could tell me what had
become of Lee, as I knew that he intended to continue with
them during the whole voyage.

G

" Oh, yes; we had a letter from him about a week ago. When we left Port Phillip, in 1852, he sailed with us to India, and then went on to China, and returned with us to London. He behaved so well during the whole voyage that the Captain and officers were vastly pleased with him. He not only worked well himself but he had great influence with the other men, and helped considerably to keep them in good humour and at their duty. At the end of the cruise he had the whole of his wages to receive together with a handsome bonus; and when we sailed on this voyage he came with us working his way out as a sailor passenger, and bringing his wife and little daughter with him. We left him at Melbourne, and in his letter he says that he got work the day after landing, and that his wages being £5 a week, he feels very comfortable and happy."

If he is living now I have no doubt he is a prosperous and a happy man. If he should ever read these words he will recognize his own likeness, and I daresay will still hold the advice I gave him in honour. But with whatever feeling of gratitude he may think of me, I feel sure that I shall ever regard him with yet higher respect : for my experience of life has taught me that it is an easier thing to give, than to take and act upon even the wisest advice.

.   .   .   .   .   .

Woolner kept a log on his homeward voyage while on the *Queen of the South*, beginning it July 23.

Sunday, July 23.—We are in Bass' Straits; yesterday weighed anchor about 3.0 m. p.m., passed the Heads at 5.30 p.m., the pilot left 6.10 p.m. A large party accompanied us to the Heads then left us by the *Lioness* steamer : there was great hurrahing and cheering in taking leave, perhaps the last for some of us. This morning is delightfully bright and we are favored with a glorious breeze sending us along at about 10 knots. The passengers seem a very respectable set of people and I see no disagreeable ones yet and hope this experience may hold out. I hoped when I returned to England to have had the friends with me I came out with, but now I cannot anticipate seeing them for 2 years at the least. I most sincerely hope neither will regret coming here. When I first saw Australia its hills were soaked in romantic richness and a halo of promise crowned it with glory; I thought if the result in reality were rich as the seeming to me I should find all the vague hopes of youth fulfilled. I have found them infinitely surpassed and am made proud and happy.

Evening.—Been going on at a good pace all day with steam and canvas. I have been on deck most of the time, either looking at the water or walking with Mrs. Wilson. It is beginning to rain now but the wind keeps up.

.   .   .   .   .   .

Tuesday, July 25.—We have a good sea and wind going at a satisfactory pace. Feathered the screw at $7\frac{1}{2}$ a.m. I rose at 8 and had a pleasant walk on deck before breakfast: after, I blew an honorable cloud on the main deck chatting with Mr. Graham.

.   .   .   .   .   .

Sea-birds are floating easily around the ship, their earnest heads pointing with set determination towards the water; it is the way they do business, these beautiful creatures, and seek the essential wherewithal.

Night.—The ocean looks most dreary and desolate; a thick wet mist is over everything and the air soaks chilly into one.

.   .   .   .   .   .

Thursday, July 27.—After dinner I went into the second officer's cabin to see his log and have a yarn : found him a very intelligent fellow and fond of poetry, particularly Tennyson's, he has his poems and sets great store by them : he is going to lend me his log to copy, so I shall have it correct.

.   .   .   .   .   .

Friday, July 28.—Last night the weather was unusually rough and pitched our poor ship about any how : sometimes it felt as if two gigantic hands were shaking it to pieces. I got very little sleep after 2 p.m. and was not sorry to see thro' my scuttle a roundish blotch of light in the eastern vapor that I knew to be the sun. Did not rise till 8.30 a.m.

. . . . . .

Saturday, July 29.—We have had two smart hail-storms, the decks were covered with pretty icebergs in a few minutes much to the edification of the passenger boys, who instantly set about rolling it up into balls and pelting each other. We have now and then a short gleam of sunshine, but the general aspect of sea and sky is waste, hopeless and desolate : over a crumpled horizon, no ease or rest : big waves gather to ponderous bumps of water and flop down bursting about the ship's stern or temporarily shoulder her out of course, and gather up to mountainous bulks and follow us again, as if determined to drive this daring invader from the Southern desolation of waters or swallow it up and let it settle to the bottom. The good ship seems to notice very little these stern waves, but bounds merrily on, jauntily as one of the wild seabirds that wheel about and flutter on her emerald wake or float away beyond the reach of sight.

. . . . . .

Sunday, July 30.—About 10.30 a.m. a savage squall came on from the South East quarter : it roared thro' the rigging like the thundering rush of a mighty furnace and tore the sea up in tumultuous splashy masses, obliterating all around with vapors lashed from the commotion; broad, sodden snowflakes filled the air, falling with an infinite complexity of lines, and the chilly air keenly bit thro' clothing, however thickly laid on. I stood it some time but when my pipe was finished I turned into the saloon where the temperature is pleasant enough. Prayers have been read here by the Doctor, but I did not attend them, being engaged another way.

. . . . . .

Nothing could seem more cheerless than a glance on deck : everything looks stiff with wet, the ropes look particularly obstinate and decks false in slipperiness : sailors and officers move awkwardly and slowly, knees bent, elbows sticking outwards, their souwesters and oilskins

SKETCH FOR CAWNPORE MEMORIAL, 1861
(Never executed.)

[*To face page* 34.

shining and dripping, boots saturated thro' and thro'. Passengers are not troublesome on deck; I saw one standing under the poop awning, more like a mere bundle of clothes with something inside to keep it upright than an active living creature. This weather makes the soul shrink within small compass, as the mercury settles in the thermometer; we use what vitality we have to keep ourselves warm and seem to spare no surplus for fun, vague chatting or anything not strictly essential; therefore we may pick out some one and walk the poop side by side with him for an hour at a time, but do very little talking all the while; that is reserved till we come below, stand over the saloon fire and get thawed, what may be done in that way. We are going about 8 knots now.

. . . .

One thing, a person is forced to have a certain amount of exercise whatever his inclination, for the trouble of keeping balance is considerable even when sitting, and standing is a tax on attentive dexterity that if carried much farther would bid fair to rival the efforts of a tight rope dancer. I saw one albatross this afternoon, the first of this voyage : numerous of those innocent-looking birds called Cape pigeons have been with us since we entered Bass's Straits : the ship never seems so solitary with them circling around.

Monday, July 31.—Another night of tumbling : my berth is of smallest dimensions, more fit for a coffin as regards size, still there was play enough to give my unfortunate ribs a considerable bruising.

. . . . . .

I find it next to impossible to read this weather, being obliged to bestow so much attention on keeping warm. I cannot wonder at the Laplanders and others of the same kind being such senseless phlegmatic beings, for they must absorb all their intellect in getting food and keeping warm, just as bears do. I think men of temperate climates are usually more vigorous than inhabitants of hot countries, but not the men from regions of almost perpetual frost, they are the most dwarfish and insignificant on the earth.

. . . .

[Referring to the want of fresh vegetables on board—which Woolner thought so important.]

Monday, July 31.—If I were an influential individual I would see to these things; but when a person has no hubbub reputation, no matter if he talk the wisdom of a cherub no one will hear him.

Night.—The day has been lovely in contrast with the preceding ones; one short squall came from the west about 3 p.m. which sent the ladies off the poop in a hurry, but we only enjoyed the outskirts as it veered off the southard: it was a glorious sight to watch the difference of where it had been to where it was beating ocean with a mist; there, dazzling waves of light dashed forward in triumphant splendor and made a dim horizon wane dimmer; opposite, was no horizon at all, the squall-cloud plucked the billows up into itself and wrangled and ground them to spray and mist: thro' all this commotion, high above it nearly to the zenith rose the magnificent grace of a rainbow, under which the noble ship seemed entering to a stranger world.

Tuesday, August 1.

Last evening I had a read at Ruskin's first vol. of *Modern Painters* and derived much pleasure from the wisdom of the principles enunciated and the forcible grace of the language they are expressed in. I am convinced the work must do an incalculable amount of good, for it states truths hitherto but dimly understood by many fine artists and totally disregarded by the bulk—I see no evidence of unjust bias in the author, not more than his propositions justify, and I apprehend no man can be too fond of nature and truth. Artists and critics object to this book the same way that unhealthy people object to the physician's injunctions to take exercise and face the pure air of heaven, but if they wish to enjoy long life they must do as they are recommended.

The sweet birds keep with us still, tho' not in great number: lovely companions in the southern waste. I

have no beautiful sunrises or sunsets to note down here;
we rarely see aught but the dull grey uniformity, sometimes
lit with misty sunshine : this afternoon the sun fought
behind a great accumulation of dull grey vapor scudded
with paler mist, and sent down a fan of light broken to
lashes, against which rolled a heavy weight of billows.

Wednesday, August 2.

The sun was victorious this afternoon before sinking,
and bursting thro' a mountain of cloud hurled down a
pyramid of glory to the sea, which heaved a black sullen
mass ponderous as lead. From the great vapor-bulk a
few grey showers were glancing downwards and opposite,
in the south-eastern sky, dimly seen was the opalescent
ghost of a mighty rainbow. I was looking on with a very
orthodox poetic spirit when the abrupt ringing of the bell
announced dinner, of course poetics vanished as beautiful
clouds before a strong wind, for in this bracing southern
cold it is astonishing how the appetite of man develops
and how everything celestial takes fright at this ravenous
wolf !

Saturday, August 5.—Last night I had a good long read
at Ruskin, and enjoyed it as much as was possible in such
a confusion of voices; it delights me the downright hearty
way he cuts up and exposes the ignorant conceits and tame-
ness of the over-lauded old masters as much as it pleases
me the keen, magnificent exposition of Turner's greatness
and the delicate beauties of minor landscape artists. I
should like to hear some of his criticism on the works of
Anthony, who is now a man of note in the world. I suppose taking into account every kind of scenery and style
of treating them, Ruskin understands landscape better
than any other man.

Sunday, August 6.

Night.—The day has been bright throughout, not one

squall or hail drift : the poop and main deck were covered with people; many that had never appeared before, brought out from their cabins by the warm sunshine as moths are from cocoons, and some disported in gay garments, and men manufactured smoke from dried tobacco leaf, leisurely walking ; children ran wildly about trying to catch one another.

Tuesday, August 8.

At 2 p.m. we had to go off our course on another tack. I read a little of Ruskin and finished the first vol. of *Modern Painters.* He must have worked hard during his life to accumulate such an extraordinary amount of truth as is shown in this vol. alone : the character of water is wonderfully rendered, he seems while writing to be a sea-god he understands its nature so perfectly; I have no doubt the rocks and mountains are equally faithful, but I do not know this so well. The trees are truth itself.

Thursday, August 10.

The sea is a great commotion, a pale grey broken with glaring light and transparent shadows and big rolls of foam that burst and over-run the surface of their parent waves. Plenty of the Cape birds accompany us, but I have not seen any they call whale-birds, tho' one would expect to find them here. The Cape birds fly round our ship at night, several people told me they saw them wheeling about in the moonlight. . . . This journal-keeping makes me at times feel fearfully literary ! I do so because I resolved to write something every day and am glad of what may help to feed my resolution.

Unhappy literary men ! poor squirrels in the wheel; doomed to perpetual pawing in your mills to please your many-headed master the public : your kind master who throws a nut or two for giving him a ticklish eye-pleasure in his listless hour, at the cost of your own health, liberty and life itself. Well my good literaries, if you will make squirrels of yourselves you must not wonder the public catch and put you in a cage.

. . . . .

Wednesday, August 16.—The breeze continues, we are going nearly 8 knots. Just as breakfast was over a real genuine iceberg made its appearance off the windward quarter (north) for our edification; there was no mistaking the solidity of this monster of the deep : it rose sheer from the water in a perpendicular line on one side to about 100 ft., then ran along in abrupt craggy points to half its length and gradually sloped till it fell again sheer into the sea; it was pale cold grey with a faint belief of greenness pervading the hollows, but no colour was decidedly distinguishable for a mist that hung in that direction. It seemed to me 8 miles distant, some said only 5, others 12 : the truth of which never will be known. We are in the region of danger at last and the need of keeping a sharp look out is evident : at night it is a matter not to be treated as a joke by any means, for objects cannot be seen any great distance then, particularly ice, which in colour is so similar to the ocean.

. . . . .

Thursday, August 17.

. . . .

I find it pleasant to meet anyone here who has an idea superior to the rooting for riches, for there is a doleful lack of such spirits. A sea voyage would not be so dull an experience if there were minds to associate with; want of this makes it so oppressive : for what human soul can sympathise with bees, ants and squirrels, which those are who regard the storing of wealth as the main object of life? This supposes them honorable in the means of acquiring their desires, which is seldom the case with men possessed of this debasing passion; usually they convert themselves into foxes, rats, ferrets, rapacious wolves, hyenas, serpents, tigers, sharks and sometimes even far worse, into absolute demons, unfit for earth, scorned of heaven, fit only for purification in hell-fire. A sad pity that self-denial is not as assiduously taught the young as the multiplication table is ground into them ! Prudence may be instilled into youths without making its cash aspect the goal of life, just as a mother's care for her child may recommend him keeping his feet dry without making dry feet the great object of his life.

. . . . . .

Friday, August 18.—The morning is bright but remarkably cold, I think the coldest we have had. Several more Icebergs have been seen; one beautiful specimen was seen at the northward; at first it appeared like a great castle on the extreme edge of a table-rock; then changed to a rocky island with sharp mountain spires; the highest peaks were dark grey shimmered with greenish light, the lower part was bathed in an opalescent halo that climbed up the icy gorges like incense; and on the east and one great mass shone a mound of light in the form of a grave. When I first saw it, it stood dark against a light sky afterwards changed to ghostly white sheets hung on a sky of darkness. There are many of the beautiful birds about us to-day, and the boys catch them with fish hooks.

. . . . . .

Wednesday, August 23.—I think I will never make a voyage in one of these steamers again, for a voyage under any circumstance is a detestable thing to undergo, a hateful waste of one's life, a thorough case of being buried alive, a blot of stagnation, but particularly all these when you cannot sit in your cabin and read, must be loitering idly about against your will; this is fearful ruination to every faculty, causing laxity of life, carelessness of thought, laziness and universal deadness. Of course this intellectual havoc refers to myself only, the others are not much affected by the life on shipboard, they are men who have made their fortunes in business and going home to enjoy them; they have no exertion of mind but to think how to spend their money in the pleasantest way.

. . . . . .

Saturday, August 26.—Wind S.W.S., course N.E.N.: consequently the wind is right aft, but not very strong;

THE PIPING SHEPHERD.   FRONTISPIECE TO THE " GOLDEN TREASURY,"
1861
From the original drawing by T. Woolner belonging to Miss Palgrave.

[*To face page* 90.

very cold, ice lies about in snug corners. They put the steam on last night and took it off this morning. The sea is a world of agitation, waves covered with a net of foam fibres like the ribs of leaves; clouds are harsh and hard against the white coldness, the sun breaks through in places and transmutes the water to dazzling silver that baffles observation. It seems to grow colder as, we advance, the counteracting pleasure I feel is that we must grow warmer ere long : I like to put down our position from day to day and feel we are gradually conquering space; space, the hard, the cruel ! [I read yesterday a beautiful tale of a poor sailor who loved a girl and married her; he had been in the coasting trade and lived comfortably till two children were born to him, when he felt the need of more profits for his labor and engaged in a ship bound for a distant part of the world : the ship was wrecked and he thrown on a desert island. His wife waited anxiously his return, till her slender means vanished and then had to sell all her goods; she then went away from all she knew and in secret worked to support her children, which at last brought them to utter misery and near starvation, her strength being insufficient. Just at this time a man who had loved her before her marriage discovered her and took the children to support and aided her in many ways also. At last a sailor appeared who assured the poor woman by certain signs that her husband was really drowned. Hitherto she lived in hope of his return but now all was over : her kind friend in due time asked her to become his wife, at last in gratitude she consented. They had been wedded many years when one bleak night the true husband came back : he went to the house and stood outside and between the curtains saw his wife and her husband, his own son and daughter—now grown to a lovely girl—sitting happily round the fire; his wife was kissing a baby sleeping on her breast—what a haven of happiness in that warm room ! What a hell of wretchedness within himself ! The man would not mar that joy by discovering himself, and felt he returned " Too late," so went his way. Many years after this a villager going

to church noticed an old man apparently asleep on the
grave of the woman which was beside her husband's; they
had both been long dead, and going to wake him found
him dead. They discovered a lock of hair in his poor old
wrinkled hand, and one old villager to whom he had con-
fided his secret, recognized him and related what he knew.
He said when the man returned and saw their comfort he
was resolved to leave his country again saying " there is
no place here for me."]

.   .   .   .   .   .

Monday, August 28.—Wet, sleety and uncomfortable
moving : wind right aft but very light; the ship rolls a
great deal. They hoisted the main royal this morning,
this looks like expectation of light weather. Another
extraordinary event ! Last night I was awakened by a
strange noise near me and as I lay in a dim half uncon
scious state it seemed like the peculiar cry of an opossum;
but as I had not heard of anyone having such a creature
on board I thought I might be mistaken and perhaps it
might be an infant wailing; then again I knew of no infant
so young as to warrant such a feeble cry, therefore in my
doubt I gave up the mystery and fell asleep. When I
came into the saloon this morning I discovered my opossum was a real baby born about the time I heard the
squeaking wail, and on mentioning my experience in the
matter it afforded a joke about the ship : I have not the
least doubt the youngster will be called " Opossum "
henceforth. The event took place in the cabin next mine,
so I have cheering prospects of plenty of midnight music
the rest of the voyage. I can scarcely wonder the little
babe cried at being brought into such a cold uncomfortable world, amid such sea tumbling and discomfort : one
thing, it may prepare it for the buffets it must undergo
in this life of trouble, so all may prove as it should be.
This is the 3rd child produced on the *Queen of the South*
this voyage.

Thursday, August 31.—Going along under close reefed
topsails fore and mainsail. The sea is in grand commotion
alive in every particle. There is a squall on now and the

sky is dark : before this the clouds were solid sharp and hard against a hard crystaline blue, but these squalls like anger obliterate beauty. Last night while sitting in the saloon reading Coleridge I was startled by a prodigious concussion overhead; every one thought the deck was coming in.

Friday, September 1.

Last night read *Bacon's Essays* with the same delight I ever have when reading those masterpieces of thought and expression. Except Carlyle's no other Essays in our language can mate with them in any way that I have read or heard of. His mind is as pregnant with thought as a pomegranate is full of seed and sheds truth as the sun does light.

Thursday, September 14.

We saw a ship coming towards us about 2 p.m., and deep excitement occurred among our folks all eager for English news; after awhile she shortened sail, and we saw she intended speaking us : she turned round by our larboard bow, and when close enough told us her name and country—*Wilhelm* of Hamburgh just sailed from Cadiz; our Captain asked what news ? The answer was " England is war with de Russe."

I saw one flying fish to-day, being the second I have seen this voyage; also a Portuguese man-of-war, a small creature like a nautilus.

Saturday, September 16.

There are many flying fish about, they look like swallows in the graceful turns and undulations of their flight : some are splendid, the under part of the wing being brilliant crimson and their backs dusky blue with white shining tails. Made good runs the last two days.

Monday, September 18.

.　　　.　　　.　　　.　　　.　　　.

Last night I went down into my cabin intending to note
the brilliant phosphorescent light in the wake of the vessel
but the heat was too dense and uncomfortable and I could
not stand it.　I never before saw the light so bright and in
such vast quantity : on the dark waves the spots shone
like stars and in the depths their reflection could be seen,
likewise the wake itself was a solid mass of smothered light
and looked the galaxy in the heavens; it could be seen for
about a ¼ of a mile : at first the sky was quite dark when
the light shone most brilliantly, but soon after the breeze
freshened and blew the sky clear when the light became
faint and nearly died away, except in here and there a few
scattered sparks.

.　　　.　　　.　　　.　　　.　　　.

Tuesday, September 19.

.　　　.　　　.　　　.　　　.　　　.

We glide proudly over the ocean, our noble ship throwing
forth a wedge of foam from its bows : the good ship goes
its steady course loaded with responsibility,—many anxious
human creatures with their strange hopes and fitful passions;
thousands of letters pregnant with value or burning with
emotion, and least, tho' sad to say, often regarded as
first, immense treasure in solid gold.　The breeze is most
favorable for us and shows no sign of lulling, which fact
acts most beneficially on our captain and passengers
generally.　I will write to Melbourne to-day.　I only wish
I had a private place in which I could do it.

.　　　.　　　.　　　.　　　.　　　.

Thursday, September 21.—Glorious morning, delicate
cooling breeze from the north, but though pleasant it
serves us little in making way.　Still under steam : a most
grievous pity our ship is so foul for we lose nearly half the
advantage of our screw; the poor *Queen* labours thro'
the water like a big boat or a woman swimming encumbered
with her garments.　This morning I have been soaked in
perspiration thro' overhauling my boxes to get some things
out : the heat is not the only annoyance, the coal dust is

[*Photograph by* W. *Jeffrey.*

BROTHER AND SISTER; OR, DEAF AND DUMB, 1862

[*To face page* 95.

bestowed so bountifully amidst our goods we cannot use them without immediately becoming covered with the same and appearing like dirty sweeps, blacksmiths or tinkers. The day is most charming and if with this atmosphere we could do as we would it would indeed be happiness.

.   .   .   .

Sunday, September 24.—We came to anchor yesterday between 1 and 2 o'clock. I went on shore with a party and landed about 3 p.m., and after enjoying ourselves walking about the town (St. Jago) and gardens looking at the tropical growth, we returned to the ship between 6 and 7. This morning I went on shore to see the market and returned at midday. The day is crammed full of excitement, bartering for fruit and seeing the stock get on board : the swine were the drollest possible sight, they seemed to entertain a particular aversion to being slung up in the air and testified their disapprobation by most terrible squeaks and shrieks.

Night.—Weighed anchor about 3.40 p.m., we are now steering northward. I think I have seen more strangeness the last two days than I ever saw before in the same length of time : the completely idle animal life of the St. Jago niggers and half-castes, etc., struck me as the most decidedly different existence to what I had ever seen; the Portuguese soldiers with their correct uniforms and weak serious visages I have seen the like of in France; the poor slap-dab buildings I know the correspondencies of; even the vegetation I had mostly seen before, tho' never looking comfortable; but this lolling, swimming, dreaming, vacuous life I never had a definite notion of before; these creatures seem bred in the earth from contact of the sun; born, live, die and are buried in the sun's heat. All strong, healthy and well-built, some are of exquisite symmetry and perfect form; I saw women that would be a mine of value to an artist, and children that reminded me of Titania's Indian fancy, so round, sweet-faced and perfect. These creatures feed on bananas, sugar-cane, potatoes and cocoa nuts, for which they need scarcely do more than gather and devour; they love beads on their wrists and necks and on their children's ankles : the men tie a rag round their loins; women wear something linen just over the breasts, which often falls as low as their feet, tho' by no means always : brats always naked. They are all remarkably civil and pleased to be noticed for the sentiment itself, besides the " dampar," or sixpence, they anticipate. There is none of the contempt shown by the Portuguese natives towards the niggers that is practised by the Americans to their niggers; they all appear snug enough together.

.   .   .   .   .   .

Monday, September 25.—Most brilliant morning, fine breeze : a great number of dusky sea birds floating round and about us. We are in sight of 1 island and lately passed another. We lost 2 sailors at Porto Praya, and took 3 others in that were runaway seamen from ships that went in there for provisions.

Night.—We let go the anchor in St. Vincent's harbor about 5.10 p.m. after a delightful sail all day. This island is a most desolate conglomerate of stony volcanic rubbish; the whole length of the island I scarcely saw ½ a dozen spots of greenness some not more than 3 feet square : in one part up a mountain of loose stones I saw several spots that proved to be goats; how the creatures got there would puzzle a King George; it proves there must be something in the vegetable line or how could the goats live? They are hardy animals, but not strong enough to digest rock I should be inclined to imagine. I see not the remotest sign of a tree, the inhabitants obtain chief part of their provision from St. Jago, and gain their living by the coal. The custom house officer who boarded us had no news of the war, and many were disappointed : I cannot confess to a similar mortification for I had thought very little of the matter, well knowing I could not change the state of affairs whatever excitement I might dissipate in : I suppose I shall hear some at Southampton and can rest satisfied with tolerable fortitude till then.

.   .   .   .   .   .

T. Woolner to His Father, Thomas Woolner

"*Queen of the South*,"
Harbour of St. Vincent's Island,
September 26, 1854.

My dear Father,

You will be surprised to see a letter from me dated from on board ship. I left Port Phillip July 22nd and arrived here yesterday evening. We came by way of Cape Horn and merely called in here to coal. St. Vincents being the general depot for the G.S.S.S. Com.'s ships to call for coal on their way to and from Australia and India.

.   .   .   .   .   .

The ship is so very foul she loses on the average more than 4 knots an hour. I am thoroughly thro' and thro' sick of being on board, and lying at anchor in harbor surrounded by mountains of coarse loose sort of stone that can scarcely produce a grass blade or the most miserable shrub. I see some ugly looking vultures manage to claw out a scraggy existence or I should say the island was incapable of sustaining a living creature. I also saw the track of some land-crabs but it was in the direction and indeed led into a burying ground, I naturally conclude the gaudy monstrosities feed upon the dead. Altogether I should call St. Vincents the reverse of an earthly paradise.

We had our victualling arrangements so unskilfully performed that we fell short after being at sea only 40 days and had to put in at St. Jago, another of the Cape de Verdes, for provisions. There was a vast quantity of fowls, ducks, turkeys taken on board there, but the man who had charge being drunk knew not what he did, stowed them away with the pigs, and going to look at them the next morning found over 100 killed and destroyed by said pigs so that they had to be cast overboard. St. Jago is not like this place except in being a volcanic district, for it is so fertile it not only supplies this rock with all it wants, but numerous ships that continuously call to renovate the larder : they are nearly half niggers there, being 8000 slaves and 10,000 freemen.

The man is shouting to be quick. I must finish in hurry.

Your affectionate son,
Thomas Woolner.

H

Wednesday, September 27.

.   .   .   .   .   .

The women here mostly are anything but beauties, not
so finely formed as the Jago ones, nor did they appear
such a merry easy going set of creatures altogether : I
believe this difference must be occasioned by the soil itself
and influences of the weather. Here is aridity, choking
dust and no greenness except a few scrubby pine looking
stumps, stony hills that cannot grow a grass blade and
clouds floating about that will not rain : there is luxurious
vegetation growing without much attention, their hardest
work seems eating rich fruit the earth throws forth : and
looking round they see green mountains plunging into the
clouds as a beast thrusts its head into a thicket for shade :
the one life is a wandering over a dust heap for scraps,
the other wallows joyously in the midst of plenty, shining
on the fat of the land. At this place I went along the plain
some distance to a well where the town gets supplied with
water : it was just such a one as we read of in extremely
old books, such as Homer and the Bible : there I saw
Rebecca standing on the stone coping of the well drawing
up water, each round dusky arm alternately down and
aloft : her garments most generously disposed : I apprehend she was scarcely well accustomed to a European
stare, for as I stood looking upon her scarf-bound head,
slightly turned aside, and watched the smile tremulous on
her lips—it might be fancy—but I thought I saw through
that dark cheek of hers the rich pomegranate flushing into
bloom. The way of carrying water has the oldest and most
romantic effect; one I saw with the bottom of the red
earthenware vessel on the palm of her hand, not with her
fingers towards you, but towards her own back, which gave
a most delightfully graceful effect : the most common way
is to carry the jars on their heads without wadding or
padding of any kind.

.   .   .   .   .   .

Thursday, September 28.—Dirt, noise and confusion
throughout the ship, for the foul process of coaling goes
on with proper vigour : when we shall get away I know

not but some time this afternoon I suppose. The water is
remarkably green; anyone sitting near catches the reflection and looks verdant in the extreme : fancy a green head
of hair ! but such is the fact, I could not well have believed
it without seeing : it is more like green paint than an
ethereal thing like reflection, several times I have been
quite deceived. The water is so clear the bottom can be
seen distinctly; there are innumerable fishes of all kinds.
I saw a shark this morning floating lazily thro' the wave
and sometimes thrusting up his dorsal fin.

Sunday, October 1.

Another vessel just hove in sight : at first it showed like
a minute sparkle on the fire waters then grew into a pale
butterfly, now it swells a proud ship manifest to all. The
day has grown very warm. I saw one of the finest fields
of cirri at noon that ever was; every form of mottling that
could be conceived; cluster of curved shells raying in
graduated succession, breadths of vapor scarce seen
curdling into substance, and millions of whirling little
manes rampant thro' the sky.

Monday, October 2.

Night.—When I rose this morning I little thought the
fortune of beauty was in store for me I enjoyed to-night.
A wondrous sunset ! An immortal dower to all who saw
it. One might as well attempt to describe the countless
variety of form in the splashing waves of the ocean; the
universe of intricacy in a great forest or the complex
passions that agitate all the nations of the earth, as yield
even a faint notion of the heavenly splendour that shone
upon our gazing as we stood looking with loving eyes
upon the sun's departure to-night. North, South, East
and West, the perfect circumference of the sky was crowded
to astonishment with delicate to ponderous passages of
fineness or power : it was a ring of magnificence, and the
sun was the precious jewel in that rich setting. Round

the sun was a wreath of deep burning light—the lower sky
was red hot—not to be looked at far less written down;
flames dashed from the glowing sky as sparks flash from
beaten iron; the water was fluid metal : above the densest
body of fire lay a plain of clear crystalline sapphire, so pure,
serene and beautiful, had the bright forms of silver sparkle
shining there been angels of God singing everlasting joy
one could not wonder more;—had a long, plaintive wail
for past dismay come floating over the sea, and continued
warbling love and pity to all mankind, till evil hearts
melted in delicious sympathy, and giant Wrong dropt his
sword and chain like things accursed to the lowest darkness
of ocean, and long-suffering man, regenerated, had leaped
like the morning, from his long, black dream, I say these
things had not given me any surprise ! "What would life
be without such sights as these ? "

  · · · · · ·

Friday, October 6.—A delightful morning, fine breeze not
in our favor so much as might be wished. I felt something in the air this morning that vividly reminded me of
England; I could fully believe and hold the fact that I
was drawing near : it might be the iron gray sea laced over
with threads of froth and bursting foam, or the hard gray
sky of dark clouds fleeced with rainy vapor and shattered
thro' with lovely openings of azure, or the fresh chill wind.

  · · · · · ·

 Sunday, October 8.

     · · · ·

There was a poor weary storm-tossed lark settled .on
the ship this morning; it trembled with fear and weakness
looking around upon us with its full clear eyes : one fellow
made a dab and frightened it off : I saw it a few seconds
struggling with the wind and lost it in a great glare of
sunshine that lay on the water. A ship passed us early
this morning which the Captain says was a man of war.
We shall soon be in the thick of the ships. At noon we
were 740 miles from Start Point : now we are less than
1000 I feel getting near home. A fine brig has just passed
on the port side. The breeze is delightful and swells the

XVI.

I had been sitting by her tomb
    In torpor one dark night;
When fitful tremors shook the doom
Of cold, lethargic, settled gloom,
    That weighed upon my sight:

And while I sat, and sickly heaves
    Disturbed my spirits' sloth,
A wind came blown o'er distant sheaves,
That hissing, tore and lashed the leaves
    And lashed the undergrowth:

It roared and howled, it raged about
    With some determined aim;
And storming up the night, brought out
The moon, that like a happy shout,
    Called forth my Lady's name

In sudden splendour on the stone.

[Photograph by H. Dixon.

SPECIMEN OF WOOLNER'S HANDWRITING
Verses from MS. of *My Beautiful Lady.*

[To face page 100.

sails quite hard with plumpness : the foam flies from us in
broad sheets and glitter in the sun. I have been standing
on the forecastle where the action of the ship can be seen
more vividly than elsewhere, and really sometimes she
looks as if she enjoyed the tumbling.

Tuesday, October 10.

Night.—Not many more of them here. Going along
well, 8 knots full. After dinner soon after sundown I saw
a meteor float along the air close to the ship, it passed by
the beam and half round the stern then vanished. I have
read of souls departing in a flame of light and could almost
imagine this a vital spark of some one quitting this con-
tentious world. I hope not. It was the purest light I
ever saw and the most serenely lovely.

Wednesday, October 11.—Last night put away my writing to join in a game of whist with Mr. Peel and others :
I am not fond of card playing but as we play only for
pastime and not money there is no harm. When I went
to bed we were going with a glorious breeze about 9½ knots,
but this morning found a head wind.

Thursday, October 12.

Night.—Abreast the celebrated Eddystone Lighthouse :
we did not expect to hug the land so closely and the Start
was to have been our next indication of land. I have seen
plenty of seaweed floating in patches to-day; even this link
between sea and land tho' trifling is thrice welcome. I saw
dotted in various points on the horizon 13 craft at once;
we spoke one and learned the war continues and Sebastopol
is taken !

For myself though I have occasionally enjoyed a little
intercourse, and the sunsets, the mellow flow of light
around the moon, the wild splashing of ocean, the noon-
day clouds, the sailors' cheerful activity, and the skill of

command, my chief enjoyment has been within myself what was in no way connected with the ship, the people on the ship or the ocean on which we rode : I have had genuine joy, deep and everlasting : and as it has been during the voyage I must ever recur to it with satisfaction as a pleasant portion of life. Throughout my noting are numerous complaints, some sharp and vexing at the time, but they grow dim in the mist of distant time, and as I approach my glorious country these things diminish to small specks of remembrance and I can feel joy alone for what has brought me to her again, and as I look back from the coming years surely the prime feeling will be kindliness and gratitude towards our good ship *Queen of the South*.

.   .   .   .   .

Friday, October 13.—When I finished the above last night I went on deck and saw the Start Light; we came abreast about $10\frac{1}{2}$ p.m.   I saw the land when I woke this morning and could not lie in bed comfortably under the circumstances, and so dressed and came on deck to look at the dear pale cliffs, a comfort to my eyes, ease to my soul, as food to a hungry man this sight to my desires.

So Woolner returned to England from his gold-digging adventures, the hard open-air life had done him a world of good, both in health and spirits, and he did not regret his experiences. He was strengthened and refreshed, and felt that he could now gain his living by his art and get enough portrait work to do to enable him, with the money thus earned, to carry out his ideal artistic aspirations. He was little changed in appearance, and the frontispiece represents him as he then was.[1]   He came back to London hoping to get the Wentworth Statue to do, leaving Sydney where he had plenty of work, on the chance of getting the commission.   While he was in Melbourne and Sydney he modelled many medallion portraits, most of which have been cast in bronze; of especial merit among them

---

[1] He did not grow a beard until 1858, when he wrote to Mrs. Tennyson : "Tell Hallam he will not know me unless he try to imagine me with a cocoanut mat tied round my chin !! when perhaps he may manage it."

may be mentioned those of W. C. Wentworth, Governor Latrobe, Sir Charles Fitzroy, William Fanning, the boy Charlie Howitt and his sister Edith Howitt. The treatment of the hair in these medallions is a notable feature. Woolner often worked himself on the bronzes, after their return from the foundry, giving them a quality and surface rarely seen in any other medallions.

Before Woolner went to Australia he had many friends, among the earliest he numbered Dante Gabriel Rossetti, William Rossetti and the other members of the Rossetti family, Frederic George Stephens, William Allingham, Ford Madox Brown, Coventry Patmore and his wife (" The Angel "), Alfred Tennyson and Mrs. Tennyson, Thomas Carlyle and Mrs. Carlyle, Robert Browning and Mrs. Browning, W. B. Scott and his wife, and members of the Orme family. When he returned to England, between the years 1855 and 1865 his art brought him into a vast circle of friends and acquaintances, and it is hardly exaggeration to say he came in contact in one way or another with most of the people of note in the artistic and literary world of his day. His truthfulness and enthusiasm made him beloved of his friends, but there is no doubt his outspoken opinions and sentiments did not help him in a worldly sense. If he thought a work of art carelessly executed he would say so : he could not praise what he did not think good or which showed a want of the best efforts of the artist, be he painter, sculptor or writer. Careless work or slack work he heartily condemned.

CHAPTER IV

THE next ten years of the sculptor's life will be told almost entirely by means of letters; the greater number being those written to him, although his letters to Mrs. Tennyson have fortunately been preserved.

T. WOOLNER TO MRS. TENNYSON

15, *Mary Street,*
Regent's Park,
October 23, 1854.

MY DEAR MRS. TENNYSON,
I hope you will forgive me for not keeping my promise to write to you from Australia, but really I could have told you nothing that would have interested you, . . . and I only trespass on your time now because I am anxious to hear of you and Mr. Tennyson and your little sons, who are most splendid looking boys I hear from Mrs. Patmore. . . .
I am come to England to try to obtain the execution of a statue of William Wentworth that is to be placed in Sydney : rather a long distance to travel on a chance, but I have solid grounds for hoping it will be given to me or I should not have left Australia for another year, as my works in Sydney were very much liked and I could obtain plenty of employment, taking likenesses only of course, but in this department of art the colonists were fully willing to give encouragement. . . . I was not successful in my mining expedition and did not find nearly enough gold to pay the expenses necessary : but I by no means regret having visited the magnificent country, some of the scenes in which gave me more pleasure than any I ever saw before, being more wild, vast and solitary. I hear of many books, articles, letters, etc., denying the delicious purity of Australian air.

. . . .

I found it all that could be desired everywhere except

in Melbourne, where the hot winds almost stifle the inhabitants occasionally.

Give my kindest regards to Mr. Tennyson and tell him his vol. of Poems was the richest intellectual enjoyment I had during my 2 years and ¼ of exile, it was to me the only link that connected savagery and civilisation.
Believe me,
My dear Mrs. Tennyson,
Ever truly yours,
THOMAS WOOLNER.

P.S.—The specimen I send is an instance of how the gold is frequently found, amalgamated with quartz, and is more interesting than mere gold and I thought you would prefer it.

T. WOOLNER TO MRS. TENNYSON

15, *Mary Street,*
Regent's Park,
December 25, 1854.

MY DEAR MRS. TENNYSON,

I have been thinking of the medallion and have concluded it will be better to make another entirely of a smaller size : the present one could easily be altered but the size I strongly object to : a head or a figure should never be more than half size unless full life sized, and this is nearly ¾.

Tell Mr. Tennyson it will not require a great deal of time as I am so well acquainted with his features now, and he need not anticipate it as an extraordinarily formidable task : Millais told me he read him some new poems of such marvellous beauty, that they surpassed anything he had ever done before, which of course I find too hard to believe true, as I do not believe perfection can be more than perfect.

I am delighted to hear Rossetti and Millais are going to illustrate the poems, with Hunt, they are the only men who ought to presume to tread upon that enchanted ground.
Ever sincerely yours,
THOMAS WOOLNER.

MRS. TENNYSON TO T. WOOLNER

Farringford,
March 29, 1855.

DEAR MR. WOOLNER,

Many thanks for your kind letter. We cannot quarrel with you if you borrow a little sunshine from imagination to throw over your visit at Farringford, however puritanical we may be in our worship of truth.

. . . . . .

Hallam is obliged now to make the best he can of his Mother. His chief delight is Mr. Burchell and he exclaims " Fudge " with roars of laughter a hundred times together. He insists on having this book and no other after dinner. Alfred laughs at him because I maintain it is on account of the superior grace of the designs. Little Lionel lifts his hands in a very pretty way to the " Madonna and Child " when he comes into the Drawing-room and says " Lady ! Pretty ! Baby ! " if you could not admire his taste you would at least like to see him clap his little hands as he does sometimes at this picture. We have had snow and hail since you left. I have another letter to write, so farewell. There are three more tiny poems added to " Maud."

Very sincerely yours,
EMILY TENNYSON.

T. WOOLNER TO MRS. TENNYSON

27, Rutland Street,
Hampstead Road,
November 18, 1855.

MY DEAR MRS. TENNYSON,

. . . . . .

As regards doing a bust, it is what I have wished many years, to do one of him, and I know nothing that would please me so much. I was going to model a group to be exhibited next year in the R. Academy, but if you can persuade him to let me do his bust, I would postpone the modelling of my group and exhibit it the following year instead. If he will let me, will you at the same time allow me to make a medallion of you, for I feel certain I should be able to do one both he and you would be pleased with.

. . . . . .

[*Photograph by Kent and Lacey.*

DR. ALEXANDER WAUGH, MINISTER OF THE SCOTCH
PRESBYTERIAN CHURCH
From a Tassie gem, 1791.

[*To face page* 107.

Patmore has just called. . . . He has completed the 2nd vol. of the *Angel* except 5 idylls and intends publishing as soon as it is completed. I saw a review of a Poem by " Festus " and in an extract occurred, the word " Psychopompous ! "

. . . . .

I think this the most curious instance of departure from simplicity I have seen for a long time.

. . . . .

Yours sincerely,
THOMAS WOOLNER.

MRS. TENNYSON TO T. WOOLNER

Farringford,
November 21, 1855.

DEAR MR. WOOLNER,

Many thanks for your kind letter. I am sure you will know I did not for one moment mean to ask you to give up more time to us than you have already done. I only felt I must tell you how it was that another was going to do a bust of Alfred,[1] because it seemed to me after all your labour you would have a right to be hurt, if you did not know how it came to pass, and I cannot help wishing it were you who had to do it and to say also, that if you still wished it you should have an opportunity of fulfilling your wish. But then we both think you ought not to give up that group. If you wished to do the bust it could be done I suppose any time you are here and finished when you had not other work in hand. Perhaps it is presumptuous to talk thus considering the uncertainties of life. What you say of my medallion is most kind, but some way I cannot feel it right to let you waste your time on my lean face which should have been drawn ten years ago at least, if at all. But, if you think I say this with the slightest feeling you would not make a medallion we should both like, you are very much mistaken. Do you not remember how much we admired your ladies? Perhaps you do not but I do !

. . . . .

Alfred's kindest remembrances,

Most truly yours,
EMILY TENNYSON.

[1] Bust by Brodie.

T. Woolner to Mrs. Tennyson

27, *Rutland Street,*
Hampstead Road,
December 23, 1855.

My dear Mrs. Tennyson,

.   .   .   .   .   .

You must think me very ungrateful to have so long neglected answering your kind beautiful letter, but it is not quite my fault, as I have had to wait the convenience of others to discover when I should be free from petty engagements. I think my road is clear at last. I have been modelling a posthumous medallion, which has taken me 6 times as long as it need have, because the deceased's friends were too inert or busy to come and see it.

.   .   .   .   .   .

What you say of your own medallion, that it should have been done 10 years ago, I can scarcely agree with; for tho' probably your face may have been rounder then, I know the expression was no better and I think not so good : the expression of persons whose minds are fixed upon high and holy things grows better every instant of their lives, thro' growing in fact nearer to that perfection they contemplate. I feel confident your face is admirably adapted for sculpture, therefore I hope you will be resigned to your fate. . . .

I saw Moxon a few days ago, he seemed in high glee that the illustrations were being completed so quickly, his only complaint was of G. Rossetti, but he is now, I believe, hard at work upon them.

.   .   .   .   .   .

Yours very sincerely,
Thomas Woolner.

Mrs. Tennyson to T. Woolner

Farringford,
January 1, 1856.

A happy New Year to you, Dear Mr. Woolner, lovely visions fixed for ever in marble to astonish and delight the world, and whatever else your heart most longs for, and whatever there is good for you, whether you long for it or not !

Many thanks for your kind letter. The time you mention will, I think, be quite convenient. If any unexpected hindrance should arise I will tell you. At present Alfred is at the Grange, but he had no intention of staying more than three or four days. We must catch him as we can for the few sittings you will want. I hope it may be warm enough for us to be in the Drawing-room for I fear the Study would not be so good a light for you.

. . . . .

The chicks are threatening. I must get a little walk before they do more than threaten. The children are well. They have been charmed to-day by a kite which Uncle Weld has made for them. Hallam wanted to know " if Hallam would go up to the sky with a string? " and Baby began flying a letter of mine for his kite.

Very sincerely yours,
EMILY TENNYSON.

T. WOOLNER TO MRS. TENNYSON

27, *Rutland Street,*
Hampstead Road,
January 6, 1856.

MY DEAR MRS. TENNYSON,

I return your pleasant greetings for the new year tho' you need them not, having already all the good this earth affords, a husband glorious and mighty among men, children lovely as they can be, the honor of your friends and the infinite treasure of desert; what can enrich these? I can but hope you will live many many long years to enjoy your blessings.

I think it will be of no consequence where the bust is modelled.

. . . . .

I feel certain he [1] anticipates the operation with shoulder-shrugging horror and I feel sorry to torture him, but as it is a duty I owe myself and country I nerve myself to disregard the fact: I owe it to myself, because in all probability I shall never have another head to equal his so long as I live, therefore ought to make the most of it: to my country, for in some future age how many would regret if there were no adequate representation of him? I hope to lure him into complacency by doing such a likeness of you as will please him, and reward your trouble in sitting by doing his bust in a way that will satisfy you; such are my purposes and wiles. Moxon told me if business

[1] Tennyson.

went satisfactorily with him this spring he would give me a commission to do it in marble.

I was glad to read what you told me of Hallam and baby; I long to see them for they interest me excessively.

Give my kindest remembrances to the great man, and with many thanks for your kindness

Ever truly yours

THOMAS WOOLNER.

T. WOOLNER TO MRS. TENNYSON

27, *Rutland Street,*
Hampstead Road,
March 17, 1856.

MY DEAR MRS. TENNYSON,

I merely write a few words in haste to accompany Luchesi who brings the box.

I am delighted to send you a Myall box—violet scented wood—which I begged from an Australian friend yesterday —he turned the box himself in Australia; inside is a little lump of gold for Lionel, which he can have made into a pin when he arrives at the proper manly proportions— there is a whip that will not wear out for Hallam, and so he can thrash away fearlessly. There are some things for Apollo to clean the tubes of his pipes with, and some of the kind of birdseye weed I smoke.

I likewise send said Apollo some blank books of which he stood in need : there is one for his pocket, that he may be tempted to set down the lovely lines he makes while out walking instead of trusting to a treacherous memory—the writing will not rub out tell him : there is one thick book wherein I wish you would persuade him to write down all the exquisite pictures he has ready formed in words so that they may not be lost, it grieves me to think what risk they run of fading out.

There is a small india-rubber house which is to serve Hallam for a model in the development of his constructive propensities, and a rare virtue for a child's toy, it will not break.

Luchesi will only make the mould of the bust at Farring-ford but will cast it in town; I asked him to cast the

forehead of the original and just the tip of his nose, for if
I do the bust in marble they will be an assurance to me.

[No signature.]

Mrs. Tennyson to T. Woolner

Farringford,
March 20, 1856.

Dear Mr. Woolner,

There is one I can answer for as half inclined to
cry seeing so many kindly appropriate remembrances.
We feel there is one friend at least who does not find
the Solent a Lethe. Accept our best thanks. The boys
were as delighted as you could desire them to be. All
the balls danced together and the licence to whip Mamma
were particularly charming.

The little stretcher Hallam appropriated as "mys"
and began forthwith exercising himself. "Apollo did not
strike the lyre" on the occasion of your departure but he
mourned in sober honest prose and said how sorry he was
you were gone. Baby asked for you and Hallam said
you were "gone over the great towns." Luchesi says
the bust is not at all injured by waiting. Alfred watered
it sedulously on Tuesday and Wednesday.

.   .   .   .   .   .

We have had our noses taken according to order and
A. has had his forehead and hand taken. . . . "Merlin"
goes on grandly. I think "Trust me not at all" or
"Trust me all in all" has grown into an exquisite song.
I hope your kind gifts will preserve many a precious scrap.

[No signature.]

T. Woolner to Mrs. Tennyson

27, Rutland Street,
Hampstead Road,
April 15, 1856.

My dear Mrs. Tennyson,

.   .   .   .   .   .

How sorry I am you are not finally settled about your
house; I had been flattering myself your bothers were
nearly ended, or they would be when the sale was over.

Moxon has not been to see the bust tho' I expect him
every day : all who have admire it very much; some
say it is by far the finest thing I have done and everybody

who knows the original says the likeness is as striking as possible : but I think no one has admired it so much as Millais who went quite into raptures at the sight of it, and told me to tell you he thought it " splendid," he said no other word would express his feeling with regard to it : as a proof of his sincerity he gave me a commission to do a bust of himself,[1] which I am to do when he comes to live in London and he means to have in either marble or bronze; he said he would likewise have one of his wife if he could afford it, but at present this is uncertain.

I am delighted that " Merlin " is written safely down : how I wish I could hear it; I quite envy those fortunates who have.

My dearest remembrances to the great man and your Darlings.

Ever sincerely,
Thomas Woolner.

Mrs. Tennyson to T. Woolner

Farringford,
April 18, 1856.

Dear Mr. Woolner,
What a wonderful medallion have you sent. Wonderful in delicacy ! I congratulate you that after all your unheard of labours and misfortunes the result is so admirable. The only thing I would suggest is the scraping away of a little of the nose underneath the nostril all along to the point so as to shorten the nose a wee bit; if this would not bother you and if you think it right.

We were delighted to hear what Millais said and did. I do hope that little statue of yours [2] will do great things for you. We shall look with warm interest for any proofs of appreciation.

We both of us went to the Grand Review [of the Fleet] in the little Solent and saw things very comfortably and well. The sight was magnificent. I wish you had been there. I got a ticket by mistake and so I came to be there. I am glad I went. The firing along the whole

---

[1] This Bust was not made.   [2] The statue of " Love."

ALICE GERTRUDE WOOLNER

From a painting by Arthur Hughes.

[*To face page* 113.

line when the Queen was saluted, the clearing of the smoke when ships and distant hills began to be seen again, the long line of ships standing up still and grand like an avenue of sphinxes, the cheering, the manning the yards, the great ships turning in slow majesty one after the other. We are glad to have seen so grand a sight.

Poor Mr. Angus Fletcher pray tell him with our kind regards how sorry we are to hear of his lameness. It must be a great trial.

.   .   .   .   .   .

Alfred's love and the boys'.

Most truly yours,
EMILY TENNYSON.

T. WOOLNER TO MRS. TENNYSON

April 29 [1856].

MY DEAR MRS. TENNYSON,

I am rejoiced to find you are so well satisfied with the medallion and have no doubt that the suggestion concerning the nose is correct, for I have never found you wrong in any you have made hitherto : so soon as the box arrives I will look to it. I have always taken your hints but in one instance, and now find I was wrong in not doing so : I refer to making the right jaw of the bust a trifle thicker as you wished and I did not see; now I see clearly it requires that addition. . ... I am heartily glad you both enjoyed the naval review so much; I am sure it must have been a splendid exhibition of power : . . . Give him [Tennyson] my most devoted love and your little darlings.

Ever sincerely,
THOMAS WOOLNER.

T. WOOLNER TO MRS. TENNYSON

27, *Rutland Street,*
Hampstead Road,
May 28 [1856].

MY DEAR MRS. TENNYSON,

I was delighted to hear from you again. . . . I have at last finished your med. and I think it looks very well; I feel sure there is some of your character, for various persons who have seen it remarked upon the extreme sensitiveness it displayed, and some said it was

I

the most sensitive face they ever saw. . . . I saw the
illustrations, some time ago and liked some of Millais'
extremely : the one I preferred is I imagine that you
mentioned—it is a young man leaning on a stick and a
lovely girl talking to him, there were two from " Dora "
and one from the " Sisters " I liked very much ; that old
tower with the wild sky I thought extraordinarily fine,
in nearly all Millais' was great excellency but one of
lovers embracing on sea-shore, which I did not like at all.
. . . It is a pity you have not seen the Exhibition of R.A.
this year, Hunt's " Scapegoat " is wonderful, some of
Millais are exceedingly good in colour, one of them, the
" Blind Girl " is good in expression likewise. Hunt has
not sold his picture and is not likely to now for a long
time. . . . Ruskin has been cutting it up and praised
some of the worst pictures in the place ; he has made such
an obvious mess of it this year that his enemies are dancing
for delight. Hunt says as he has no wife and youngsters
he cares very little for it. . . . I should like Ruskin to
know what he never knew—the want of money for a year
or two ; then he might come to doubt his infallibility and
give an artist working on the right road the benefit of any
little doubt that might arise. The little despot imagines
himself the Pope of Art and would wear 3 crowns as a
right, only they would make him look funny in London !

Very sincerely yours,
THOMAS WOOLNER.

MRS. TENNYSON TO T. WOOLNER

Farringford,
June 10, 1856.

DEAR MR. WOOLNER,

I know you take so kind an interest in us that you
will be glad to hear we are here at last in our home for
life, I hope. I know we have your good wishes for all good
to us in it. I am as you may suppose a good deal knocked
up but I write now partly because I am not sure whether
you are waiting to hear from me, before you fulfil your
kind promise of sending the medallion.

.   .   .   .   .   .

Alfred has nobly stood out all the bustle and bother
of the removal, helping to unpack and himself to place
the things. The boys are charmed at getting back.
Hallam said " may I stay ? " He still retains so much

recollection of you that he persists in calling a stranger kind to him, Mr. Woolner.

Alfred does not know I am writing or he would send kind messages. Be of good cheer the bad days are, I hope, behind you. The night behind and only the day before you.

Most truly yours,
EMILY TENNYSON.

T. WOOLNER TO MRS. TENNYSON

27, Rutland Street,
July 24, 1856.

MY DEAR MRS. TENNYSON,

. . . I was at the Brownings last night; I took them a cast of Mr. Ten.'s med : they were immensely pleased—meant to have it framed and carry it about with them wherever they went. Browning said no likeness could possibly be better. I have improved it since you saw the photograph—it was upon your hint that it " looked scornful tho' very grand : " I watched his face and now have put a slight touch of sweetness which I think is of golden value, and now I consider it the *very best* med : I have done. I have a cast for you when you please to claim it—perhaps you will let me know about when you mean to settle again. My love to pets and their father.

Yours truly,
T. WOOLNER.

T. WOOLNER TO MRS. TENNYSON

27, Rutland Street,
Hampstead Road,
August 16 [1856].

MY DEAR MRS. TENNYSON,

. . . I have been busy at work upon a med : of Robert Browning and have made it so like folks make a great fuss who have seen, his wife seems not to know how to express enough praise. . . . I am very glad Browning is pleased for I have a great admiration for his books except one, and his character I think noble and chivalric to the highest degree. The statue of Bacon is for the New Museum Oxford; but it is not a thing I can well be congratulated upon, for 2 or 3 more such commissions would lodge me in prison for debt. . . . I am anxious to

know how the Arthur poems progress?   I hope they will
not be long before they leap forth into light—Mrs. Browning
has just begun sending to Press a poem 11,000 lines long !
Carlyle sent Patmore a letter praising the *Espousals* up
to the skies.   I saw one of Rossetti's designs for the book [1]
—most lovely. . . .

Yours truly,
THOMAS WOOLNER.

[1] Poems by Alfred Tennyson, illustrated, 1857.

CHAPTER V

Sir John Simeon to T. Woolner

Swainston,
Isle of Wight,
September 10 [1856].

My dear Sir,
    I am just returned home after a short absence, and find on my arrival your most valued and acceptable gift. I really have not words to tell you how fine I think the medallion,[1] and how admirable I consider the likeness. Your kindness is not, I assure you, thrown away, for the likeness of our incomparable friend which I owe to you, will be to me a constant source of deep and daily pleasure. . . . Believe me always,

Yours most truly,
JOHN SIMEON.

T. Woolner, Esq.

James Spedding to T. Woolner

60 *L.I.F.,*
Saturday, September [1856].

My dear Woolner,
    I hoped to call on you this afternoon, but I am overwhelmed with proof-sheets. Your medallion of the Laureate is magnificent, and puts all competitors out of the field. Am I to understand that it is mine to keep— or only to admire for a while?

Yrs. in a hurry,
Jas. Spedding.

[1] Medallion of Alfred Tennyson.

117

WILLIAM ALLINGHAM TO T. WOOLNER

Lane Ballyshannon,
September 4, 1856.

DEAR WOOLNER,

.   .   .   .   .

. . . Emerson's *English Traits* (which I am just writing for) is to me the literary event of the year. I respect America on account of that one just man.

It's comically disgusting to see the *Athenæum's* enumeration of distinguished American writers, Irving, Bancroft, Prescott, Hawthorn, Longfellow, *habitually* ignoring (a good word here) Emerson. What eloquence his is! Sweeter than honey, more cordial than wine. I wish you would tell me some news, however curtly, of yourself, and the rest. I hear from nobody almost. Have you been with Browning? Where is he?

Ever yours,
W. ALLINGHAM.

T. WOOLNER TO MRS. EMILY PATMORE

Wallington,
near Newcastle-on-Tyne,
September 14 [1856].

MY DEAR MRS. PATMORE,

The above address will explain why you received no answer to your kind note of the 8th. I left London last Sunday early by steamer for Newcastle, arrived there on Monday night, arrived here Wednesday morning. The Trevelyans are charming persons. Sir Walter a grave dignified man; very kind and hospitable, and of wide experience in all scientific matters and general knowledge. Lady Trevelyan is full of life and splendid geniality. I could almost agree in Scott's extravagant praise, that she was " the best woman in the whole world." Such a place! such copses and woods and bullrushy ponds with water-hens, etc. Such gardens with old rich brick walls encrusted with romance and peach trees and apple trees—one 76 feet from tip to tip. O, such a place to luxuriate in! I should have called to see you before I started but was working till the last hour. I am so indolent I can scarce bring myself to spare time to write even if I had anything to say. I had a letter from Sir J. Simeon—in a most delighted state about my new

T. W.

THE SCULPTOR AMONG HIS MEN

[*To face page* 119.

medallion of Apollo, says it will be a "constant source of deep and daily pleasure," had a letter from J. Spedding who says it is "magnificent and puts all competition out of the field." From him, this is praise immense and I feel a sort of tingling pleasure as I think of it, for I have a sincere admiration for Spedding.

Excuse this silly gossip.

Yours very truly,

THOMAS WOOLNER.

I expect to start for Edinburgh in a few days. I yearn to see a picturesque city.

T. WOOLNER TO MRS. EMILY PATMORE

Wallington,
near Newcastle-on-Tyne,
[*September* 1856].

MY DEAR MRS. PATMORE,

. . . I should have been delighted to meet the magnates you mention, but you see my reason for not doing so in the above address.

I stay here till Monday when Munro and I start for Jedburgh on foot, thence rail to Edinburgh. The country about the border is I hear fine in the extreme, and they say it would be cruel to miss it. I had an immense treat yesterday. Sir Walter took Munro and me to see Sir John Swinburne's Turner drawings : they are some of the most marvellous art I ever saw—infinite in beauty and interest, a chapter might be written upon each. They are not mounted under glass but in a folio and Miss Swinburne always carries them with her when she travels. Old Sir John is as fine a picture as any drawing, rather more so, the old boy is 96, and as cheerful as any man half that age; and takes as much interest in all that goes on—a handsome looking old fellow. I should not have said so much of him only that he has been a great encourager of art in his day and therefore entitled to my little homage. What a wonderful country this ! ! ! I can scarcely persuade myself to leave it; and if possible the people are nicer than the glorious country. I had heard wonderful accounts of them and find my fancy had not over-colored them in any way and that I had not believed in a thousandth part of their worth. I expect

to be in London in a fortnight or thereabouts. My kind
regards to Mr. Patmore.

                        Yours very sincerely,
                              THOMAS WOOLNER.

            VERNON LUSHINGTON [1] TO T. WOOLNER

                                    Ockham Park,
                                    Ripley, Surrey,
                                    October 2, 1856.
MY DEAR WOOLNER,
      I have got my father's consent for you to take a
medallion of him for me. He is at liberty, I believe all
this month, but would *much prefer* your coming soon.—
Now can you come? and if so, when? Write please by
return of post and tell me. Do not settle about the 21st,
because my father has to be at Bath on that day, to make
some utterance in the Denison case; and I think the
earlier you choose the better, so as to get it over and out
of his mind. Suppose we say, Monday in next week, and
stay as long as you like. Of course I shall be here to keep
you company.

                        Yours very truly,
                              VERNON LUSHINGTON.

            ROBERT BROWNING TO T. WOOLNER

                                    3, *Parade,*
                                    West Cowes,
                                    October 1856.
MY DEAR WOOLNER,
      Your kind & pleasant note has just reached me :
our stay here ends on Monday; hence we proceed for
(perhaps) a week to Taunton; and the remaining fortnight—the autumn—half of October we shall pass at
Devonshire Place. Who knows but you may return
before we set out for Italy again? You make it seem a
long journey now—taking us as it does, from such kind
faces, and admirable right hands. The first thing I shall
do, will be to write to Rossetti. In any case, believe I
carry away memories I run no risk of losing in another
year's absence—if it is to be *that*, and no longer. And

      [1] Vernon Lushington was an early friend of Woolner's, some years his
junior, and he was a generous and enthusiastic admirer of the Sculptor.
Through the young barrister Woolner had the pleasure of knowing the
Rt. Hon. Stephen Lushington and his family.

my wife, (here, correcting proofs at my elbow) bids me
thank you as heartily, and promise for her to remember
us entirely. You must know how we shall watch your
ways, that have begun so—— On the whole, I hope to see
you before we go : if that may not be, send the cast when
you please—and have the goodness not to forget my commission of the *frames*—which the maker can leave. And
you shall have one good-bye word from

Yours faithfully ever,
ROBERT BROWNING.

T. WOOLNER TO MRS. TENNYSON

27, Rutland Street,
October 13 [1856].

MY DEAR MRS. TENNYSON,

> . . . .

Moxon has arranged with the engraver to do the plate
from the new medallion [1] entirely, and he has promised
Moxon to get it done very quickly in consideration of the
importance of doing so. I saw one of the engravings of
Rossetti's design for " Mariana " and think it perfectly
lovely. I know you will be charmed with it. Saw another
of Millais' on the block—as good as possible—some of
Hunt's are remarkably fine, two most splendid, one was
badly cut I fancy.

Browning goes in a few days to Florence already his
wife suffers from the vile weather and has a severe hollow
cough most distressing to her.

> . . . . . .

I hope your little boys are well.

Ever truly,
THOMAS WOOLNER.

T. WOOLNER TO MRS. TENNYSON

27, Rutland Street,
Hampstead Road,
November 6, 1856.

MY DEAR MRS. TENNYSON,

> . . . . . .

I hear that Millais has done a most wonderful design
from the Lord of Burleigh which is being cut in the wood :

---

[1] The medallion of Alfred Tennyson The frontispiece to the Illustrated
Edition of Tennyson's Poems.

a friend of mine—a good judge, says it is finer than any design he has ever done before. Moxon complains loudly that he cannot get the blocks from Rossetti.

I have finished my medallion of Dr. Lushington which gives great satisfaction to the family. They are most delightful persons and I enjoyed my visit to them very much; Vernon, my friend, is one of the kindest and nicest fellows living I think.

I do not get on fast with my marble bust but have now commenced working on it again, and if I escape interruptions expect to get it in little over a month finished.

.   .   .   .   .   .

I suppose you know that Browning is gone to Florence again : which I am sorry for, as he is a first rate man and most delightful companion : I know a great many men of one kind and another but only a few that I really and thoroughly like and he is one of my favourites—you may quite depend that he means any thing he says— what does not frequently happen to one I am sorry to say.

I hope you will hear of some place to suit you among those delightful Lakes for your " change of air " next year. I always look back upon Coniston with a satisfied poetic love, for the happy week I spent there, now more than 6 years ago. I think it the happiest week I ever spent, it gladdens me even at this time and will I think so long as I live.

.   .   .   .   .   .

I was rejoiced to hear from Moxon that the poem " Courage poor heart of Stone " was to be put into the next edition of Maud : I think that of immense import- ance in bridging over what lies between the sadness and the madness.

.   .   .   .   .   .

Ever truly yours,
THOMAS WOOLNER.

MRS. TENNYSON TO T. WOOLNER

Farringford,
November 11, 1856.

MY DEAR MR. WOOLNER,
        The beautiful boxful has arrived quite safely to-day. Accept our best thanks. Dr. and Mrs. Mann are here and are delighted as well as A. and myself with

the delicate yet lofty beauty of the medallion and with
the grandeur of the bust.

.   .   .   .   .   .

Sir John Simeon was so pleased with his medallion and
not less with the maker thereof if I may be permitted to
say so. Your facts of Natural History seem to have had
a great charm for him.

Our boys are well. I wish you could see them. I am
so pleased the medallion and the bust are such great
successes. The bust is A.'s favourite and mine also I
think. The medallion strikes the Manns most at
first.

.   .   .   .   .   .

Very sincerely yours,
EMILY TENNYSON.

T. WOOLNER TO MRS. TENNYSON

27, *Rutland Street,*
Hampstead Road,
November 25, 1856.

MY DEAR MRS. TENNYSON,

.   .   .   .   .   .

I am glad to have seen Lady Franklin, I shall never
forget the unutterable sadness of that face. What did
you think of the miniature poet Read? Allingham said
you might put him in a snuff box then into a waistcoat
pocket. . . . I do not know when I can give myself the
treat of coming to Farringford : my work takes me so
long. . . . I have worked 3 weeks upon the face of my
bust and think it will take me a month longer to finish
the entire bust. . . . After this is done I must finish
Bacon.[1] . . . I have not seen Vernon Lushington yet
but . . . I know there is nothing could possibly delight
him so much as to visit you. . . . I have been very much
pleased with Mrs. Browning's book. There are a few
things I do not think to be true, but when a work contains so much of good I feel it almost ungrateful to find
out faults.

Ever truly yours,
THOMAS WOOLNER.

[1] Dr. Acland of Oxford wrote of this work : " Bacon is the best statue—
and it shall have on every account the best place."

T. Woolner to Mrs. Tennyson

December [1856].

[He thought very highly of " Aurora Leigh," and writes about the poem thus—]

I am heartily glad that you are pleased with " Aurora Leigh," I felt sure you would. Mrs. Browning distinctly meant it for a novel written in metre. I imagine she had a great deal to say, more than she could speak in finished poetry, and as verse was to her far more natural than prose, she adopted the most fluent way of expressing herself. I think she makes a little too much of the social questions, making it too pamphletty—the same thing is illustrated in too many ways, making the book unnecessarily long. . . . I could go on writing a long time now in admiration, for save a few things such I have mentioned, I do thoroughly admire it — the wholesome aspiration that uplifts and illuminates the whole. I long to write and tell her how much I have enjoyed the reading of it, but I can find no time for these luxuries.

William Bell Scott to T. Woolner

Newcastle,
December 4, 1856.

My dear Woolner,

Your Browning came all right a day or two ago. Many thanks for it. . . . The medallion is a splendid piece of work, quite equal to Carlisle [Carlyle] I think, but what a different subject you have had to handle. . . . Some men's works rise in one's estimation infinitely after knowing the authors, and in all cases the peculiarities and characteristics receive great additional interest. But the connection between Browning's face and his works seems to me as little understandable as well can be. Of course his conversation would connect the two immediately but his head is I think the most unprepossessing poet's head it is well possible to imagine. Both the Brownings are certainly greatly and profoundly endowed, the first things of Mrs. B.'s I recollect quite carried me away, but *his* last volumes contain more wonderful lights than any books I know. Her new poem I have not yet read, but I have the notices in the *Spectator* & *Athenæum*. . . .

Your long silence was too bad, if I had not heard of you,
I should have feared you were not well. . . . My picture
is finished, and so far pleases myself, if it confirms the
confidence the Trevelyans have in my handywork the
next will be begun with tremendous pleasure. . . .

Believe me,

My dear Woolner,

Yours,

WILLIAM B. SCOTT.

MRS. TENNYSON TO T. WOOLNER

Farringford,
December 16, 1856.

DEAR MR. WOOLNER,
    I know how much you care for the Brownings so
I am going to tell you the good news we heard from Sir
John Simeon yesterday, that Mr. Kenyon has left them
a good deal of money. If this bring them to live sometimes in the Isle of Wight will it not be delightful ! Many
a happy meeting may you have with them at Farringford.

    A. has taken to rolling the lawn. I must go out to
him. The bairns are well.

Most sincerely yours,

EMILY TENNYSON.

T. WOOLNER TO MRS. TENNYSON

27, *Rutland Street,*
Hampstead Road,
December 17, 1856.

MY DEAR MRS. TENNYSON,
    I am sure there never was one in the whole world
kinder than you, every letter you send me is a fresh
proof. . . . That is fine fun you write of—the Brownings
having plenty of money left them. I do not care much
about it tho'; for they are very well circumstanced in
these matters I believe. . . . If I heard that poor Mrs.
Browning had recovered her strength enough to enable
her to dwell in England, that indeed would delight me :
for at present you know it is utterly impossible for her to
endure an English winter. All the best ladies I know are
delicate : Mrs. Carlyle has been ill a long time; she
scarcely sees any one and cannot get out and she looks

dreadfully weak, it grieves me to look at her. Sir Walter and Lady Trevelyan are in town, but my pleasure has been shadowed in consequence of the same thing; she is so weak and delicate. . . . They are both of the best I ever knew, and I cannot say which is most to be admired. I wish you knew them, for I feel certain that you would thoroughly love Lady Trevelyan : . . . One thing I know you would like, she really worships your great lord, and what I admire in her, she has breadth to take in Browning also;—for I seldom find one who fervently admires both; an admirer of one generally thinks it to be his duty to pitch vigorously into the other. Browning told me he often found men trying to make friends with him by picking holes in Tennyson : he said : " If a man want to make a friend of me, he cannot begin a plan more fatal to his hopes than by finding fault with him : for I thoroughly admire everything he has written, and for a man to find fault with that, is finding fault with my own taste and judgment." That is how I like to hear a man talk.

Since I wrote the above I have been to spend an hour or two with the Trevelyans. . . . They have the greatest interest in my artistic well being and seem to like my things extremely : in fact so much that I expect some day they will give me an order to make something for their grand hall at Wallington, for they have been asking me if I could suggest any appropriate subject, what size I thought figures ought to be, &c. It is late and I will finish another time—will smoke one pipe, then put up the shutters.

.   .   .   .   .   .

My love to your sweet little boys and their illustrious sire.

Ever yours,
THOMAS WOOLNER.

W. B. SCOTT TO T. WOOLNER

Newcastle,
December 22, 1856.

MY DEAR WOOLNER,

I have just learned by a letter from Lady Trevelyan that you are to do something for the centre of the hall— you are to put the finishing crown upon the work—the

THERE SHALL BE ONE FOLD AND ONE SHEPHERD

IN MEMORY OF MARY ELLEN WIFE OF ARCHIBALD PEEL AND DAUGHTER
OF SIR ROGER AND LADY PALMER ... WHO DIED 9TH SEPTR 1863 AGED 31
ALSO IN MEMORY OF THEIR FIRSTBORN ARCHIBALD ROGER, WHO DIED 1ST
FEBRUARY 1860 AGED ONE YEAR AND SEVEN MONTHS

HEAVENLY WELCOME
Monument in Wrexham Church.

[To face page 126.

jolliest piece of news I have heard for a long time.[1] . . .
I write now to tell you I have sent off the box to-day
with a picture inside which you will I hope like in some
degree.   It is an old thing of mine but has always been
a favourite of my own.   It is the *Burgher watch on an
old stone wall*, with the least faint glimmer of evening. . . .
We are now reading " Aurora Leigh."   You say there is
in it the *finest writing* Mrs. Browning has ever done.   I
quite agree with you it is superb in writing, and makes
other poets seem parched and poor, but after all it is a
novel in verse, another *Jane Eyre*. . . .

Yours most truly,
W. B. SCOTT.

MRS. TENNYSON TO T. WOOLNER

Farringford,
December 24, 1856.

DEAR MR. WOOLNER,

This is Christmas Eve and the first in our own
house.   It is saddened by Lionel's being ill as he was
when you were here nearly two years ago.   He was
recovering then.   He has been very unwell since Friday
last, and this is why I have not been able to answer your
kind note before.

.   .   .   .   .

I am so glad you have made such good and pleasant
friends as the Trevelyans.   Next time they want change
of air and may this be long if they only want it for health's
sake !   but when next they do want it, recommend
Freshwater.

I hope you are having a merry Christmas, and that a
happy New Year is coming for you.

.   .   .   .   .

I thought the Brownings had been poor or I should
not so much have rejoiced over their acquisition of money.
I think it is a bad thing to get into the habit of overprizing wealth, whether for one's self or others, and it
seems an overprizing to desire more than food and raiment
and Farringford. . . .

[No signature.]

[1] It was W. B. Scott who induced Woolner to visit Sir Walter and
Lady Trevelyan; and he generously rejoices that they have given his
friend a commission.   Lady Trevelyan had written to ask Woolner to
stay with them, and Scott's representations settled the matter, and a
happy and long friendship was the result.

T. Woolner to Mrs. Tennyson

27, *Rutland Street, N.W.,*
December 30, 1856.

My dear Mrs. Tennyson,

.　　　.　　　.　　　.　　　.

I have nothing of any importance to tell as I go out but little, except to break up my evenings at parties where I spend my time wishing myself at home and doing things that need doing. Gabriel Rossetti a few evenings ago showed me two fresh designs he had done on the wood, one was St. Cecilia who was just dead, fallen back into the arms of an angel : the angel's expression was remarkable for the vivid spiritual light that shone thro' his face; I do not know if it will be possible for the engraver to render this, but if so, Rossetti may think himself fortunate : the background is a most elaborate piece of work. The other is a design of the 7 queens placing King Arthur in the barge and is an interesting thing.

Probably you have heard or read of the death of Thomas Seddon a friend of all our set : he was with Hunt in the Holy Land. He died at Cairo.

.　　　.　　　.　　　.　　　.

With kindest wishes,
Very truly yours,
Thomas Woolner.

James Spedding to T. Woolner

60 *L. I. F.* (*W.C.*),
February 6, 1857.

My dear Woolner,

Could you by accident breakfast with me next Sunday at 10 ? Nobody will be with me except Froude, the historian (whom by the way you might like to see) but I want to speak to you about a matter in which you will take an interest. We have got leave from Lord Verulam to have an engraving of the boy-bust of Bacon for one of our volumes. F. Holl is to engrave it; but how will it be best to get a copy made for him to engrave from ? Drawing from the round is out of his ordinary line, and would take too much time; and he did not seem to know anybody whom he could confidently recommend to do it. Do you ever do such things yourself ?

If not, you must at least know of somebody who could be trusted to make a faithful drawing. If you cannot come to breakfast on Sunday let me know when I shall find you at your studio.

Yrs very Truly,
JAS. SPEDDING.

T. WOOLNER TO MRS. TENNYSON

27, *Rutland Street, N.W.*,
February 11, 1857.

MY DEAR MRS. TENNYSON,

Mr. Jenner called with his brother[1] Dr. Jenner upon me a week or two ago, and was perfectly entranced with my bust, did not seem as if he could tear himself from it. Talk of hero-worship! I think that I never saw anything like it before. Told me he thought " In Memoriam " the highest revelation that we ever had for guidance, and the more the English nation came to that view the greater it would become. And he talked with me a long time show- ing himself to great advantage in these high matters. He does not look the least like a tradesman, but something between a great city merchant and a country gentleman.

I met Mr. Froude at James Spedding's on Sunday morning where I went to meet him at breakfast. He is a handsome, clever quiet looking man, with a musical voice. I was a good deal impressed with him.

At a party on Monday evening I was introduced to Lord Byron's grand-daughter, Lady Annabella King,[2] as the " real maker of the wonderful bust "; many years ago, when she was a child I gave her some lessons in modelling and she remembered me in a moment and said that she had been wondering who I was all the evening, and whether I could be the same person she had known; also she said " Altho' I never heard them mention your name, yet when they were talking of this bust I felt a presentiment that it *must* be of you they

---

[1] Afterwards Sir William Jenner.

[2] Lady Annabella King was not the only young lady Woolner helped with her modelling. Miss Bonham-Carter modelled her statuette of Miss Florence Nightingale with the Lamp under his supervision and guidance, and he also taught Miss Alice Helps, daughter of Sir Arthur Helps, in later days.

were talking." Of course I am bound to consider this very complimentary coming from such an illustrious young lady. But seriously, the enthusiasm this bust creates is something extraordinary, most of which I attribute to the subject, tho' doing so is not so flattering to myself.

With kindest regards,
Very truly yours,
THOMAS WOOLNER.

MRS. TENNYSON TO T. WOOLNER

Farringford,
February 13, 1857.

MY DEAR MR. WOOLNER,
    It was very pleasant to get your note enclosing the other. . . . I am delighted about the bust,[1] and I do hope it will hold so many thousands[2] in its hands, that the one poor little Australian thousand will have no chance of tempting you back across the great ocean.

Forgive these stupid lines but I was so glad to hear some faint echo of the praise that comes to you. I could not forbear writing by return of post to tell you so.

Ever most truly yours,
EMILY TENNYSON.

T. WOOLNER TO MRS. TENNYSON

27, *Rutland Street, N.W.,*
March 8, 1857.

MY DEAR MRS. TENNYSON,
    I have only a few minutes just to tell you that my bust is finished, and send you a card or two, thinking you might know some who would like to see it. . . . I expect a good many next week, or this week perhaps I should call it; Ruskin came yesterday and was more pleased than any one, since Millais saw it, has been : he said that he was "very glad to know that such a thing could be done" and he shook my hand violently several times congratulating me on my "great success" as he called

---

[1] Tennyson.
[2] Woolner had received an invitation to return to Australia and promised work to the amount of one thousand.

it, and when he was going away said, "I consider that bust to be a triumph of Art." Now if he would say this in print it would make my fortune, but unhappily it quite hurts his feelings to have to praise anything without colour.

.   .   .   .

Very truly yours,
THOMAS WOOLNER.

W. B. SCOTT TO T. WOOLNER

Newcastle,
March 8, 1857.

MY DEAR WOOLNER,

Last time I wrote you I quite forgot the little picture of the Harvest moon, and now will you have the kindness to send it in to the Academy on reception day? . . . It appears the sculpture room is to be reformed— are you going to try your luck again with something? From all I hear your bust of Tennyson must be about completion. Everybody says great things of it. That being done and your monumental philosopher, you will be thinking of the centre of the saloon at Wallington. Do you recollect the scheme of the pictorial part? Four pictures on each of the two sides . . . all Northumbrian subjects. . . . You may be sure we in these northern regions are looking forward with tremendous interest to your design. . . . Will you thank D. G. R. for me on the receipt of the numbers of the Magazine. His " burden of Nineveh " comes home to me, it is the right stuff.

Yours,
W. B. SCOTT.

T. WOOLNER TO MRS. TENNYSON

27, Rutland Street, N.W.,
March 16 [1857 ?].

MY DEAR MRS. TENNYSON,

.   .   .   .   .   .

I have been awaiting a satisfactory answer from V. Lushington. . . . I know you will like him greatly for he is one of the dearest fellows living. . . . Mrs. and Mr. Weld came to-day and liked my bust [1] very much.

---

[1] The beardless bust of Tennyson.

Mrs. and Mr. Maurice ditto. Mr. M. said it ought to be in the new National Portrait Gallery for said he, " if they do not have him who will they have? " Of all the persons who have been to see it I fancy Carlyle was the most delighted—said it was a thorough success, absolutely perfect, &c.—and made a great fuss. . . .

Very sincerely,
THOMAS WOOLNER.

MRS. TENNYSON TO T. WOOLNER

Farringford,
March 18, 1857.

MY DEAR MR. WOOLNER,

Our best thanks for the reviews. I cannot tell you how glad we are that the bust should be recognised not unworthily. Surely this is the beginning of a happier day for you.

.   .   .   .   .   .

I quite agree with what you say about big parties and my own private belief is, that it is not thus people get known in a way in which those worthy of being known care to be known. I must not say more to-day than our kindest regards and best wishes.

Most sincerely yours,
EMILY TENNYSON.

I wish the public could compel A. by Act of Parliament to cut off his beard ! We had the Simeons and Camerons here last night. I wished you could have met them. On Monday they assembled here also to keep Lionel's birthday, three years old.

D. G. ROSSETTI TO T. WOOLNER

Friday, March 27, 1857.

DEAR WOOLNER,

.   .   .   .   .

I shall be looking you up for a jaw, when we can settle some matters, I want to introduce you to Linton the engraver who would like to know you, and has a project for an illustrated Mr. & Mrs. Browning [1] to be *done solely* by ourselves & under our control. You ought to

---

[1] This project was never carried out.

join, with portraits certainly & I think with design too. Ought you not? The affair had better not be spoken of to any one yet, except Hunt if you should see him— indeed no one I think till Linton has spoken to Chapman & Hall.

Your
D. G. R.

I only got your note last night.

T. Woolner to Mrs. Tennyson

27, Rutland Street, N.W.,
April 28, 1857.

My dear Mrs. Tennyson,

Many thanks for several kind little notes telegraphing the great man's movements: I am glad that he has come to this part of the kingdom for I have no doubt the change will be of service.

.   .   .   .   .   .

I was grieved to hear the death of Mr. Barrett, not on the old gentleman's account but because I know the distress it will occasion to poor Mrs. Browning, who quite worshipped the old man however unworthy of it he was. He never would be reconciled to her after her marriage, but adopted the somewhat odd plan of hating her for the deed. Poor Mrs. Browning bribed the butler to let her father's dining room blind remain up a little way that she might obtain one glimpse of him from the street, before she started for Florence. She was so weak the poor little creature had to hold on by area rails while she looked her last at her cruel father, then went home and spent the evening in crying.

Another of the old gentleman's whims was not to allow either of his sons to learn any business or profession. . . .

.   .   .   .   .   .

I saw Vernon Lushington last night; he said that he saw Mrs. Carlyle on Saturday night and that she was looking very ill and thin; this is not brilliant, but that she sees anybody is an improvement. I greatly want to see her but it is of no use going so far as it is a great chance for any one to do so.

Ever truly yours,
Thomas Woolner.

T. Woolner to Mrs. Tennyson

27, *Rutland Street, N.W.*,
May 29, 1857..

My dear Mrs. Tennyson,

I have been working hard at little Lushington and shall soon be at a standstill for some of the family to come and look at it. Next week I expect a lot of persons to come and see my Lord Bacon, which is finished and ready to go to its destination : I intend starting it on the 10th June.

For my own part, as I think I have told you before, a visit to your house does me more harm than good, for, I am such a long time so fastidious that no kind of society hardly pleases me, the women do not seem refined enough and the men seen to have dwindled : I must except two, the Carlyles : I saw them on the evening of my return and had the pleasure of finding Mrs. Carlyle considerably better than I have seen her for a long time. Carlyle was sad, almost broken down with the huge difficulties he has still to grapple with in conquering the man whom no other could conquer.

Sincerely yours,
Thomas Woolner.

T. Woolner to Mrs. Tennyson

27, *Rutland Street, N.W.*,
June 25, 1857.

My dear Mrs. Tennyson,

Mr. Lear is in town but I have not yet been able to see him, he is so very busy and says he ought to go to 756 places every evening !

I had a note from Professor Thompson the other day, in which he told me that the Manchester authorities had given my bust the place of honour in the exhibition there.

I cannot send a long note for I am killingly busy working all day and half the night to finish a sketch I am doing for Wentworth's statue : for it seems the Sydney people *will* have a statue after all. Unfortunately I work with no or but little hope as Wentworth knows nothing

DR. JOHN HENRY NEWMAN, 1867

Taken in the Library of Keble College.

[To face page 134.

of art and will not understand my sketch, and fully
believes I know very little of art and seems to have no
confidence—he has been going to Marochetti and Munro.

. . . . . .

He wanted Gibson to do his statue but he refused
saying his hands were full of work, the truth is Gibson
is unable to do a modern statue, and when obliged to do
one he puts his man in a sheet or a blanket—is it not
odd?

Very sincerely,
THOMAS WOOLNER.

I have been several times to Mrs. Prinsep's and have
enjoyed my visits greatly. I always meet interesting
persons. Last Sunday there were Thackeray, Bayard
Taylor, Kinglake, Watts & Hunt. I also saw Mrs.
Brookfield.

T. WOOLNER TO W. M. ROSSETTI

Manchester,
August 2, 1857.

DEAR WILLIAM,
I have not been able before to write. . . . The
Art Treasures Ex. does not close until the end of Oct.
This is a most fearfully busy place, no rest for mind or
body, din, clatter, thunder, dust, smoke, showers of black
smuts, & therefore, as you may suppose not exactly the
place I like. . . . But the Art Treasures are worth any
amount of inconvenience—wonderful—only too rich—you
are bewildered with the amount. The w-colors of Turner,
W. Hunt, D. Cox are without exaggeration transcendently
beautiful. Mulreadys from the life marvellous, the best
I ever saw. . . . I went to hear Dickens read his *Xmas
Carol,* he did it admirably : the Free Trade Hall was
quite full of hearers. I wish you were here. . . . Mr.
Fairbairn's children are most interesting little things and
I suspect that I shall be able to make something good of
them. Tennyson was delighted with Art Treasures, liked
his reception among Manchesterians, they have an immense
reverence for him. I am going to-morrow to stay at
house of Frank Jewsbury, Esq., 92, Stockport Road—if
you should have anything to write about. . . . Kindest
regards to your Mother and sisters.

Yours ever,
THOMAS WOOLNER.

T. WOOLNER TO MRS. TENNYSON

27, *Rutland Street,*
Hampstead Road, N.W.,
August 18, 1857.

MY DEAR MRS. TENNYSON,

I have scarcely got the Manchester smoke and din out of me yet and feel the greatest difficulty in setting to work. I arrived in London at 10 on Saturday night, having had as pleasant a ride with Mr. Stephen Spring Rice as was possible under the circumstances.

.   .   .   .   .   .

I went on Sunday evening to see Carlyle who enquired most kindly after you both and was grieved to hear of your husband's illness. . . . I am anxious to know how he is getting on, do send me a line if you please just to say.

.   .   .   .   .   .

I never heard Carlyle talk more solemnly than he did the other evening about the condition which our statesmen are bringing our country to : he did not at all run into fierce declaiming and denunciation but talked calmly and keenly for fully an hour on India, China and the causes of the outbreaks in a style quite different to parliamentary debates.

.   .   .   .   .   .

Very sincerely,
THOMAS WOOLNER.

Carlyle spoke with profound contempt of Ruskin because the little Art Deity called "Aurora Leigh" the finest poem by far of the present age, and gave him a copy to read.

T. WOOLNER TO MRS. TENNYSON

27, *Rutland Street,*
Hampstead Road, N.W.,
August 23, 1857.

MY DEAR MRS. TENNYSON,

.   .   .   .   .

In my last letter I forgot to tell you how miserable my pussy was after I left here for Manchester : poor puss came in as usual at my tea time and as I was absent he looked quite unhappy and would not take his milk when given to him, and after coming fruitlessly for several evenings ceased coming altogether. When I came back on Saturday night he made a deal of fuss, jumped upon my knee—a liberty he never takes at any other time—sat down and purred most triumphantly. On Sunday evening we had tea $\frac{1}{2}$ an hour earlier than usual and when puss came in I was absent; he could scarcely believe it, but went up to my brother several times to examine him, and at last having come to the conclusion that his senses did not deceive him, he sat looking at my vacant chair and would not be consoled either with milk or bread and butter. Who will ever persuade me that pussies have no affections? The truth is very few persons treat them with proper respect, and animals understand a slight or insult a great deal more clearly than we give them credit for.

I am going on with my sketch for Mr. Fairbairn's children but at present I cannot say satisfactorily: I find it so hard to fix my mind upon one subject after having had it dissipated upon many as I had at the Manchester Ex: and railway travelling always upsets my head for work for some time.

．　　．　　．　　．

I should like to go and live in Paris for a year or two: I think that if I get the Fairbairn children's heads modelled and can secure a commission from the Trevelyans I may be able to manage it. It would be a great thing for me, as I found the Paris atmosphere dry and well suited to me; and besides I should not have such a fearful deal of my time occupied with friends and folks of my acquaintance. . .

I was grieved to see the death of Sir Henry Lawrence announced, for, from what I have been able to gather he was by far the most able man in India : his brother is also a very fine fellow, but we are not overdone with great men. I am going to see the Patmores this evening.

．　　．　　．　　．

Very sincerely,
THOMAS WOOLNER.

T. WOOLNER TO MRS. TENNYSON

27, *Rutland Street, N.W.,*
October 13 [1857 ?].

MY DEAR MRS. TENNYSON,

What of all things in the world think you I have been doing? Novel-reading! I have finished off *Pamela* and am now deep in *Clarissa Harlowe :* I am enchanted with her, the fine sensibilities and choice suggestions of her beauty, her noble indomitable soul; as for the scamp Lovelace, his character is perfection as a piece of art, if art can be perfect without perfect adherence to truth : I say this for I do not believe it possible to find a man with such consummate gifts, so keenly alive to all that is good and refined that could pursue an angel-hearted girl with such relentless villainy for such a fantastical object. This is the chief objection I have to the work, but my admiration is manifold and too complex to express in a few words : there are 7 vols. I am deep into the 4th and feel no sign of lagging interest : surely this is something remarkable in a reflective kind of novel as I may call this. I am the more pleased with this Clarissa as modern writers have not the power of delineating noble women : of all modern female characters "Maud" is the only one that peculiarly delights me; I love Clarissa's character and because her character is so thoroughly developed & Maud because there are only a few divine suggestions and all the rest left to the imagination. . . . I finished my Fairbairn sketch and have almost done the Trevelyans one. . . . I will in some other letter give you my meaning in the sketch for Trevelyans : I hope they will like it for I feel sure of being able to make an attractive and interesting group of it. I hope that Ruskin who has been staying with them, has not set their minds against having a piece of sculpture at all, for he is quite capable of such a thing, and he openly avows that he " hates sculpture." . . .

Very sincerely,
THOMAS WOOLNER.

MRS. TENNYSON TO T. WOOLNER

Wednesday, December 16 [1857 ?].

MY DEAR MR. WOOLNER,

We did not mean to have gone but when they came and took us in a fly what could we do ? Not that we should have gone had they not told us Mr. Maurice could not come. The boys are both very crazy about coming to see you. I hope we shall manage to be with you to-morrow about 4 and then perhaps you may come with us, we are to go to Mrs. Prinsep's on Friday. I do badly to stay in a a house, and should always like my private house like a snail to moor alongside of that of a friend.

Very sincerely yours,
EMILY TENNYSON.

T. Woolner to Mrs. Tennyson

27, *Rutland Street, N.W.*,
December 17, 1857.

My dear Mrs. Tennyson,

I want immensely to finish off your med: because I hate to have incomplete things about me, and I know if I make it perfect it will be a great delight to many of your friends, for altho' you do very little in the visiting way, you are the most popular lady I ever knew : it would be of no use for me to come only for 2 or 3 days, as it takes 2 days to allow the railway shaking to subside with me, and I can never work upon any very delicate work unless I feel quite calm and settled.

I went by Mrs. Cameron's invitation to the Prescotts' on Tuesday evening to look at private theatricals in which Miss Cameron took a chief part : she really did it remarkably well, in fact, if she had not been so obviously young, she might have been mistaken for an experienced actress; her movement was perfectly unembarrassed and expressive and her voice was just as natural, as if she were taking her tea and chatting with a few private friends : the old satirist Thackeray sat next to me and he seemed to be extremely amused, turned to Mrs. Cameron " Never let her act again, or she will be ruined from this moment." I suppose he meant in consequence of her great success and the elicited plaudits. Lord Monteagle and Mr. Spring Rice were there. I believe there was to have been a ball after the supper but Hunt and I came away immediately the acting was over. . . .

Very truly
Thomas Woolner.

CHAPTER VI

VERNON LUSHINGTON TO T. WOOLNER

St. George's Hall, Liverpool,
January 6, 1858.

DEAR WOOLNER,

I have received both your notes, they came both together. And the worst is my answer must be a wet blanket to your scheme. . . . I have this however to tell you that I have just come back from smoking a pipe with our friend Mr. Miller : and he bids me say, he will be just *delighted*, if you will come and see *him*, " come straight " he says, " to 9 Everton Brow and take up your bed there." There you shall see Turners, Millaises, Winduses almost as many as you will, and one of the heartiest of human kind that now walk on terra firma. I am sure you would enjoy it. I hope all things prosper with you at Manchester. One of my hopes in the world is to see you recognised at your proper worth.

As for me & the Law, we get on pretty well. I am like a farmer *jogging* to market;—not yet having reached market.

Yours affectionately,
VERNON LUSHINGTON.

T. WOOLNER TO MRS. TENNYSON

Northwood, Manchester,
January 11, 1858.

MY DEAR MRS. TENNYSON,

. . . . . .

I have an awfully tough job in these children, and often fancy the difficulty will prove insurmountable.

Mrs. and Mr. Fairbairn have gone away for a week, and intend visiting Lord Ward and D. of Newcastle : Mrs. Fairbairn was half afraid to go because the little boy was seized with a violent fit of crying just as she was starting : the Dr. came and said the pain in his knee which caused the crying was only temporary.

I have been once to see the Jewsburys and they made no end of affectionate enquiries for their great hero : Miss Geraldine Jewsbury says that they have never ceased talking of the night he visited them and feel and vow eternal gratitude toward me for having taken him there, in fact, she says, it was the culmination of their existence, and to crown it all, his introducing you to Mrs. Jewsbury was to make the remainder of their days golden or something of the kind.

You will think I must have plenty of spare time to run on gossiping thus. . . .

Very sincerely,
Thomas Woolner.

T. Woolner to Mrs. Tennyson

27, Rutland Street, N.W.,
February 11, 1858.

My dear Mrs. Tennyson,
          I have at last reached Babylon in the South and can have my chat to you again; I could not do so before as my life has been a model of perpetual motion ever since I left Fairbairns, and when I was there I had no extra time, but was engaged in no end of ways and at last found it quite impossible to fulfil all my intentions and the intentions of others towards me, so made a clean run of it and went away to Liverpool where I stayed three days with Mr. Miller—a gentleman who owns a valuable collection of pictures and is extremely hospitable to artists. I was hugely delighted with the great Liverpool Dock five miles long, the largest and best in the whole world : the day I was there the ships, from one end to the other, were decked in all their colours, and as there was plenty of wind the scene was very gay. What I found most interesting was to watch the ships discharging cargo, with the strange countenances of the sailors and their foreign costumes.

From Liverpool I went to Newcastle and stayed a few days with my friend W. B. Scott : while there I went to hear Gerald Massey deliver a lecture on Pre-Raphaelitism; it was very good and stated the truth of the movement in a popular and attractive manner.

.   .   .   .   .

From Newcastle I went to Wallington and really enjoyed

several days, during the day going out with the keeper shooting hares, pheasants &c., a most glorious way of seeing the country, besides exercising the prerogative of humanity in bringing the feathered race within bounds; In the evening sitting and chatting with Lady Trevelyan and Sir Walter and a beautiful young lady a niece of theirs.

On my way home I called at York and stayed a few days with a friend; the most notable thing I did there was to convert a whole family to the true faith in matters poetical by reading *The Miller's Daughter* and *The Gardener's Daughter, The Sisters* and a few minor things. They were nice kind persons with a good amount of sense and taste, but somehow they were unable to penetrate the meaning and catch the music: when I had done reading they said they had never heard anything so lovely in all their lives, and that they always should have admired it if they had properly understood it. So you see, to a person of frantic philanthropies, such as I am for instance, chances are always turning up where a little good may be done !

.   .   .   .   .

I enclose a pretty lace collar for my little friend Hallam; It was made by Lady Trevelyan expressly for him and as it was for such a distinguished child as the son of our living Apollo, of course she took extra pains in stitching it up : she sat up late the night before I came away to get it done.

.   .   .   .   .

Very sincerely yours,
THOMAS WOOLNER.

I did a med : of Fairbairn when I was there, he makes a very good one.

W. B. SCOTT TO T. WOOLNER

Miss Hare's Balcony House,
Tynemouth,
February 23, 1858.

MY DEAR WOOLNER,
          Thanks for your letter, numerous and fervent in proportion to the agony indured by the writer of said missive. It is too bad to ask you to write I plainly see, so we in these parts must be content to have all the fewer letters however much coveted. But why can't you live with the world shut out, you bachelor sculptor ? If you had a wife and no studio out of the house, I am afraid no

THE LORD'S PRAYER; OR, TREVELYAN GROUP

[*To face page* 142.

amount of income would compass solitude, but as you are—more especially with the doctrine you express about *work* (*which* I apprehend to be a nuisance at all times and under all circumstances save when it is called for by the good of others) to wish and to have lie so close one would say, they may be comprehended in one. Here we are in front of the sea, which is to-day like a waste of snowdrift under the pressure of a southeast wind, making the window blinds bellow like sails, and ventilating this room in a most anti-sanitary manner, dreadful for one's hands. The effect is quite other than what I want, so I have an excuse for retiring to the fire and answering your letter my dear old smoker. . . .

My wife sends her kindest remembrances and wishes you were here still.

Yours ever,

W. B. Scott.

T. Woolner to Mrs. Tennyson

27, Rut'and Street, N.W.,
February 22, 1858.

My dear Mrs. Tennyson,

I was highly delighted to receive your letter and the little letters and messages : I was surprised that Hallam had made such progress in writing, and how prettily put together his words were.

I have not commenced modelling either Fairbairn's or the Trevelyan group but am going on with the marble bust of little Lushington and cleaning up a few casts of my Tennyson bust. I received a message from Mr. Ruxton, the chief and projector of the American Ex : of English pictures at New York, that if I would send my bust over to Boston a Dr. Bellows of that town would undoubtedly buy it : Dr. B. says he feels inclined to buy it unseen, having heard so much about [it] from Emerson. I suppose Emerson must have read about it and had mentioned it in his correspondence.

Have you seen and do you like W. Morris' poems ? I have not seen them to read yet, but long ago he read me some which I thought contained some original ideas and an extraordinary power of entering the far-back old knightly way of looking at things. He is one of the men who worked at the mural Arthur pictures at Oxford, but is not experienced as an artist. I am afraid from all I gather that those pictures are not the marvels of art persons might be led to suppose who only listened to the rhapsodies of Ruskin from himself or diluted through his disciples : I have heard only one person who is totally unexperienced give an opinion upon them, and altho' he admits any amount of originality, yet at the same time confesses that it does not fulfil its object.

.   .   .   .   .   .

I saw James Spedding a week ago sitting in his little back room correcting Bacon proof sheets as usual; I stayed and smoked a cigar with the judicious philosopher and heard him defend Lord Palmerston's policy toward Louis Napoleon and chat upon various things; he made kind enquiries of you all, said he had not heard of you for nearly two months.

I suppose you do not take much interest in the hubble-bubble of selfish politics; but if you did you would not receive much hope from such characters as S. Warren, Bulwer and Disraeli being three of our rulers. " It's a sad thing " Carlyle once said to me " when a man cannot respect the government of his country." I am afraid we have been in that predicament for some time past and seem likely so to continue.

.   .   .   .   .   .

Very sincerely
THOMAS WOOLNER.

I wish indeed I had been dining with you when Sir John was or at any time.

MRS. TENNYSON TO T. WOOLNER

Farringford,
February 25, 1858.

MY DEAR MR. WOOLNER,
Many thanks for both the letters. If you could have seen the quiet smile at one moment, the shout of delight at another as the letter moved them, I think you would have felt repaid for the trouble of writing it.

.   .   .   .   .   .

But for that bust it does seem a very great shame that it should leave England. We had heard that Trinity

College had offered £200 for it. I do not know what the price fixed on it is but I have that feeling for Trinity that as far as feeling goes I would rather have it there than elsewhere, though I know it ought to be in London.

. . . . . .

Alfred says " tell him not to part with that to America he is sure to find a purchaser in England." I do hope you will soon come to us.

> With Alfred's and the boys' love and thanks,
> Most truly yours,
> EMILY TENNYSON.

T. WOOLNER TO MRS. TENNYSON

> 27, *Rutland Street,*
> *Hampstead Road, N.W.,*
> *March* 11 [1858].

MY DEAR MRS. TENNYSON.

I was at J. Parker's on Tuesday evening and there saw Matthew Arnold, first time since I saw him at Tent Lodge in 1850 : . . . he made kind enquiries after you who seem to have taken his fancy exceedingly. He was a regular swell, in brilliant white kid gloves, glittering boots and costume cut in most perfect fashion. He had a long talk with Patmore : whose countenance the whole time beamed radiant joy with the satisfaction of holding intercourse with such a high Oxford don of critical propensities. You were mistaken in supposing Trinity College had offered £200 for my bust; if they had the bust should have been in their Library long ago. . . . I went and saw the immortal Thomas and his wife the other evening : I am happy to say she is getting thro' this winter far better than she did the last . . . He—the grim one—was almost pleased for he has nearly completed his 2 first Vols. of *Frederick.* He was talking chiefly upon the barbaric ignorance of the English in matters historical, and retailed an anecdote which he said was almost incredible, only as it happened to himself he could manage to believe it :—He was at a nobleman's house where were collected some of the chief lawyers and statesmen of the land, and happening to mention the battle of Tcherzsne between the Russians and Turks in 1770, he said not one of these distinguished persons had ever heard of it ! . . .

> With kindest wishes,
> Very sincerely,
> THOMAS WOOLNER.

L

27, *Rutland Street,*
Hampstead Road, N.W.,
April 2, 1858.

MY DEAR MRS. TENNYSON,

.   .   .   .   .   .

I went to spend the day at Cambridge the Sunday before last, but was so pleased with the place that I stayed Monday likewise. I had never been there before and found plenty to interest me among those stately old colleges, for they are so filled with associations of mighty men : a person might spend a week there agreeably if not profitably, probably both; but my stay was so short that I could only glance at the lions and the rarities. I saw Milton's mulberry tree, planted by his own hand they say. I went to Trinity, saw the proud Master who showed me the statue of Bacon, which is only a modernised copy of the old one in St. Michael's Church at St. Albans; also the statue of Milton by Roubilliac, which is a very good specimen of a very bad manner. After looking at these the high dignitary took me into the library and showed me the statue of Byron by Thorwaldsen.

Mr. Clark the tutor of Trinity kindly invited me to dine in Hall, and I found it very interesting to see the hundreds of students in their old quaint gowns busily employed doing honour to substantial things : after dinner a long grace in Latin, then we adjourned to Accommodation Room, where I had a long chat with Professor Thompson upon Greek Art chiefly Phidian; I found him an extremely interesting dignitary and most appallingly knowing in matters Greek.

I stayed with Mr. Macmillan the publisher : he was extraordinarily kind in showing me about, and he has such a keen appreciation for all high things in poetry and other literature that he is a very agreeable companion.

.   .   .   .   .   .

I called and saw Mrs. Carlyle and am sorry to say she looks most dreadfully ill : she had got through the winter very well until two warm days came about ten days ago, when she was tempted by the genial air to go out of doors for ten minutes each day and doing so gave her fresh cold. She feels it irksome to remain in so long having been shut up for twelve weeks : she looks worn and sad, I did not see the grim man, but he is I believe pretty well and hard at work bringing his 2 first vols. of *Frederick* to a close.

After this I took steamboat and train and went to see Mrs. Cameron; I met Miss Cameron with a large brown paper bag full of hot-cross buns, which she was taking to some hospital patients close by !

.   .   .   .   .

I saw Patmore the other night at J. Parker's and he was talking a great deal to me of a new poem called *Anastasia,* which he says contains some of the finest things he ever read, and that for fine imagery Shelley is nothing to him : I have not had an opportunity of seeing it yet but I daresay you have as all poems are sent to Farringford. Patmore's own book is selling off well at last : so his turn has come at last; his *Angel* has not met the respect she deserved at the hands of the British Public, and now I suppose said Public mean to recompense him for old neglect : as you may naturally suppose P. is in good spirits.

At Parker's I also met Froude, who is an extremely serious man; he said he should greatly like me to model a bust of the high and puissant Thomas Carlyle, for he believes that Carlyle and Tennyson are the only men of the present time whose heads will be cared for 200 years hence. It does seem a pity such a prodigious genius should not have his countenance recorded faithfully in a durable material. The difficulty would be to get him to sit, in fact it would be a formidable undertaking, for the dragon might open fire at any moment.

.   .   .   .   .

Believe me,
Ever sincerely,
THOMAS WOOLNER.

HALLAM TENNYSON TO T. WOOLNER

Farringford,
April 28, 1858.

MY DEAR MR. WOOLNER,
Love and kisses. I used to love you and you used to love me and you played with me. I love you and you love me. What games did you play with me when you were here? Have you forgotten them? Mamma has not been well but now she is better and papa is making a beautiful summer-house, and would you like to come and see it? Mamma has been wheeled in the little carriage

and papa draws it, and papa says mamma must come to the summer-house and papa painted the summer-house all by himself. I want very much to see you.

Your affectionate

HALLAM TENNYSON.

T. WOOLNER TO MRS. TENNYSON

27, *Rutland Street,*
Hampstead Road, N.W.,
May 2, 1858.

MY DEAR MRS. TENNYSON,

I have been half expecting to do a bust of Sir James Brooke; T. Fairbairn says if he can be induced to sit to me he will have it done in marble : Mr. Novelli, T. Fairbairn's most intimate friend knows, the Rajah well and is going to do his best towards that object; this is one reason why I must be here and on the alert, in case of an opportunity offering. I have finished the bust of little Lushington, which took me a long time.

I will write again when I have seen Hunt and Mrs. Carlyle.

Tell Hallam I should very much like to see the summer-house and see his Papa's style of painting upon it. I expect it is in the broad anti-pre-Raphaelite style. And Lionel tell him his letter was a very pretty letter, but I was not perfectly clear as to its meaning in some parts, but I saw it was very affectionate, which I was very glad to see; and tell them both I hope soon to love and kiss them really instead of in letters, for the love in letters is not so sweet as when we can see it with our eyes.

With kindest wishes,

Ever sincerely,

THOMAS WOOLNER.

T. WOOLNER TO MRS. TENNYSON

27, *Rutland Street,*
Hampstead Road, N.W.,
June 7, 1858.

MY DEAR MRS. TENNYSON,

I should have written before but was waiting for *Mrs. Carlyle's* answer : I went twice to Chelsea unsuccessfully to see her, and as I could not spare time for another attempt, I wrote your message to her : the enclosed will explain the rest : when you write to me, please send it back for I never like to destroy her letters—unless, of course, you wish to keep it. You will see the mighty man of genius is not so easily managed as a pet bird. I think if he could see his wife's weak state so keenly as he can spiritual truths, he would not let his plans interfere with her little projects for health-seeking. The last two years have made sad havoc in her constitution.

.   .   .   .   .   .

I have seen a good deal of Palgrave of late and find him an exceedingly nice fellow : of course I feel somewhat awed before a man who has read the whole of Plato in the Greek, but as he is not oppressive with his learning we get on very well together, and his high regard for the Lord Farringford is pleasant common ground for us both.

I cannot tell you how I admire the new poem of " Guenevere " ; it seems to me the best of the three, not in execution for they are all perfect, but the subject being more complex and difficult, there was scope for greater subtlety of power. In the whole range of our literature there is not a finer scene than where the King moves away from the Abbey. I most earnestly wish you could persuade him to do the Maid of Astolat, not only for the extreme beauty of the subject, but for the sake of introducing much of Sir Launcelot, he being a character of such terrible importance to the " Guenevere " poem, and the immense suggestions arising from the poor lady's death.

.   .   .   .   .   .

I am working at Fairbairn's group, but getting on very slowly : if one is not content to do work in the old conventional manner, the difficulties he draws upon himself are not light.

I went to Burlington House on Friday, a huge party; saw Mrs. Prinsep there, the only fine looking woman in the room; she was most admirably dressed; I have to dine at her house next Sunday.

.   .   .   .   .   .

My love to your darling little pets; tell them I will write when I get some time and something to say.

Ever sincerely,

THOMAS WOOLNER.

Mrs. Carlyle to T. Woolner

5, Cheyne Row, Chelsea,
Thursday [*June* 1858].

DEAR MR. WOOLNER,

I was very vexed, in fact savage at finding your card again ! It was such an unlikely accident my being out that day ! My husband, having no proof-sheets on hand, was suddenly struck with my " thinness " and " paleness " and decided on taking me " a few miles on a railway to try if that would put any life into me ! " and we were away *trying* when you called.

As to Farringford I need no *representations* to make me feel its desirableness ! The idea of being *in the country with the Tennysons* is quite tempting enough; independent of " beauty of scenery " etc. etc. ! But till Mr. C. is gone to Scotland, and has settled *his* further plans, it is no use, I know, entertaining a plan of my own. There is talk of my meeting him in Yorkshire and in various parts of Great Britain ! I must just wait till I know if I am *wanted*, before I think about what I wish. If I am allowed " to wander at my own sweet will," however, and Mrs. Tennyson's angelic invitation be still open then, I should really, I think, be able to muster *faith* and *hope* and even physical *strength* enough to go to her for a few days.

I wish Tait had not painted Nero as big as a sheep ! *That* is what provokes me; more than being transmitted to " Posterity " in " wrong perspective " and with a " frightful table cover ! "

Yours very truly,
JANE CARLYLE.

Sunday! Oh my gracious ! I took this note to the post myself with some others on Monday afternoon and I find it in the pocket of my dress this morning.

W. B. Scott to T. Woolner

Newcastle,
September 19, 1858.

MY DEAR WOOLNER,

I was very glad to hear from you the other day. . . . I can tell you that Italy is all that has been said, sung or painted, and that the old masters were greater than I previously believed them to have been. . . . If one had gone early and with the old reverence, it is far from certain that

VIRGILIA BEWAILING THE BANISHMENT OF CORIOLANUS, 1867
From the plaster model.

[*To face page* 150.

the result would have been good, the authority of the past would have possibly enslaved one, but as it is I hope to derive only good, I who am infinitely little of a hero worshipper. Venice I found little to my taste. It is only a show and easily exhausted. Titian and Paul Veronese are pompous coves and always" going in " for the splendour and sumptuosity—qualities my cynical nature hates, and as for Tintoret he is an intolerable libertine although in many regards his great " Crucifixion " in San Roco is one of the 2 or 3 most notable pictures I have ever seen. Then there is nothing in Venice but the Venetian School (properly enough) and when these 3 great gladiatorial individuals have been mentioned, we must fall back on the Bellini and a few others nobler and purer than the gladiators but exhaustible. There is the bronze of Collione which *you* know but little else in sculpture.

Florence is the glorious place—city and country, art and nature, never to be forgotten; great churches and galleries endlessly interesting, and as one is neither a catalogue-maker nor picture dealer there is Fiesole and San Miniato and other places about. The Brownings were gone to Paris so I did not see them which was a disappointment. What lots of work you seem to have in hand now. I suppose if one asks this day 5 years how the group for the hall is getting on one may hear something of it.

Yours ever,
W. B. Scott.

T. Woolner to Mrs. Tennyson

27, Rutland Street,
Hampstead Road, N.W.,
October 12, 1858.

My dear Mrs. Tennyson,

Having been busily employed enjoying myself merely it was not natural that I should have any time to spare, for it is only industrious persons who ever have any leisure, and I should have written to you long ago to tell you that you made a serious mistake in supposing that you saw my lip curl with contempt when you were criticising my work; I would rather my lips were split into a hare lip than it should ever show contempt for anything you said :

.   .   .   .   .   .

As to your fear that I did not know your admiration for my bust, it is quite groundless I assure you, and I never want higher praise so long as I live than I have had from you, and I know it to be impossible for me to receive any that I can value more highly; and so you may imagine how delighted I am that you were so impressed by the grim Warrior of Venice, for that is my special favourite of all the middle-age sculpture I have ever seen. Do you remember that I pointed out parts of the horse's head as in some respects inferior to the other portions of the work? Since then I have learned more about it, and find that the sculptor considered himself shabbily treated by the Venetian Senate and left Venice and the statue with the horse's head incomplete, and it had to be finished by some inferior man. The Senate were in such a rage that they passed sentence of death upon Verocchio, who snapped his fingers at them and grinned: after some years the old rascals wanted a piece of sculpture done and humbly—I suppose—invited him back, and as he considered Venice rather a nice place he consented.

I am charmed to think that you have had Mr. Maurice with you, for you must have enjoyed having intercourse with such a lofty soul: and Ludlow too, he is a very fine fellow, I have the highest respect for him. These with Sir John Simeon must have been a glorious party.

. . . . . .

While I was with the Rajah his friend Novelli, who is also Fairbairn's *most* intimate friend, asked me to come to Aberystwyth and spend a few days with him; I intended not to go anywhere when I had done the bust but considering what an important man he was, and how tough a job it is going through a London winter with no country given health to support one, and also feeling in a very unsettled state of mind, I promised to go, and very glad I am that I did go, for I feel as strong again as when I went. . . . and I enjoyed myself mightily. He is one of the most fascinating men I ever met, he has the soul of a poet with the profoundest comprehension of business in its minutest details: the Rajah calls him Prince of British Merchants; and altho' this Prince has one of the most enormous businesses in the World, he wields it all as lightly as a lady plays with a feather; he perfectly astounds me by his cleverness, for his accomplishments never seem to end; he plays the piano exquisitely and his own compositions make one think he has devoted his whole life to the art of music; to see him play billiards one would think he must have been a billiard marker, for he beats any gentleman player and gives long odds. I shall tell you plenty about him when I see you. Fairbairn always promised me as the highest compliment he could pay me, that he would introduce me to his friend Novelli, and altho' I believed he was a nice fellow from his report, yet I never imagined him to approach what I really found him. To make his happiness complete he has a most charming wife and two children.

. . . . . .

You did not tell me a word about the " Lady of Astolat," she is the lady who claims the chief of my interest at present, and therefore of course I want to know how the poor young creature goes on in this rough world. You will think this the most egotistical letter you ever read, but I must tell you what Novelli said of my bust of the illustrious Poet; he said that it was the *only* bust he ever saw in his life that thoroughly satisfied him and came up to what he thought a bust should be : and I think it is because he has such a high idea of my artistic power thro' this work that he has taken such a great liking to me—so you see, hard work after a while does bring some fruits.

. . . . . .

Very sincerely yours,
THOMAS WOOLNER.

T. WOOLNER TO MRS. TENNYSON

27, *Rutland Street,*
Hampstead Road, N.W.,
October 22 [1858].

MY DEAR MRS. TENNYSON,
. . . I went on Saturday Evening to see the Carlyles, who made the kindest enquiries of you and yours. Mrs. Carlyle looked much better as to her health than I have seen her for some time but more sad than I think I ever saw her before, in fact it made me feel quite sad to see her. Carlyle himself was remarkably well, in excellent spirits and a good temper : we talked a great deal about Oliver Cromwell—for I want some time to get up a statue —and a great deal of the Rajah Brooke : Carlyle has the greatest admiration for him, which I am pleased to say is mutual; I am going to take the Rajah to see the grim philosopher some evening when he comes to town to stay : it will be good fun to see them together—the man whose

pen talks strong words and the man who talks thro' cannon-thunder and with sharp swords. . . . I am busy now preparing to commence upon my Trevelyan group : there is a great deal of fidgetting work measuring, carpentring, and dirty fuss with clay, &c., before one can set to work upon a large subject of this kind. . . . I went and dined with Frank Palgrave on Sunday : he had plenty to tell me of his holiday trip &c. I spent a pleasant half day and am going next Sunday to Kew to see Dr. Hooker his cousin, whom I met once at Hampstead. . . . Old Sir Francis is almost enthusiastic about Carlyle's *Frederick*, says that [it] is by far the best thing C. has done. He generally thinks and speaks of him as a wild man. . . . I went to Holman Hunt's the other evening and met Lear who shewed all his sketches done in Holy Land : I think that they are the most beautiful things he has ever done : if you have not seen them I hope you will, for they would give much delight and interest you extremely, not only for the mystery and history attached to the places themselves but also for the excessive fineness, tenderness and beauty of the art displayed in them. One of the finest, a comprehensive view of Petra I think, by sunrise, he is going to execute large in oil for Mr. Fairbairn. . . . Allingham passed thro' London a few days ago : he had been spending a week with the Brownings at Paris . . . the Brownings are back in Florence by now. . . .

Very sincerely yours,
THOMAS WOOLNER.

T. WOOLNER TO MRS. TENNYSON

27, *Rutland Street, N.W.,*
October 26 [1858 ?].

MY DEAR MRS. TENNYSON,

.   .   .   .   .   .

I went with Frank Palgrave on Sunday to Kew to see his cousin Dr. Hooker and spent a delightful day going thro' the glasshouses and museums, the Dr. very kindly pointing out the rare plants and telling of their peculiar properties. One plant called " Moving Plant " particularly struck me— at the base of every leaf are two small leaves that are continually moving up and down and in short jerks, and they look as if they were telegraphing to each other; if you have not seen it, you could scarcely have seen anything so odd.

There is another water plant the leaves of which are skeletons and are never anything else, the young ones are born skeletons and grow to full sized skeletons and die such, and I hope are decently buried as such ! Dr. Hooker also showed me a curious property of the Euphorbia; if you break a leaf off and touch a drop of water with the white juice that exudes therefrom, the water will instantaneously disperse ! There are plenty of other things he showed us that would interest you to see, but would not much interest you to read of unless they were written by a scientific pen. Both the Dr. and his wife are delightful persons. I believe old Sir William is a very fine fellow, but I did not see him.

I went to a Council Meeting of our College [1] yesterday; it was called in consequence of Mr. Maurice having resigned his Principalship, which he did because one of the Council had long been trying to counteract his teaching and had even ridiculed him in a public print. We managed it all rightly, begged Mr. Maurice to withdraw his resignation and said that his views should be strictly respected, and finally gave the offender a sound dressing which I hope will prove beneficial to him.

At the Council I met Ludlow who told what a delightful time he had spent at yours. I daresay that you will think me rude for telling how loud he was in your praises. I never heard him praise anybody or anything so highly before since I have known him. What an uncommonly nice old lady, Ludlow's mother is ! She is one of the few persons—the very few—that I have met in my life who fully coincide with my notions of womanly delicacy—I daresay that I am somewhat fastidious on this point and puritanical.

I have now really begun my Trevelyan group and have been all day making the skeleton and putting on the clay : I expect the Trevelyans in town in about a few days and they would naturally have been considerably disgusted had I made no commencement.

I see by the papers that the poor Rajah is ill and at Manchester. I had received a note from him a day or two before saying that on the 20th he should be back at his own cottage in Godstone, and I had written saying how rejoiced I was that he would so soon be back to quietness.

Very sincerely yours,
THOMAS WOOLNER.

[1] Working Men's College.

T. Woolner to Mrs. Tennyson

27, *Rutland Street, N.W.*,
November 14, 1858.

My dear Mrs. Tennyson,

I ought to have written before to thank you for your last two kind notes, but the truth is I have been held prisoner by Frederick William of Prussia of late, and you know what a stern and unrelenting mortal he is, and what small chance there is of getting away when he once lays hold of you. I have been immensely delighted with the book and the only things I have had to find serious fault with are the great number of genealogies, which are pleasant enough to those who like such things, but personally I find them a bore. The amount of learning Carlyle has managed to cram into his two vols: is tremendous, and I do not wonder that he has been ill or nearly so ever since he commenced upon the work. I notice he comes down rather hard upon poets every now and then throughout the work; which I do not altogether see the fun of, for surely everybody is not called upon to write history, and those who possess the gift of song surely have a right to exercise it. But you know, Carlyle always will say what he pleases and he never seems to care much who will or who will not like it.

.   .   .   .   .   .

I am working at my Trevelyan group but as yet do not make any great show, for sculpture is of all arts the slowest to make a display. I wish above all things that I had some lovely sharp cut face to model from for my lady; no-one can imagine the immense want it is to me.

I forget if I told you that I went and spent a Sunday at Oxford a fortnight ago, went to see Woodward [1] anent the design for the chief entrance to the Mus : the design was approved of.

.   .   .   .   .   .

I grieve to say that Woodward is in a most delicate state of health, in fact his life looks as weak as a little candle in the open air. He is the most splendid genius we have in architecture, and his loss would not be made up in a hurry.

.   .   .   .   .   .

Very sincerely yours,
Thomas Woolner.

[1] Benjamin Woodward, the architect.

ACHILLES SHOUTING FROM THE TRENCHES
One of the bas-reliefs around Gladstone Bust in Bodleian.

[To face page 157.

F. T. PALGRAVE TO T. WOOLNER

Hampstead, N.W.,
January 12, 1859.

DEAR WOOLNER,

If it is agreeable, would *Saturday* next do for you to come to dinner at 6–6.15 ? The same younger friends of mine, by name Grove, are coming.

It was *not* with reference to the medallion of Mrs. Tennyson that I put my question, but in order to answer a friend who had asked me. But it is very kind in you to offer me one; and if you will have one really to spare, I should value it much as a bit of your work. By a defect in mind, I suppose, portraits as such, of friends, give me no pleasure. I am glad for your sake, others don't feel thus; and I am delighted that you finished the work to your satisfaction, that you had so long a holiday, and that you saw the great and beloved Jowett. . . .

Ever y^rs
F. T. PALGRAVE.

JAMES SPEDDING TO T. WOOLNER

60, *L. I. F.*,
July 10, 1858.

MY DEAR WOOLNER,

I am afraid it won't do for me.[1] I do not find my clubbish tendencies increase with years; and I grow every day a worse member of the few societies to which I belong. The evening hours are my best working hours; and when the rest of the world goes abroad I feel an irresistible attraction towards home. Whether it is the effect of years, or of my particular kind of occupation, or the development of a disposition naturally inclined to solitude, I don't know : but so it is. I have no doubt the society will be an excellent institution for those who have an affinity to it; but I should be a drone, and deserve the fate which drones have to undergo when the hive is full. I am glad to hear that you have likewise Maurice's head in hand.

Yrs. ever.
JAS. SPEDDING.

[1] This was probably in reply to a request from Woolner to propose Mr. Spedding as an honorary member of the Hogarth Club or the Working Men's College.

T. Woolner to Mrs. Tennyson

27, *Rutland Street,*
Hampstead Road, N.W.,
August 3, 1858.

My dear Mrs. Tennyson,
        My kindest thanks for your kindness in sending me
news of the letter you received.

.   .   .   .   .

I went on Saturday to Godstone to see the Rajah of
Sarāwak and stayed till Monday when we came up to town
together.   I found him a character that England may well
be proud of :   I have rarely met a man I liked so well at once,
for I felt as if I had known him all my life ;   he is so
thoroughly frank and honest and has such a fine sympathetic nature.   He has the slow weighty movement of the
head that you see in a lion, and tho' he roars with laughter
and is full of geniality, you see when talking of hostile
matters his mouth clench like a vice with determination
wholly irresistible.   He is a man who inspires me with
entire confidence in the inexhaustibility of his resources ;
if one barrier of his is beaten down it is only to encounter
another and a stronger, and so on until the enemy gives up.
I could go running on about him for pages and tire you out
of all patience, so will say nothing of his active capacious
forehead &c., but as I am going to do a bust of him I hope
to have some day a chance of showing you what he is
like more amply than I can in words.   He asked me to go
and see him whenever I liked.
        I am in a state of furious vexation for my things have
returned from the R. Academy Ex :   grievously injured ;
glass of med : smashed, med : injured : and a figure of
St. John has his nose crushed to pieces ; and persons tell so
many lies I cannot discover who did the mischief.

.   .   .   .   .

Very truly yours,
Thomas Woolner.

T. Woolner to Mrs. Tennyson

27, *Rutland Street,*
Hampstead Road, N.W.,
January 16, 1859.

My dear Mrs. Tennyson,
        Hurrying, scurrying, worrying, toiling, moiling, and

to be whirling like a distracted teetotum, has been my fate
since I left Farringford over a week ago. This is the first
disengaged time I have had since that time or I should have
written earlier.

. . . . . .

I dined with the Trevelyans on Wednesday and on Thursday they came to my studio; Lady T. was delighted with
your med : and said that it looked 20 years younger than
the old one but I battled with this monstrous exaggeration
and reduced her to 10 years, which she stood out for heroic-
ally, and said that tho' she did not like the other much yet
this she thought charming and beautiful. They were
immensely pleased with the great Rajah's bust but I do not
think they liked Maurice's; which is curious, for every one
else who has seen it has been very much so : I daresay it
is because they do not know the original.

On Thursday evening I went to Letherhead in Surrey to
see a great beauty whom I have long been promised a sight
of—my friend who mentioned her having thought she would
do for my Trevelyan Lady. Altho' it certainly was an
awful bore leaving my work yet I was munificently repaid
for the lady, Miss Waugh [1] was one of the grandest creatures
I ever saw and her face is not far from what I want for my
Lady : I hope to get her to sit.—I stayed all the next
day at Letherhead to try and make friends with her and I
am rather in hopes that I succeeded; but whether I did or
not, I did her a great deal of good, for I converted her to
Browning and almost—of course not quite—but almost
made her look with suspicion upon that schoolgirl poet
Longfellow; Tennyson was her established poet, but she
looked with a gentle eye upon the Yankee and could make
neither head nor tail of the great Robert : but by taking a
good deal of pains I made the Yankee sink into comparative
insignificance with the subtle, sturdy and craggy English-
man overloaded with Italian tendencies. I should not
have taken so much trouble with her mental development
had she not been so majestically beautiful, for my sense of
fitness was violated in knowing that such an imperial looking creature should have anything like serious admiration
for Longfellow, and yet turn from Robert Browning as
from a thing of not much importance. I will tell you
more of her if I manage to get her head to do, but now
I cannot write you a long letter.

[1] Miss Waugh married W. Holman Hunt in 1865.

There were all sorts of persons called upon me the last week I was away from home : the Rajah passed thro' London *en route* for Somerset and wanted to see me : Fairbairn called, having come up from Man :[1] on business : a gentleman called who said he thought of having a marble of the Rajah—not heard if he has made up his mind yet : Mrs. and Mr. Maurice called to see his bust, and my man at the studio had not the sense to put it in a proper light and position to show them.—Curiously—you know I was complaining that Frank R. Cox would not publish his " Break, Break, Break " and when I got home I found a copy with his card ; he actually has brought it out at last ; he called on me to ask your address, I suppose that he wants to send you a copy. My love to my little pets and tell them that I miss my fun very much and I wish they could come to me, for I shall quite forget how to tell stories before I see them again if I do not mind what I am about.

> .   .   .   .   .   .

> Yours very sincerely,
> THOMAS WOOLNER.

MRS. TENNYSON TO T. WOOLNER

Farringford,
February 1, 1859.

MY DEAR MR. WOOLNER,

Mr. Cox[2] was so good as to send me the song, and I fully meant to have acknowledged it yesterday but post time came before I had done so, having as usual many other letters to write.

> .   .   .   .   .   .

I think the music very beautiful. The wailing accompaniment of the beginning specially so. If I dare I should object to the long notes of the second stanza, " Well " is not according to the metre of the poem. We both hope it will not be long before we hear you sing it and then who knows, perhaps I may give you a hard task and ask you to sing mine too, and you are not to say I have stolen the theme because it happens to be strangely like Mr. Cox's,

---

[1] Manchester.
[2] Mr. Frank Cox, the musician, gave Woolner lessons in singing, he was fond of singing ballads and he had a good voice. He asked Mr. Cox if he would ever be first-rate, tip-top, and as the musician replied he would never be that, he discontinued his lessons.

though of course, wanting much of the beauty and all the science because mine was done before my marriage.

.   .   .   .   .

Ever yours most truly,
EMILY TENNYSON.

T. WOOLNER TO MRS. TENNYSON.

27, *Rutland Street, N.W.*,
February 8, 1859.

MY DEAR MRS. TENNYSON,

.   .   .   .   .   .

I have just returned from T. Parker's and it is very late. . . . There were plenty of folk at Parker's; Mr. Maurice looking benign as ever : Froude, polished, judicial and keen, Grant, Vernon Harcourt, Masson and plenty of others.

.   .   .   .   .   .

I will send your Med : in a few days : I have it in a gold frame and it looks I think bright and pleasant : everybody who sees it is delighted and says " what a beautiful profile she has "; you must pardon my gossip or you will think me an Irishman who wishes to flatter.

.   .   .   .   .   .

Ever truly yours,
THOMAS WOOLNER.

I will send the Stothard's " Boadicea " when I send your med : also a photograph of self which I promised : it makes me rather an upstart guy, but it's no matter.

.   .   .   .   .   .

T. WOOLNER TO MRS. TENNYSON

27, *Rutland Street,*
Hampstead Road, N.W.,
February 12, 1859.

MY DEAR MRS. TENNYSON,

There was no need to ask me to have the things framed for they were already done : I started the case containing them this day.

.   .   .   .   .   .

In the opposite corner of the case will be found the photograph of my beautiful and majestic countenance, which of course will illuminate the whole of the house with its brightness ! Next will be found your Med : it is a beautifully clear cast and the best that has been taken : I intended to

M

have kept it for myself, but on second thoughts determined
on sending it to cheer the poetic mind ; not that any person
but myself could detect the least difference in the casts,
only I thought it the greatest compliment to send him
quite the best. . . . Please to let it be hung up as near
Lear's little picture as possible and on a level with the eyes
of a person ordinarily tall.

At the bottom of the case will be found Stothard's
" Boadicea," an extremely choice and beautiful engraving,
I think quite the most complete of all Stothard's works : so
that I hope Poetry will appreciate Art and not stick this
work up against the ceiling.

. . . . . .

I wanted to pay Mr. Maurice a compliment, for the great
trouble which I gave him in sitting to me for his bust, and
therefore I made Mrs. Maurice a present of your Med :
framed in the same way that yours is, and on Thursday evening I went and took it to them : you cannot imagine the
delight it gave them both, they praised it as highly as it is
possible to praise such a little thing, and made many
minute observations regarding the features which showed
how well they knew the original ; and I am sure if the old
saying be true that when a person's face grows hot, some
one is praising said person, I am sure that your flesh must
have been burnt dry upon your face, as the apples are
sometimes parched dry upon the trees under an Australian
sun ! the affection that Mrs. Maurice feels for you is something extraordinary :

I went last evening to Palgrave's to meet Froude, Grant[1]
and Grove at dinner. We were very comfortable : Froude
is a really nice fellow, beside being a magnate in history,
and has most exceedingly gentlemanly manners. I am
sure that I should be immensely fond of Grant if I knew a
great deal of him. Palgrave is extraordinarily kind to
one and is always doing some good-natured thing or
another.

Fairbairn called to see how the bust of the Rajah is
getting on and was very well pleased with my progress.
He had just received a letter from the Rajah.

. . . . . .

I am going to Uxbridge to-morrow to see the Trevelyans
who are staying with her Sister Mrs. Hilliard, who is one

----

[1] Sir Alexander Grant.

of the most delightful little gossippy creatures that ever lived. . . .

Ever sincerely yours,
THOMAS WOOLNER.

MRS. TENNYSON TO T. WOOLNER

Farringford,
February 15, 1859.

MY DEAR MR. WOOLNER,
The box has arrived quite safely, and the contents give great delight. A. says of my medallion he does not see how it could be better, so you see he is not ungrateful for your generosity. Hallam seemed extremely pleased with it. You see I take this to be more of you than yourself for I begin with it. Your noble self [1] is not so noble as I would have made it.

. . . . . .

We had had the wit to find out what a fine engraving [2] that is before your letter came which pleased me. We thank you most heartily for all.

. . . . . .

I am sure you would love Sir Alexander. I wish I might call him Grant, man-fashion. What a pleasant chronicle your letters always are.

. . . . . .

The " Maid of Astolat " is quite finished now, all but last touches, I do not think you will find her all unworthy of your ideal. A. is better again and very cheerful.
Good-bye my dear Mr. Woolner, all good be with you.
Believe us, with Alfred's love and theirs,
Very gratefully and sincerely yours,
A. E. H. L. TENNYSON.

[1] Photograph of T. Woolner.
[2] The " Boadicea " by Stothard.

CHAPTER VII

THOMAS CARLYLE TO THOMAS WOOLNER.

Chelsea,
March 3, 1859.

DEAR WOOLNER,

I called yesterday, 4 to 5 p.m., at the Studio, but found nobody—was proud I had found the House again, so that I might call another time.

I want you, in the meanwhile, to persuade the Secretary of the *Hogarth Club* (in some friendly way, for I would not hurt his feelings on any account) to cease altogether sending me the *business* letters &c. of that Institution,—to which I wish honestly well; hoping always I may look at your exhibited works, or the like, one day; but do not take hold farther, nor ever intend to do, least of all in present circumstances. Such letters are not only a waste of trouble and postage stamps to your society, but there is implied a kind of untruth in the affair : in short they are becoming, in their great frequency and miscellaneous complexion (of which I enclose you a specimen with appendix) an afflictive phenomenon more or less; and I beg you, in a cunning silent way, stop them !

When anything that can interest a general member of the Community is afoot I shall be happy to hear tell of it.

.   .   .   .   .   .

Excuse my headlong message (headlong form of ditto) : I am in more haste, and with a heavier burden on my back, than is good for me just now.

Yours ever truly,
T. CARLYLE.

The Hogarth Club, formed in 1856, consisted of a number of young men of talent and genius in Literature and Art, but more especially of Art, who primarily founded the Club for the purpose of showing their pictures and sculpture.

IN MEMORIAM
Four children in Paradise.

[To face page 164.

In 1860 it numbered among its honorary members such names as Carlyle, Tennyson, Browning, Thackeray, Richard Owen, J. F. Lewis, W. Mulready and R. W. Emerson.

Carlyle's letter requests that no more notices of the Club's ordinary proceedings be sent him !

A Book of Club Rules and List of Members, 1860, bound in parchment, contains the names of nearly all the interesting British artistic and literary men of the time.

T. WOOLNER TO MRS. TENNYSON

27, *Rutland Street, N.W.,*
March 20 [1859].

MY DEAR MRS. TENNYSON,

I have become so disgracefully dissipated that I have been unable to write to you before, for last week I actually dined out four times and had the other evenings engaged out likewise.

I saw Fairbairn on Friday night who is in town for the purpose of working in the Sarāwak business; the Rajah himself was expected in town yesterday.

. . . . . .

I was at the Prinseps' two or three Sundays ago and was asking Watts what he intended to send to the R.A. Ex: and I asked if he meant to send the Poet's portrait, but he said he had no thought of doing so for that he thought doing so would not be agreeable : but I said I imagined that since he has been so much exhibited already, I did not think he cared anything about it. But I inwardly determined to ask you, for I think it a pity that it should not be seen by the world, in order to help correct the base and false impression given by Brodie's bust and Mayall's photographs : for altho' the view of the character chosen is not what altogether satisfies either you or me, still it is a high and noble work of art and would do a great deal of good in assisting public taste, and unless there were any real objection it would be a pity not to let it be publicly seen. Will you kindly let me know? then if you and he consent I will tell Watts.

. . . . . .

My friend Watts, who wrote on *India Heroes* is going, I grieve to say, to Australia again; he has accepted an appointment of £1000 a year to edit the *Argus*. I think it a pity for Watts to cast himself away thus, for I think him one of the cleverest political writers we have.

.   .   .   .   .   .

I forget if I told you that I went a short time ago to see Hunt's picture and how wonderfully he is going on with it : really every time I see it I think it promises to be greater than ever I thought it before. I am happy to say that he has quite resolved to exhibit it alone and not to send it to the R.A.

.   .   .   .   .   .

Hoping that Hallam and the little Lion are flourishing vigorously,

Ever sincerely yours,
THOMAS WOOLNER.

March 21.—Yesterday Fairbairn and Novelli called at my studio to see the Rajah's bust. They told me of a great scheme they have on hand to make an appeal to the nation on behalf of Sir James as the Government has refused to do anything for him.

.   .   .   .   .   .

I am sorry to trouble you,[1] but I cannot help it; but you who are high up in the world have to undergo these bothers in common course; the high branches are often stirred and blown about while the grasses and weeds below enjoy an enviable placidity.

Again truly yours,
THOMAS WOOLNER.

MRS. TENNYSON TO T. WOOLNER

Farringford,
March 23, 1859.

MY DEAR MR. WOOLNER,

What a wicked woman I should be if I thought it a trouble ! Why is it not a glory to be able to pay a tribute in any way however humble to a great work and to a great man. I have told Alfred that if you do not hear to the contrary before Sunday, you may conclude that the portrait may be exhibited and that his name may be put on the Committee. I entirely agree with what you say about the protrait. Mr. Watts thinks I want a particular expression, but it is not that I want, I *only*

---

[1] Request for Tennyson to sign the appeal.

want what has scarcely yet been given in the world, the man at his highest stamp forever so long as canvas will last. You know the lines that exactly express what I do want [1] so I hope will Mr. Watts some day. Nevertheless the portrait is, as you say, " a high and noble work of art," and it ought to be known to the world for its own sake and the sake of the artist.

What you tell me of the poor Rajah's [2] state is sad indeed, sadder for us than for him. He must feel that he has done a good day's work. We may well fear that when he is gone we have none left to do such another.

What glorious friends you have, Fairbairns, Novellis, Brooke and others! Have you quite perfected yourself in the song? I am sorry that your Watts [3] is to leave England. We cannot spare such men.

. . . . . .

Love from the boys.
Most truly yours,
EMILY TENNYSON.

T. WOOLNER TO THOMAS CARLYLE

27, *Rutland Street,*
Hampstead Road, N.W.,
March 27 [1859].

DEAR MR. CARLYLE,
The Rajah's address is—Sir James Brooke, K.C.B., Beach House, Dawlish, Devon.

Mr. Knox the gentleman who wrote the paper which I enclosed says that he knows nothing could possibly have so cheering an effect upon the Rajah as your sympathy expressed directly from yourself, as he has more respect for your opinion than that of any other person. And I think Mr. Knox was more pleased to know that

---

[1] " As when a painter, poring on a face,
　　Divinely through all hindrance finds the man
　　Behind it, and so paints him that his face,
　　The shape and colour of a mind and life,
　　Lives for his children, ever at its best."—ELAINE.

[2] Rajah Brooke.
[3] H. E. Watts, editor of the *Argus* in Australia, afterwards a writer in *The Standard* in England. He was an early friend of Woolner's, and in future years became a great friend of his children.

you were going to write to the Rajah than if you had allowed your name to be on the Committee.

Very truly yours,
THOMAS WOOLNER.

T. WOOLNER TO MRS. TENNYSON

27, Rutland Street, N.W.,
March 27, 1859.

MY DEAR MRS. TENNYSON,

I have been out from home every evening and could not before thank you for your kind notes. I went to L. H. House [1] last evening and had the pleasure of hearing the " Maid of Astolat " read. I think it all that can be possibly desired and its completeness struck me equally with its versatility. I think if there is one portion more beautiful than any other, it is that which was the most difficult to do, and which you thought the only part likely to jar upon the modern mind; I mean that where the Lily Maid herself makes love to Launcelot just before he takes his final leave; nothing could have been more perfect and nothing more sublimely modest; in fact I think this particular part a consummate triumph of poetic skill; and this very boldness of the girl's evidently springs from the most absolute purity of heart; and this with shadow of doom that we feel surely to be creeping over her, create a pathos in the hapless maiden's favour, which, together with the sense of what Launcelot loses in the loss of her love, actually are the poem.

.   .   .   .   .   .

I am working fearfully hard to try and get my Rajah done for the R.A. Ex. I do not yet know if Fairbairn will like it sent there : I rather want it because Foley is to have the arrangement of the sculpture this year and he does me the honor to think well of my efforts : he told me that for many years he had felt nothing but disgust at the way the R. Academy had treated me : these were his actual words ; and coming from an academician you will admit that I must have been a victim : and for no other reason than that people praise my works ; which to old stupid academicians is gall and wormwood.

There was a sale of pictures on Sat : at Christie's of which some were lovely.

.   .   .   .   .   .

[1] Little Holland House.

There was one of the best Turner drawings I ever saw,
" Lake of Zug," a rising sun smiting the mists that over-
hang a blue valley of water shadowed by blue mountains
and transforming all the zenith cloudlets into silver and
gold. I certainly should like to be nabob enough to buy
just one of Turner's drawings, for there is a charm in his
things that attract me more than the paintings of almost
any other artist.

Mrs. Prinsep had to dine with Thackeray last night,
and she left early to be back in time for the reading of
" Astolat " and she said that the fierce old satirist was
snarly because she would leave, even tho' she told him that
she would and could dine with him any day throughout
the year, but that she saw Tennyson only on rare chances.

Sir J. Simeon came to see me on Friday and was very
pleased with my Rajah; and he praised your med: very
much also; he said that at first it did not please him altogether, but that now it did. I forget if I told you what a
fuss Novelli and Fairbairn made with it and a great
Scindian Warrior one of Napier's heroes, that he was fond
of and who fought at Hyderabad and Meanee said it was
the most beautiful expression he ever saw on a human
face.

I have Mr. Norman's med: quite finished and put into
its frame, which instead of a red inner rim has a deep
rich blue one, and I think the effect superb : I never tried
this colour before and am so satisfied with the effect that
I shall generally adopt it I think. I should like you to
see this med : for I think it is the best piece of modelling
that I ever did. My time is up and I must not gossip any
longer : I have to snatch at a few minutes for writing just
as a hungry horse might snap at a stray twig or two while
dragging his loaded waggon along the lane.

.   .   .   .   .

Ever sincerely yours,
THOMAS WOOLNER.

DR. JOSEPH HOOKER TO THOMAS WOOLNER

Royal Gardens, Kew,
April 30, 1859.

MY DEAR SIR,
A very kind & liberal friend of science & of my
Father's, is very anxious that there should be executed

a good portrait or bust of the latter, & has requested me to see what can be done in the matter.

There have been many portraits executed of my Father & all more or less failures, owing to his variable features, & it has struck me that sculpture might succeed better. Of this I am no judge myself & I know of no one to whom I could better apply than to yourself. Will you kindly tell me whether, should my friends approve of having a bust, you would feel inclined to undertake it, & upon what terms? Perhaps you would like to see the subject first—(it is in many respects a famous one for your art) & if so I should be delighted to see you here whenever most convenient to you, & you will always find luncheon at 1 p.m. . . . Mrs. Hooker desires her best compliments.

Ever truly yrs
JOS. D. HOOKER.

T. WOOLNER TO MRS. TENNYSON

27, *Rutland Street,*
Hampstead Road, N.W.,
May 13 [1859].

MY DEAR MRS. TENNYSON,

. . . . . .

I am heartily glad that the poems are going on : I do not understand much about correcting proof sheets, but can scarcely regard it as such a severe task and unpoetical employment as you seem to hint at : while the poet is down here upon the earth, he must do something earthly; and what can touch more delicately upon it than for the poet to correct his own immortal thoughts in that particular form by which they are to be made known to all the world, and for all time to come?

I am perfectly sure that those poems from their very greatness will be widely and fiercely abused. An original poet always is so with every new work he produces : men make up their minds upon works already done, and a new work from the necessity of the case disturbs that impression previously made. It always was and always will be so. If a poet produces works just in the key of former works, the many would applaud him, but the few would say that he was growing mannered and declining; and they would be right; but when he produces a new work the few applaud, the many howl, and they are wrong : but before long the howl weakens, and by the time another

IN MEMORIAM G. B., 1872

[*To face page* 171.

work is ready, the howl has grown into shouts of admiration. I know this from observing the change of opinion with regard to "The Princess" and "Maud"; both extremely new and unlike anything either he or anyone had done before : and I confess that I hope to see the same abuse heaped upon these new Idylls for it will be an ominous sign when a poet's works are at once loudly and widely admitted, for then he may say to himself with Phocian "What mistake have I committed?" or begin to suspect that he has not made an advance. Of course I am vexed at human creatures being so thoughtless to abuse what they do not understand, and what they ought to profit from, and still more hurt to know how such wicked folly disturbs the maker of what called it all forth; but I had rather see him enraged than declining, and as the growth of greatness is ever accompanied with clamour, I say then welcome clamour. Great men have greater views, are loftier and see farther than other men; and at the same time being taller and bigger, assuredly they must have a greater stress of the storm to bear than those who are far beneath them. But I must leave off, or you will say I am growing didactic and unfitting myself for the pursuit of art.

I cannot get on satisfactorily with my Fairbairn group, for interruptions; I am doing a med: of Mr. Knox, a splendid man, friend of Novelli's, Rajah's, Fairbairn's and others; he has a beautiful face, but I wish that I had not had to do it until the children were finished : also I have commenced a bust of Sir William Hooker at Kew; he will make a fine bust I think; but he is a difficult subject; all artists hitherto have signally failed, but I do not mean to fail if I can help it. They are all charming persons, he and Lady Hooker, Dr. and Mrs. Hooker, and so I hope to please them with the likeness, for they are very anxious about it.

. . . . . .

You will be glad to hear that the Rajah is getting better, and his spirits improving; so after all I begin to hope that we shall have the grand fellow with us some few years yet.

. . . . . .

My love to the fine little fellows; tell them not to pluck up all the wild flowers from the woods !

Very truly yours,

THOMAS WOOLNER.

Woolner went down to Kew to model the bust of Sir William Hooker, the famous botanist, and became great friends with Dr. Hooker's children—Sir William's grandchildren. They were allowed to watch the sculptor at work and insisted the Bust ought to have arms and hands, and they were so upset at there being none that to please them he put little hands sticking out of the shoulders! and then to quiet them gave each a lump of clay to try and model themselves; to pinch and punch the soft substance is a never failing pleasure to children.

CHAPTER VIII

Doctors' Commons,
Tuesday.

DEAR WOOLNER,

Montagu Butler a friend of mine (and Fellow of Trinity) has written to me proposing that some of us Trinity men should join together, buy your Tennyson and present it to the College Library at Cambridge. What do *you* say to this? Would you be satisfied with your masterpiece resting *there* to the end of time? I think you must have seen our Library when you went to Cambridge searching for Bacons; and know otherwise what rank our Trinity College as a place of education has and has long had in the sight of all the land. Your Tennyson if it got there would find itself in company of many distinguished heads by undistinguished sculptors; also in the presence of Thorwaldsen's Byron;—in some respects there could be no fitter home for it than Trin: Coll: as so much of Tennyson's history is connected with the place; but on the other hand no one cares for Art in Cambridge and your handiwork would seldom be beheld by any seeing eye. However please think of it, and write me word as soon as possible whether you would agree to such a destination, & what price you set upon your head. The scheme you see, is only just conceived, but I think we might carry it out, as M. Butler, tho' quite young, has much influence. . . .

Yours affy,
VERNON LUSHINGTON.

MRS. TENNYSON TO T. WOOLNER

Farringford,
May 25, 1859.

MY DEAR MR. WOOLNER,

What an interesting chronicle your letters always are! I have to go and look after A.'s room and see that it is made as comfortable as may be in its unfinished state

for the evening.   It is a queer thing now with ceiling away,
for which the builders excuse themselves with reasons to
my unconstructive mind not good.   In spite of this A. pro-
nounces it a charming room and I quite agree. . . . There
I am on my third page without having said a word of that
for which I write.

My hearty congratulations, that at last the bust [1] question
is settled for I am sure it must have been fretting you this
long while.

. . . . . .

A. is gone to Brooke.   The boys have just been in
chasing each other with a mad glee born of the south wind
perhaps.   They are going as they fancy to gather all the
daisies on the Lawn.

Most sincerely yours,
EMILY TENNYSON.

T. WOOLNER TO MRS. TENNYSON

Rutland Street, N.W.,
June 15, 1859.

MY DEAR MRS. TENNYSON,

I have heard from Macmillan that he has obtained
possession of the bust and now has it safe in custody : he
says in reply to my regrets for troubling him so much " The
trouble is nothing and the pleasure great; so say no more
about it." You see what a good fellow he is. He tells
me that after all he believes the bust will be placed in
either combination room or the Master's Lodge; so that
I suppose the remonstrance has produced fitting fruit.

I heard last night that he was in town and was dining
at the Prinseps' on Sunday : I met Mrs. Prinsep at Hallé's,
where I was invited to hear him and Joaichim (if that's
how he spells it) play : it assuredly was the most marvellous play that ever fascinated my hearing, it was more than
magical, it was almost heavenly. They played the pieces
of Beethoven, and the indescribable agitation, the unutterable yearning reaching nearly to death, then the pause,
and then wild mad exultation of triumphant passion sub-
siding through sweet varieties into continuous tendernesses
of melodious sound, were rendered in a way that made
the listeners well nigh believe that the instruments had
vital souls.

I believe that these two men are admitted to be the best

[1] Bust of Tennyson.

in the world in their respective ways, and I must say that they almost reveal new forces in nature it seems to me.

.   .   .   .   .   .

I have just received home my bust of Sir William Hooker cast all safely; so that now I have no more anxiety upon that matter.[1] How I wish that grim old gentleman Carlyle would let me do his bust : what a nuisance it is that the men who are most worthy of being handed down visibly to posterity are the most hard to come at.

.   .   .   .   .   .

That lightning which I mentioned to you on Sunday split a tree and killed a man in St. James's Park.

Ever truly yours,
THOMAS WOOLNER.

EDMUND LAW LUSHINGTON TO T. WOOLNER

Park House,
September 5, 1859.

DEAR MR. WOOLNER,
The bust[2] & stand both have arrived quite safe, & have been set up in the place that seemed best suited for them, in the drawing room. It is a very beautiful work, & the more one looks at it the [more] surprising it seems that you sh^d. have succeeded in giving so near a likeness.

I am much obliged to you for the pains you have taken in ordering the stand : Mrs. A. T. is still with us, I hope rather better for a little quiet, but far from well.   He has returned from his summer excursion, & I fear we are not likely to detain them much longer. . . .

Yours very Truly,
E. L. LUSHINGTON.

T. WOOLNER TO MRS. TENNYSON

27, *Rutland Street,*
Hampstead Road, N.W.,
October 15 [1859].

MY DEAR MRS. TENNYSON,

.   .   .   .   .   .

I have been back from my country change about a week

[1] It was this bust when carved in marble that had the accident at the Royal Academy in 1860; it is therefore curious he should have felt so free from anxiety about this particular bust.

[2] Bust of Edward Henry, son of Professor Edmund Lushington.

and have seen a few friends and am gradually settling down again into a respectable working character; which is what I have not been for some weeks; my time having been employed taking walks, bathing, shooting partridges, riding, playing billiards, smoking and dancing!—in fact a country gentleman's life: Do you not despise me? the result of all this dissipation was a robust state of health, to such a degree, that I felt it in my conscience to make puns.

.   .   .   .   .   .

Last evening I went and took tea with the Carlyles. He was unusually well and so pleasant and entertaining that I did not leave him till nearly 12: he talked a great deal about snakes: and we discussed French matters at some length: I was anxious to hear what he thought of the stupendous naval preparations being carried on over the way with such astounding rapidity: he does not like them at all and thinks it means mischief.

.   .   .   .   .   .

You will be glad to hear that Mrs. Carlyle is much better than when she left London: she looks better than I have seen her look for fully twelve months: she had been in a great way for some time in consequence of a cart having passed over the neck of her "Nero"; but after a few days he recovered and her grief assuaged. They both made very kind enquiries of you, but I was not able to give such a good account as I wished.

.   .   .   .   .   .

I went on Sunday to see the Patmores, who were all well; he read me some of the parts of his new poem which were much the same as the former in tone of thought and subject, but for finish I think they beat anything he has hitherto done. He lent me some poems by William Barnes that he and Venables rave about as being such a mighty poet: I have read a few, and the ideas appear to me good, so far as I can understand them thro' the dismal lingo called Dorset dialect, which he has chosen to imprison them in: and there is a true feeling for freshness and purity of country air and scenery; and a good rough idea of shrewd humour that reminds one of Burns.

.   .   .   .   .   .

I am, my dear Mrs. Tennyson,
Sincerely yours,
THOMAS WOOLNER.

MRS. TENNYSON TO T. WOOLNER

Farringford,
October 20, 1859.

DEAR MR. WOOLNER,

It was very pleasant to hear from you again and I thank you for your welcome letter. I should long ago have written to you had I not been so ill this summer that the Doctor forbad my writing.

I am inclined to think a country gentleman's life a very wholesome one in many ways, so to me your holiday appears pleasant and good. I and the boys spent all our time at the Lushingtons'.[1] Days with them have their own peculiar charm to me and this was not wanting, only I was not in a state to enjoy it to the full. The boys liked the novelty of playfellows and got initiated in cricket and other things.

The little bust[2] looked touching and beautiful in its place and I wished to have told you so then. I trust many more beautiful things are in petto.

Alfred's love and the boys'.
Most truly yours,
EMILY TENNYSON.

VERNON LUSHINGTON TO T. WOOLNER

Liverpool,
November 1, 1859.

MY DEAR WOOLNER,

Good news. The mighty Master & his men have at last graciously condescended to accept your *Masterpiece* & even with thanks. Into the College Library itself they won't allow it to go, that being devoted to the dead men, but they offer to place it in the *Vestibule* of the Library, to be promoted we hope, in due time, when old Tennyson himself is promoted. To this we offer no objections, seeing no probability of obtaining better terms, & wishing to have the business settled; so into the Vestibule your Bust goes. What sort of a place (this Vestibule is, for exhibition purposes, I cannot say, never having looked upon it in that light, but simply as a

[1] Maidstone.
[2] Marble bust by Woolner of the son of Edmund Lushington.

N

Vestibule. I am almost afraid it is " for a charnel dungeon
fitter," but we must make the best of it. Could you go
down to Cambridge, next week, to help them to choose the
fittest spot, and to insinuate your opinion as to the most
proper kind of pedestal ? for it is to be on a pedestal says
the Master. Your time I know is precious enough, but it
would be a good & kind errand; & you would receive
a hearty welcome from many. I return to Babylon this
evening : let us meet soon, & hear of your summer doings,
& see your worthy face again. *What* weather ! never do
I remember such a grim stormy October : here at Liverpool we feel what storms mean—brave men & helpless
women hurled to sudden death, sorrow brought home to
hundreds of families—not without due tribulation do we
do our business in the great waters.

Your affec. friend,
VERNON LUSHINGTON.

T. WOOLNER TO MRS. TENNYSON

Cambridge,
November [1859.]

MY DEAR MRS. TENNYSON,
    . . . I am down here for the purpose of seeing the
Master [1] about the bust. . . . The greatest man of the world
was pleasant and sweet as possible and agreed with everything I suggested concerning position, light, pedestal &c.
The light, . . . will be favourable : and altho' not in so
dignified a position as if it were in the Library itself, still
it will be in a much better light, and I shall be perfectly
satisfied. There appears to be a great deal of interest concerning it among the magnates here. . . . I was talking with
a great Preacher, Mr. Rowlson [2] here this morning—here
they regard him as an extraordinary man—and he told
me that Gladstone was reading some of the " Idylls " to a
few friends, he among the number, and that at one portion
both Gladstone himself and Lord Granville . . . burst
into tears before all the company . . . which does show
that they are susceptible of tender sentiments. What a
charming man Clark [3] of Trinity is ! He is as courteous and
kind as any man can be. Montagu Butler, one of those
who were most active in the bust affair is elected Master
of Harrow : he is the youngest they ever had there. . . .

---

[1] Dr. Whewell.   [2] Rolleston.
[3] The Public Orator, Cambridge.

GUINIVERE, 1872

[*To face page* 178.

Punch, or the *London Charivari.* November 12, 1859.

THE LAUREATE'S BUST AT TRINITY.[1]

(A fragment of an Idyll.)

So the stately bust abode
For many a month, unseen, among the Dons.
Nor in the lodge, nor in the library,
Upon its pedestal appeared, to be
A mark for reverence of green gownsman-hood,
Of grief to ancient fogies, and reproof
To those who knew not Alfred, being hard
And narrowed in their honour to old names
Of poets, who had vogue when *they* were young,
And not admitting later bards; but now,
Last week, a rumour widely blown about,
Walking the windy circle of the Press,
Came, that stern Whewell, with the Seniors,
Who rule the destinies of Trinity,
Had of the sanctuary barred accèss
Unto the bust of Alfred Tennyson,
By Woolner carved, subscribed for by the youth
Who loved the Poet, hoped to see him set
Within the Library of Trinity,
One great man more o' the house, among the great,
Who grace that still Valhalla, ranged in row,
Along the chequered marbles of the floor,
Two stately ranks—to where the fragrant limes
Look thro' the far end window, cool and green.
A band it is, of high companionship,—
Chief, Newton, and the broad-browed Verulam,
And others only less than these in arts
Or science : names that England holds on high.
Among whom, hoped the youth, would soon be set,
The living likeness of a living Bard,—
Great Alfred Tennyson, the Laureate,
Whom Trinity most loves of living sons.
But other thought had Whewell and the Dons,
Deeming such honour only due to those
Upon whose greatness Death has set his seal.
So fixed their faces hard, and shut the doors
Upon the living Poet : for, said one,
" It is too soon," and when they heard the phrase,
Others caught up the cue, and chorussed it,
Until, the poet echoing " Soon ? too soon ? "
As if in wrath, Whewell looked up, and said :—
" O Laureate, if indeed you list to try,
Try, and unfix our purpose in the thing."
Whereat *full shrilly sang* th' excluded bard,

" Soon, soon, so soon ! Whewell looks stern and chill,
Soon, soon, so soon ! but I can enter still."
" Too soon, *too soon !* You cannot enter now."

---

[1] Reprinted by the special permission of the Proprietors of *Punch*.

"I am not dead : of that I do repent.
But to my living prayer, oh now relent."
"Too soon, too soon ! You cannot enter now."

"Honour in life is sweet : my fame is wide.
Let me to stand at Dryden's, Byron's side."
"Too soon, too soon ! You cannot enter now."

"Honour that comes in life is rare as sweet;
I cannot taste it long : for life is fleet."
"No, no, too soon ! You cannot enter now."

So sang the Laureate, while all stonily,
Their chins upon their hands, as men that had
No entrails to be moved, sat the stern Dons.

T. Woolner to Mrs. Tennyson

27, *Rutland Street,*
Hampstead Road, N.W.,
November 13 [1859].

My dear Mrs. Tennyson,
   I was going to write to you some time since to tell
you that the Cambridge Magnates had resolved on putting
the bust in the Vestibule of the Trinity Library but chancing
to meet Vernon [Lushington] accidentally he told me that
he had already written to apprise you. . . . I think it a
fair compromise between the original to have it placed in
the Library itself and the utter rejection of it by Dr.
Whewell and his brother Dons; . . . I hope the subject
may at last rest peacefully, for in all conscience from first
to last, there has been storm enough of one kind and
another sounding round the marble head . . . Palgrave
I am sorry to say still keeps unwell . . . he came round
to my room the other evening to meet Holman Hunt,
and they talked dreary semi-archaic-conjectural lore anent
Gospel evidences nearly all the time they stayed. . . .
                                          [No Signature.]

Thus the bust which had caused so much talk and
discussion found its resting place in the vestibule of
Trinity College. Woolner carved replicas of this work,
one for Mr. Charles Buxton and one for Mr. Charles Jenner
of Easter Duddingston, who on the death of the Laureate
generously gave it to Hallam Lord Tennyson to place in
Westminster Abbey, in Poets' Corner.

CHAPTER IX

MRS. TENNYSON TO T. WOOLNER

Farringford,
November 16, 1859.

MY DEAR MR. WOOLNER,

If you are satisfied we are, and so now there is nothing more to be desired but the advantageous light. We are sorry to hear about Mr. Palgrave. For the most part I agree with you about Religious books, and yet, however dimly shadowed, there are ideas and truths in Mr. Maurice's book that can only be ridiculed because too great for the comprehension of the mocker. As a man speaks of his friend and so kindles an ardour of affection in the heart of another man for the friend whom he loves and reverences, so some good men can speak of Christ and make Him seem more lovely than He would otherwise do to hearts stranger or estranged, and this is what we want to see—Christ as it were face to face—to know Him heart with heart. The Word is the Word still however abused is it not ? Pardon me I am as bad as a religious book.

We had Sir John Simeon dining with us the day before yesterday and to-day he comes again with Mr. Charles Wynne. We have had Kingsleys, Gattys, and others besides staying with us and on Monday we expect Mrs. Cameron and her little boys.

.   .   .   .

The Kingsleys were so very pleasant.

I wish you would give Alfred something to do. He is pretty well but for want of this.

.   .   .   .   .   .

Alfred's love and the boys'.

Most truly yours,
EMILY TENNYSON.

You do not tell me how your work proceeds which is, you know, always very interesting news to us.

[*November 23, 1859.*]

Extract from letter of T. WOOLNER TO MRS. TENNYSON

.   .   .   .   .   .

I had a pleasant trip at Cambridge or stay I ought to say, for the journey cannot be called pleasant. I was introduced to Sedgwick and had a good long chat with the patriarch, and I have considerable hope of being able to get the fine old fellow to sit for a bust; which would be a grand thing, as it has rarely been my lot to contemplate so magnificent a head as his. He looks to have a most powerful intellect, and his nature is evidently most simple and natural; with great kindness, broad generous humour and the sternest dislike to rascals. Clark, that delightful man says he thinks there will be no difficulty in getting him to sit; and if he succeeds there will be another great man added to my gallery. Sedgwick expressed himself strongly that the bust was not put into the library at once; thought it absurd etc. I forget if I told you that altho' not so dignified in position the bust would be in a superior light as regards displaying the art of the bust; which assuredly is what I care mostly for. . . .

I am going on Saturday to stay Sunday, back on Monday morning, to Brighton to see Knox, a friend of Novelli, Fairbairn and other of my friends; he is one of the chief leader writers on *The Times* and has been ill for a long time poor fellow, I grieve to say, and as he thinks it would please him to have a chat with your humble servant, it will be very delightful to run down to see him. . . . Have you heard of Frank Stone's death ?

But possibly you have not heard the cause. A friend of his told me of it yesterday. It appears that he has long been troubled with heart disease and the election of the R.A. coming on he fell into a most agitated state, fearing that he might not be made an R.A. As he feared, it proved; for a friend announced that Phillip was elected and that he, Frank, had not had one vote; this to his poor weak mind was the crack of doom; his heart broke and he went home and died straightway. . . .

Ever sincerely yours,
THOMAS WOOLNER,

[*The Autumn of* 1859 ?]

Extract from letter of T. WOOLNER TO MRS. TENNYSON

.   .   .   .   .   .

I went and spent a long evening with Carlyle on Monday last : he was not in good spirits ; in fact he has not been at all well since that laborious continental journey last year, the details of which he told me, and I do not wonder at his discomfiture. I tried hard to persuade him to cut work altogether for a few months, on the plea that it would be all the better for his book, and he confessed that he had not done so much in three months as he was accustomed to do in so many weeks when in a higher tone of health. So that considering Mrs. Carlyle absolutely needs country air, for she has been unwell for a long time, and I did not see her on that evening, I think he will soon really attend to his health and cease working for awhile. Ruskin came in while I was there and commenced a buzz of inflated rapture upon a piece of charlatanry called " Victory," by Marochetti, now being shown at Apsley House ; . . . Ruskin's inflation was met in a manner that I think one so utterly good and kind as you could not with your utmost efforts imagine ; but we certainly gave that conceited creature something to reflect upon. When he was gone we both agreed that a man who took Marochetti as his ideal sculptor, Louis Napoleon as his favourite king and politician, and Spurgeon for his best beloved theologian, was certainly an unsafe guide for women and the youths of England ; for beside these, his trusting admirers are few. . .

Sunday Night.—I have just returned from Slough, where I passed a pleasant day. W. Rossetti went also, and we paid a visit to classic Stoke Pogis, and did the proper thing by quoting " Ye distant spires, etc : " and looked upon the humble homes where " the rude forefathers of the hamlet sleep." It was really a charming scene, rendered impressive by a poor funeral which was performed at the time : we looked on at distance till it was done and the mourners had all dispersed, when we entered the graveyard and were to some degree appalled by the lively energy shown by the gravedigger and little boys filling up the grave ; the boys evidently enjoyed the keenest delight, and worked with a will that I never before saw shown except in men digging for gold. I could not avoid feeling that it was in part unseemly, this wild haste to get a fellow creature thoroughly covered away from sight.

I forgot to mention in my last note, how delighted I was with the bold little poem of "Riflemen." It has been much admired, quoted and alluded to; as well it might, for it is like a gun booming of danger fast coming upon us. I am rejoiced to find that Rifle Corps are being formed all over the country; not by any means too soon, as we may find out to our cost before long.

Believe me,
Ever truly yours,
THOMAS WOOLNER.

Extract from a letter of WOOLNER'S TO MRS. TENNYSON

December 5, 1859.

I grieve to hear that the Poet is not well, and most sincerely hope that if a subject for a poem will make him better that he will soon succeed in pleasing himself. I wish I could persuade him to do the tale of the Sailor which I told him of years ago I should think,[1] for I think it capable in his hands of growing into one of the greatest of poems, altho told of persons not princes, philosophers, or chiefs. I daresay he has forgotten it. . . .

Extract from a letter of WILLIAM ALLINGHAM TO T. WOOLNER

Lane, Ballyshannon,
December 21, 1859.

Tremble (here is an aphorism I make) when you find yourself in company with a stupid person, for you know not when or how he may injure you; and you cannot defend yourself.

THOMAS COMBE [2] TO T. WOOLNER

Oxford,
December 21, 1859.

DEAR SIR,
      It gives Mrs. Combe and myself much pleasure to hear from our mutual friend Mr. Hunt that you assent to accompany him to Oxford on Saturday next. Hunt

---

[1] This story alluded to is the story of the Fisherman—written out later for the Laureate by Woolner.

[2] Mr. Combe, of the Clarendon Press, was a most kind friend of Woolner's, and he commissioned him to make a bust of himself and one of Dr. John Henry Newman, afterwards Cardinal Newman.

CRANESDEN

[Photograph by Glanville, Tunbridge Wells.

[To face page 185.

is not famed for his punctuality, we shall be glad to see
you as early in the day as is convenient, but pray do not
be later than four as we dine at five in order not to interfere with the Meeting at Magdalen, which I hope you will
enjoy.

Yours faithfully,
THE. COMBE.

EDWARD LEAR TO T. WOOLNER

9^{4to,} V. Condotti, Roma,
February 16, 1860.

MY DEAR WOOLNER,

o my deerunkel [1]—Mr. Edward Wilson has brought
me your letter of Jan.y 19th this afternoon, at 4 p.m.
So I walked round the Borghese villa with him, & thought
him a very nice fellow ;—& if he hadn't been so, I should
have seen what I could of him : for your sake unkel. I have
asked him to dine tomorrow, tête-à-tête, & shall feed him
with stewed beef & maccaroni & you may depend on my
doing all I can for him, as far as my little possible goes.
For in 10 days (his limit of time here) much cannot be done.
With regard to Naples & other parts of Hitterly, I fear
I can do less. . . . Tell my pa he is a nasty unnatural
old brute of a parient, as lets his own flesh & blood pine &
fret away in furrin parts, without his never writing nothink
to them. I am immensely glad you give such a good
account of dead Daddy—& long to hear of the picture being
finished. I approve of both your dancings, . . . a couple
of little apes as you both of you be ! For all that I wish
you were both of you here. I really do wish you could
come before I go hence and am no more seen in Rome, for
I hate the place more & more & more & more. I heard of
your being at Farringford from Mrs. Tennyson. . . . Don't
you delight in Tithonus ? I am glad you went over to
Swainston : Sir J. Simeon has done himself & his religion
credit by his good & manly letter. Thank you for what
you say of my pictures : it is a really great pleasure to
know that Fairbairn likes his Petra so much. . . . Dear
me ! I wish you could come out here for a little time . .
you might see all Rome so quietly as you never would have
another roppertunity of doing. So might Pa. I am glad

---

[1] Edward Lear called Woolner his " unkel," and Holman Hunt his
" pa " and his " Daddy " ! Edward Lear was much their senior.

to hear of your doing Sir W. Hooker & Sedgwick . . . my plans are much changed since I came here, and I find I must put off Palestine till Autumn. And thus I am going on with paintings of Palermo, Dead Sea, Parnassus. . . . Beirût, & Damascus, with some drawings,—But I also wish to paint the Seeders of Lebanon from the big Seeders at Sir J. Simeon's before I come to town. I am convinced of this : a man cannot too perpetually & too wiggorously keep a beginning & a setting forth of new themes for work : if so be he goes on to finish them. After I've done all the above toppicks, I trust to go to Jerusalem & after that perhaps to the troppicle regents, & the Specific highlands and never comes a Hewropean trader & a lustrous creeper

my unkel Tom.   niy pa

in a flag sliding over summer trailers which accounts for the same.

O my belovydunkel, my eyes are tired with the light, and my 'ed is a ākin : so I can't right any maw, beinng half asleep. Give my love to my dear pa, & to Brother Bob Martineau, & to my Grandfather Maddox Brown, which I always keep seeing his picture of " Work " before me.—(o my !) . . . Good-bye my dear boy. I am truly glad you are going on so well. Write me a line by post some day for it is a pleasure to hear of you.

> And believe me,
> Dear Woolner,
> Yours affly.
> EDWARD LEAR.

Do write & send me the address of your Studio.—I hope though, you'll get a block of marble for the little Fairbairns soon.

Woolner having received a commission to do the bust of Professor Adam Sedgwick, the geologist—the Professor wrote to suggest dates for the sittings to take place.

PROFESSOR SEDGWICK TO T. WOOLNER

Trinity College,
February 24, 1860.

DEAR SIR,
It was not without extreme reluctance that I consented to sit. Not that I was insensible to the honour my friends intended me, but I did not like to put them to so much cost : & perhaps I was selfish in my reluctance, as I do not much like the kind of durance that is inflicted in a sitting. Clark told me (if I mistake not) that you were willing to come down to Cambridge, & that the work, while I was " in the stocks " might be gone thro' at Cambridge. If so, I am at this moment ready; and I only wish you had a better block to work upon. It will be hard for you to turn my old, withered, wooden face to good account. But this is your look out & not mine. But if it do not fall in with your arrangements to be so long at Cambridge I must put off the sitting till the warmer weather of spring when I may come up to London & attend your appointment in your own Studio. The worst of it is, that during all the spring months I am in the possession of that vile adhesive fiend, suppressed gout; & that I continue a perfect model of melancholy or vile temper. I have no hopes of escape from this annual & most unwelcome visit. . . .
I am, Dear Sir,
Very truly yours,
A. SEDGWICK.

Besides the irksomeness of sitting, the great geologist felt a terror at first of having his bust done—thinking he had to lie on the floor and have the liquid plaster of Paris poured over his face ! and his relief and satisfaction were great when the sculptor told him he had only to sit in a chair and chat. During the taking of the portrait the sitter and artist became very good friends. There is rather an amusing anecdote in connection with this bust. Under the marble bust is a space where the name is usually cut in, but in this bust Woolner had carved there also a fossil fish, one of the Professor's discoveries—a lady coming one day to the studio to see the work exclaimed : " How lucky Mr. Woolner, there should happen to be the fossil in that particular bit of marble ! " [1]

T. WOOLNER TO MRS. TENNYSON

27, Rutland Street,
Hampstead Road, N.W.,
February 26, 1860.

MY DEAR MRS. TENNYSON,

. . . I was to have gone to Mr. Jowett next Sunday but instead have to go next week to Cambridge to begin Prof: Sedgwick . . . the Professor is so old and subject to illnesses that it was thought by his friends highly desirable I should lose no time in doing him. My bust of Sir W. Hooker is now done and it appears to please the judges who have seen it in an extraordinary manner :—Sir C. Eastlake says that this bust settles the question of color and statuary; that when marble is wrought to such a point of perfection it leaves nothing to be desired—and that when he looks at it he forgets that it is marble and can think of nothing but the man. This coming from such a high official authority who is always considered particularly chary of praise is of value. . . . The Trevelyans called on me the other day; and fortunately I had done something considerable to their group. . . . My love to the Poet; tell him that Fairbairn says " Tithonus " is one of the greatest poems in the world, and one of the most perfect. . . .

Very sincerely yours,
THOMAS WOOLNER.

T. WOOLNER TO MRS. TENNYSON

Trinity College,
Cambridge,
March 21, 1860.

MY DEAR MRS. TENNYSON,

I have managed the old gentleman's head at last,[2] which will be finished or nearly so tomorrow. Everyone who has seen it declares it most successful, and the enthusiasm expressed is all I can possibly desire. It certainly was a tough job, and has taken about a week longer than I

---

[1] The fossil was the Areolepis Sedgwickii.   [2] Professor Sedgwick.

calculated : I have now to do a medallion of Clark before I return to town. . . . I know you will like Clark very much : I have known but very few men I like so well, and here his popularity is quite next to Sedgwick himself. . . . I went to-day to see the University boat pull fast; they are now in training for the great match to come off between Oxford and Cambridge on the 31st. It was a truly beautiful sight to see the 8 strong young men pull together so perfectly that it looked like one creature, and the boat like one life. . . .

[Signature missing.]

T. Woolner to Mrs. Tennyson

27, Rutland Street,
Hampstead Road, N.W.,
April 11, 1860.

MY DEAR MRS. TENNYSON,

I will not stultify my own counsel by giving you work to read much writing and will only say how greatly Clark was delighted with his visit, which would have been an absolutely perfect joy if it had not been shadowed by knowing how unwell you were.

I hope the dear little boys are getting rid of their enemy, for it grieves my heart to see them imprisoned like chickens under a coop—but the approaching warm weather will be their friend.

.   .   .   .   .   .

I entreat you not on any account to write back until you are quite well again. My best love to the Poet—tell him I will try and write out the points of that Sailor's story.[1]

With kindest wishes,
Ever truly yours,
THOMAS WOOLNER.

Mrs. Tennyson to T. Woolner

Farringford,
April 27, 1860.

MY DEAR MR. WOOLNER,

I could scarcely help crying when I heard of your irreparable loss,[2] not your loss only, but all people's.

.   .   .   .   .   .

[1] The story of " The Fisherman."
[2] The deplorable accident at the Royal Academy, when the nose of the marble bust of Sir William Hooker was broken.

A. is quite pleased to see how neat the new gardener has made a great part of the kitchen-garden and besides he allows A. to dig, a delight forbidden by Merwood, and to be told that you are doing a great deal of good instead of mischief is a pleasant change indeed! I won't write more, but I cannot help telling you that I cannot get your loss out of my mind, though alas this will not repair it.

DR. JOSEPH HOOKER TO T. WOOLNER

Royal Gardens, Kew,
Thursday [*May* 1860].

MY DEAR WOOLNER

I am deeply concerned to hear of the grievous disaster that has befallen you—much more I assure you my dear fellow for your own sake than for that of the *bust.* Your fame is secure, come what may of *that,* & though my Barometer of sympathy rises to " high disappointment " on the score of so splendid a rendering of my Dad being spoiled, that is nothing to the depth of sympathy with you to which it falls. As to my thermometer it is smashed, having bolted up far above Passion point on reading the conclusion of your note. That such an accident should have occurred is bad enough, but through carelessness, & with such an insult coupled is beyond all sufferance.

Come on Sunday my good Woolner & mind you & Novelli stay over dinner. . . .

Ever sincerely yours,
JOS. D. HOOKER.

MRS. JOSEPH HOOKER TO T. WOOLNER.

[*May* 1860.]

MY DEAR MR. WOOLNER,

I must put a few lines in Joseph's envelope to tell you how very sorry I am to hear of the misfortune which has occurred to you. I am thoroughly indignant, so much that I feel quite glad it will not be in my power to see the Academy this year. I don't think I could enter the rooms with any degree of patience. It is really too bad, & the impossibility of getting redress makes it more insupportable. I am really very, very much grieved for you, to have all the labor of so many months ruined it seems as if no indignation could be too great to bestow on those horrid Academicians. I hope Sunday will be a fine day, & a little warmer than it is now.

Ever yrs sincerely,
FRANCES HOOKER.

These letters show the intense sympathy felt for the sculptor in the damage to a work thought so highly of by judges of Art.

LADY HOOKER [1] TO T. WOOLNER.

Royal Gardens, Kew, W.,
May 1 [1860.]

DEAR SIR,
I hardly know how to thank you for your kind gift— so beautiful in itself, & so specially interesting to me. I should have liked to make my acknowledgements in person, but you know, I daresay, that I am wholly laid up, unable for the last half year or more to stand alone—much less to walk : in fact, *come* as I tell my husband, *to my 2nd, childhood.* Most indignant have I felt at the cruel careless-ness with which your laborious & beautiful work, of Sir Wm. Hooker's bust, has been mutilated. It strikes me that nothing would so much induce the Royal Academicians to make you good amends, as your expressing a determina-tion to exhibit it, the bust without a nose. They could not refuse this :—& I will venture to say that no sculptor's work would attract such attention as yours ! Public notice would be the more called to the beauty of the still perfect portion. And, after all, the Elgin marbles have well accustomed spectators to this special deficiency : so that the loss of the nose no longer looks grotesque, but a mark of the real antique !—I hardly think however that the officials of the Royal Academy would welcome such a semblance of the chisel of Phidias or Praxiteles.

I am very much yrs.
MARIA HOOKER.

T. WOOLNER TO MRS. TENNYSON

27, *Rutland Street,*
Hampstead Road, N.W.,
May 2, 1860.

MY DEAR MRS. TENNYSON,

The disaster to my bust of Hooker has caused an extra-

[1] Wife of Sir William Hooker.

ordinary amount of sorrow and indignation; one would almost fancy that it had been some great man killed thro' shameful negligence, instead of a mere piece of marble work destroyed. It is a most lamentable loss to me, for I think that I have received higher praise for this than for anything I have done. I patched up the nose with borax for the R.A. Ex: for I thought they might as well have the benefit of their own handiwork for the season; yesterday I received a note from Millais saying that the mending did not show in the least; if so, then of course, whatever merits there are must be partially concealed likewise; he said the bust was " MOST EXQUISITE " underlined twice, " marvellously finished," and " the best thing " he had seen; then as a climax, said he liked it " better than Tennyson's."

A great deal of my time is occupied during the evenings answering letters of sympathy; for the affair seems to have spread wonderfully fast; and from what people say I think if the R.A. persist in refusing to pay the price of the bust that it will do them a great deal of harm.

. . . . .

Novelli, Hunt, Palgrave and I went to Kew and spent the afternoon and evening with Dr. and Mrs. Hooker, spending a pleasant time as you may suppose in such good society. The gardens are beginning to look cheery and bright.

[Signature missing.]

[*Photograph by L. Caswall-Smith.*

" FEEDING THE HUNGRY "

One of the bas-reliefs on the Wigton Fountain. The central figure is a portrait of the
sculptor's wife.

[*To face page* 193.

CHAPTER X

T. Woolner to Mrs. Tennyson

27, Rutland Street,
Hampstead Road, N.W.,
May 17, 1860.

My dear Mrs. Tennyson,

. . . Yesterday I had to go and see a cast taken of the left hand of Lady Noel Byron, wife of the poet. The summons said it was essential that an honorable man should do it, or I should not have been troubled. I do not much like taking casts of any one dead, but could not refuse in this case, as I know so many of their friends. But I am glad I did go, for a nobler sight I never saw—she looked as if she were living, and had just dropped to sleep, and as proud as a queen in all her splendour. I think there never was anything finer than her brow and nose. . . . She seems to have been almost adored by those about her. . . . By a happy fluke I discovered the name of the little bird mentioned in "Elaine" as making the ear weary by repetition of one particular passage of notes. It is the "Willow Wren," and begins to sing in April. Be so good as to tell this to your Husband and it will rejoice his un-ornithological heart. I went and spent last Sunday with Patmore at Finchley, and read part of his new poem, which is remarkably good in execution, and I think very original in idea. Perhaps you know that the Angel has been granted the heavenly gift of another male cherub, which is No. 6. . . . You must have heard of the prodigious success of Hunt's picture [1] in a popular sense, nothing like it in modern times . . . it is so unusual that a fashionable public goes mad about anything more dignified than a Crystal Palace, crinoline or a Railway King. . . .

Ever truly yours,

Thomas Woolner.

[1] "The Finding of Christ in the Temple."

27, *Rutland Street,*
Hampstead Road, N.W.,
June 24, 1860.

MY DEAR MRS. TENNYSON,

·   ·   ·   ·   ·

I went to see the Review yesterday, and was rather amused to see the extraordinary popularity of the movement : Hyde Park was nearly full; the trees were full of men and boys; you never saw such unlovely fruit, some of which were too ripe and fell to the ground bringing big branches with them : the surrounding houses and balconies and roofs were full; all the adjacent streets were full and a vivid fever of excitement I am told pervaded the whole of London. I was with an Indian Officer who was with Sir Hugh Rose in his campaign, and when the guns began to boom at the Queen's approach, I asked him if the sound did not make him feel very much at home : for I think I never saw a man look so pleased; it brought to mind his battles, and he told me of them with a delight and ecstasy that made me think war could not be so bad as it looked, to the warriors; and although he was wounded fearfully, he regarded the wounds as trifles compared to the delightful excitement of battle : he is a direct descendant from Dr. Donne, the old poet.

·   ·   ·   ·   ·

I am going to Oxford on Tuesday for the R. Association, my address there will be *Thos. Combe, Esq., Clarendon Press.* I suppose I shall stay a week, partly with him and with Jowett. I do not much wish to see the ceremonies, but Hunt engaged a long time ago for me without consulting me in the least, so I was obliged to go; and going is no great harm, for I do about as much work in a week as I ought to do in an hour, if I were in a fitting state for work. Woodward wants me to take my design for the doorway down, and intimates that he thinks after all they will be forced to have it :—I suppose for this simple reason, that they are not able with all their learning to suggest a better subject.

·   ·   ·   ·   ·

I want sadly to get on with the Trevelyans' Group, but the want of a fitting face so checks me that I cannot get up any interest for it.

I hoped to have this Sunday all to myself, but last night

on arriving found a note from Novelli asking me to his house in the hope that he shall get Clark, for us to talk matters over, I suppose connected with the Macaulay's and Hallam's statues : but my impression is, that altho' I have friends on both committees, Marochetti has more.

.   .   .   .   .   .

How long will you remain at Farringford? Because I should exceedingly like to run down just to see you, for when I was last down I can scarcely be said to have seen you; . . . The chief drag I have on my wheel now is the bust of William Fairbairn; for I am sorry to say the fine old gentleman is not strict in keeping his engagements, and has kept me waiting many times without any fruit whatever, and I cannot get on with the work at all; and the only reason why I can go to Oxford is that he is going too, and I can be sure he will not be able to sit.

My love to the Poet and the boys.

.   .   .   .   .   .

I cannot tell you how thankful I am for your letters : your last I keep always with me and read in choice moments; as one would look at a beautiful locket miniature, always in some strange way hoping to get nearer the spirit of what the picture speaks of.

.   .   .   .   .   .

Ever sincerely yours,
THOMAS WOOLNER.

ROBERT BROWNING TO T. WOOLNER

Florence, June 15, 1860.

DEAR WOOLNER,

I happen to have an occasion of sending to England—I was your debtor for a long, kind—most welcome letter, introducing Mr. Wilson to us. I don't write often, & may easily do myself great injustice, but not, I really think, in your mind—so fresh is its kindness in my memory. I follow your career with true delight, as I see one work succeed another in the registry of the newspapers—but I need no assurance of your genius.

Will you like to have, for our sakes, these photographs, just done in Rome? The horseman is Pen on his pony, from a capital little painting by Hamilton Wild, an American artist of achievement & promise besides.

We have just returned from Rome—and go presently to

Siena for the hot months. . . . There is no England for us this year—but next year, if all goes as we hope, you will see us again. Meanwhile be sure of the true regard of my wife & of yours most sincerely ever

ROBERT BROWNING.

You will find the photographs left for you at Chapman's, 193 Piccadilly.

EDWARD LEAR TO T. WOOLNER

15, *Stratford Place, W.*,
June 25, 1860.

MY DEAR UNCLE,

Which your letter of April 9 was very welcome & should have been replied to b4, only it came when I was all in a bussel a leaving Rome—I tried to get to you yesterday—but only reached Mrs. Martineau's house before it was too late to retrace my steps :—but some day I shall

hope to come & look you up, & meanwhile if you are passing here, I am full of small unfinished works, some of which might interest you, particklar 2 views of Palermo, with portraits of Garibaldi in the foreground, as I am on the point of taking up & down Bond St. with a box for shillings.

I saw Edward Wilson a day or two ago. My father [1] I have seen several times, & am as glad of his success as if I had got double myself. He is a blessed old parient he is. The best criticism I have yet heard on his picture [2] was last week, when a very fine gentleman objected to the " commonplace air " of the Virgin & added " No well-bred woman would ever enter a room in such a *fussy* manner."—This, however absurd,—is really a fact.

I have been some days at Farringford with F. Lushington. All are pretty well there, Mrs. A. better than I had expected. Mrs. Cameron absolutely sent up a grand piano by 8 men from her house for me to sing at !!!!!!!

W. G. Clark was at a fish dinner on Fryday last at Grinidge. I hear you suffered brutally from the R.A. porters, as to Sedgwick's bust.[3] What are you now

---

[1] W. Holman Hunt. [2] " The Finding of Christ in the Temple."
[3] Bust of Sir William Hooker, not Sedgwick.

about? I write in haste: but thank you for your letter nevertheless.

Yrs. sincerely,
EDWARD LEAR.

T. WOOLNER TO MRS. TENNYSON

27, Rutland Street,
Hampstead Road, N.W.,
Wednesday, July 25, 1860.

MY DEAR MRS. TENNYSON,

.   .   .   .   .   .

I am sorry to tell you that Carlyle is sadly knocked up with this hateful weather and hard work. I was to have taken the Rajah to him last evening, but the Rajah having a bad cold dared not go out, so I went alone. Carlyle is going next week to the most northerly point of Scotland to stay with Sir Something Sinclair, and thinks 2 months of doing nothing may set him up again. He was wonderfully kind and tender in his manner. Mrs. Carlyle is much better than I have seen her for a long time.

The Rajah is much stronger than he was this time last year; and he tells me his relations with the English Government are more satisfactory than they had been for a long time before and he seems hopeful. He likes Hunt's picture and Darwin's book exceedingly.

I went on Saturday to spend Sunday at the Prescotts' and there were a pleasant party—Brookfield, Venables, Lord Overstone, Hunt, Dean Trench and others. Venables and I went two long walks on Sunday and he was very pleasant, and really interesting. You know, altho' he is such an honourable truthful man, he does not often condescend to be very agreeable to any but his old friends; therefore I considered myself fortunate.

[No signature.]

MRS. TENNYSON TO T. WOOLNER

Grasby,
August 18, 1860.

MY DEAR MR. WOOLNER,
        I have written to A. how it rained and how we were deluded yesterday, but I must not let the post go without a few words of thanks for all your goodness, the crowning

act with which I hold the giving up your work to go with
A. May the journey [1] be fabulously delightful to both !

All best wishes for you. When I am a little rested I shall
begin the poem, to be ready to give it up when required.
Most truly yours,
EMILY TENNYSON.

T. WOOLNER TO F. T. PALGRAVE

Bideford,
Tuesday, August, 1860.

MY DEAR PALGRAVE,
I am deputed to write and say that you must be
at Tintagel instead of Penzance, if you please, by Friday
or thereabouts; at any rate we shall remain there until
you come. . . .
Excuse this being so badly written I mean as to forms
of letters not to composition, I let that take its chance,
for there is a waiter dodging and fidgetting around me and
makes my nerves as irritable as a bee tied up in a bottle. . . .
Thine ever,
THOMAS WOOLNER.

T. WOOLNER TO MRS. TENNYSON

Tintagel, Cornwall,
August 25, 1860.

MY DEAR MRS. TENNYSON,

Palgrave arrived this afternoon, and I was going back
in his fly to Launceston, indeed had my things packed,
bill paid etc., but your Husband and Palgrave urged me
so strongly to stay that prudence, desire to get to work,
hatred of continuous wet, and everything gave way and I
consented to stay a short time longer. I hope that now
I am so near I shall be gratified by a sight of the Land's
End; for that I have the greater part of my life longed to
see, although I know perfectly well it will be much like
many rocky scenes of my experiences; but I am rather
like a baby and want to do something that sounds
grand.
My object in writing is not to tell you this, but to ask

[1] The journey in Devon and Cornwall.

if you will kindly send on my poem [1] to Lady Trevelyan
when you have done with it.

Ours was a remarkably pretty tour if the weather had
been decent—Bath was splendid, Bideford interesting, and
Clovelly is the most picturesque gem I ever saw; Bude
was wild and desolate and fascinating, but not so much
as Boss Castle, which is one of the most savagely rugged
things in nature I should think; this place would be en-
chanting under ordinary circumstances, the broad sweeping
simple country—quaint, queer looking cottages, terrible
rocks and mysterious caverns, and ruins of grim old castle,
inaccessible on one side and not easy of approach on the
other. There is no comfortable bathing which is a serious
disadvantage, for the sea is so roary and rough that none
but a good swimmer could enter with impunity.

> Yours ever truly,
> THOMAS WOOLNER.

T. WOOLNER TO MRS. TENNYSON

> 27, *Rutland Street,*
> *Hampstead Road, N.W.,*
> *October 8, 1860.*

MY DEAR MRS. TENNYSON,

I had a pleasant little chat with the great Greek
professor the other day; he was anticipating a few days
of delightful holiday at Farringford he told me.

Palgrave called in this evening; he is busy reading all
the Poets for the purpose of making a collection [2] to publish
which he intends to beat that of Allingham. I am rather
fond of such books, for I can dip from gem to gem without the
trouble of getting up to take books down from the shelves.

I cannot write so much as I could wish for it is so late,
and the fire having gone out without asking my permission like a bad servant, it has grown colder than is pleasant,
so wishing my best love to the Poet and my pets.

> Am,
> Ever truly yours,
> THOMAS WOOLNER.

---

[1] " My Beautiful Lady."   [2] *The Golden Treasury.*

THE REV. H. MONTAGU BUTLER TO T. WOOLNER

Harrow,
October 12, 1860.

DEAR MR. WOOLNER,

I shall feel very glad if you are able to execute for me a work in which I am much interested. I intend to offer to the Master of Trinity a Bust of the late Archdeacon Hare, to be placed in the College Library.

The Archdeacon, you are perhaps aware, was brother-in-law of Mr. Maurice, and he was for a long time a resident Fellow of Trinity. In testimony of his affection for the College he left it an exceedingly large and valuable present of books.

He was in short one of our undoubted benefactors as well as (in my opinion) one of our greatest ornaments in modern times. Such a man deserves a permanent mark of respect, and my own affectionate reverence for his memory makes me rejoice that it should fall to me to pay it.

Mr. Maurice has been kind enough to inform me that there are two extant portraits of Hare; the one by Richmond, the other, less satisfactory but in some respects characteristic, by S. Lawrence. These belong to Mrs. Hare, and Mr. Maurice authorises me to say that they would be placed at your disposal, and that the family would to the best of their power furnish you with hints suggested by personal recollection.

My wish is that the Bust should be in marble, and as good a one as you can make. I put the matter very bluntly but I do not see that I can put it more accurately.

You will oblige me by letting me know what the entire cost would be; but I do not anticipate that any difficulty can arise between us on this point. The commission of course must be conditional on the assent of the Master of Trinity to accept the Bust, but it is impossible that he can hesitate. To say nothing of higher claims, which every Trinity man know to be irresistible, Hare was an intimate personal friend of Whewell. . . . Your name will, I am sure, be a guarantee to him, as it is to Mr. Maurice and myself, that all that marble can do for a face no longer living will be done by your hand and mind.

Believe me,
Very truly yours,
H. MONTAGU BUTLER.

HEAD OF OPHELIA, 1874

[*To face page* 200.

MRS. CARLYLE TO T. WOOLNER

5, *Great Cheyne Row,*
Chelsea,
[*November 22, 1860.*]

1000 thanks dear Mr. Woolner !

I can't make up my mind yet which of the Photographs I like best. The little one is the most characteristic; exactly the attitude in which you stand on our hearthrug ! But the larger one will be best for hanging on a wall. So I mean to frame both, the little one alongside of Kate Stanley. I will ask the immortal Mr. Tait, the first time I can get up the steam to go to his house, if he have an unspoiled copy of Lady A. I was vexed, after promising you one, to have none better than *that* to give you. I am sorry for your cat's Influenza [It is a clear case of Influenza !] but it would have been worse if she had given way to passion, as her mother has just done, and done no end of mischief in attempting a great crime ! For several days there had been *that* in her eyes when raised to my canary, which filled my heart with alarm. I sent express for a carpenter, and had the cage attached to the drawing-room ceiling, with an elaborate apparatus of chain and pulley and weight. " Most EXPENSIVE ! " (as my Scotch servant exclaimed with clasped hands over a Picture of the *Virgin and Child* in the National Gallery !) and there had it swung for two days, to Mr. C.'s intense disgust, who regards thy pet as " *the most inanely chimerical of all* "—the cat meanwhile spending all its spare time in gazing up at the bird with eyes aflame ! But it was safe *now*—I thought ! and went out for a walk. On my return Charlotte met me with " Oh ! whatever *do* you think the cat has gone and done ? " " Eaten my canary ? " —" No, *far worse !*—pulled down the cage and the weight, and broke the chain and upset the little table and broken everything on it ! "—" And not eaten the canary ? "— " Oh, I suppose the dreadful crash she made frightened *herself ;* for I met *her* running down stairs as I ran up— tho' the cage was on the floor, and the door open and the canary in *such* a way ! " You never saw such a scene of devastation. The carpet was covered with fragments of a pretty terra cotta basket given me by Lady Airlie—and fragments of the glass which covered it, and with the earth and ferns that had been growing in it and with birdseed, and bits of brass chain, and I can't tell what all ! That is what one gets by breeding up a cat !—She had rushed right out at the back door and didn't show her face for twenty-four hours after !—And now I don't know where the poor bird will be safe. Come soon.

Affectionately yours,
JANE CARLYLE.

MRS. TENNYSON TO T. WOOLNER

Farringford,
December 7, 1860.

MY DEAR MR. WOOLNER,

We shall miss you very much at Christmas I need not say. Let us know when anything is settled about Sedgwick, please. I heartily agree with you in your dislike of money affairs and I become more and more convinced that money lies at the root of at least half the sin and sorrow of the world. Beyond all price to me would be a worthy subject for Alfred, one which would fix him whether he would or no.

The boys' love and Alfred's, the boys both shout out " I hope he will come soon."

Most truly yours,
EMILY TENNYSON.

JAMES ANTHONY FROUDE TO T. WOOLNER

6, Clifton Place,
Hyde Park, W.,
Sunday, December 8 [1860].

MY DEAR WOOLNER,

I am sure you will forgive my trespassing upon you with a matter on which no one living can give so good an opinion as you can give. My brother-in-law Mr. Warre of the Isle of Thanet has lately died, and his family wish to place a really handsome monument over the vault. There is no alternative in a monument between what is beautiful & what is hideous.

If the feeling is not definitely pleased it is disgusted.

Can you tell me where to go for designs—or could you be induced to sketch a design yourself ? [1]—Were there a chance of persuading you I would call on you to talk it over.

Ever faithfully & truly yours,
J. A. FROUDE.

[1] Woolner designed the tablet, which was erected in Ramsgate.

T. WOOLNER TO MRS. TENNYSON

27, *Rutland Street,*
Hampstead Road, N.W.,
December 9, 1860.

MY DEAR MRS. TENNYSON,

.   .   .   .   .   .

Palgrave has nearly finished making his selections from the Poets,[1] and has throughout shown the most extraordinary interest in his work; in fact he scarcely seems to think of anything else than the work he is engaged upon. He certainly has an astonishingly acute and quick mind in reading an enormous amount and extracting the best things.

.   .   .   .   .   .

Novelli came this morning to see Sedgwick and was so delighted that he said it was unquestionably the best bust I had done.

.   .   .   .   .   .

I forget if I told you in my last note how remarkably well Mrs. Carlyle is this year, and generally she is laid up an invalid the whole winter. I was there the other evening and they told me a good joke of Ruskin. She sat next him at dinner at Ld. Ashburton's, and Ruskin was full of glee at the thought of having been chosen to decide as one of the judges on the Melbourne Shakespeare statue affair, and she told him that he and Carlyle would never agree, but asked, who he would appoint, supposing he were sole judge, to make Shakespeare's statue; he said that undoubtedly he should appoint *Richmond,* the portrait draughtsman and that he considered Richmond could do it better than any other man in England. This is quite serious and not the least in joke on his part. I merely give it to you as an instance of the flimsiness and folly to which a man's mind may arrive, when he lives fattening upon the adulation of ladies and weak young men, chiefly landscape painters.

.   .   .   .   .   .

My love to the Poet and the boys who are I hope vigorous.

Ever truly yours,
THOMAS WOOLNER.

[1] *The Golden Treasury.*

T. Woolner to Mrs. Tennyson

27, *Rutland Street,*
Hampstead Road, N.W.,
February 13, 1861.

My dear Mrs. Tennyson,

.   .   .   .   .   .

I have placed the Sedgwick at Trin: Col: Lib: [1] in the vestibule beside the Tennyson and everyone is delighted with it I believe. It is in a most excellent light and looks better than in my own study. I met Kingsley at Macmillan's and he was exceedingly kind to me, and insisted on my going to his house as he wanted to introduce me to his wife.

.   .   .   .   .   .

My love to the Poet and the boys. I have not heard any news for a long while of them.

Ever truly yours,
Thomas Woolner.

James Anthony Froude to T. Woolner

Clifton Place,
Tuesday, July 2 [1861].

My dear Woolner,

The Ramsgate Tablet had better be sent down as soon as it is ready. . . . I will try to get to you again to see the Cawnpore sketch [2]—the figure appeared to me intensely expressive but expressive of unthinkable agony. The child appeared as if it had just dropped from the hands.

Did you mean that?

Ever faithfully & truly yours,
J. A. Froude.

[1] Library.
[2] A design for the Cawnpore Memorial. A sketch in plaster, which represents a mother with her arms stretched out in despair and agony, and the child dead at her feet.

T. WOOLNER TO MRS. TENNYSON

27, *Rutland Street,*
Hampstead Road, N.W.,
October 5, 1861.

MY DEAR MRS. TENNYSON,

You know that one of the dearest wishes of my soul was to get a house in town where I could also have my studios; this has at last been accomplished : I have paid the whole of the money £1200 and now you may regard me as a Nabob swelling with importance. Palgrave is now living in the house but I shall not be able to do so until the studios are finished building, which will be in about 2 months. I think it will be a most beautiful place, with five rooms for workshops besides a large kitchen below in which I can stow away things not in immediate use, and this advantage is equal to another shop.

This house in Welbeck St : Cavendish Sq : is the result of about 6 years' searching, and several months of such annoyance that I think a little more would have driven me into a deadly fever of illness; I have been obliged to consent with my eyes wide open to be plundered to the extent of £300; this is bad enough, but not so bad as all the worry added to it has been. Now I suppose I shall be always tormented with servants : really human life is by no means a joke.

I am getting on very well with my Fairbairn Group the marble has turned out most perfect and excites the admiration of all who see it, for the tone and texture are most choice. I have just completed a Tennyson bust in marble for Chas : Buxton M.P. for Maidstone : this also has turned out excellent marble. I have just finished a marble bust of W. Shaen, he is the happy man who possesses the only complete dwelling house built by poor Woodward whose death I suppose you have heard of. I have finished models of Arch : Hare and Prof : Henslow, and am now doing Mr. Fairbairn in marble : so you see that altho' nearly badgered to death I have not been idle; but all my hard work seems to bring me nothing but more worry and I see no chance for any ultimate reward.

You have no notion of what a changed fellow Palgrave is; he is perfectly cheerful, even hopeful, and his kindness and thoughtfulness in everything that he can do to serve any good turn are more than I can tell. His *Golden Treasury* has been such a marked success, in fact extraordinary, that it has cheered him wonderfully. I am in hopes he will fall in love and marry some girl, for there will be abundance of room in my big wilderness of a house for him.

. . . .

I saw that Sir J. Simeon had consoled himself again : Froude had done ditto. I see that Patmore in his new poem in Macs : Mag : [1] warmly advocates the practice of this kind of consolation.

. . . . . .

Most truly yours,
THOMAS WOOLNER.

T. WOOLNER TO COVENTRY PATMORE

27, *Rutland Street*,
Hampstead Road, N.W.,
October 6, 1861.

DEAR PATMORE,
I called on you to-night but found the gate barred, the bell rung but did not open it, so I had to go away without seeing you. I am bound to say that it was not far from 10 P.M. which is I suppose late for country.

I saw Macmillan who wants me to do an idea for Mrs. Patmore's book which I confess will not be easy. I told it him merely as a thing I should like to do if space on page permitted &c : but both he and Masson were tickled with the notion that they scorned to admit any other could be more appropriate as regards Art; the consequence is that I shall have as much study of composition for this trifling thing as I should have in designing a group for marble—but we must take the world as it goes. I finished the purchase of my house £1200 !—think of the vast and majestic sum ! I puff and blow with importance; I am a grampus snorting thro' the seas of difficulty. Palgrave is already established in the new house; the studies progress well. I have been rejoiced to hear good accounts of Mrs. Patmore. I hope they may continue good throughout the winter.

Ever yours,
THOS. WOOLNER.

[1] *Macmillan's.*

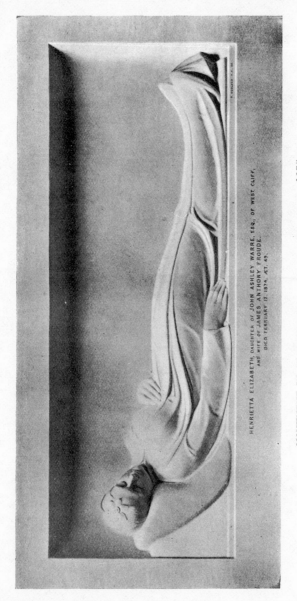

HENRIETTA ELIZABETH, DAUGHTER OF JOHN ASHLEY WARRE, ESQ, OF WEST CLIFF,
AND WIFE OF JAMES ANTHONY FROUDE.
DIED FEBRUARY 12, 1874, ÆT. 43.

MONUMENT IN ST. LAWRENCE CHURCH, RAMSGATE, 1875

To face page 207.

Mrs. Tennyson to T. Woolner

Farringford,
October 8, 1861.

My dear Mr. Woolner,

Tho' not yet free from the cruel bondage of the seventy or eighty letters we found on our return, to which number there have been daily additions, yet I cannot help saying we are so very glad that you have a house fitted to your purposes, and in a quarter likely to make you still better known than you are.

We rejoice too, of the pleasant news of Mr. Palgrave and *The Golden Treasury*.

.   .   .   .   .   .

We wished you could have seen the divine expression of St. Firmin (I think it was) in one of the screens of the Cathedral at Amiens. The sword is uplifted over the martyr to strike and certainly there is a heavenly glory in his face not to be forgotten. And a wonderful drama too in the surrounding group. They are statuettes, all coloured.

.   .   .   .   .   .

But, do you know, I will whisper this in your ear, that the beauty of Farringford is dearer to me than that of any of those places.

[No signature.]

CHAPTER XI

WOOLNER wrote out for his friend Tennyson the story of
" The Fisherman " he had told him years ago, and which
he had read himself on board ship returning from Australia :
a note in his diary on November 11, 1861, states : " Took
Tennyson the Fisherman story." This tale was made
by the Poet into the beautiful poem of " Enoch Arden,"
one of the most touching in the English language.

THE FISHERMAN'S STORY

A Fisherman, who belonged to one of the coast towns of
either Norfolk or Suffolk, had always regarded one little
girl, a playfellow and daughter of a neighbour, as belonging
peculiarly to himself. I am not aware that he had any
special reason for so doing beyond his own strong will and
inclination. However this may be, when he had reached
an age to seriously ponder such things, to work hard, save
money, buy a smack, make a home for this girl as his wife
—was to him the very meaning of his life. In due course
all these intentions were fulfilled and he was happy.

For some years he was as much so as a human being
can be ; he was healthy, wedded to one whom he had loved
from infancy ; and was moreover gladdened with three
children.

After he had been married wellnigh 7 years he began
to grow anxious and somewhat desponding, and all his
wife could do was insufficient to cheer him to serenity
again, but after this depression and care had gone on for
some months he at length formed his resolution, and
communicated it to her.

It was this—he found that the utmost exertion would
do no more than barely support his family with the

common necessaries of life, and therefore he would sell his little well beloved vessel, with the money stock a shop of general goods, and set his wife up in business, which he hoped would support her and children till his return, for he meant to enter as boatswain a ship bound for China, and if needed do this twice, and with the wages that he would save, enter into partnership of some larger vessel, which he reasonably calculated would bring him profits enough not only to maintain his family well, but would enable him to educate his children, which, as he had ever been of a gentle nature he considered as indispensable for them as food itself.

For the first time in her life his wife tried to thwart his project by opposition : she entreated him by all means in her power to give up the thought of leaving her, his children and his country; but all her entreaties failed, for he firmly believed that this was his only escape from seeing his children grow up in ignorance and his wife ultimately dwelling in squalor, so that at last she yielded; the smack was sold, the shop purchased and stored and he was soon successful in getting such an engagement as he desired. And then came the dreadful day of parting.

She mourned as if his absence were his grave; but after awhile set herself to do her best with the shop and children. She never did really well but managed to get some kind of a living for awhile, tho' not having been bred to barter she found at length her small stock decrease, without its bringing back the wherewithal to replenish it. Year after year slipped by and she heard no tidings of her husband, and found herself in deep poverty and her heart sick with hopelessness.

It appears that there was a rich miller living near the town, who also had been a playfellow both of the fisher-boy and of the girl, and like the fisherboy, her lover. He had never married but had in silence loved on without hope. He was of a high and noble nature, and when he became aware of the woman's distress endeavoured by many ways to benefit her; but for a long time he was unsuccessful. At last, when her state had become most

P

wretched, he went to see her and urged her by the love she bore her husband's children to let him at least send them to school, and when her husband returned, if she wished, she could return what little he might have spent on them. She could not resist this offer, as she thought in duty to her husband and children both.

But what chiefly determined her in accepting his assistance was the death of her youngest child, who she feared all too truly had fallen a sacrifice to those wants that money alone can provide. Thus matters stood for some time, till by degrees the two remaining children came to love him so much that he claimed the right to send them presents, books, flour etc., and many things for their support.

Things went on in this way for 8 years and a half, and no news whatever came of her husband, beyond the fact that the ship in which he was returning from China was wrecked in the Southern Seas, and all hands lost. At the end of this time the miller came to her and said, that she must now know that all chance of again seeing her husband return was beyond hope. That while there was the vaguest hope even he had avoided the topic, but now felt he might speak of it safely without fear of misconstruction. He said she had suffered bitterly and long like a true wife, and now he thought in justice to herself she might enter on a new life and if she would, he should consider it the highest reward that could come to him if she would consent to be his wife; he said she knew that he loved her children as if they were his own, and that he wished to be a father to them. She was overwhelmed with grief and gratitude, and could never thank him enough for his more than human kindness to her and hers, but implored him not to urge her as she felt her husband *must* be living.

He at that time urged no longer but continued, if possible, to double his kindness. At the end of another year he opened the question again, and this time she so far entertained his proposal as to promise, that if he would add to his generosity by waiting one year longer, she would then if no tidings came become his wife : he thought this an uncalled for delay but consented. At the stipulated time he again made his attack, and she promised to become his wife; but notwithstanding her promise she continued through various excuses to delay the marriage for 6 months longer, making in all 11 years since her husband departed.

The husband himself, after a successful and profitable voyage to China, was returning by way of the Southern Seas when the ship met with a tremendous storm which wrecked her, and he, with only two companions clinging to a mast, were drifted ashore upon an island in the S. Pacific Ocean, where one of them soon died, and 3 years after the other, so that for 12 years he lived alone upon the island like a wild man, he having lived there 15 years in all; at the end of which time a vessel, also returning from China having met a long course of baffling winds, and being distressed for water, made this island for the purpose of filling their casks, where they found this man, and brought him back to England.

He lost no time in reaching his native town where everything seemed familiar, yet bodefully strange.

He himself was so changed and worn that he had no fear of being known. He went to the house where he had left his wife and found it passed into other hands. At length he found courage to make enquiries and learned what had taken place.

It was on a damp, chill autumnal evening when he sought the miller's house just outside the town. He passed unnoticed through the garden, and saw a light in the parlour; he went close and looked in, where he saw the miller, stout, rosy and happy, with a two years old child on his knee, and his own daughter a beautiful girl of 18 leaning over his shoulder playing with the child; opposite the miller sat his wife, looking calm and happy, talking to his own son, a lad of 16 or so. He saw the service set for tea, the candles were not lit, for it was what in those parts they call " between the lights," and they were enjoying themselves by the light of the fire. The sight of this domestic peacefulness and delight contrasting with his own black desolation made the poor man groan, and in his deep agony turn from what was bitterer to feel than death.

He left the garden and fell down on the ground, praying God to give him strength not to mar the happiness he had seen by any disclosure of himself, but he could not destroy the happiness of a whole family and must be ever wretched himself. He determined then that while he lived they should never know his fate, and went down to the wharves and gained a poor livelihood by porterage, unloading ships and doing any little jobs he could get for about a year, when he was taken with an illness which soon brought him near the end. When he felt his time had nigh come, he disclosed his whole story to an old woman with whom he lodged, (and who had originally given him the history of his wife's widow-life and marriage with the miller), under solemn promise that she would not reveal it until his decease, when she was to go and tell his wife all she knew, and that he died praying of his God to bless her and her family.

Farringford,
December 5, 1861.

MY DEAR MR. WOOLNER,

. . . . .

What a pleasure it will be to them[1] and us to see you again. It seems so long since you were here. I am very glad your rooms will be so beautiful. People may say what they like, but beauty is a great help in life and not merely an unnecessary indulgence.

. . . . .

Yes, he has done a little of the " Fisherman." It is indeed an heroic story. Commend us heartily to the Carlyles and with love from Alfred and the boys,

Believe me,

Most truly yours,

EMILY TENNYSON.

Thank you for the beautiful shepherd.[2]

[1] Hallam and Lionel.
[2] The " Piping Boy," frontispiece to *The Golden Treasury.*

THE LISTENING BOY

Sketch for an imaginary memorial to a deaf child.

Extract from Mrs. TENNYSON's letter to T. WOOLNER.

December 12, 1861.

. . . .

I hope you will think what A. has done of the " Fisherman " as grand and beautiful as I do.

. . . . . .

What you say about work for sensitive minds—Idleness to them *is* far the hardest work, it saps the very roots of life.

. . . . . .

Ever most truly yours,
EMILY TENNYSON.

T. WOOLNER TO F. T. PALGRAVE

27, Rutland Street,
Hampstead Road, N.W.,
December 31, 1861.

DEAR PALGRAVE,

. . . The Palace progresses; the smells are dreadful, the confusion dire. O'Shea [1] is doing his work like a man, and the corbels are bursting forth into violets, roses, thistles, ivies, geraniums & other things lovelier than their names. He does not complain of the stone having been cut away, he says it does very well for his purpose : . . . so fast is his progress that unless your brother come early O'Shea will have done and fled, for such rapidity of workmanship I never saw, he does 3 corbels a day ! I thought he would take a day each. . . .

Thine
T. WOOLNER.

MRS. TENNYSON TO T. WOOLNER

Farringford,
February 11, 1862.

Thank you, my dear Mr. Woolner.

. . . .

The " Fisherman " [2] is to have a previous training I think in his boyhood. A. has been talking to Captain Hamond about it. There would not be sufficient bettering of his condition in a mere sailor's pay. This is why the

---

[1] O'Shea, a very accomplished stonemason, who carved the corbels in the studios at 29 Welbeck Street.
[2] " Enoch Arden."

boatswain is important. I hope you were not vexed by trouble thrown away as much as I was vexed that you should have thrown it away. Tho' no good and kind act is ever really thrown away, is it ?

Alfred varies but on the whole is better. He and the boys send love.

Believe me,

Ever most truly yours,

EMILY TENNYSON.

CHAPTER XII

T. WOOLNER TO MRS. TENNYSON

29, *Welbeck Street, W.,*
February 19, 1862.

MY DEAR MRS. TENNYSON,

. . . I saw and spent nearly two hours with Browning on Sunday, and found him as interesting as ever. He is cut to the quick at his wife's death and sometimes, when anything verges near the subject his voice stops altogether, and his manner pierces one's soul with grief; yet notwithstanding the awe which such overwhelming sorrow commands, I could not help feeling a kind of deep and wild delight, that I really saw a man who could feel the death of a wife, as one's old-fashioned notions thought a wife's death ought to be felt. It was to me a gust of fresh wholesome air; for truly the way the world lives with regard to the greatest and highest things is well nigh enough to make belief in them sicken and die altogether; and it needs the occasional sight of how a true woman or a great man feels and lives for a poor or ordinary individual to be able to sustain anything of a large heroic faith. I forget if I told you that I should have to do a figure of P. Consort for the N. Mus : Oxford, to be presented to the City. Unfortunately it is not marble and only stone, but I must make the best I can of it. . . .

Ever yours truly,
THOS : WOOLNER.

MRS. TENNYSON TO T. WOOLNER

Farringford,
March 20, 1862.

MY DEAR MR. WOOLNER,

. . . . .

I feel very anxious to see your group [1] not so much for the sake of the delight I feel sure I shall have in it, but to reassure myself that it has a beauty which must speak to

[1] " Constance and Arthur," deaf and dumb.

215

every one. I want that you should do beautiful things, for I think these have the language common to all, and I have now grown very impatient for popularity for you. Do not scorn me or it. The human heart reveals many things even without the illuminating brain.

The Duke of Argyll has promised to speak to the Queen himself and this seems the best thing that could be done, for he is to speak Alfred's impressions of your power and standing, and his own impression of these impressions is, that there never was such a partisan as he laughingly calls him.

.   .   .   .   .   .

Believe me, with Alfred's love and the boys',
Most truly yours,
EMILY TENNYSON.

There is the following entry in Woolner's diary : April 24, 1862. " Robert Browning called to leave stanza for group." Browning was so struck by the pathos of the marble group of Thomas Fairbairn's children, Constance and Arthur, exhibited in the great International Exhibition, he wrote the following lines printed by kind permission of Mr. John Murray. The manuscript of these lines by Robert Browning, Woolner sent to Mr. Fairbairn who had given him the commission.

DEAF AND DUMB CHILDREN

Only the prism's obstruction shows aright
The secret of a sunbeam, breaks its light
Into a jewelled bow from blankest white;
   So may a glory from defect arise:
Only by Deafness may the vexed Love wreak
Its insuppressive sense on brow and cheek,
Only by Dumbness adequately speak
   As favoured mouth could never, through the eyes.

MRS. CARLYLE TO T. WOOLNER

5, Cheyne Row,
Chelsea,
Wednesday [March 27, 1862].

MY DEAR MR. WOOLNER,
Can you come to tea on Friday (the day after to-morrow) at eight o'clock. It would be a charity towards my Husband ! A pretty little new-married girl is to bring her Husband to make acquaintance with Mr. C. that

evening; and I don't, for my part, see the least in the world how the said Mr. C. is to get thro' it, without your or some as efficient help!

He has been doing what he could about the Herbert Statue; but whether the least good will come of his speaking God, or the Devil, knows!

Faithfully yours,
JANE W. CARLYLE.

PROFESSOR SEDGWICK TO T. WOOLNER

Langcliff, near Settle,
May 19, 1862.

MY DEAR FRIEND.

The very serious illness of my Niece brought me down to this place on Saturday, the 3rd of this month. At the end of the week following she seemed so convalescent that I went to spend a few days at Dent—my native village—where my Nephew and his family now live in the old Parsonage. To my great grief I heard that she had suffered a relapse; and I consequently returned thither at the end of last week. To my great joy I learnt at the Settle Station . . . my Niece was much better . . . These facts cannot be of any interest to you, and I only state them as my apology for not having answered your two letters . . . this letter will not leave Settle till the evening. You will see from these dates, that it was *literally impossible* for me to communicate with any member of the Macaulay Committee. Had I been present I should have mentioned your name as a sculptor of genius who would devote himself with all his energies to the work of art, if appointed to it by the Committee . . . I may at the same time, say with truth, that I shall on personal grounds rejoice should they have selected you as their Sculptor. . . .

I remain, dear Woolner,
Very faithfully yours,
A. SEDGWICK.

THOMAS WOOLNER, ESQ.,
29, *Welbeck Street.*

PROFESSOR SEDGWICK TO T. WOOLNER

Langcliff, near Settle,
May 24, 1862.

MY DEAR WOOLNER,

All the family news I can send is good . . . My Niece is *slowly* recovering; but steadily: & I now feel very confident hopes that she will next week be able to go with me to a most comfortable Hotel which overlooks Morecambe Bay—one of the finest—nay, the *very finest*, of the Bays in the north of England. . . . The weather is not so warm & lovely as it was for the first three weeks of this month : but we are so near the rock in the fields all around us, that the land soon drinks up the rain, & our soil requires refreshing with frequent showers. All the hills around us, show us grey precipices of Carboniferous limestone—the most picturesque limestone rock in England —*e. g.* the scenery of Cheddar; Clifton; Chepstow & Tintern; the High Peak of Derbyshire; Ingleborough; Easdale etc. etc. etc. If you have not seen all these places, go and see them, that you may learn how sweetly, tho' a little roughly, dame Nature knew how, in olden times to sculpture stone work in this Island of ours . . . I yesterday drove up the valley of the Upper Ribble to Horton, where I had spent some happy days when I was a schoolboy. . . . I saw the tombstones of some whom I had personally known, & of them I had known less familiarly; but they had left no living representatives in the wild & retired district. Not a soul was living in the neighbourhood of whom I had any knowledge—such blanks are common with me now. Yet I have a constant longing to gaze at spots which I have gazed at 60 or 70 years since.

"Past and to come seem *best,* things present *worst.*" I think these words are in Shakespeare. . . . My memory paints brightly the days of my early life, & I well may call them *best;* & I am now working my way thro' the 8th decade of " *labour* and *sorrow* " which *I cannot truly* call " the *best.*" . . . I am writing to congratulate you on the unanimous decision of the Macaulay Committee. I heartily rejoice at it. . . . May God speed you well in all the future works of your life ! May your past life, however long continued, be *ever bright* in *memory;* and may your future ever be full of good *hope.* . . .

Ever truly yours,

A. SEDGWICK.

From Woolner's Diary, July 5, 1862—

" Finished writing out Suffolk story, ' The Sermon,' [1] for A. T."

---

[1] In February, 1864, an entry in Woolner's Diary states : "A. Tennyson called and dined—went with him to Spedding's rooms where he read me his new Poem of ' The Sermon ' so called at present."

[*Photograph by Kent and Lacey.*

BLUECOAT BOY GROUP
From plaster model.

[*To face page* 219.

It will be seen " The Sermon " was the title Woolner
gave the tale. Tennyson taking the main points for his
lovely poem named it " Aylmer's Field." The receipt
of the MS. was acknowledged by Mrs. Tennyson from
Farringford a few days later in a letter dated July 10.

" THE SERMON.

" There never was anything like it; that Sermon will
never be forgotten, it was the death of both of them."
They were some such words that took my attention late
one summer evening, when my grandfather and an old
rustic were chatting together of the county families that
were flourishing or had passed away. I [1] was a very young
child, but as my memory for tales that interested me has
always been vivid, I think all the points will be accurate. I
cannot remember a single name and doubt if I ever took
notice of any at the time.

The Sermon was preached at the burial of the only child
of a wealthy Suffolk Baronet, the sole representative of
what had been a powerful family. His daughter was
regarded as the beauty of the county, and adored by all
the villagers and tenantry on her father's lands. It was
her constant practice to go among them bestowing kind-
nesses among the women and children, and she was often
accompanied by a young man, who was brother of the
Rector of the parish where she dwelt.

This young man's family had always been on the most
familiar terms with the Baronet's, and tho' many years
her elder he had been her constant playmate when they
were children, and as they grew their intercourse ripened
into devoted love. The youth spent most of his time at
the Hall, and no bar was put upon their intimacy, until the
parents of the lady began to think of marrying her, and
neighbours to hint that it was dangerous to allow their
daughter to spend so much time with him, as her feelings
might become entangled, etc. The parents seem not to
have had eyes of lynxes, but suspicion once roused to the
true state of the case, their observation soon left no doubt

[1] Thomas Woolner.

in their minds as to the mutual love, nor did their resolution
halt as to means of stopping it; for they at once forbad the
youth their house and reproached him cruelly for having
abused the family confidence, taken advantage of their
generous hospitality to steal the affections of their only
daughter, the only child they had to uphold the grandeur
of their position : it was wicked, mean and disgraceful
in one of no fortune ever to have thought of such a thing.
There was nothing left for him under the circumstances
but to submit for the present. He received all possible
sympathy from his brother the Rector, who certainly was
astonished at the turn things took, for tho' perhaps he
may not have put it into actual language ever in his own
mind, yet considering the immemorial intimacy of the
two families, the apparent affection the parents bore the
young man, and the encouragement they always gave to
his visits, he could not help dimly thinking that they meant
to give their daughter to him. For awhile the youth was
overwhelmed with this disaster; but partly his brother's
wise exhortations and in part from his own energy of
character he at length aroused himself to action and
determined on his course.

He had always been educated with a view to the Bar and
went thro' the preliminary studies, but had delayed pur-
suing his course from time to time, held in thrall by the
sweet society of the girl he loved. But he now resolved to
go straight to London, work incessantly at his law, make a
name and fortune and return a great man and demand his
beloved in marriage, and he fully believed that there was
nothing could prevent the fulfilment of all this.

As the parents had declared open war and he knew the
girl loved him perfectly, he felt no hesitation in taking
his own course, and contrived to obtain a short dangerous
meeting with her one night, when she promised that
nothing in life should induce her to act unfaithfully towards
him, and he promised that let happen what would she
might rely on him : and they arranged to write to each
other occasionally to relate how things stood. The parents
were glad when he had gone, but as their daughter was

reserved and unlike what she had always been to them hitherto, they saw they had lost her confidence, and suspecting she might keep up some correspondence with her lover, they used every means until they discovered the fact, probably through the Postmaster of the place, and then resolutely destroyed every letter which passed between the pair.

At first the young lady continued her angel visits— angel in goodness not in rarity—to the cottages where her pensive sweetness and deeper expressed sympathies endeared her still more to their primitive and reverential inmates : but gradually her sadness grew heavier and her visits more seldom, and often attacks of illness would suspend them altogether. Gossip was pretty active among the villagers during all this time and as may be supposed, so far as they dared, the character of the Baronet and his wife were roughly handled for their flint-hearted cruelty in killing the sweet lady whom they almost worshipped : the youth too was a huge favourite with them all; for his frank, joyous, vigorous nature won every heart to admiration and they said he was made for her.

The course of things had gone on in this way for nearly a year and a half; the parents had grown more stern and cruel as they saw their daughter estranged from them more and more and she rejected at once and resolutely, every suitor they had trotted out for her benefit, and had even forbidden her charitable visits to the tenantry : in fact everything which they knew she took interest in was denied her. She was never allowed to see the Rector save during service at church, and she could get no tidings the most remote from the youth, and tho' she knew his faithfulness too well to doubt, yet this poor troubled unfed belief was insufficient to satisfy her soul and the natural consequence followed. She lost her health, her sleep, and became so frail and weak that probably some accidental illness attacking a form so well prepared to receive it, made a short story of her sorrows, and she died with a suddenness that struck her parents with absolute horror.

The youth had been only too faithful to his resolution to

achieve success. He had worked with an energy that astounded even the most energetic workers at the Law: all day and half thro' the night despite the serious remonstrances of friends, he ground and toiled. Already high authorities spoke of him as one destined for the highest honours, and he himself almost began to see something like light breaking thro' the difficult ways. He had not much time for sadness, for altho' his brother kept him informed in a way softened by his own kindliness of the young lady so far as he knew, he regarded his troubles as certain to come to end, and every account did more to stimulate his already overtasked brain to fresh exertions than make him dwell on the contemplation of her sufferings. But of late, as his brother could give him no detailed information of his love, some dreadful sensation kept starting up and taking possession of his mind, and he ever strove by more fiercely determined labour, as his only salvation to keep this horrible feeling at bay; and during these mortal struggles of his soul he received a letter from his brother announcing the girl's sudden death.

This was almost too much for any human being to bear. The whole structure of his life that he had been piling up with such energetic and loving endeavour crushed down with its whole weight upon him, and his reason snapt like the overdrawn cord of a bow. One cannot reason on what a man does who is mad. In those days when men dared not go from the Bank to Paddington except in companies of twenty or more every gentleman kept arms; and he during the paroxysm of despair on the receipt of these evil tidings, seized a weapon and slew himself, and fell, a bloody protestation against insatiable vanity and inexorable fate.

With this calamity raw upon his soul it was the Rector's duty to preach the funeral sermon for the lost Beauty.. He was a man who seemed very much the opposite of this brother, not joyous, bright and rapid but deliberate earnest and profound, altho' perfectly frank and straightforward, he always gave the notion of holding the most of his force in reserve; in fact altho' as simple as a child a man in no way to be trifled with. He had always been immeasurably fond of the lady, and had it been possible her love for his beloved young brother would have increased his love; he had watched their career with something of saddened tho' peculiarly vivid interest which was ever his wont to take in all lovely things : and he had endeavoured to come to some kind of understanding with the parents vainly, but tho' he from his character and position could not be treated with the flagrant scorn his brother suffered, still their haughty conduct made it clear to him that in time only was there any hope. From the wonderful beauty of the girl, her wealth and historic name, the number of rejected suitors, her sufferings and sudden death, her romantic love, the interest attached to the young man's family, his high abilities and accomplishments and terrible end, the Rector's own lofty nature and well known passionate eloquence all combined to create an extraordinary interest and sensation of increasing awe, as the day came on which the sermon had to be preached. People came from far and near, both great and small, till the church was overcrowded with a pained multitude. But whatever they may have expected the result of the sermon went beyond their utmost imagining.

From sepulchral silence the Rector spoke tenderly and long, dwelt upon the sweetness and lowliness of Christ's nature and His infinite love for all mankind, how born lowly He lived lowly, and used His whole life striving to knit men together in brotherly love; and lastly and by the agonies of death bequeathing to mankind the glory of His immortal love, yielded His precious life to seal and witness His sincerity. He had taught men the worthlessness of worldly riches compared to those spiritual treasures which the very poorest might store up in his soul; and that even a King arrayed in all his glory could not equal a wild lily of the field, yet with sorrow he saw how little heed was given to those truths, for which their Saviour had laboured and died in ignominy amid the taunts and sneers of a Jewish multitude, like a felon nailed to a cross. He saw that riches were sought for and prized as greedily as they had ever been; that pride in empty honours seemed to strengthen with the ages of the world.

He said they had all congregated to solemnise the burial of a fair young sister in whom, if ever to any mortal creature, the gentle Spirit of Christ had entered. One so fair and good that she carried the brightness of sunshine with her as she moved, and left cheerfulness, happy memories and gratitude wherever she had been.

Angel-faced and angel-hearted she seemed lent to us by her Maker as testimony of His bountiful goodness, as an inspiration and a sign of what may be attained by worship and devoted adherence to His will on this earth. Then was it possible any wretch could be found in this great land, that for more than a thousand years had been taught by lifelong service of zealous priests of His Word and the blood quenched in flame of holy martyrs; was it possible any being could be found, who could wilfully injure one so innocently sweet and sacred in her whole life; was there any savage or abandoned outcast even who could regard one so gifted with other feelings than joy and wonder?

With sickened heart and humiliation he was bound to say that such had been found! but where? from the purlieus of vice and degradation? No, not there! And if he could lift his voice into a high loud cry of all the nations of the earth, and proclaim where such had been found, as with the trump of doom, it would awaken a universal shock of incredulity as something too monstrous, too far from nature to be believed, but so it is, the breakers of this beautiful vessel were her own parents! They it was who denied her access to her little cottage flocks, that she fed with happiness of spiritual food. They who strove to make her false to her love and false to her God in Heaven: and seeing her droop and pine and sicken day by day, could only harden more their hard hearts and pile upon her gentle spirit the load of oppression yet more heavily, till the burden was too sore to be borne, and she the Darling of all hearts could find peace nowhere but in the stillness of death. Of what value now can be all their pride of ancestry

and boundless wealth, and what can save them from the
hissing scorn of their fellow mortals, and the burning stings
of their own conscience—parents solitary, childless and
unloved ! His mind borne on a storm of passion, denounced
pride and avarice and hardheartedness and all those dreadful
worldly vices that had brought about this fearful calamity,
till there were sobbings and moanings and deep groans
throughout the congregation and great agitation. The
mother uttered a sharp cry and fell into a fit, causing a wild
commotion throughout the church, while the Baronet sat
in a paralysis of stupor seemingly unmindful of everything,
and they had to be taken home in their coach, where the
mother after a few days' acute suffering died. The Baronet
lived a year or two longer an utterly changed man, shut
up from visitors and incapable of managing his affairs in
any way, in fact almost an imbecile till he died.

The estate passed into the hands of one of another
family, who demolished the house and let all the land out
in farms under the management of an agent; so that the
villages changed their character entirely and the beautiful
young mistress the tenantry had all so loved, was seen
through memory as the spirit of a golden time that departed with her; and for long years after the Rector was
thought of as the avenging angel to wreak judgment upon
those hardhearted ones who caused all the desolation;
and with this belief the old men might well say " there
never was anything like it : that sermon will never be
forgotten : it was the death of them both."

Mrs. Tennyson to T. Woolner

Farringford,
July 10, 1862.

My dear Mr. Woolner,

The story [1] is very grand and very finely told we
think. The arrangement and form are so good. Best
thanks for it. Yes, Mrs. George Patmore wrote to me
simply announcing the death. It is a terrible thing for
him indeed.

[1] " Aylmer's Field."

Q

Do you know that your name was almost the last word she spoke?

. . . . . .

I felt sure you would like Dr. Temple. There is a child-like transparency about him I think but I do not know him well.

. . . . .

I feel that I have not half enough thanked you for having taken so much trouble about the story, nor expressed what I think of its grand capabilities. I hope he will do it.

[Signature missing.]

MRS. CARLYLE TO T. WOOLNER

Holme Hill,
Thornhill,
DUMFRIES ! ! !
August 13 [1862].

MY DEAR MR. WOOLNER,
　　A thousand thanks for having done for me so much more than you led me to hope ! I shall be glad and thankful to possess even a plain photograph of Mrs. Twisleton; for either money or love or for the credit of Mr. Dickinson's name ! The long letter amounts to this, it seems to me, " if we had known that the obscure looking Female who stalked quite promiscuously into our shop had borne the not obscure title of Mrs. Thomas Carlyle, we would have treated her with less abruptness and hauteur ! "—But on any terms as I have said, I shall gratefully receive the photograph which can be got nowhere else !
　　Go and see my unfortunate Husband who, like " the last rose of summer is left blooming alone " at Cheyne Row ! And go often, if you please, till I come back ! I cannot expand myself on paper, because of the pen ! which is a steel one, and it is like writing with the point of a scewer ![1] Tell me if anything happens to you while I am here—and believe me always,

　　　　　　　　　　Affectionately yours,
　　　　　　　　　　JANE W. CARLYLE.

In after years the Sculptor's wife had a very similar experience. One evening when dining out, she was taken in to dinner by a somebody who had not caught her name,

---

[1] Skewer.

and who thought a good deal of himself, and took little trouble to entertain his neighbour. After dinner, in the drawing-room he came up to her and said, " Mrs. Woolner, if I had known who you were I should have paid you more attention ! "

THE REV. H. MONTAGU BUTLER TO T. WOOLNER

Harrow, October 7, 1862.

DEAR MR. WOOLNER,

Many pressing duties during the last ten days—a time here of much anxiety—have combined to make me *appear* ungrateful for your kindness. . . . The three Photographs, in that singularly graceful and appropriate frame, will be among my favourite art treasures. The frame will hang in an honoured place in my study, and will have as a near neighbour a lithograph of Hare's much loved Library which Mrs. Hare most kindly gave me some months ago. . . Judging from the Photographs I feel most thankful that I was led to ask you to undertake the very difficult task of making the Bust of a man you had never seen. I only saw him once, but the likeness seems to me most excellent, giving a very earnest & faithful record of a very earnest & high-minded man. I shall be much surprised if Hare's dearest friends and persons who can judge wisely of a work of art, are not pretty unanimous in gratitude to you.

You have enabled me to gratify far more fully than I could have hoped for a longing desire to show my affectionate reverence for Trinity, while paying respect to the memory of an illustrious Trinity man. This is indeed a great service.

And now I have to confess a barefaced act of robbery. I positively refuse to restore the *fourth* of the four Photographs that you first sent me. The other three shall return forthwith. But the fourth, which gives a peculiar profile of Hare such as I fancy I remember, I must & will keep.

Will you be kind enough to let me know what I owe you ? . . . .

Believe me to be

Very truly yours,

H. MONTAGU BUTLER.

T. WOOLNER TO F. T. PALGRAVE

Burton Park, Petworth,
October 12, 1862.

MY DEAR PALGRAVE,

I have been day after day intending to write to you.
. . . Take my heartiest thanks for your most generous
letter. I gratefully accept your permission to say no
more about the £500 till the time comes when I can repay
you.

. . . You are assuredly the most generous fellow I have
ever known and had it not been for you I should never have
made the start which I think I now have made. I could
not help showing your letter to Fairbairn who has the most
affectionate interest in everything relating to you and he
said on returning it " This is a most noble fellow." Mrs.
Fairbairn says that she takes more interest in seeing Hunt,
you and me well married than in any other friends of hers.
I always told you that the Fairbairns liked you very much
but I never knew myself till now how vivid their affection
was towards you. Your mention of the Ladye [1] gives
me a very agreeable notion of her character, and I feel
quite sure that you have chosen wisely. . . . I feel a great
desire to make her acquaintance . . . . I leave here to-
morrow for Sir John Simeon's, I. of Wight—then if I can
shall spend a few days with the Tennysons *en route* home.
My holiday has done me a world of good. . . . I spent the
best part of two days with the mighty Thomas to help get
those phos. of him and am glad they have turned out so
well. . . .

Affectionately thine,
THOS. WOOLNER.

The following letter is in answer to an invitation from
Woolner asking Carlyle to come and spend the evening with
him at Welbeck Street to meet Captain Sherard Osborn,
Mr. Lay and Mr. Gladstone—the two former being well
versed in matters concerning China.

[1] F. T. Palgrave's *fiancée*, Miss Cecil Milnes-Gaskell.

LORD LAWRENCE, CALCUTTA, 1875

[*To face page* 229.

T. Carlyle to Thomas Woolner

Chelsea,
November 30, 1862.

Dear Woolner,

If I could but get myself under way, on such a voyage at night! But alas, I fear that will be impossible on Tuesday.

Pirates are fair game on all waters, on the part of all men. But does Captⁿ Osborn know for certain that the *Taepings* [1] require to be shot? One Mr. Meadows, a very ingenious man, who had been 12 years in China, and is gone back, had, when I saw him, the idea that the Taepings were intrinsically in the *right ;* and that it was the unworthy Phantasm of an " Emperor " and his yellow Cousins who got hopelessly out of square!

Yours always truly,
T. Carlyle.

T. Woolner to Mrs. Tennyson

29, Welbeck Street, W.,
December 2, 1862.

My dear Mrs. Tennyson,

. . . . .

I had a glorious night this day week with Sherard Osborn and Mr. Lay his chief: I learned more of Chinese nature and the future politics of their government than I ever knew before. Both of them are coming here this evening and Mr. Gladstone is coming too to discuss matters Chinese; so that I expect it will be highly entertaining. S. Osborn said he enjoyed the evening he spent here with the Bard hugely, and told me shyly that he almost worshipped Tennyson. Froude also told me that he did not know how to express his gratitude to me for having given him the chance of meeting the Bard again.

. . . . .

I should like you to see a wonderful Eagle by Haehnel that we have here.

My love to the boys.

Most truly yours,
Thos : Woolner.

[1] Note by Mr. Alexander Carlyle. " A political party in China. See Irving's *Annals of our Time*, p. 320.—A. C."

Mrs. Tennyson to T. Woolner

Farringford,
December 5, 1862.

My dear Mr. Woolner,

.   .   .   .   .   .

I rejoice to hear that you are so busy. You must not spend spare minutes in writing when reading is so much better for you. Yes, A. is going on with the poem.[1] He takes walks often now that the tourists are gone. I think the beginning of the poem very fine, my chief objection to it is that it must necessarily be so indignant in its tone.

.   .   .   .   .   .

With Alfred's love I am,
Most truly yours,
Emily Tennyson.

[1863] Woolner went in the beginning of the year to Wallington, Newcastle and York, and met amongst others his old friend W. B. Scott, with whom he went long walks on the moors. Soon after his return to London he received the following letter offering him the commission to do the Statue of John Robert Godley.

Sir John Simeon to T. Woolner

Swainston,
February 3 [1863.]

My dear Woolner,

The Colony of Canterbury New Zealand are desirous of putting up a Bronze-statue to their Founder John Godley, who was one of my oldest and dearest friends. The carrying out of this intention has been entrusted to a Committee in England consisting of Lord R^d Cavendish, C. Wynne, Godley's brother-in-law, Ld Lyttleton & myself with power to add to our numbers. The other members of the Committee have thought fit to place the matter in my hands, & I have accepted the responsibility of undertaking its main conduct. It will give me the greatest pleasure if you will undertake the work. I wish you had known Godley well. You may have met him with me. He was one of the truest and noblest of men, with qualities of head and heart combined that I have never seen equalled. Devotion to duty & unbending determination to do the

---

[1] " Aylmer's Field."

work he had to perform were his principal characteristics. We have Photographs & a miniature of him, not much you will say, but his portrait is very indelibly engraved on the hearts of many attached friends who knew & loved him, & who will all put their memories at y^r service. The Statue is meant to be in bronze & the Sum voted is £1500. Not enough I believe, but there is not practically any limit. . . . Write soon & say you accept the task assigned.

Yrs most truly,
JOHN SIMEON.

Woolner was delighted to undertake the work; on his acceptance he received the following letter.

Swainston,
February 6, 1863.

MY DEAR WOOLNER,
     Many thanks for y^r note—I am delighted that you are able to undertake the Statue. I forgot to say that it was meant to be in Bronze, but I take if for granted that that material is as much in y^r department as marble. Will you give me one line on this point by return of post ? . . .

Y^{rs} in haste very truly,
JOHN SIMEON.

On March 4, he received the official confirmation of the commission to execute a colossal statue of Godley in bronze.

CHAPTER XIII

About this time Woolner saw a great deal of the Carlyles. On April 28 [1] he describes a visit of special interest : " Mrs. Carlyle called upon me one afternoon. She wanted me to take tea at her house and go afterwards with her husband to the Hanover Sq. Rooms to hear Chas. Dickens read, as she said that Dickens had sent Carlyle 2 tickets with an intimation that it would do him good to hear a little reading. She was not strong enough to go with him, and he had made it a condition that she must persuade me to go with him or he would not go himself. I went to Chelsea, had tea, and we took a cab to Hanover Sq. We found the room crowded, and soon after we were seated C. Dickens appeared I need scarcely say amidst loud welcomes. He was the best reader I ever heard, and the changes of voice and manner suitable to the various characters were so easy and natural they appeared before the audience like veritable living beings. But I must say with regret that the performance was a terrible strain upon the reader's vital energies, as it was clear that his whole mind was concentrated upon the long continuous effort. The Reading was divided into two parts of an hour each, with an interval for rest of 10 minutes. When the 1st part was over Dickens came and took Carlyle away to an inner room, and in a minute or two after Carlyle came to fetch me ' to have some brandy and water ' but I said I wanted no brandy & water; he insisted that I must have some, and I went accordingly. Within the room the brandy soon appeared and each poured out a portion for himself and Carlyle took his glass and nodding to Dickens said : ' Charley, you carry a whole company of actors under your

[1] 1863.

232

own hat.' The second part of the Reading was equally
well done, and Carlyle had nothing but praises to bestow
upon it, but I confess to being filled with doleful forebodings
as to the effect of these readings upon the writer's health, as
I thought he must be using up his splendid faculties too
rapidly."—T. WOOLNER.

As early as 1861 Woolner had been given the commission
to design figures and reliefs for the New Assize Courts in
Manchester, and from 1863 to 1867 he was at work on these.[1]
The circular alto-relief of the Judgment of Solomon had
on either side of it a figure of the good woman and the
drunken woman; and in writing about them in 1863, Mr.
Alfred Waterhouse, the architect of the Assize Courts, says :
" The Solomon Women have come to hand. We are all
delighted with your virtuous woman, and disgusted as we
ought to be with the awful example."

T. WOOLNER TO COVENTRY PATMORE

29, Welbeck Street, W.,
February 23, 1863.

MY DEAR PATMORE,
          I read your letter to Froude and thought it most
satisfactory as a statement of your notion of the critics'
cunning and of Froude's own courtesy. I sent it on to
him. . . . You think far too highly of any trifling service
that I wish to render you, and are much too modest in
thinking you have no claims. To have lived a simple
dignified life, thoroughly eschewing the gaudy vulgarities
that delight so many : at great sacrifices to have steadily
thro' sharp difficulties pursued one object that you truly
believed would benefit your fellow creatures, and to have
done this with infinite temptation for luring you into
an easier path resisted, seems to me to constitute very
strong claims upon any one who has been able to recognize
the worth of such a life as yours—I can only hope that the
unknown enemies who fill the Press may have their minds
changed and not bespatter your idea so thickly with mud
that the public cannot see what it is and how it is fashioned.
I do not marvel at the thought which haunts your life;

---

[1] There were eight figures of England's greatest lawgivers, a large statue
of Moses with the Tables of the Law, and two bas-reliefs.

tho' the same vivid happiness that you have known you can hardly know again, the present natural gloom will give way to something far different and better. I have seen after some almost painfully magnificent sunset a passage of darkness followed by light transcendently tender : and it has seemed that the pathetic beauty I saw there hanging over the mysterious earth came on me with even a dearer sympathy, gave my spirit a sense of deeper rest, and more spoke to me hints of immortality, than when I had gazed upon its fullest glory : and altho' my spirit may have been overcast with mournfulness, yet the pathos held within itself something more sacred and sweeter than joy. So that in my vision I see you for years to come, amid a rich harvest from your labours, and beholding your children flourishing like young vines around (I write in tropes and images but you will know my meaning). So you must cheer up and not, or try not to think too much of what drags with such strong temptation. I most deeply and warmly sympathize with all your trials and grief, and trust that time will deal gently by you.

Ever truly yours,
THOS : WOOLNER.

COVENTRY PATMORE TO T. WOOLNER

May 26 [1863 ?].

MY DEAR WOOLNER,

When you have finished reading vol. 2 of the " Angel " I should be much pleased if you would write me a line or two as to its general effect upon you.

I value your opinion very much, and if there is anything that strikes you either as wanting or superfluous I should be glad to have the opportunity of considering of it, before coming out with the final one-vol. edition.

Ever truly yours,
COVENTRY PATMORE.

WILLIAM ALLINGHAM TO T. WOOLNER

Lymington,
May 29 [1863].

MY DEAR WOOLNER,

How are you getting on these fine days ? I find this place charming, walked on Wednesday to Beaulieu, 7 or 8 miles, where in rich wooded vale stand the remnants of King John's Abbey, not ruins because part is the present Church, & in the Abbot's House dwells now and again the D. of Buccleuch, lord of the manor, who shuts up roads here, though he couldn't stop the Thames Embankment.

The jolliest thing is a farm house called Abbey Walls, with the monks' huge barn (225 feet long) still in use as a barn, though not in its full old size. The nightingales were singing everywhere. When will you come down & walk or boat to Beaulieu or elsewhere? I am in lodgings (Mrs. Rice's) on the shore road, facing the Isle of W. but have taken a cottage & hope to be in it in a week or two. Have been twice on the Island, but seen nothing of the Tennysons. Have you any news of them lately? T. will likely be going somewhere on a summer tour shortly? I should like very much to see him but hesitate to call.

Yours always,
W. ALLINGHAM.

MRS. COMBE TO T. WOOLNER

University Press, Oxford,
August 17 [1863].

DEAR MR. WOOLNER,
    I rejoice the cast has come out so well and has elicited such favorable testimony from your friends. Of this however I am certain—that none of them can admire it as much as I do. No, not even Hunt. . . . We are to quit Oxford mid-day Wednesday for Dover, whence by way of Calais we shall proceed to Brussels. . . .

    19*th*.—Since writing the above, dear Mr. Woolner, St. John Baptist has arrived and is safe in the Sisters' keeping. The opening scene was exciting and the pleasure of the good Sisters when the beautiful embodiment of their patron Saint was revealed to them was quite touching. Miss Nelson was happily returned and her sweet mild eyes beamed with delight. Sister Jane and I quitted at last disturbed by a host of sins of omission. The little I have read of your poem has highly impressed me. . . .

    With our most kind regards,
Believe me ever,
Dear Mr. Woolner,
Yours very sincerely,
M. COMBE.

THOMAS COMBE TO T. WOOLNER

August 18, 1863.

MY DEAR WOOLNER,

.   .   .   .   .   .

Your " beautiful Lady " shall be corrected as you desire & another proof sent to you.   Then it will be plain sailing, and we shall soon get thro' it.   Will you sell the copyright ?

I am delighted to hear that you are to bust Gladstone— he has a good head and will do you credit.   Y^r Sun is *coming out* & you may prepare for greater things. . . . The next proofs I send to Hawarden. . . .

Thanks for kind wishes.   St. John is come.

Yours very truly,

TH. COMBE.

Woolner had been given a commission to do the bust of the Rt. Hon. W. E. Gladstone, and in August Mr. Gladstone wrote to suggest various times for the sittings.

RT. HON. W. E. GLADSTONE TO T. WOOLNER

Hawarden, Chester,
August 14, 1863.

DEAR MR. WOOLNER,

Mr. Palgrave has conveyed to me your kind offer. I have written to him all my doubts & scruples & in conscience I wish I could dissuade you.   But all human affairs mainly turn upon woman, and my wife insists upon my leaving you to your fate.   I have therefore only to say that the choice lies between (1) Your coming here between this time & the 30th, & I am to say my Mother-in-law, and standing Host, would be most happy to see you.   (2) Your doing the like considerably later in the year. (3) My sitting to you in Welbeck Street on the occasion of my visits to town which would begin probably to be pretty steady from about the middle of October.   Pray choose what may suit you.   If you came here the 2.45 train is good & you would come on from Chester to Broughton, letting us know.

Believe me,

Very truly yours,

W. E. GLADSTONE.

ALFRED TENNYSON, 1873
Exhibited in 1876.

[*To face page* 237.

T. Woolner to Rt. Hon. W. E. Gladstone

29, *Welbeck Street, W.,*
August 17, 1863.

Dear Mr. Gladstone.

I have long wished to make a bust of you, but knowing the great value of your time I never had enough boldness to take measures for the purpose, so that you must know how proud and grateful I now feel at being allowed to fulfil my wishes; and I beg you will give Mrs. Gladstone my sincere thanks for having rendered such efficient aid, and assurances that my best efforts will not be wanting to do justice to her good offices. As you kindly give me my choice and I rather dread delays, I will take advantage of No. 1 proposition and start to-morrow (18th) by the 2.45 train for Hawarden. I have sent my clay, modelling stool, etc., off to-day addressed to you to avoid mistakes : your servants will consider them uncouth and unintelligible arrivals, and might have refused them with a name they did not know attached. Pray give your brother-in-law my kindest thanks for generously giving me this early opportunity of doing what I have so long wished to do.

Most truly yours,
Thos: Woolner.

Woolner arrived at Hawarden on August 18, prepared the clay the next day, and the day after he began to model the bust which he finished on 31st. He had a very pleasant and interesting visit, and soon made friends with Mr. Gladstone's young sons Henry and Herbert. Mrs. Gladstone was most kind and helpful arranging for as many sittings as she could. Both Mr. Gladstone and Woolner prided themselves on their quickness in dressing, and one evening they raced each other and both came out of their rooms at the same moment !

This bust of Mr. Gladstone was carved later on by the Sculptor and placed in the Bodleian Library, Oxford, and on three sides of the pedestal were inserted marble bas-reliefs, subjects from Homer's *Iliad*, designed as a compliment to Mr. Gladstone's study and knowledge of Greek art. The three subjects are—

Thetis imploring Zeus; Achilles shouting from the Trenches; Thetis rousing Achilles.

Woolner carved and gave to the Royal Academy as his Diploma work the bas-relief of " Achilles shouting from the Trenches," upon his election as Royal Academician in 1874.

A third was carved for Mr. Charles Jenner.

Mrs. W. E. Gladstone to T. Woolner

> Penmaenmawr,
> September 14 [1863].

Dear Mr. Woolner,

The arrival of the valuable photograph caused quite a sensation. I had already seized upon it and placed it in my room—till your letter arrived, and now I will take care it is placed in " the Temple of Peace," it is *excellent*, & with its autograph very valuable & *much prized*. Many thanks to you for being so kind as to send it to us— all so well framed and good throughout. I rejoice in what you tell me about the bust—& am not surprised it is approved of—you deserve it should have succeeded for you have searched deeply and stamped upon it what makes it so valuable, God's gifts written upon that countenance ! I shall long to see it in marble. We are enjoying bathing and mountains and peace, such a snug party—the dear little boys are gone wh. is a loss reminding one that complete happiness is not *to last* here. I shall give them your message—they will not forget how kind you were to them —poor darlings at the end of their journey to school they were both found fast asleep in the train like the babes in the wood. All here desire to be most kindly remembered.

> Believe me,
> Yours sincerely,
> Cath. Gladstone.

My Husband is to go to the Queen at Balmoral next week.

Mrs. Tennyson to T. Woolner

> Farringford,
> Freshwater, I.W.,
> October 6, 1863.

My dear Mr. Woolner,

．　　　　．　　　　．　　　　．

When are you coming ? We hear you have made a very successful bust of Gladstone, and that you have been visit-

ing Froude. I hope you have been happy. Success, too,
to " The Beautiful Lady," who is dawning on the world.
     With the kind love of A. and the boys,
          Ever most truly yours,
               EMILY TENNYSON.

          T. WOOLNER TO MRS. TENNYSON

                              Salcombe,
                              Kingsbridge, Devon,
                                   October 8, 1863.
MY DEAR MRS. TENNYSON,

     .   .   .   .   .   .

   I have been at this place a week with Froude and
have had one lovely day. But altho' the weather has
been bad, yet with the kindness of my host and hostess
and the real beauty of the scenery despite rain, I have
enjoyed my holiday greatly. I had first to go into the
remote wilds of Staffordshire to see a Captain friend, bosom
friend of Sherard Osborn, married; it took much coin and
time to do it, but the sight of the whole thing was so interesting it quite repaid the trouble. The lady was so
beloved that the town of Leek gave itself a holiday, and
all the population crowded the church and streets to see the
marriage and procession of carriages : the prettiest part
of the show was 210 little girls clad in white and with a
blue ribbon adorned with silver anchor across each breast,
and wreaths of flowers on their heads : a certain number
of them lined the porch, and path of churchyard and steps
strewing flowers as the bridal procession passed. The
lady is a great heiress, and these little girls were the scholars
of a big school which she had established for them. They
had a ball in the evening, and it was a sight to see the
energy of those young creatures dancing. If the brave
deserve the fair, the Captain certainly did his bride, for he
fought the *Lee* gunboat for many hours within 90 yards of
one of the Taku forts on the Peiho, and had his vessel sunk
by the Chinese shot, and he had with his few surviving
men to cling for 5 hours, fired at the whole time by those
Johnnys, on the stump of his mainmast, which was all
that remained out of water.

     .   .   .   .   .   .

   I had a most pleasant visit at Hawarden Castle doing
Mr. Gladstone's bust : it seemed to have been almost the
entire study of Mrs. Gladstone to manage how to let me

have the most of him for my purpose; and nothing could have been better than the way he underwent the necessary infliction of sitting. I found him a most fascinating man in every way, and his remarks on books and history, human nature, and politics were all most interesting and instructive. It would have done your heart good to have heard the way in which he talked of the Bard's Poems; and the extraordinarily close acquaintance which he showed concerning them.

It is very kind of you to ask me, but I have not the least notion when I shall be able to see you again, for after I leave here I have to stay a few days at Nettlecombe with Arch: Jermyn, brother of Lady Trevelyan and then I must get back to work.

.   .   .   .   .   .

My poem will not cost me any money or I should not have printed it; but it has cost me a great deal of work. Mr. Combe of Oxford asked me to read it, and he liked it so much that he was determined to have it brought out; so that I had no more bother beyond finishing up the proofs : best thanks for your good wishes. My best love to the Poet and the boys.

Ever most truly yours,
THOS: WOOLNER.

MRS. TENNYSON TO T. WOOLNER

Farringford,
Freshwater, I.W.,
October 24, 1863.

MY DEAR MR. WOOLNER,

"My Beautiful Lady" has come to me to-day, thanks to your kind remembrance. I have only just caught sight of her as Alfred immediately took her to his room. I shall not see her well until we have another tutor.

.   .   .   .   .   .

I hope you are gaining strength and freshness for renewed work. He will not give "The Sermon" up, though I advise him, wicked creature that I am, you will say. I long for him to be at the "Sangreal," feeling sure that is his work and the days are going fast for him and for me. He continues better, so do I.

With kindest love from him and the boys,
Ever most truly yours,
EMILY TENNYSON.

COVENTRY PATMORE TO T. WOOLNER

December 3, 1863.

DEAR WOOLNER,

I got back the MSS. I told you about. There seems to have been nothing worse than carelessness in the delay.

I opened " Fraser " yesterday just where the writer abused the finest image in your Poem,[1] and one of the finest in any Poem—that about the moonlight bringing forth the name like a shout. Nothing could be bolder and more entirely unexaggerated at the same time.

Yours ever truly,

C. PATMORE.

T. WOOLNER TO MRS. TENNYSON

29, Welbeck Street, W.,
December 10, 1863.

MY DEAR MRS. TENNYSON,

.   .   .   .   .   .

I am hard at work on Macaulay, and Godley, and some of the Manchester statues. Macaulay having had a fat undefined face, I find it extremely difficult to get the likeness at all satisfactory : Godley's is much better for the purpose, being a thin man.

.   .   .   .   .   .

I am glad you were pleased with my book on reading it again; but I cannot well understand how you call it blame, when you say the Lady does not talk so well as yourself. She may talk fitly and yet need not be represented as knowing so much as you—for you must remember that she is meant to be only a young girl.

.   .   .   .   .

You will be pleased to hear that Haehnel,[2] that fine German sculptor of animals you have heard me talk of, has received a good number of orders for bronzes and is now on the fair road to be appreciated, and will be able

[1] " My Beautiful Lady."—The lines referred to are reproduced in facsimile showing Woolner's handwriting.

[2] Woolner made the acquaintance of Julius Haehnel, the animal sculptor, in 1849 before he went to Australia, and he had the greatest admiration for his works, and many are the houses possessing bronzes of his animals through Woolner's recommendation. Amongst the finest are his " Asiatic Lion," " Prowling Lion, Lioness," " The Ostrich," " The Tiger, the Ox and the Wild Boar " (done for Sir William Gull, the well-known physician), a full description of which Woolner wrote.

R

to devote all his time to the making of more of his extra-ordinary works.

Hunt has at last finished his large picture of the Egyptian Girl, lifesize : and it is the most complete thing as regards art that he has ever done.

I expect that I shall have to run over to Ireland at Xmas to see Archy Peel [1] for a few days to study some portraits which he has at his father-in-law's place of his wife for the monument I am to do to her memory.

I am much pleased with the subject, and hope to make a pathetic and poetic work to please and help console him.

Most truly yours,
THOMAS WOOLNER.

HAEHNEL'S WILD BOAR

When we are able to give our whole admiration to a work of Art, we feel a satisfaction more perfect than when gazing on a beautiful sunset; for the sun's radiance wanes sullied with our regret at its evanescence; and it is not every sunset has the good fortune to be seen by such eyes as saw the fighting *Temeraire* tugged to her last Berth;— whereas in beholding a great thought embodied our satis-faction is deepened by a sense of its permanence, knowing that familiarity will but increase our joy and carry it on into the future. This pleasure has been given us by a German Wild Boar just completed in bronze by Julius Haehnel of Dresden for Sir William Gull.

The monster, for a creature of form so strange and of such prodigious strength, cannot fitly be called other than a monster, stands with his snout raised, eyes glitter-ing, and ears pressed sharply forward conscious of danger. But no sense of fear, and no hesitation mar the length and decisiveness of *those* mighty lines running from the ponder-

---

[1] Mr. Archibald Peel, son of General Peel, was a great sportsman and hard rider to hounds, a dear friend of the Sculptor's. They were "Tom" and " Archie " to each other always. The memorial " Heavenly Welcome " to Mr. Peel's first wife is one of if not the most beautiful of all Woolner's monuments.

ous jowl and throat deep into the chest and down to the neat and dapper hoofs in front, or from head up huge, bristling shoulders down to the eagerly set hind limbs and upraised tufted tail. The brute looks conscious of danger, but still more conscious of power, and burning to know what disturbs him that he may straightway settle accounts and return peacefully to his acorns. Indeed, he looks such " A full-acorned Boar, a German one," as would startlingly have realized his idea to Shakespeare when in these words with his customary aptness he marked off the beast : but looking at the hugeness of these proportions and the enormous strength implied, within such compactness the whole force seems light and simple, we rather feel as if some great creation of Homer had taken shape and was there before us bristling in power horrent and irresistible. This is the impression given by the artist's conception of his subject, the treatment of which in workmanship belongs to the highest rank, being a happy union of strength and delicacy; with vastness in its masses daintily varied, line blending into line by the suavity obtained only by consummate skill. The surface is so complex from indications of ligament, bone, and muscle beneath, and from innumerable unexpected starts and twistings in the growth of hair and bristles without, that no description can properly suggest a notion of its " Infinite variety "; but it is at once a gratification and a privilege to record such an original, complete, and noble work in Sculpture.

WILLIAM ALLINGHAM TO T. WOOLNER

Lymington,
February 21, 1864.

MY DEAR WOOLNER,
It has long been a load on my conscience not to have thanked you for your book. I know not if it came from you or from Macmillan, but in either case it was very welcome, arriving just in time to be carried off on a long walk into the heart of the forest in that autumn time which is now, too, part of " other years." In other years, and not very long ago, I would have criticised your poem, but now I act not thus unless asked to do it (& not always then),

& so you escape both my censures and applauses. But I could honestly praise and recollected well, on re-reading, many or most parts which had been in the *Germ*, as I had often done in the meantime.

As Tennyson is in London I daresay you are seeing him often. I was at Farringford at Christmas time. I hope if you come this way you will not fail to give me a day or two, or rather let me say as long as you can like, and see some of these landscapes and trees. I can give you a small but sufficient bedroom, my perch being Mrs. Rice's, Bath Cottage, which is about a half a mile from Lymington, on the seaward or Solentward road, for 'tis hardly a sea, unless you are on it in an open boat & in a stiff gale as I was last week. I hear nothing of any Londoners. Send me a line at least to say you forgive my non-acknowledging remissness.

Do you care a bit about Shakespeare monuments? I wish they would ask you to make a big, bold Statue, place it on the centre of new Blackfriars Bridge (near where stood the Globe Theatre on the right and the Blackfriars Theatre on the left bank of the Thames) rising boldly above a specially designed parapet, & call the said bridge Shakespeare Bridge for ever & a day. Nowhere I think is a statue so effective as on a bridge, & this is certainly Shakespeare's part of London.

Always truly yours,
W. ALLINGHAM.

Please say has Mrs. Clough come in to live in town? Do you ever see Browning?

ROBERT BROWNING TO T. WOOLNER

19, *Warwick Crescent,*
Upper Westbourne Terrace,
February 24, 1864.

MY DEAR WOOLNER—(I won't return your unkindness and Mister you)—I feel sorry indeed that I am engaged doubly, —that is, to dine and then go elsewhere, on Friday : I never see enough of Tennyson, nor yet to talk with him about subjects we either of us value at three straws, I suppose : but I always enjoy smelling (even) his tobacco smoke : tell him so, with my true love. Something like which, you

THE CRUCIFIXION.   A REREDOS
From the plaster model, 1876.

[*To face page* 244.

must please to take too, dear Woolner, for all your kindness (except as excepted against) to

Yours ever
ROBERT BROWNING.

Palgrave the Traveller I like hugely.

In 1864 the figure of Moses, for the Manchester Assize Courts, was in its position, but fault was found with it and criticisms hurled at it. A Lancashire man felt impelled to write the following letter—

MOSES AND HIS CRITICS

To the Editor of the *Manchester Guardian*.

SIR,—Our Lancashire habit of "heaving half a brick" at a new-comer has led us to fling a good many heavy witticisms and criticisms at an illustrious stranger who has lately shown himself in our city. I allude to the figure of Moses designed by Mr. Woolner, and lately placed on the great gable of our new Assize Courts. This is what might have been expected; and a like welcome has, I should imagine, been given to every public statue that has been put up in England for many a long day—it is our English way of enjoying anything new. . . .

I am, sir, your obedient servant,

A CONSERVATIVE.

March 12, 1864.

At the same time this quatrain was printed in a newspaper—

THE STATUE OF "MOSES" AT THE NEW ASSIZE COURTS

The architect, upon his topmost work,
The Hebrew lawgiver in stone imposes.
Is he not right? A place for trying suits
Is certainly the very place for Moses.

CHAPTER XIV

HENRY N. GLADSTONE TO T. WOOLNER

Cliveden,
Maidenhead,
April 2, 1864.

MY DEAR MR. WOOLNER,

I must write you a line to thank you for your beautiful book—it is the first really beautiful book I have had in my life. I also thank you for your letter explaining about the book—I received them both with great joy this morning when I was in London   Papa, Mama, Mary, Herbert and I are come here to stay till Monday, it belongs to the Duchess of Sutherland, it is one of the most beautiful places in England, the river Thames runs just at the bottom of the garden.   There are such lots of Dukes, Duchesses, Earls, Lords and Hon. that Herbert and I do not know what to do with them.

I am
Your very affectionate
HENRY N. GLADSTONE.

THOMAS WOOLNER, ESQ.

I hope to come to your house some day to see the bust you spoke of but I am afraid it cannot be these holidays.

MRS. COMBE TO T. WOOLNER

The Clarendon Press,
April 14 [1864].

MY DEAR MR. WOOLNER,

.   .   .   .   .   .

I shall be greatly obliged by your ordering two sets of the photographs from the Bust framed in compartments, one of which I wish sent to our niece, Miss Nattali . . . the other to me.   The Bust [1] excites the most unqualified admiration from all who have seen it, both as a likeness and work of art. . . .

[1] Marble bust of Thomas Combe by Woolner.

246

My husband begs his friendly regards, and with the assurance of mine, and that the high and increasing gratification I derive from the Bust, will ensure you a high place on my list of Benefactors,

Believe me,

Dear Mr. Woolner,

Yours very sincerely,

M. COMBE.

T. WOOLNER TO MRS. TENNYSON

29, Welbeck Street, W.,
May 13, 1864.

MY DEAR MRS. TENNYSON,

. . . . . .

Sir John Simeon called to see me a few days back and is greatly pleased with my statue of his friend Godley. Artists and others who have seen it say that I have solved the difficulty of modern costume in sculpture.

Most truly yours,

THOS: WOOLNER.

[The following letter is in answer to a request by Woolner to Carlyle to sign a paper.]

THOMAS CARLYLE TO THOMAS WOOLNER

117, Marina,
St. Leonard's-on-Sea,
May 31, 1864.

DEAR WOOLNER,

I at once sign, and return;—I would even walk in suppliant procession to the Hon. House (if necessary), bareheaded and in sackcloth and ashes, entreating said Hon. Long-eared Assembly to deliver us from that most absurd of all Farce-Tragedies daily played under their supervision.

We are all doing rather well here; well, considering. My poor Mrs., I cannot but flatter myself, continues slowly to improve, tho' her sufferings are still very great. I myself complain most of my intolerable *bankrupt* Printer, and the delays he occasions. Without work *done*, there is no real triumph to be had over one's multifarious confusions here and elsewhere.

The air, the sea, the green land, and fine old-fashioned

Country Hamlets, the rides by shore and silent lanes white with hawthorn: all is beautiful here;—on one's first egress, such a sky as is *miraculous* to London eyes, every morning.

To work, to work! For the *night* cometh withal.

Yours ever,

T. Carlyle.

On the first of June, Woolner became engaged to Alice Gertrude, daughter of George and Mary Waugh. She was the youngest but one of the family of six daughters and two sons. Sweet, gentle, self-effacing, although lovely, devoid of personal vanity and jealousy, she was then and always absolutely unworldly, she was hardly more than a girl at the date of her engagement, but her future husband at that age had realized her nature, and held in true reverence her "lofty young soul," and by her own family she was idolized. The Sculptor received a great number of letters of affectionate congratulation from his many friends, showing their sympathetic joy in his happiness—it is only possible to print a few of them; almost the first was from Mrs. Tennyson, written from Farringford—from Thomas Carlyle, Edward Lear and Mrs. Froude. Among many others were notes from the Hookers, Trevelyans, W. Rossetti, Pollocks, Ford Madox Brown—and the Combes of Oxford.

Mrs. Tennyson to T. Woolner

Farringford,
June 6, 1864.

My dear Mr. Woolner,

It is indeed glorious news and we are heartily glad to have it. May all your fondest hopes be more than realised! I cannot but think she must be worthy of your choice, and if so, they can scarcely fail of fulfilling themselves. Where truth and love are, the elements of eternal youth grow ever younger in its strength; how should it be otherwise? Do not let the marriage be long delayed. You will both come and see us soon. I trust you have found what you want to make a good bust. So many will be grateful to you for it.

A. and the boys are gone to-day with Mr. Allingham,

Edmund Lushington and Mr. Wilson to Beaulieu. They have a lovely day for the old sanctuary of many memories.

. . . . .

All best wishes,
From yours most sincerely,
EMILY TENNYSON.

6, *Clifton Place,*
June 7 [1864].

MRS. FROUDE TO T. WOOLNER

MY DEAR MR. WOOLNER,

The children & I are quite delighted to hear the great news—Anthony is at the Record Office but I can't wait till he returns to write—I am so glad you followed my sagacious advice for indeed it is *great* happiness & I trust you will have it to the fullest extent.

The children returned from their walk yesterday reporting that they had seen " Mr. Woolner walking with a tall young lady—oh ! *so* pretty & we think he must ' be beloved to her ' (their expression for such matters)—for we passed him quite close & he never saw us ! "

Your note explains this sad neglect of your former friends & I am delighted to think that the surmises of the youthful minds were so correct. We shall be very anxious to see Miss Waugh & I hope we shall all be well acquainted some day—I am sure you would choose somebody *very* charming.

With warm congratulations . . .
Yours very sincerely,
H. E. FROUDE.

T. CARLYLE TO THOMAS WOOLNER

117, *Marina,*
St. Leonard's-on-Sea,
June 11, 1864.

DEAR WOOLNER,

Your Letter from The Grange, last Sunday, was naturally very interesting to us ! My poor Wife is still too weak for writing, almost ever : but both she and I, and she bids me say so, are delighted to hear of your getting an eligible young Wife,—which we are aware is the crown and keystone of all comfortable *Housekeeping*, and expect will be a very great improvement to you, in that and all other respects. Solomon said long ago, " He that getteth a good wife, getteth a good thing "; and I never heard anybody contradict him,—nor will I myself, by a long way !

In early times I used to hear a great deal of your fair Bride's Grandfather; " Dr. Waugh," oracle of all Scotchmen in that strange London, and much talked of at home among the Dissenting Religious Circles;—an excellent reasonable solid kind of man, I do still understand. Whom if a certain Young Person resemble, it will be well with her and Another ! Very seriously we wish, to her and to you, all manner of prosperity, and a fortunate and useful life together.

We still imagine there is improvement visible here from week to week,—at least I do, rather more and not *less* confidently as we go on; and am for my own share at length got thoroughly busy again; which is an immense point in my favour. Everything is lovely exceedingly in these green environs, in this bright sea and sky;—and, till July unkennel London on it, the place is nearly empty of foreign guests. Except indeed a few Gipsies, squatted comfortably in some woody bank, on one's evening ride.

Yours ever truly (tho' in haste),

T. CARLYLE.

EDWARD LEAR TO ALICE GERTRUDE WAUGH

15, *Stratford Place,*
Oxford Street, W.,
June 24, 1864.

DEAR MADAM,

Although I have not as yet the pleasure of your acquaintance, I cannot help begging you to do me the favour of accepting a small drawing,[1] which my friend Thomas Woolner—who I gladly hear is soon to call you his wife,—will bring you. If you will please me by hanging up this little offering in your future home, you will often, I would hope, be reminded that among the many who will wish you & Woolner long years of happiness none do so more sincerely or more hopefully than,

Dear Madam,

Yours very truly,

EDWARD LEAR.

---

[1] A water-colour drawing of Corfu.

Rt. Hon. W. E. Gladstone to T. Woolner

11, Carlton House Terrace, S.W.,
June 25, 1864.

Dear Mr. Woolner,

Through my wife I understood that I might pay you an evening visit & see your guest.[1] If you will be at home this evening about nine, please send a *verbal* Yes by the bearer.

Yours most truly,
W. E. Gladstone.

Rt. Hon. W. E. Gladstone to T. Woolner

11, Carlton House Terrace, S.W.,
June 28, 1864.

Dear Mr. Woolner,

I am sorry to report that I find the House of Commons list, the only one over which I have any power, hopelessly crammed for the days over which the coming debate is likely to extend. On Tennyson's behalf I have appealed to the Speaker as I thought you would wish and he will treat the case as special & give him a place on Monday next.

He should be there *before* half past four. . . .

Sincerely yours,
W. E. Gladstone.

Thomas Carlyle to Thomas Woolner

St. Leonards,
June 28, 1864.

Dear Woolner,

You were right as to Addiscombe; next morning we heard it was let. Various projects were canvassed, other kind possibilities there still were, but all had their difficulties : the end was, We are to stay here till July is out; by which time, it is hoped, a slow journey toward Scotland may be undertaken—my Brother superintending; I returning then to Cheyne Row, and waiting,—with Work and Silence as company. This is what suits me best; and her too, I really think.

There has been a *little* more of sleep (not at all a *much*) since you were here; and aspects are slightly brightening again. For this is the " *Place* of Hope ! " Your amiable

---

[1] Alfred Tennyson, the Laureate.

Young Lady sent flowers today; thank her, and say you
wish her well (unless perhaps you have hinted that already !).

Yours ever truly,

T. CARLYLE.

Farringford,
Freshwater,
Isle of Wight,
July 11, 1864.

MRS. TENNYSON TO T. WOOLNER

MY DEAR MR. WOOLNER,

I cannot tell you how sorry I am that my intention
of writing to you the very day A. returned has not been
fulfilled till now. . . . I rejoice at the happy account he
gives of you and the family so soon to be nearest to you.
I hope it will not be later than September. The months
of our short life are precious. Why should they drag
wearily with absence when they might go winged with
presence, which sentence I take to be worthy of Queen
Elizabeth herself, in its elaborateness or whatever else it
might be called.

I hope you think he has given your stories [1] well. I
wish he would give mine now and do the " Sangreal " for
me, not but that I heartily adopt " Enoch Arden."

Ever most truly yours,

EMILY TENNYSON.

T. WOOLNER TO MRS. TENNYSON

29, *Welbeck Street, W.,*
July 14, 1864.

MY DEAR MRS. TENNYSON,

I think the stories are rendered beautifully. The
" Aylmer's Field " contains some of the most exquisite passages ever written, and is very complete in its key. But
I am not certain whether it is the key that pleases me
most—whether it is not too beautiful almost—and whether
something more stern and craggy would not have seemed
to me more appropriate; but of all this I am by no means
sure.

---

[1] " Enoch Arden " and " Aylmer's Field."

CHARLES KINGSLEY, 1876

[*To face page* 252.

Please give my kindest love to the boys. Tell the Bard that Gladstone was highly pleased—he was pleased with the Danish Speech. " It is indeed something to have pleased such a man "—said he.

This is my first moment since receiving yours.

Most truly yours,

Thos: Woolner.

James Anthony Froude to T. Woolner

Salcombe,
August 30 [1864].

My dear Woolner,

. . . When is the execution? I have been urging on the children the propriety of their writing to you on the subject. They loudly and angrily refuse, but in the tone of their refusal show how much they are interested nevertheless. A word from you will be very welcome.

" Aylmer's Field " is the grandest thing I have read of Tennyson's—and " Tithonus " too—how beautiful it is.

Affect^{ly} yours,

J. A. Froude.

Children were very fond of Woolner, and many of his friends' children were highly excited at his approaching marriage. One little girl, on first hearing of his engagement, clasped her hands together, saying she wished she could be one of Mr. Woolner's " brides "!

Woolner was married on September 6, at Saint James's Church, Paddington, and the honeymoon was spent in Guernsey at L'Ancrasse; while there they saw much of Paul Naftel, the water-colour painter, and his wife.

They returned to England about the middle of October, staying on the way at Dartmouth, Exeter and Salisbury. They then settled down at 29, Welbeck Street, which remained their home all their lives.

The portrait by Arthur Hughes of the young wife, painted very shortly after her marriage shows her very much as she was at the date of her engagement; and although altogether it is the best portrait of her and is very charming, neither it nor any other has ever quite done her justice.

The picture was bought with a wedding cheque given by F. T. Palgrave to his friend Woolner.

In answer to a letter from Woolner asking Arthur Hughes to paint the portrait, he wrote : " About the picture *of course* I shall be delighted to do what you want done, am ever so much flattered to have been selected."

MRS. CARLYLE TO T. WOOLNER

5, Cheyne Row, Chelsea,
Saturday [October 1864].

DEAR FRIEND,

When your note was delivered here to-day, I was on my way to call for " the young Wife," who is and will ever remain associated in my mind with the loveliest roses ! *The roses* were all I could see of her at St. Leonards ! I have since seen her graceful and gracious figure on paper ; and shall now see her face to face, and if she make you as happy as I want you to be, I shall love her with all my heart. Yes, thank God, I am much better than when I left St. Leonards ; but I had best not " crow till I am out of the wood." I am still but catching a glimpse of open country between the trees ! I am not " well " and not strong, am not confident, only *less suffering* for the time being and with a feeling of *Hope* struggling slowly and doubtfully to Life in me, like a poor wretch fished out of the Depths by the Humane Society's drags, and this is why that having driven to-day as far as Harley Street to call for your Wife ; I suddenly took fright and returned home *re infecta.* My back is so weak and stiff from this terrible long illness that I can hardly stand upright, and can walk only a few yards with painful difficulty ; getting in and out of a carriage is more trying to me than scrambling over a wall six feet high used to be, in the blessed time when I had " no *nerves,*" or didn't know that I had any ! Now, if there had been no young wife in the case I could have driven up to your door and called you out to transact our interview in the carriage. But the nearer I got, the more I felt it too great a liberty, to propose to a young wife, a stranger to me, that *she* should come out and sit in my " neat Fly ! " And to *stagger* in, after my present fashion of walking, to the young wife and stranger was a disregard to *appearances* which I could not, at the last *supreme* moment, attain to ! So, I just turned back ; more shame to me ! If you will come and bring Her here, I shall be greatly obliged to you. I drive out every day at one o'clock and

come in at three—either before or after these two hours
I am visible till nine at night, when I go to my room. I
dine at four in the Drawing-room, and have got it so fixed
in my head that *eating*, instead of being a vulgar trans-
action for ME is a benefit conferred on my Husband and
Friends; that I no longer feel ashamed to eat before wit-
nesses; so you can choose your hour with the exception of
just the two I have named.

God bless you,
Affectionately yours,
JANE CARLYLE.

T. WOOLNER TO MRS. TENNYSON

29, Welbeck Street, W.,
November 3, 1864.

MY DEAR MRS. TENNYSON,

When I wrote a short time back I forgot to ask you
to tell the Bard that he can have his attic as usual whenever he comes to town and likes to have it; the only difference he will find in my present arrangements will be a double
welcome, and a more careful eye to watch over his comforts. If he comes in the winter he must have his attic
to sleep and smoke in.

I do not find that my experience agrees with the Bard's
opinion of his " Aylmer's Field "; for he thought it was
and would be regarded as the least effective of the new
poems, whereas I hear good judges say quite the contrary.
Froude by no means a light authority, told me the other
day he thought it the " finest piece of writing that Tennyson had ever done." Anyway the Bard's own forebodings
as to the non-success of the book must be dispelled by this
time, for as regards sale and popular opinion and praises,
it must have surpassed everything he has ever done. I
only hope it will inspire him to write heaps more poems;
for now he has only to think out a good subject and write
it straight off; as his command over language is quite
absolute now, and the verses must fashion themselves so
perfectly in his mind at once as scarcely to require correc-
tion. I wish he would write a set of songs in lyrical metres,
for since Burns he is almost the only poet who has been
able to do a song.

I have seen Mrs. Carlyle since I wrote and was charmed

to find how well she was looking : she is too weak to do much more than stand upright; but her spirits are good, and her state may almost be called a resurrection from the dead.

.   .   .   .   .   .

I am sorry to tell you that Hunt has made up his mind he says to go to the East for 2 or 3 years, and means to start in about 2 months. It seems a pity he should go to stay so long in that dangerous climate, but he has got the notion of painting religious pictures and it is of no use trying to dissuade him.

Palgrave went off this morning to Yorkshire with his wife to stay some time. I went with him to see the new statues from Rome at the B. Museum and found they were poor rubbish mostly, and of no value, save to show what muffs there were among the ancients as well as in our own time, but the newspapers have a different opinion upon what they do not understand.

Most truly yours,
T. WOOLNER.

MRS. TENNYSON TO T. WOOLNER

Farringford,
Freshwater,
Isle of Wight,
November 4, 1864.

MY DEAR MR. WOOLNER,

Mr. Wilson arrived yesterday and he has kindly taken the boys for me this morning, so I will not let it pass without a few lines of thanks for your welcome letter, and of affectionate congratulation from us on your marriage, which all who have the pleasure of knowing your bride think so very happy. May it indeed be so ever more and more. We looked for you both at the appointed time, and now we will look for you whenever you bid us do so, and let it not be long.

.   .   .   .   .   .

Thanks for what you say about the new poem,[1] but for you it would not have been. Do you like the idea of the Selection in sixpenny parts for the working man ? And I wonder whether you would approve of my notion of having headings and tail pieces, if had at all, made out of flowers,

[1] " Aylmer's Field."

emblematic of the Colonies by way of telling the world that one considers that the Colonists too are among the people of England.   Each Colony I think ought to have its flower or tree emblem but as far as I can make it has not, so all that could be done would be to have kinds of typical plants—cotton, coffee, eucalyptus, acacia, rice, maize, vine, wheat, etc., bread fruit tree, fern tree, palm and pine.

.   .   .   .   .   .

We hope that in consideration of our being so far away from town, you have chosen a tankard or gold bracelets or whatever you will by way of memorial of our good wishes.

.   .   .   .   .   .

With love and best wishes from Alfred and the boys to yourself and all kind greetings from us all to your Alice.
Believe me,
Most truly yours,
EMILY TENNYSON.

T. WOOLNER TO MRS. TENNYSON

29, Welbeck Street, W.,
November 17, 1864.

MY DEAR MRS. TENNYSON,
      The Bard's room is all prepared and he can enter at will.
      A thousand thanks !—the cheque came safely to hand. I had been looking out but was not satisfied with what I saw, but now I have got a glorious silver mug, 90 years old and there will be engraved upon it " Given by Alfred and Emily Tennyson to Thomas Woolner Sep : 6, 1864 "—my wedding day.   I shall look quite splendid.
      I will tell the Bard what I think of your projects of woodcuts for the 6d. Numbers.
      Alice has returned to me again, having been absent a week with her mother.

.   .   .   .   .   .

She is very pleased at the notion of having to look after the Bard and make him snug.

.   .   .   .   .   .

Most truly yours,
THOS : WOOLNER.

S

MRS. TENNYSON TO MRS. WOOLNER

Farringford,
Freshwater,
Isle of Wight,
February 11, 1865.

MY DEAR MRS WOOLNER,

We shall be delighted to welcome Mr. Woolner and for as long a time as he can stay, yourself also if you change your mind.

.   .   .   .   .   .

Lionel was the other day singing the sweetness of the days that were past, when the sculptor with hair like a torch was here, in Latin verse—so Mr. Woolner will perceive he is of a constant mind.   Hoping that we may send him back quite well,

Believe me,
Very truly yours,
EMILY TENNYSON.

St. Mary's,
March 24, 1865.

T. WOOLNER TO MRS. TENNYSON

MY DEAR MRS. TENNYSON,

I returned last night from Seaton, having spent a most pleasant time.   Lady Ashburton was kindness itself and there was no state or grandeur.   Carlyle was charming, and his talk was interesting in every way; he, Sir W. Trevelyan and I used to go out riding together nearly every day.   Last Tuesday the whole party made an expedition to the house I told you of (St. Mary's), and had luncheon in the open air, on the step of the terrace on which the house stands.

Carlyle has given up the notion of buying it, but says that if he were ten years younger and able to enter a new kind of life he should not wish a happier looking spot.   The house is built of solid stone; the rooms are wainscoted all round, the ceilings also are of pine polished; and most beautifully finished throughout.   There are 100 acres of land with a cottage for farm man &c., and the price asked is £2000.

.   .   .   .   .   .

Lady Ashburton was anxious I should buy it and offered to lend me as much of the money as I liked, but of course a big house to me would be like buying a pack of hounds.

I went on Wednesday to see Clevelands, a place near there,

SIR COWASJEE JEHANGHIR READYMONEY.   MARBLE STATUE,
BOMBAY, 1876

[*To face page* 259.

and it was without exception to my mind, the loveliest place I have ever seen even as it stands now; so that what it must be in the time of the leaf surpasses my imagination to perceive.

. . . . .

I think there is no chance of Carlyle coming to I. of Wight, for he said that as soon as the Seaforth Lodge engagement was over he wàs due in Scotland to stay with some of his family for a long time, and he does not expect to be back before the end of autumn or something like that, so that I shall be all that time without seeing the dear old philosopher.

. . . . .

Most truly yours,
THOS : WOOLNER.

ROBERT BROWNING TO T. WOOLNER

19, *Warwick Crescent,*
Upper Westbourne Terrace, W.,
May 25, 1865.

MY DEAR WOOLNER,

Will you tell Mr. Jowett that I am most grateful for his goodness, and accept it with the utmost pleasure !

As for you we are old friends now, and your own goodness is much as usual.

I write at once—but will call on you before the time, to arrange how we meet & go together : how pleasant it will be !—at least to

Yours ever truly
ROBERT BROWNING.

Of course I am very thankful to Mrs. Pattison also—as you must kindly assure her—but indeed one's breath is taken away by you & your friends.

CHAPTER XV

WOOLNER was in the habit of taking his workmen, modellers and carvers for an outing in the country every summer. He is seen whilst on one of these friendly expeditions in the group, on the left of the white haired old man in the centre, Jimmy Holland by name; he was an old Sailor who did odd jobs in the studio such as beating up the clay—damping the cloths to keep the clay models moist, fetching and carrying tools and stoking the furnace. This old fellow, Jimmy, was proud of telling how, when Nelson left England for the last time, he laid his hand on Jimmy, then a boy, to steady himself getting into the boat which was to take him to his flag-ship. Another experience of his, was when on board the ship which took Napoleon to St. Helena. One day as the Exile paced the deck, he stopped and accosted Jimmy, (he often spoke to the sailors when in the humour,) and asked : " How long since you saw your Mudder and Farder ? " and Jimmy answered : " I should 'a' seen 'em a long time ago if it hadn't 'a' been for *you!!* " pointing his forefinger impressively at the Emperor, who with hands behind his back, walked off laughing softly to himself.

Another worker in the studio who came on and off for many years was W. F. Woodington, son of Woodington the sculptor, and the following little anecdote about him is recorded in Woolner's words.

" One day in 1838, Woodington, the sculptor of one of the reliefs on the base of the Nelson column, was on a steam boat returning from a trip to Margate; and in the midst of a great blazing sunset he saw the old *Temeraire* drawn along by a steam tug. The sight was so magnificent that it struck him as being an unusually fine subject for a picture, and he noted all the points he thought would constitute its glory if presented on canvas. But he was not the only person on board who took professional notice of the splendid sight, for he saw Turner himself there, also noticing and busy making little sketches on cards. He pointed him out to his companion as Turner the great Landscape Painter. When Woodington went home he made a sketch of the subject while all the incidents were fresh in his memory, intending at some future favorable ₚopportunity to paint a picture; the intention ultimately proving to be one of those instances of goodness that pave the way to another but not a better world !—On the year following, going to the R.A. Ex : what was his amazement on beholding the veritable scene that had so delighted him again blazing before him in all its glory ! He now saw that Turner had not been busy making those little sketches on cards for nothing; for here was a result beyond anything of the kind ever seen in paint before.   I scarcely need say that Woodington felt no inclination to begin painting his intended picture of the *Old Temeraire*."

T. WOOLNER.

MRS. TENNYSON TO T. WOOLNER

Farringford,
July 24, 1865.

MY DEAR MR. WOOLNER,

Many thanks for your kind letter and our best wishes for the beautiful Fanny [1] and Mr. Hunt. I trust that the marriage will not only make them happy but add, if possible, to your own happiness and Mrs. Woolner's. Do you know we went round by St. Mary's ? We had to hurry back to see Professor Owen so there was no possibility of trying to find Lady Ashburton.

Our boys are with us and well.   Great is the joy of having them as you will know. They are very brown and a good deal altered considering the short time. But they keep their old simplicity though somewhat of the old grace is gone, only for a time I hope.

With our love,
Ever most truly yours,
EMILY TENNYSON.

[1] Eldest sister of Mrs. Woolner and the first Mrs. Holman-Hunt.

T. Woolner to Mrs. Tennyson

29, *Welbeck Street, W.,*
July 27, 1865.

My dear Mrs. Tennyson,

. . . The Emperor [1] has accepted my bust of Cobden,[2] and the correspondence on the subject is soon I believe to be published in the papers. I have nearly finished the model of Peel's Monument; and Watkiss Lloyd, who saw it, says I shall have nothing to do but babies and Angels for years after this is exhibited. The Angels I should like very well, but as for the babies I profess no especial admiration for the pretty squalling little creatures. . . .

Lady and Sir Walter Trevelyan were here yesterday, . . . she was in such a state of delight with my bust of Carlyle that I really hoped it would take the form of ordering a copy in bronze ! . . . .

Most truly yours,
Thomas Woolner.

T. Woolner to Rt. Hon. W. E. Gladstone

Clifton Hill House,
Clifton, Bristol,
August 9, 1865.

Dear Mr. Gladstone,

I met the member for Chester a short time ago and he told me that you were going to be some time at Hawarden Castle. I therefore gave directions for one of the medallions of Tennyson to be sent down to you and I hope you will do it the honour of letting it be hung up in the Temple of Peace : the original himself was very pleased that you liked it for both he and Mrs. Tennyson say they like it better than any other likeness that has been done of him.

I am at this place doing a bust of Dr. Symonds, who has an excellent face for sculpture. I forgot to mention to you when you were at my studio, that my statue of Godley was finished in bronze and exhibiting in the Italian Court at S. Kensington, it may probably be there 2 or 3 months longer, and should you chance to go there any time you may be in town I should much like you to see it before it

---

[1] The Emperor of the French, Louis Napoleon: Napoleon III.

[2] Woolner carved four busts of Richard Cobden : one for Mrs. Cobden; one in the National Portrait Gallery, London; one in Westminster Abbey; and the one above mentioned. There are many letters from Mrs. Cobden about the bust expressing her enthusiastic admiration of it.

goes to N. Zealand. Please give my kind remembrances to Mrs. Gladstone and your family.

Very sincerely yours,
THOS : WOOLNER.

RT. HON. W. E. GLADSTONE TO T. WOOLNER

Hawarden,
August 11, 1865.

DEAR MR. WOOLNER,

Your kind & most acceptable present [1] has arrived in safety and the work is much & unanimously admired. It is most pleasant to have it in view and though my room (which has been shifted) is more than ever full of books, I shall make this a *sine quâ non*. Believe me,

Very faithfully yours,
W. E. GLADSTONE.

Will you remember me kindly to Dr. Symonds, my slight acquaintance with whom I am ever anxious to improve?

T. WOOLNER TO F. T. PALGRAVE

29, Welbeck Street, W.,
August 21, 1865.

DEAR FRANK,

. . . I was quietly getting my breakfast at Clifton about 8 when the telegraphic message came summoning me. . . . Had it been two days later the bust of Dr. Symonds would have been completed and now I must go tomorrow or next day to finish him off. The Doctor says he thinks it a great success, and remarked just what Gladstone did—that seeing me model gave him a totally new idea of art; he seemed to have no notion that in serious art every touch had to be treated with the same care as the pointing a rifle at long range. . . . I went one day to Wells and was hugely pleased with the elegance of the chapter-house which looks like a gigantic mushroom of fairy lightness. The famed sculptures I thought about as bad and no better than nearly all the Gothic sculpture I ever saw, poor and ugly in composition, grotesque in meaning and of almost blank ignorance as to human form. . . .

Yours affectionately,
THOS : WOOLNER.

[1] The medallion of Tennyson framed.

LETTER FROM MRS. CARLYLE TO T. WOOLNER

4, *Langhorne Gardens,*
Folkestone,
Wednesday [August, 1865].

How nice! I have no doubt it is lovely! Such a Mother! And such a Father! Pray give it a kiss for me, a whole shower of kisses. I hope to see it with my bodily eyes before long. I return to Chelsea on Monday next till then I am here with Miss Bromley and the Pugs.

Mr. Carlyle too is longing for home. Can know no rest till he gets there! Poor despised Chelsea has risen in value of late—I should not wonder, so great is his impatience to get back to London (!!!) that he will start off without awaiting my return, and plump down on those terrified servants all by himself! this week! My arm continues free of pain, and I can use my hand to a certain small extent, for example I write this note with the lame hand! and since I have been here I have knitted a pair of what shall I say? Garters! Upon my honour.

Dear love to the pretty wee Wife,
Affectionately yours,
JANE CARLYLE.

T. WOOLNER TO F. T. PALGRAVE

September 2, 1865.

DEAR FRANK,
. . . I began the medallion of Emily Rhodes, to my grief that it should be such an insignificant thing when she would have made so admirable a bust. . . . Arthur Hughes has sent home the picture of Alice, and I think it looks lovely only that the red of the shawl attracts from the countenance. £100 is his charge for a portrait in that style finished up like it, tho' he made a difference to me being an artist. Instead therefore of considering the money spent on doing up the house &c., which you gave me a wedding present for that purpose I am going to consider, this picture as your present : my wife has always been saying she wanted me to get something beautiful that your name might [be] associated with, and now I do not think I can do better. . . .

Most sincerely thine,
THOS: WOOLNER.

T. WOOLNER TO F. T. PALGRAVE

29, *Welbeck Street, W.*,
September 11, 1865.

MY DEAR FRANK,

I finished the model of the lovely Emily Rhodes to-day and it gives vivid satisfaction to all concerned . . . it does not look in the least like a portrait but like some Greek poetic face. In about 2 days I shall have finished the model of Alfred for Manchester, then I hope to be off to Scotland for a fortnight.

I have finished Giffy's [1] book and have for the last fortnight scarcely thought of any thing else, I found it so absorbing; the description of the shipwreck is worthy of being part of an epic poem & you move about among the cities, their suburbs, and their inhabitants as if you were really a traveller among them. . . . I went to see Carlyle this evening and found him vigorously reading at Racine who seems just now to give him especial admiration.

Affly yours,
THOS : WOOLNER.

T. WOOLNER TO MRS. TENNYSON

29, *Welbeck Street, W.*,
October 3, 1865.

MY DEAR MRS. TENNYSON,

I have just returned to Babylon and its horrid roaring, having been touring in the Highlands and other places for 17 days.

When I was at Leek Miss Gaunt, a lady who lives there and who met the Bard a year or two ago at Buxton I think, told me a story that happened among her acquaintance, so like " Enoch Arden " that I thought it worth while to let you know.—Two fellows made love to the same lady, one was a poor sailor, the other a rich banker man :—the lady (strange to tell) actually married the sailor. The sailor was a gentleman sailor only a poor one. After living with her and having three or four children born he had to go to sea, and his ship was lost. For many years nothing was heard of the sailor, and in the meantime the rich banker turned up, and did great things for lady and children on the grounds of old friendship, and ultimately persuaded her to marry him. They lived together happily and had several

---

[1] Gifford Palgrave, the traveller.

children. One day home came the sailor without a penny, and chanced to go to his own friends before looking for his wife and heard the whole story. As you may suppose he felt the reverse of merry on the occasion; but after consulting a great deal at length determined not to reveal himself to her, and, went away and has never been heard of since. His friends all suppose him dead, and have in consequence told the circumstance. The happy ones are alive now, living in luxury in some Midland town. Miss Gaunt told me their names, but charged me not to repeat them, and the name of the town which I have forgotten.

· · · · · ·

I saw Palgrave this morning for a few minutes and he looked like a squire, so rosy and brown and robust with his six weeks' holiday in lovely Wales. How curious it seems that the loveliest countries have the most hideous barbarous natives. I have been about parts of Scotland fit for the abodes of archangels, but the life there huddling within the ugly hovels seems scarcely human from its set hardness and brutish coarseness.

I suppose you heard of the death of Miss Bonham-Carter. There never was a finer creature in intelligence and active goodness.

With love to the Bard,
Most truly yours,
THOS : WOOLNER.

MRS. TENNYSON TO T. WOOLNER

Farringford,
October 5, 1865.

MY DEAR MR. WOOLNER,

I wish some good soul would make you so rich that you need not live in roaring smoky London.

· · · · · ·

The other day we had yet another story of (not told us) like "Enoch Arden." It makes one fear the women do not wait so long as they should. I like better that old German story, where the faithful Baroness is dispensing of her goods to the poor and one bold beggar embracing her is about to be knocked down by an attendant, when the beggar says, "My friend there is no need for that, behold your Master!"

[*Photograph by Lock and Whitfield.*

THOMAS WOOLNER, R.A., 1877

[*To face page* 266.

Mr. Jenner is quite princely in his generosity. I hope you will say that we feel him so.

. . . . . .

With kindest regards,
Believe me,
Most truly yours,
EMILY TENNYSON.

T. WOOLNER TO MRS. TENNYSON

29, Welbeck Street, W.,
October 9, 1865.

MY DEAR MRS TENNYSON,
. . . The Palgraves called yesterday to see the babe. He (Palgrave) was flourishing with life and vigour as usual. . . . Frank is very busy preparing his Art Essays for the Press to come out by Xmas. I hear from Arthur Hughes who told me he had been working hard at "Enoch Arden" and that Payne pressed him sharply as to time, but I advised him not to be pressed on any account so as to run any risk of doing the designs hastily, for art is a thing that will not admit of hasty and sudden freaks from publishers, however enterprising. . . .

With all kind remembrances,
Most truly yours,
THOS : WOOLNER.

MRS. TENNYSON TO T. WOOLNER

Farringford,
Freshwater,
Isle of Wight,
November 8, 1865.

MY DEAR MR. WOOLNER,

. . . . .

I do not doubt that Mr. Patmore will make a good use of his riches. He was very generous as a poor man and I do not think he will be less so as a rich.

Stepmothers must in modern story be made always good instead of always bad, as they used to be. I think one hears of so many good ones. For instance Lady Simeon. Sir John has just left us having paid a bachelor visit while his wife is away with her little boy for change of air.

. . . . .

I am glad you have a little bit of imaginative work to do though not one you would perhaps have chosen, yet it

must be a relief from the busts of dead men or living either.
You are rather vicious about the National Ode, but I shall
hand you over to Mrs. Woolner for punishment.   Tell her
for once she must forego her nature.

With love to her,
Believe me,
Most truly yours,
EMILY TENNYSON.

THOMAS COMBE TO T. WOOLNER

Oxford,
November 14, 1865.

MY DEAR WOOLNER,

.   .   .   .   .   .

   Dr. Acland asked me if he could purchase a cast of
y^r bust & I volunteered to give him one—plain plaster.
I sh^d prefer for all our sakes but then it sh^d be under glass
to prevent the maids rubbing my face every morning with a
dirty duster.   So it will be best to paint me. . . . A new
spirit has certainly come over Hunt for he [has] written
me a second letter before I had answered the first and in a
more spritely style than I have seen for months [& years]
He tells me the bands ([bans] were asked last Sunday so I
am anticipating the next and most important act.   I don't
think it would be prudent to go to Jerusalem at present—
the risque will diminish daily to other places.
   . . . Mrs. Pat will probably put in P.S. so I have only
to give my love to Alices two & say

I am yours very truly,

T.C.

T. WOOLNER TO F. T. PALGRAVE

Farringford,
Freshwater, I. W.,
November 28, 1865.

DEAR FRANK,
   I am much obliged for your good services [anent]
"the Gladstone Mem" and am highly delighted at the notion
of Homeric basso-relievos, Tennyson thinks Achilles crying
out from the trenches on one side, and Andromache watch-
ing from a tower the body of Hector being dragged round
the walls on the other, with Homer himself in the front
won't be a good choice of subject.   I shall be back in town
on Friday, and then I shall talk with you on the subject :

I am almost afraid to make my experiments with the bust itself, for as it now stands it is exactly as I conceived it originally, and I fear any change would weaken the sense of its oneness, the soul of Art; and I think it more strictly appropriate that he should look the living man surmounting the ideal subjects, to avoid any possibility of being mistaken for the poet himself instead of his commentator. This change has done my eye a great deal of good. . . .

> Yours
> THOS : WOOLNER.

THOMAS COMBE TO T. WOOLNER

Oxford,
December 12, 1865.

MY DEAR SCULPTOR,

Dr. Acland told me on Saturday that he had received the bust[1] and was so pleased with it that he thought it as delightful to look at as the marble. I shall certainly consider myself yr. debtor for it & also the one sent to the Nattalis—you shall make me a present some years hence.

I have another subject for you, Dr. Newman, as fine a head as any you have done. I have promised it to my wife who will write to the Doctor for his assent. What a glorious evening you must have had with Gladstone, Hunt etc. etc.—he must indeed have been pleased to stay so late. I doubt not the Memorial does delight him for he has a large love for Oxford & ever will have—I regret having been so *dummy* as to relinquish the bust . . . you must put out all yr. strength on the pedestal—let it (be ?) *original* like no other pedestal. . . .

> Our love to Both.
> Yours ever
> TH. COMBE.

MRS. TENNYSON TO T. WOOLNER

Farringford,
December 19, 1865.

MY DEAR MR. WOOLNER,

Now you must let me write myself to say that Alfred has arrived safely this morning by the 12.30 boat, having slept at Lymington and dined and breakfasted with

---

[1] Plaster cast of Bust of Thomas Combe.

Mr. Allingham, and tell you how grateful I feel to Mrs. Woolner and yourself for all the enjoyment you have given him. His letters have always had such a happy tone, that I am sure that none of the trouble you have taken to amuse him has been thrown away.

The boys are already looking much better. We have got a second and bigger pony for them.

.   .   .   .   .   .

Believe me,
With all kindest remembrances to you both,
Most truly yours,
EMILY TENNYSON.

RT. HON. W. E. GLADSTONE TO T. WOOLNER

Hawarden,
December 26, 1865.

DEAR MR. WOOLNER

I have not by me the Act respecting the New Law Courts : but I do not know that the First Comm^r of Works has any *Status* in the Commission except that of a member : and I am of opinion that the controul of the Treasury is chiefly general and financial.

For my own part I am unable to follow the general course of proceedings : but I give attention when needed through the Two Treasury members. As regards Mr. Waterhouse personally I gather that there is a very favourable feeling towards him : but that his surrender of the duty of framing the block plans was reluctantly required as absolutely necessary to secure anything like equality of footing.

As regards competition, I have no strongly formed opinion : but this question is one which I think could only be raised in the sense you desire, by the legal & independent members of the Commission. While I am very sensible of the force of the considerations which you urge, I can only offer to send your letter, if you think fit, to the Lord Chancellor, the head of the Commission.

Wishing you & Mrs. Woolner a happy Christmas—
I remain most faithfully yours
W. E. GLADSTONE.

I think G. Hardy would make a very good bust, Still if they put him opposite to me in the Bodleian I hope mine will run away.

WILLIAM ALLINGHAM TO T. WOOLNER

Lymington,
February 18, 1866.

MY DEAR WOOLNER,

I should be thankful for a line or two from you, how are you all? & how manage the Tennysons in their new circumstances? I had a pleasant walk of 5 miles with T, when he passed thro' here. The Wight is now to me "a dissolute island" (as we say), totally uninhabited, yet it looks pretty to-day, blue gray hills behind the slip of blueish sea, and there's greenness and sunshine on the Hampshire foreground. What wind, what wet we have had. Many a fine tree lies uprooted. Pylewell Park yesterday looked like a battlefield of the Giants, huge elms lay cumbering the torn sward. I would you were here this fine day for a walk & talk.

Ireland's fit of illness goes on, not a fever, but a fit of mumps or boils, as it were, ugly and disagreeable. A brother of mine who manages a bank in Waterford thinks too much has been made of Fenianism by the authorities. On the peasantry he thinks it has no hold at all. Certainly if the Gov^t are going to make concessions to Ireland just now, they ought also to make repressions, & show the kind hand as a strong hand. *Ireland and England cannot properly be governed alike.* I liked Gladstone's speech in the Irish Debate, but he or anybody could scarcely venture to take steps of needful boldness in the matter.

Always yours,
W. ALLINGHAM.

I beg leave to present my best respects to your wife & daughter, tho' as yet unintroduced.

The Oratory,
Birmingham,
March 1, 1866.

MY DEAR MRS. COMBE,

Thank you for your very kind letter. . . . As to your proposal that I should sit to Mr. Woolner, as you may suppose, at first it startled me—but it is too kind and too flattering to admit of my declining it—and you must say so, if you please, with my most sincere acknowledgments to Mr. Combe. . . .

[This is an extract from a letter of Dr. Newman's to Mrs. Combe.]

Dr. John Henry Newman to T. Woolner

The Oratory,
Birmingham,
June 9, 1866.

My dear Sir,

I propose, if all is well, presenting myself to you on Tuesday morning the 19th at any hour you may fix after eleven. And then I will come to you, as you wish, morning after morning, till you have done with me. And I will not forget the photographs.

Very truly yours,
JOHN H. NEWMAN.

Thos. Woolner, Esq.

F. T. Palgrave to T. Woolner

Sea View House,
Swanage,
September 14, 1866.

Dear Woolner,

. . . Gifford in his hasty notes before leaving, mentioned seeing you, and I hope you managed to have a pleasant evening or two together. He has not yet exhausted all the *stimulus* of his character, & would not heartily acquiesce in an English life at present : yet it is with great regret that we see him leave us again : and I am sure he will have wanted all the encouragement of his friends to inspirit him for the Euxine. . . . We hope to send the children to London on Wednesday next & to go ourselves to Salisbury, Glastonbury, & Wells : returning to York Gate on Monday. . . . We have had but a discomfortable autumn, but like this place extremely. It is much like Freshwater only on a larger scale & with a total freedom from Cockneys & . . .

Ever very truly yours,
F. T. PALGRAVE.

I have begun an essay on Crabbe, and find it very interesting work.

T. Woolner to F. T. Palgrave

September 16, 1866.

Dear Frank,

. . . I was glad to hear from Giffy that you liked the place you are at so well and which he seemed also to

"GODIVA," 1878

[To face page 273.

have enjoyed very much. He looked rather dull at the leaving all his old friends for such a bleak region, and for an indefinite time : he could not do with rest as his daily life for the present, I am sure, but he has had of moving about rather more than even his restlessness can digest comfortably. I spent a very pleasant evening with him and your other brothers, who had come up to wish the traveller God-speed—and he also came to our house two evenings. . . . I have finished Prescott's model; Mrs. Prescott says it is perfect, and that all the friends she has sent to see it speak not only in praise but in rapture of it. It is a satisfaction to have pleased her and this was not an easy task; it is of course quite a different looking thing to when you saw it. I have been working hard at Fowler's bust and have done save a little scraping in holes and corners. . . .

Yours ever,
T. WOOLNER.

WILLIAM ALLINGHAM TO T. WOOLNER

Lymington,
October 5, 1866.

MY DEAR WOOLNER,

Many thanks for your friendly note of some time ago. I have been intending to write, but now that I begin, have little more to say than to wish you all good luck in your visit to Italy. You are not quite gone yet I suppose ? Who knows but one of my winter days here will be brightened up by a letter from Rome, at least I will hope so.

The Tennysons came back to Farringford, I have not seen them but hear they are pretty well. . . . We have had wet and stormy weather, then a few fine days, almost too hot, now grey and misty sky over the changing woods.

Poor unlucky Ireland has again a bad harvest and is in very low spirits, the only relief, as usual, for her children an escape to America. No people want good governing so much as the Irish, or would (even yet, however late) take with it better but alas ! I go on reading old Irish History and shall perhaps get some light upon it. As to writing upon it, or on anything (save for the market) that is a thankless task. However, one goes on, and finds compensation.

Any chance at all of your running down here for a couple of days before you start ? I long for a long walk and talk,

T

and we could go over to Farringford. Did you see a paper of mine on Clough in last *Fraser?* Mrs. Clough wished me to write, I think, but most probably will not be satisfied. 'Tis inadequate certainly—very, but honest, and that's all about it. A paper in *Cornhill* (by whom?) takes nearly the same view of A.H.C.

Kindest regards I beg leave to send to your Wife and Daughter and with best wishes remain,

Always truly yours,
W. ALLINGHAM.

WILLIAM ALLINGHAM TO T. WOOLNER

Lymington,
December 12, 1866.

MY DEAR WOOLNER,

I went over and saw Tennyson the day before yesterday. All well at Farringford intending as you know to go after Christmas to lodgings at a farm house in Surrey. Mrs. Tennyson told me that you are expected at Farringford for Christmas, and asked me too, but I was booked some time ago to go to London for that holiday. 'Tis only for three or four days and I hope I shall find you hereabouts on my return. Pray tell me your plans, I should be sorry to miss you.

An intimation came the other day of my election to the Century Club, which no doubt I to owe you, so please be thanked accordingly. . . .

I am digging away at old Irish Annals, plenty of materials, but O in such confusion! I can't possibly get the books &c here which I want; none to borrow, a few must be bought painfully! others waited for.

Tell me, is Carlyle in London, and will he be at Christmas? I am specially desirous to know this.

What changes of weather we have, Saturday bright and frosty, Sunday muggy and overcast, Monday bright and springlike, Tuesday general fog, Wednesday mild and moist. But this is not amusing and I am come to the end of my tether, so pray accept kind regards for your wife, children and self from

Yours always,
W. ALLINGHAM.

My friends in Ireland don't express any alarm about the Fenians, it is chiefly no doubt an American game.

T. WOOLNER TO WILLIAM ALLINGHAM.

29, *Welbeck Street, W.,*
February 9, 1867.

MY DEAR ALLINGHAM,

I could not as I expected find time to send you a letter from Rome and was unable to send to any one save my wife, & had to write to her when I was so tired I could scarcely do anything but sleep.

But tho' I did not write I bore you in mind and when I went to visit the grave of Shelley I gathered a violet from it to send you; but now the poor shrivelled little thing seems a mockery and makes me almost ashamed to send it; but it will serve to show you my will was good to write tho' my opportunity was nil.

It was a lovely bright morning and tho' January the flowers were so gay, the grass so cheerful, and the tall cypresses looked so stately and sentinel-like that you felt it would be no great mischance to lie snugly there among the English dead—I went also to the grave of Keats and there were no flowers growing upon it; but there was a ragged, weedy, half wild look which in the warm balmy sunshine made it some way seem appropriate to the shade of the lovely young poet. I lingered round it and felt as if I were leaving a dearly loved friend when I had to go. I cannot attempt to explain or give an account of the Art of Italy; it would take three volumes of large proportions to tell you all my opinions, and would take many months to condense those opinions into the bounds of a letter! I must reserve chat on this and many other subjects till I have my long-wished-for walk with you in the New Forest, and I hope this year will be more fortunate to me in this respect than years and seasons have been heretofore.

When you have a few minutes tell me how you are going on, and what you are working at. I saw Carlyle at Mentone and was delighted to find the dear old fellow in good spirits, and Lady Ashburton was rejoiced in having the mighty man to pet and honour and make cosily comfortable. He was deeply grieved at the terrible loss [1] of poor Hunt and said it contained all the elements of a tragic event. I saw Gladstone at Florence and he was leaving that day for England; he seemed to have produced a strong impression upon the Italians. Hunt was plunging deep down into

[1] Death of his wife, Fanny.

work hoping to keep the hard fixed sorrow at a kind of bay. . . . Rome is the most interesting town I was ever in save and except London, which I consider the most interesting town that has ever existed on the earth, but if I were given £1000 a year to dwell there I would refuse to do so—therefore a philosopher like you will conclude there are some objections in the place. . . .

Ever yours,
THOMAS WOOLNER.

WILLIAM ALLINGHAM TO T. WOOLNER

Lymington,
February 20, 1867.

MY DEAR WOOLNER,

Your letter was welcome, and welcome are you back to England, and thrice welcome shall you be at Lymington when you can come down. The forest is budding, primroses out in warm nooks, birds singing loudly &c. Many thanks for the Shelley violet. I have some weakness for relics and reminders. The important things however are what one preserves in memory and experience wherefore I envy you (in a friendly sense) your trip to Rome, short as it was, and dirty as that town no doubt is.

.   .   .   .   .   .

When will you come? I must bed you out. I am going on more or less (rather less than more) with Irish affairs, feel discouraged too often and can't believe I can do anything worth while. Poor Hunt's is a very sad loss. Kindest regards to your wife and babes from

Yours always,
W. ALLINGHAM.

I noted in the *Athenæum* that your beautiful " Mother and Child " is gone to South Kensington.

N.B.—Had you lived four hundred years ago you would have done supernatural ditto. But the natural is the true miracle.

CHAPTER XVI

GIFFORD PALGRAVE TO T. WOOLNER

Goukhoum-Kalé,
February 17, 1867.

DEAR WOOLNER,

The news I saw in the Papers a few days since reporting the death of your Sister-in-law at Florence, grieved me most deeply. I know that letters are in such cases poor consolers, still you and your family may like to know that you have some one who sympathizes most sincerely with your sorrow, even in this out of the way corner of the Black Sea Coast. Where I now am we are surrounded by death and illness, thanks to the marsh-fever . . . Of about 1500 soldiers the average deaths are $2\frac{1}{2}$ a day. Some how or other my own health is excellent, but I am quite an exception here. Perhaps it is riding and shooting that keeps me well : certainly not society, for here is none. But horses are cheap, and wild-duck plenty.

To give you an idea of the people of the land I send you a photograph of one, the cloak is sheepskin, so is the head-dress, the things on the breast are cartridges. When I next come to England I hope to bring with me for you some better worth having. But the inhabitants are no beauties in general. . . . Affectionate remembrance to Mrs. Woolner and yourself.

Ever yours most truly,
W. GIFFORD PALGRAVE.

EDWARD FITZGERALD TO T. WOOLNER.

Market Hill,
Woodbridge,
March 8 [1867].

SIR,

Donne tells me that you have been so good as to superintend the Packing of your Tennyson Bust : which reached me safe yesterday. For which allow me to thank you : as also for the loan of the Box. . . .When it came, a young Sailor, a great Friend of mine happened to be with me, and helped to lift the Poet out of the (saw) dust, when this was done, I said to my Man—" There is what is called A Poet, who 25 or 30 years ago might have stood up to fight you." He said " Well, sir, he's a grand looking Gentleman, and no mistake." I used to tell A.T. in those Days he had something of the Air & Look of a Sailor : and meant no ill compliment. The Sailor I now speak of is a moving statue of Strength and Pliancy too ; like one of the Elgin Marbles. . . . And this Man has a large simple, soul and Dignity of Manner, all of a piece : much more *The Gentleman* than the gentlefolks of the Place he belongs to : and very much more Ladylike than the Ladies.

Your much obliged,
EDWARD FITZGERALD.

MRS. COMBE TO T. WOOLNER.

The Clarendon Press,
May 10 [1867].

MY DEAR MR. WOOLNER,

We rejoiced to learn from Miss Smith that you were better. Do not retard from recovery by over work.[1]   I was sorry Alice was away when Miss Smith called. It is always a pleasure to her to see " The Creature," with whom she has fallen passionately in love, if only for a few minutes. . . .

Remember we are hoping to see you some early Saturday, and Alice and the children next month. Our warm love attends you all.

Believe me,
Yours affectionately
M. COMBE.

F. T. PALGRAVE TO T. WOOLNER

Mrs. Porter's,
Lyme Regis,
August 27, 1867.

DEAR WOOLNER,

I have waited to write till we should have seen Seaton, which we accomplished yesterday, *i.e.* Cecil, A.

---

[1] Woolner had suffered a bad attack of inflammation of the eyes, through overwork and straining the eyes working by artificial light, which in later years he gave up entirely.

Tennyson, & I. (He came over on Saturday & in a day or two he & I mean to go for a walk to Dartmoor, where there is some idea that Allingham will join us) . . . A T. & I walked to Beerhead, and had a very fine view of the Devonshire coast to Start Point, *i.e.* 40 miles. The drive hence to Seaton is also very pretty. We are well pleased with Lyme, which has more variety than Seaton, & as our little house is right on the beach which is sand, not only pebbles, it is the very thing for the children. . . . There is a sort of undercliff here made by landslips which is one of the wildest & richest scenes I know in England, & might last a landscape painter for years. . . . Wish us good weather for Dartmoor. The bard is very well & sends you all remembrances. . . Were you at the wedding? [1]

Ever thine,

F. T. PALGRAVE.

T. WOOLNER TO F.T. PALGRAVE

29, Welbeck Street, W.,
August 28, 1867.

DEAR PALGRAVE,

I am glad to have so good an account of Lyme for its own account and for the good it is doing you all. . . . I have been working hard at " Virgilia " [2] and shall get her done I hope this week. She creates quite an enthusiasm; Francis, who was here a few days back, declares he thinks it the finest piece of female form and style since the Fates were sculptured by the Immortal. This of course is mere ecstasy, but as all who see it say something of the sort, and moreover that it is utterly unlike anything else, I am bound to hope it may strike the knowing with respect. . . .

I was at the Peel Wedding; it was a pretty business. I thought Lady Amberley very bright and amusing.

Ever yours,

THOS : WOOLNER.

[1] Wedding of Archibald Peel.
[2] The alto-relief carved in marble for Louisa Lady Ashburton, who gave the commission. It represents " Virgilia bewailing the Banishment of Coriolanus." His arms are in her keeping. She has been gazing on a bas-relief on the wall of her chamber in which he appears as he " fluttered the Volscians in Corioli," and, overwhelmed with bitterness, she flings herself against the wall.

T. WOOLNER TO MRS. TENNYSON

29, *Welbeck Street, W.*,
December 8, 1867.

MY DEAR MRS. TENNYSON,
    I knew you would like to know of a bit of good luck
in the worldly professional sense—I am to execute the
London statue of Lord Palmerston for Palace Yard, the
finest site in the whole of London, which, of course, was
decided on when W. Cowper was Com : of Works, and he
naturally looked out for his own. The matter was placed
entirely in his hands, and his admiration for my Godley
statue would allow him to think of no other sculptor for
the veteran Statesman. Any sculptor would have crawled
100 miles on hands and knees to have got this commission.

        .   .   .   .   .   .

    I have had such an amount of admiration for " Elaine "
that I fear to show another figure, for it seems to me
impossible again, or at least soon again, to satisfy persons'
feelings so fully. The explanation is that the spectators
add the natural pathos and beauty of the story itself to my
sculpture, and thus credit me with the merit of the most
lovely love story in the world, together with all the glow
and genius which the Bard has given it. I enclose you
an account of " Elaine " from the *Athenæum*. Pray do
not hold me accountable for this paper; it was done by
an enthusiastic admirer, an old gentleman I have only seen
once or twice, but who declares that I must before long have
the world at my feet, or the sun in my pocket, or something
of the kind, and sent a few of these slips &c. to tell me he had
sent them to the newspapers all over America, in order that
the van of the human race should be made acquainted with
the latest birth of time !

        .   .   .   .   .   .

    When is the Bard really coming so far as you can guess,
for that of course is the most even you can do ?
                            Ever truly yours,
                                THOS : WOOLNER.

DR. JOSEPH HOOKER TO T. WOOLNER

Royal Gardens, Kew,
December 11, 1867.

DEAR OLD WOOLNER,
    I am very sorry to hear you are so poorly—there is
nothing like change of air for a cold or influenza. My

CAPTAIN COOK
Colossal Statue for Sydney, 1878.

[*To face page* 280.

wife has cured hers by the change to the *beastly* climate of Cambridge! Can you not come here & rusticate for a few days? . . .

Ever sincerely yrs.
JOS : D. HOOKER.

Mrs. Tennyson writes : March 6, 1868. " Joy to you, my dear Mr. Woolner, on your great good fortune, may it be only the beginning." This refers to a picture he had just bought and of which he was very proud. He began about this date to collect paintings.

There are several passages in contemporary memoirs suggesting he made a great deal of money by buying and selling pictures [1]—it was not his picture collecting that enabled him (as one writer states) " to die a wealthy man," though the term " wealthy " is a matter of opinion, but the result of hard work at his art for over forty years. Another contemporary went so far as to say " he dissipated his energies in making a collection of pictures." One has only to look at the list of works in this Life to realize how absolutely false and misleading this statement is. Since Woolner returned from Australia in 1854 all the large statues and monuments, all the busts and most of the ideal work were done, all in fact save the early plaster models done between 1842 and 1852 when he left England. The picture collecting was an expensive hobby rather than a source of wealth; and although often he received a higher price for a picture than he gave for it; in some cases he paid much more than the picture fetched in later days. Being an enthusiast, if he admired a picture and wanted it he would buy it without considering much the consequences—for fashion rules much in pictures as in other matters and whereas the beautiful works of Mulready fetched high prices thirty years ago they are now considered old fashioned and deemed of small worth. Woolner was an enthusiastic collector and really felt the joy of discovering in some out

[1] This mention of money at all, is only touched upon to correct erroneous statements that have crept about through several agencies, and, in fact, the money left did not represent by thousands what he had earned by his sculpture.

of the way spot a dirty old painting, bringing it back, cleaning it and finding it a treasure. It is the same with all collectors : the discovery of the unexpected is so delightful : just as the conchologist rejoices in finding an uncommon shell in a little heap of wet sand or pebbles and the philatelist when looking over bundles of letters sees a rare stamp on an old envelope, so does the picture collector exult in his find. Woolner had the enthusiasm of collecting in him, he collected many things besides pictures : engravings enamels, bronzes, china, and Japanese ivories and lacquers, in fact anything he thought beautiful. Adding to his collection was one of his greatest pleasures and recreations in London, after the day's work was done, for Work was his aim in life—the very reason of existence to his mind ; Work was almost a religion with him. " L'enthousiasme c'est la seule vertu " (Rostand) is almost a truth and certainly without it nothing great is achieved. Woolner studied the works of the great Masters, chiefly of the English School, with a thoroughness that characterized all he undertook. His opinion on pictures was sought by his friends and others, but as with his sculpture antagonistic critics arose to disparage his collection and his judgment ; and would behind his back " damn with faint praise " many of the works in his possession—but whatever has been said to the contrary Woolner made a collection of very beautiful pictures, the bulk of which has now been dispersed.

Mrs. Tennyson to T. Woolner

Farringford,
Freshwater, I. W.,
March 26, 1868.

My dear Mr. Woolner,
    The magnificent looking wild boar ham has arrived. I mean to prove myself no " bird of Paradise " if this needed proof, by partaking of what has always seemed to me a romantic dish. How should it not be, when it recalls to one the *Odyssey* and all sorts of beautiful myths and actual wilds and forests besides !

.   .   .   .   .   .

I beg you without a moment's delay to insure your pictures if you have not already done so. One is positively afraid of some Nemesis after so much good fortune. No, I am not. I have a kind of feeling that good fortune is good for you, and if so, I am sure that you will have it, for have we not all what is best for us?

With our love and best thanks,
Very sincerely yours,
EMILY TENNYSON.

I mean to have the ham cooked in wine and kept for some choice occasion if possible.

CHARLES DARWIN TO T. WOOLNER

Down, Bromley,
Kent, S.E.,
March 10 [1869].

MY DEAR MR. WOOLNER,
Very many thanks for the drawing : it does excellently—The " Woolnerian tip " is worth anything to me.

Yours very sincerely,
CH. DARWIN.

The infolded point of the human ear discovered by Woolner, described in the *Descent of Man.* It was when modelling his " Puck " Woolner noticed the little pointed tips that are seen in so many ears, and he exaggerated these in the statuette to a fawn-like ear giving an impish look. When Mr. Darwin sat to him he imparted to the great Naturalist his ideas on his discovery.

W. E. DARWIN TO T. WOOLNER

Southampton,
June 7 [1869 ?].

DEAR MR. WOOLNER,
The Medallion has come quite safe.
It makes a remarkably fine medallion and I like it very much—I am sure it cannot give the Wedgwoods much trouble. I do not know whether I should send this to the Wedgwoods or whether the original you have should go to them, or the reversed cast.

Yours very truly,
W. E. DARWIN.

T. WOOLNER TO MRS. TENNYSON

29, *Welbeck Street, W.,*
December 19, 1869.

MY DEAR MRS. TENNYSON,

Will you please give my best thanks to the Bard for
"The Holy Grail" which he kindly sent. I am heartily
glad to find that it is already become so popular; for I
find nothing but golden opinions of it on *all* sides: I
heard one man say that he did not know but that it was
the finest thing he had ever done. . . . I heard an anecdote
to the credit of a publisher. Morris did not like his old
ones and went to a new man—a few days back he went
to have a settlement and expected 20 or 30£, but what was
his astonishment to find placed in his hands a cheque for
£600 ! ! ! . . . .

Ever truly yours,
T. WOOLNER.

Extracts from a Long Letter from Edward Lear to T. Woolner.

Maison Guichârd,
Cannes,
May 1, 1870.

DEAR WOOLNER,

As I am not likely to see you & Mrs. Woolner this
summer. . . . I shall send a line or two, in hopes that one
day you may post one in return. I have had a long letter
from Daddy. . . . In the last letter I had written to him I
find I have knocked my head against a wall; for supposing
that he was—as he used to be—of what you & I should call
" advanced or liberal principles " in religious matters, I had
spoken about the increase of rationalistic & antimiraculous
thought, & hoped his future pictures would point or express
such progress. Whereas I find I never made a greater mistake, & that on the contrary, he is becoming a literalist
about all biblical lore, & has a holy horror of Darwin,
Deutsch . . . meanwhile if he should paint Balaam's Ass
or Gideon's Fleece it will not surprise me. . . . What are
you yourself about? & how is Mrs. Woolner & all your
children? also my little brother Cyril.[1] . . . How did you,
& how did the friends whose names you so goodnaturedly
procured as subscribers like my Corsica book? . . . What

[1] Son of Holman Hunt, aged three and a half years.

do you think as I have been & gone & done? I grow so tired of noisy lodgings, & yet am so more & more unable to think of ever wintering in England—& so unable to bear the expense of two houses & two journies annually that I have bought a bit of ground at San Remo & am actually building a house there. It was to have been like this—only the architect wouldn't let me carry out my simple principles of Art. 1. Dining Room. 2. Drawing Room. 3. Staircase window. 4. Hall windows. 5. Street-door. 6 & 7. Back & front bells. I regret extremely that I have been prevented from building on the plan. My house will be done in November, & then I shall get all my Stratford Place furniture . . . out by steamer . . . & so I shall begin 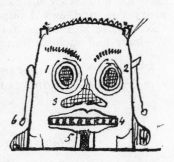 life again for the 5th & last time. As I have sold no drawings this winter & have no commissions ahead, I shall endeavour to live upon little Figs. in summertime & on worms in the winter. I shall have 28 olive trees & a small bed of onions : & a stone terrace, with a gray Parrot & 2 hedgehogs to walk up & down on it by day & by night. Anyhow I shall have a good painting room with an absolute North light. . . the room being 32 feet long by 20 broad. I hope some day you & Mrs. Woolner may see me there. . .

Yours sincerely,
EDWARD LEAR.

MRS. TENNYSON TO T. WOOLNER

Aldworth,
Black Down,
Haslemere,
October 4, 1870.

MY DEAR MR. WOOLNER,

. . . Would that some creative brain of some great Statesman could devise a mode of vital union between England and her Colonies so that they might indeed be one.

First, I would have every man among us trained to arms that we might keep the peace, then I would have everyone taught to read and write and sing and cypher, whether

he would or no or whether his parents would or no, then I
would have one great Council formed of men from all the
Colonies from England or rather Great Britain. These
should originate legislative measures for discussion in a
really imperial Parliament, which should I hope decide
how best to give most to each other, not how to keep most
each for himself or his Colony or his island; but I shall
weary you, and soon I hope you will come and talk to us
about these and other matters. I am exceeding weary.
We have had such an uninterrupted stream of guests.

.   .   .   .   .   .

Kindest remembrances to Mrs. Woolner and to " Guinivere " [1] whom A. admires much.

Most sincerely yours,

EMILY TENNYSON.

T. WOOLNER TO MRS. TENNYSON

29, *Welbeck Street, W.,*
October 9, 1870.

MY DEAR MRS. TENNYSON,
          I wish you were the Queen of England with Bacons
and Raleighs and Walsinghams to carry out your glorious
ideas, in which I need hardly say I most heartily sympathize; and none the less so because there is not the remotest
chance of their being carried out. . . .

The truth is we are a sinking people, and every sign shows
it. England has commuted her chivalrous sword by which
she gained and maintained kingdoms to a money-bag,
which she turns towards and falls down to worship, leaving
her back exposed to her enemies.

There was a time when thieves, and coarse ruffians were
called the " dangerous classes," and they are still called
so by the unthinking : but the dangerous classes are . . .
the other innumerable hosts of doctrinaires who would
put down war and make the country rich !—Rich indeed :
the King of Lydia was rich in gold; I wonder when his
enemy came and took his gold, and killed him if he remembered Solon's phrase about the value of iron ?—

These doctrinaire gentlemen mean us to lose our Colonies
one by one; and they mean India certainly to go; they
will if they can, give Ireland a constitution of their own;
and above all things here in England they mean to set Jack

---

[1] By request of Tennyson an engraving of the statue of " Guinivere "
was made as frontispiece to *The Idylls.*

[Photograph by H. Dixon.

RT. HON. W. E. GLADSTONE, 1883
Marble Bust in Guildhall.

[To face page 287.

above his master; their process for effecting this will be one they are pleased to call Universal Suffrage. They have already allowed their chief tradesman orator to announce officially from his high place on the Governmental seat, that false weights and measures are things that ought not to be interfered with, and that it would be gross tyranny to do so; and therefore, considering that there has been no official repudiation of this announcement, and that the orator is getting still his £5000 a year shows that the nation acquiesces. We may regard in spirit England's degradation completed. We cannot fight these things that get into the grain of the wood : the tree may bear lightning, or the wrestle of a thousand storms, but when the worm once enters the grain, its fall is then only a question of time. We worship commonplace men, and rich men, and quack men, and worse than all clever, good, doctrinaire men . . . who are ruining the greatness of our country on philosophical principles, and the only difference between whom and blood-stained ferocious republicans is, that the last drive you headlong into anarchy and ruin, whereas the others organize your road to destruction.—All of which things you know as well as I do; only such ideas being old and of a past age I dare not say them without exciting wrath or pity from any but a very few, and it is a comfort to say a word of truth to one who can feel a glow of England's ancient glory. My love to the Bard.

Ever yours,
T. WOOLNER.

EDWARD FITZGERALD TO T. WOOLNER.

Market Hill,
Woodbridge,
Tuesday, October (25) [1870].

DEAR SIR,

To-day we send you off the little Churchyard,[1] which won't take up much room if it does not give you much pleasure. It is not very *luminous*, as you will see, but, I think, touched with grace, one of many such little bits as he used to do, on the back of a cigar box, which I think made rather a good ground for his colour. Now, this is such a little thing that I don't wish you to spend your time writing thanks for it, only let me know if it *doesn't* reach

---

[1] A Suffolk painter.

you. I wish I had a little Nursey to send you; I have two or three rather larger ones (for which reason you might not care to have one of them) and they are not his best.

These amateurs—and I think all Painters except the best, are best in their slight sketches, done at a heat. They nearly always *muddle* when they get to working up in cold blood.

The trees are in fine colour now. And last night we had an Aurora well worth being out of London, or even Paris, to behold. " First came a white *Beam*, and then came a Rose " shelving the white one away Eastward, and then the rose followed catching up the Pleiads and Jupiter below them, and there was a grand Sword-dance half over the sky, more like Beams of Goliath than Swords, however.

Yours truly,
E. FITZGERALD.

CHARLES DARWIN TO T. WOOLNER

Down, Beckenham,
Kent, S.E.,
April 7 [1871].

MY DEAR MR. WOOLNER,

I daresay you often meet & know well painters. Could you persuade some *trustworthy* men to observe young & inexperienced girls who serve as models, & *who at first blush much*, how low down the body the blush extends. . . . Moreau says a celebrated French painter once saw a new model blushing all over her body. So that I want much to hear what the experience is of cautious & careful English artists : I always distrust memory—can you aid me ?

The tips to the ears have become quite celebrated. One Reviewer (Nature) says they ought to be called, as I suggested in joke, Angulus Woolnerianus.

A great German physiologist is very proud to find that he has the tips well developed & I believe will send me a photograph of his ears; & if a good case, I think I would have it photographed on wood engraved for new Edit. Making of course no change in my text.

Yours very sincerely,
CH. DARWIN.

CHAPTER XVII

WOOLNER was elected an Associate of the Royal Academy in 1871, and it was in this year the great Lord Lawrence came to sit to Woolner, who modelled two busts of him : the first portrait was treated in a classical manner and was without drapery; the second had a cloak around the shoulders decorated with the Star of India, and it is this bust, which, carved in marble, in 1880 was placed in Westminster Abbey, where Lord Lawrence was buried.

In the same year (1871) as the first bust was made Woolner began a sketch of a statue of Lord Lawrence— he was a magnificent subject for such a work. The statue, in which dignity and grace are blended, was cast in bronze and erected at Calcutta during his lifetime.

Of the works exhibited at the Royal Academy by Woolner in 1872, the most important was his marble statue of Sir Bartle Frere, the distinguished Governor of Bombay, in which city it was erected shortly afterwards in his honour. Woolner had had sittings from Sir Bartle Frere in 1868 for the bust shown in 1869, and the sculptor had always the keenest admiration for this great man, and their friendship, begun in 1868, lasted until Sir Bartle Frere's death.

Shown at the same time was the alto-relief " In Memoriam G. B.," which represents a beautiful boy in Paradise, seated beneath the branches of a jessamine tree, listening and waiting for his parents to join him.

At the Royal Academy was seen, besides other works, the marble bust of Charles Dickens, an elaborate piece of carving—the Sculptor had known the novelist personally, and their mutual friend Mr. Novelli had given Woolner the commission to make a bust of him; and he had been looking forward with pleasure to modelling the portrait

U   289

when unhappily Dickens's death prevented a bust from the life being executed; and Woolner was summoned to Gad's Hill to the sad task of taking a death mask of the author in 1870—from which he modelled the likeness.

The four bas-reliefs for the decoration of the fountain in memory of Mrs. George Moore, representing the Four Acts of Mercy, were exhibited also this year.

T. WOOLNER TO F. T. PALGRAVE

29, *Welbeck Street, W.,*
August 11, 1872.

DEAR PALGRAVE,

. . . . I met Fechter at a smoking party last night and was interested in the downright honest as well as keenly true opinions he expressed about sculpture. He was a sculptor for some years, he told me, and was sent to Rome for getting a chief prize : but he thought Sculpture in such a horrible state, and so wholly in the world of jobbery that he could not live such an unwholesome and painful life; and much to the indignation and grief of his father he turned actor and has enjoyed life accordingly. . . .

Wishing you sunny weather—all other good following in course.

Ever yours,
T. WOOLNER.

MRS. TENNYSON TO T. WOOLNER

Aldworth,
Black Down,
Haslemere,
October 29, 1872.

MY DEAR MR. WOOLNER,

It was a great pleasure to me to see your handwriting once again, and I must write without delay to thank you for this and for the stately " Guinivere," and to tell you how very sincerely I congratulate you on the acquisition of that fairy estate.[1] Surely such a place in such a stream and such names for itself and the village, can come to you from no cloddish son of earth. A. will be dreadfully jealous of the stream. I must look in the map and see whether you are within our ken. Be this as it may, I wish

[1] Cranesden, Mayfield.

you both and all the greatest possible enjoyment of your new possession and for the longest possible time.

.   .   .   .   .   .

Our dear old Hallam having leave from about 1 yesterday posted off here to see me, and our Lionel had also had leave from Saturday to Monday, but the brothers missed seeing each other. I wish that you could see them and we you all. A strange change in them since you were " the sculptor with the golden beard." I am so very glad that you like the Idyll.[1] It seems to me wonderfully fresh and young, to say nothing of other merits.

With my love to Mrs. Woolner,
Believe me ever,
Most sincerely yours,
EMILY TENNYSON.

This was a little estate, Cranesden, in the parish of Mayfield, Sussex. The house had formerly been a farm-house, and it is said John Maynard, Oliver Cromwell's chaplain, lived there—parts of the house were very old indeed, but the main building was Elizabethan; with the aid of his friend, the architect, Frederick Cockerell, Woolner added to it considerably, and altered it into a very charming place : an old house front from Shrewsbury was cleverly inserted in the southern wall, which was entirely in keeping with the style of architecture. Woolner had long wished to own a cottage in the country, and he laid out the grounds with great taste, and whenever he could snatch a few days' holiday, he would go down to superintend the earthworks, pond making and the planting of trees and shrubs. The house stood in about 80 acres of pasture and woodlands, and a stream ran through the copses rich in wild flowers. In the garden surrounded by sweetbriar, was a never-failing spring of the purest water. In past ages pilgrims, it is said, came to fill their bottles from it— probably on their way to Canterbury to the shrine of Thomas à Becket.

The parish church is dedicated to St. Dunstan, whose anvil and pincers are still preserved in the beautiful Old Palace, now a convent, of the Order of the Society of the

[1] " Gareth and Lynette."

Holy Child Jesus. A happy community of gracious ladies —many of the nuns devote a great part of their lives to education.

Cranesden was a house of old brick, and lay away from the village of Mayfield, which was considered by the poet Coventry Patmore "the prettiest village in Sussex." It was most picturesque, more than 500 feet above the sea, with the distinctive landmarks of the church spire and the tower of the convent. Since those days the railway has caused many new little houses to spring up, and the gas-lamps in the village rather take away from its mediæval appearance and the feeling of remoteness. Woolner, tired of the bothers of farm and land, sold Cranesden in 1882 to Lord Francis Hervey; this was a real grief to his young family, whose delight in the pretty place was unbounded.

T. WOOLNER TO VERNON LUSHINGTON

January 20, 1873.

MY DEAR VERNON,

I can scarcely tell you what I think of the death of your Father. You know he was always to me an especial admiration. His beautiful countenance, and his wisdom; his lofty nature together with childlike brightness; and the numberless valuable opinions and characteristic anecdotes that were his daily talk together made him so delightful to me, that had I been one of his own sons I could scarcely have loved and honoured him more.

His life has altogether been so beautiful and complete that to know of his end seems to me as it were the triumph over victory. It is not altogether sorrow I feel; it is rather pride that so perfect a life has become unassailable and is one of our guiding stars. This is something of what I feel when thinking of him : but how different when I think of you all. I most deeply feel with all you feel : and that the dear sun of your hospitable house has set.

It was a sad trial to my wife her Father's death; but she has been very brave.

It was most kind of you to write.

With truest sympathy,

Ever yours,

T. WOOLNER.

[*Photograph by H. Dixon.*

DOROTHY, 1883

[*To face page* 292

James Anthony Froude to T. Woolner

5, Onslow Gardens,
May 5 [1874].

My dear Woolner,

We are all agreed on the extreme beauty of your sketch—and if the execution of it lies within my means it will give me the greatest of the few melancholy pleasures now left to me if I can see that monument in St. Lawrence Church. We think it should not be larger than half size. I think myself the best size would be that of your beautiful statuette; the figure [1] twisting the flower into her hair.

. . . . . .

Ever yours most truly,
J. A. Froude.

We are all struck with the likeness which you contrived to catch even in a figure on so small a scale.

Woolner executed the monument in marble of Mrs. Froude. When it was finished in 1875 Mr. Froude wrote: "I have nothing to suggest. It is very beautiful, expressing the most perfect feeling in the most perfect way."

John Frederick Lewis, R.A., to T. Woolner

Walton-on-Thames,
May 4, 1874.

My dear Woolner,

Ill as I am—hardly able to hold the pen—I lose not a second in replying to yr astounding Letter.

I believe you to be the soul of honour or in my former healthy state of mind & body I should have thought you were jesting with my *supposed* Vanity—but I never was vain—I feel *now & have felt all my life* that tho' I did my best, all was futile. I can again say that I can hardly credit yr assertion that *such* a sum would have been offered (bonafide) for my honest, but unpretending work—your communication has upset me by its very kindness—its generous, its disinterested feeling has touched my very heart's core. Price [the owner] is a good man—he paid me my price for the picture—and I hope he is satisfied, *tho' I don't know.* However, he has behaved nobly by not pocketting his thousands. . . . The fact is, dear Woolner,

---

[1] The figure of "Love."

I am in dreamland. Forgive more, you are a fine noble
fellow & God bless you.

Most sincerely yours,

J. F. Lewis.[1]

T. Woolner, Esq., A.R.A.

T. Woolner to John Frederick Lewis, R.A.

29, Welbeck Street, W.,
May 17, 1874.

My dear Mr. Lewis,

Your letter was sent on to me at Paris, and greatly
delighted I was to know you were so pleased with the
appreciation of your wonderful picture. You do not
think so highly of your own work as your admirers, or you
would not be surprized at any amount being offered for
one of your chief pictures. I am sure Mr. Graham's offer
was *bona fide* as he asked me to find out if the possessor
would take the sum mentioned as he was willing to give it.
£10,000 is a large sum, but not much to a man worth
£100,000 a year, who wishes to gratify a keen taste. He
told me he had refused 6000 guineas for Turner's " Van
Goyen in search of a subject," and he gave 7000 for Gains-
boro's two ladies sold at Christie's last year, so that you
see he is not wedded to cash where taste is concerned.
. . . There are some delightful pictures in the Loan Coll:
at Paris, both old and modern. . . . There are the choice
works from private houses which will not be seen again by
the public. Ingres' best works are there.

Delaroche's best—the Murder of the Duke of Guise—
A wonderful portrait of a young man by Raphael. Two
fine portraits by Antonio More; superb Dutch landscapes,
and in fact to have an idea of the wealth there the Ex.
must be seen. The knic-knacs are superb and astonishing.

But I will not tire you with an account of all the delightful things I saw. It was particularly pleasant to me, for
my wife had never been on the Continent before, and everything was new as well as pleasant to her.

Gerome is very fine in the Salon this year, three pictures
are equally good—the mass there of course being fearful

---

[1] Many years after the Sculptor bought a picture by J. F. Lewis, R.A.,
of the " Khan Khalil Bazaar, Cairo," a most beautiful work of great
detail, and rich in colour and the atmosphere of an Eastern bazaar. The
picture was sold in 1895 at Messrs. Christie's.

rubbish. . . . The drawing of which so much is said, is mostly weak, and inexact, and vulgar.

With kindest wishes for your health,

Ever truly yours,

T. WOOLNER.

In June, 1874, the Hon. Henry (afterwards Sir Henry) Parkes, Premier of New South Wales, who had met Woolner when in Sydney in 1854, wrote to ask, if he, Woolner, would undertake to do a statue of Captain Cook for Sydney. The idea appealed very strongly to the Sculptor, who had a great admiration for the discoverer; and having himself spent many months in Sydney when a young man, knew the position the proposed statue was to occupy, and felt the keenest inclination to undertake the commission.

The following letter from Thomas Carlyle is the first of a series of letters about this commission, and from that time onwards were many communications to and from the Government at Sydney.

THOMAS CARLYLE TO T. WOOLNER

5, *Cheyne Row, Chelsea,*
June 10, 1874.

DEAR WOOLNER,

The enclosed letter came to me this morning in the inside of one from your old friend Parkes—who I believe is still what they call Premier at Sydney. He only seems to fear you may not be able to undertake the Captain Cook for £2000; in which sad case he asks me to " advise " who should be next applied to. I think it would be an excellent subject & well worthy of you, if you found the money offer sufficient.

In any case please communicate with Parkes as soon as possible, and let me know what you have decided on.

It is a long time since I have seen you and I myself, as is natural, go out less and less; but I hear always from time to time that everything is going well with you in your art & otherwise. Best success to you, now and ever.

Yours sincerely,

T. CARLYLE.

Owing to the height of the pedestal proposed, the statue had to be much larger than was at first contemplated, and a larger sum of money required in consequence. The lengthy correspondence in connection with the Cook Statue for two years would interest no one to read. The Agent General for New South Wales having qualms as to whether the right artist for this work had been chosen, suggested a competition in 1876 ! after Woolner had worked for many months at the design.

The opinion, on this proposition, of Sir Francis Grant, President of the Royal Academy, is expressed in his letter to Woolner dated February, 1876—

SIR FRANCIS GRANT, P.R.A., TO T. WOOLNER, R.A.

> 27, *Sussex Place,*
> *Regent's Park, N.W.,*
> *February* 11 [1876].

MY DEAR WOOLNER,
　　I am quite conversant with the correspondence which has taken place between you and Mr. Forster on behalf of the gentlemen in Australia concerning the proposed statue—and it appears to me after that correspondence to propose to throw the matter open to competition — would be an action quite unprecedented in my experience.

It would be quite unusual for any Sculptor of your eminence & acknowledged position—to enter into competition—under any circumstances. But after all that has passed—& the trouble you have already bestowed on the subject—I feel quite sure on further consideration and on a more intimate knowledge of the case they will not place you in such an unpleasant position.

> I am ever yours truly,
> FRANCIS GRANT.

Not until August did Woolner receive the official commission to execute a colossal Statue of 13 ft. for Sydney— the Statue to be in bronze. The Statue was finished in 1878, and was shewn to the public of London, in Waterloo Place.

William Allingham wrote a charming poem on it. (See June, 1878, letter to Mrs. Woolner.)

The Statue, which was much admired in London, was shipped to Australia in August—and the unveiling of the Cook Statue in February, 1879, was made the occasion of a great public holiday, and the *Sydney Morning Herald* describes " the ceremony of unveiling the Statue as the grandest spectacle which, as far as we have any knowledge, has yet taken place in Australia."

The Government Offices and the ships in harbour were gaily decorated with flags. Hundreds of people crowded into Sydney to see the ceremony, which was viewed by a crowd of over seventy thousand persons. A grand procession of sailors, marines and societies with their banners and bands having assembled around the Statue, the Governor, Sir Hercules Robinson, arrived, and before he made his speech " Rule, Britannia ! " was played and sung. Immediately after his Excellency's speech was concluded, he commanded the Statue to be unveiled, " and the men stationed near the Statue for the purpose of unveiling it, pulled the cord attached to the flag (which enveloped the Statue), and the bunting, unwinding itself from the figure on the pedestal, ran to the peak of a flagstaff and left the statue exposed to the view of the people, who greeted its appearance with loud cheering. At the same moment a merry peal rang out from the bells of St. Mary's Cathedral."

The singing of the National Anthem ended the ceremonial part of the day, but it was a long time before the people would leave the vicinity of the Statue—and hundreds lingered on to examine it.

The work won universal admiration in Australia, and is the largest statue Woolner ever designed and modelled.

T. WOOLNER TO JOHN FREDERICK LEWIS, R.A.

29, *Welbeck Street, W.,*
September 1, 1874.

MY DEAR MR. LEWIS,

Your generous soul will rejoice that poor Foley will have the last honour due to him, for our application has succeeded and he is to be buried in St. Paul's on Friday next at 12 o'clock.   He will lie close to Turner, Reynolds and James Barry, with only one grave between him and this noble company.   The sterling artists are fast passing away, and what the next generation will be like I tremble to contemplate.   With kindest wishes for your health.

Ever truly yours,

T. WOOLNER.

ALICE GERTRUDE WOOLNER, 1883

[*To face page* 299.

CHAPTER XVIII

In 1874 Woolner began to design the little Bluecoat Group for Christ's Hospital as a kind of challenge prize, the Coleridge Memorial, to be held each year by that Ward which had most distinguished itself in the work of the School during the previous year.

It was modelled early in January of 1875. The three boys represent Samuel Coleridge, Charles Lamb and Middleton. The work was partly a labour of love on Woolner's part, for the sake of the Reverend George C. Bell, headmaster of Christ's Hospital at that time, and afterwards head-master of Marlborough College, where Woolner sent his sons to be educated.

About this time, owing to distressing family reasons, which do not concern the general public, a complete break between Woolner and Holman Hunt took place.

JOHN FREDERICK LEWIS, R.A., TO T. WOOLNER

Walton-on-Thames,
November 21, 1874.

MY DEAR WOOLNER,

It causes me no little grief, when I think that my unfortunate position precludes my putting in an appearance at the R.A. on the 9th prox., but now I am almost deprived of locomotion ! It would have been to me *such* a *satisfaction* if I could have added my vote in yr. favor : but let us hope that you will not need it—and that a triumphant majority awaits you—so that my mite may not be necessary. . . .

Hoping you are well & with my respects to Mrs. Woolner, believe me,

to be always faithfully yours,
J. F. LEWIS.

T. WOOLNER, ESQ., A.R.A.

T. WOOLNER TO JOHN FREDERICK LEWIS, R.A.

29, *Welbeck Street, W.,*
November 22, 1874.

MY DEAR MR. LEWIS,

A letter from you comes like the sun thro' this dingy abomination called fog. It would have shocked me had I known such an idea as coming here this weather had even entered your head as a possibility.

So far as I am concerned election to R.A.ship is a point of no great consequence, as I care nothing for fancy titles, and do not like my time to be taken up by council meetings and the A.R.A.ship suits me very well indeed, as I get most of the fun and only a little of the work; indeed none, except teaching in the Life School which I like.

But whether I am elected or whether I am not, I would rather have had your kind and hearty letter, or your solitary vote, than nearly the whole voting of the Academy without it, or with yours in antagonism—. . .   I was going off to Venice to-morrow, but the friend [1] with whom I travel caught a sorethroat and now I have to wait till his Dr. lets him off. Except a fortnight in the Spring in Paris with my wife I have had no holiday this year and begin to feel stupid from constant work on monstrous big statues.

I gave your message to my wife, she was greatly pleased and told me whatever I said in return to " imply admiration," for you must know that she is as great an enthusiast for your work as I am myself.

Hoping for you all good,

Ever truly yours,

T. WOOLNER.

In November M. Alphonse Legros painted a portrait in oils of Woolner just before the Sculptor went on a tour on the Continent with his friend Dilberoglue. They visited Paris, Milan, Verona, whose beauties and treasures he fully enjoyed, Padua, where, he writes, the frescoes by Giotto in the Arena Chapel " I thought not only worthy of their fame, but less Archaic than I fancied from copies and

---

[1] Stauros Dilberoglue, a very delightful Greek friend, who was intimate with many of Woolner's circle. He was godfather to two of the Sculptor's children.

engravings. Among all the subjects and groups that I examined I did not find a single figure that went not straight to the purpose and intention of the work. I did not see an instance of straining for effect or of exaggeration of any kind. And in no case was a figure placed merely to fill up the composition. The chief figures are always placed to give the utmost importance without giving the impression of its having been done so : in fact I scarcely know if in the higher qualities of art the skill is not fully equal to [the] genius displayed throughout this wonderful series. The whole effect of the Chapel is luminous, refined and beatific, and is I should think the loveliest vision of the divine life on earth that was ever presented to the Mediaeval mind.

" In the Church of San Antonio, by the high altar stands a large Candelabrum by Andrea Riccio, which the guide-book says took the artist 10 years to make. It is the most sumptuous specimen of this class I have ever seen. The whole surface is covered with work of the richest kind, and balanced throughout with the nicest care, and wrought with unerring skill. But the quantity of material of art is so enormous, that no one can fully comprehend it as a whole; and it gives the impression as if a vast amount of thought and work were thrown away. How differently an old Greek artist would have designed a stand to hold lights ! A firm exquisitely designed base—a slender elegant stem, running up to branch forth into simple perfect utility; —and whatever figures or ornament were introduced pure and graceful as the buds of a white lily."

In Venice Woolner visited the important churches and saw all the notable paintings, the Saint Barbara of Palma Vecchio winning almost his greatest admiration, he calls it " this loveliest among the beauties of Venice." While there one evening twenty gondoliers sang under the window of the hotel where he was staying—one lady gave them a halfpenny !

On his return journey he went to all the art galleries of Munich—a note in his diary there states : " saw three girls fight like—dogs say ! " During his absence from England

he had been elected a Royal Academician, and he found
many letters of congratulation awaiting him on arriving
home.

T. Woolner to John Frederick Lewis, R.A.

29, *Welbeck Street, W.,*
January 17, 1875.

My dear Mr. Lewis,

It is all very well to say " do not answer this," but
I have too good a sense of my privileges to obey such an
injunction. In the " Apocrypha " I remember reading in
the days of my youth, " If thou knowest a wise man let
thy feet wear his doorstep," but as I cannot do this I may
help to wear out his door knocker.

Since my return from Venice my time has been wholly
taken up or I should have thanked you before for your
most kind and cordial letter as to my election. I have
as I said always had a shrinking from honours and committees, but now I am in the charmed circle, however I
may have got there, I must say that it is most gratifying
to find the hearty and friendly way in which I have been
welcomed by the Members, indeed they could not have
more clearly shown their satisfaction; with, of course, the
exception of the sculptors who looked sourly as usual tho'
to them I am always as amiable as one being can be to
another in ordinary life. . . .

Ever most truly yours,
T. Woolner.

John Frederick Lewis, R.A., to T. Woolner

Walton-on-Thames,
January 28, 1875.

My dear Woolner,

I have been ill enough of late to render me quite
incapable of writing—or I should have done so. I am
puzzled to know whom you allude to as " the wise man."
I doubt not that yr. " Apocryphal " friend is quite right—
but where *wisdom* is to be found is another " guess sort of
thing."

If I could pretend to wisdom, *then* shouldst thou wear
out my doorstep, but alas ! don't seek for it here when
you pass it, but be content & when you feel inclined to venture this way, a hearty welcome awaits you. I live here
like a Hermit awaiting my exit—with the dearest wife

in the world—disposed most charitably to all, & charmed to see my friends always. . . . Chantrey's £90,000 has just fallen to us. May God guide the men who will spend this money. Will they buy " Roll Calls "?. . . . I don't see much probability of my ever getting about again. I am nearly 71—so can't hope for much. That Blessed King David and 3 Score years & 10 is a bore—but I am thank God *very happy*. My respects & kind regards to Mrs. Woolner if she will deign to accept them. The same to you.

Sincerely yours,
J. F. Lewis.

Why " Mister " me ?

T. Woolner to John Frederick Lewis, R.A.

29, Welbeck Street, W.,
January 31, 1875.

My dear Lewis,

If you refuse being Mᵣed; I was much delighted with your kind letter and the hope it offered me of a pleasant glimpse of your happy life.

. . . .

I do not know what the authorities will do with Chantrey's gains, but I know that the Prince may praise and the papers may trumpet, but the Academy will not purchase " the Roll Call."

I hate the thought of 3 score years and 10 for some persons. . . . It is to me sad to think that now your genius has reached its highest glory you should be able to do less work than ever, and be tantalized with unsatisfied aspirations and unrealized visions of beauty. . . . I shall not wait for fine weather as that may be in the remote future, but, as you give permission, I shall run down to see you the first clear chance I can see. . . .

Most truly yours,
T. Woolner.

James Anthony Froude to T. Woolner

5, Onslow Gardens,
April 1 [1875].

My dear Woolner,

. . . .

I looked over the walls of St. Lawrence Church—we can have a choice of situation and at present there is every variety of light. . . . The position which I should prefer

. . . adjoins a window lately erected to the memory of my wife's father.

Ever faithfully yours,

J. A. FROUDE.

I have thought much of your Reredos. The robe blowing out is new & very fine. But if I were you I would invite opinion about the Vulture.[1] I distrust my own judgment too much to venture to give it you—but I am sure the approbation will not be unanimous.

Woolner executed a posthumous bust of Charles Kingsley, which was placed in Westminster Abbey in 1876. In 1875 Mrs. Kingsley wrote to the Sculptor: " My daughters tell me your bust is simply *magnificent, all they could* desire, and my heart bows down to you in gratitude. How he loved & delighted in your genius ! & hoped that the Westminster residence might bring him in contact with you for years to come ! "

Mrs. Kingsley was an invalid and never expected to see the marble bust. She had had a photograph of the bust sent her, and in a letter dated March 12, 1876, she writes—

" I thank you deeply, but only in my heart—words fail me. What a great artist you are. To me sculpture was always so much greater than painting, & if I had not always held this belief I sh^d now be convinced. If the photograph can be what it is—what must the marble be ? But that I shall never see." . . .

Woolner however decided she should have that pleasure, and went to the great risk of sending the marble bust down by rail to Byfleet for Mrs. Kingsley to see.

This kindly act was greatly appreciated by her. She expresses her admiration of the bust in a letter dated March 22, 1876—

My DEAR MR. WOOLNER,

It is wonderful. Especially the right side where there is the twinkle of humour about the lip, without which the grandeur even w^d have been imperfect. I cannot thank you. Words fail me.

---

[1] Apropos of this point Canon Liddon approved and said it was the only original idea on the subject for many years. The reredos represents the " Crucifixion."

Mrs. Kingsley admired the bust so much she asked the Sculptor's permission to have it engraved to illustrate one of the volumes of the Life of her husband.

T. WOOLNER TO MRS. LEWIS

29, *Welbeck Street,*
March 27, 1876.

MY DEAR MRS. LEWIS,
We were grieved to have your bad news of your glorious veteran; and the weather so abominable that I scarcely expect to have a better yet awhile. . . . You saw that my wife has returned, and the house has received its soul again. How she longs for cheery news, and to see you both again. Her day at your house is a memory steeped in romance, for your artist is her ideal of a splendid painter; and I am vain enough to think praise from her of value, as she gives it rarely. . . .
I have been too busy to write before. My love to him.
Ever yours,
T. WOOLNER.
Thanks for your kind letter.

T. WOOLNER TO F. T. PALGRAVE

29, *Welbeck Street, W.,*
April 26, 1876.

DEAR PALGRAVE,
You will see by the enclosed that I have got you many lots,[1] all good, and most of them cheap. . . .
They are so lovely that they must wait awhile before I can tear my heart to part from them. I got a few bargains. To my mind the most valuable of all the lots was 94—Portrait of Flaxman by himself: an inimitable chalk drawing highly finished, and certainly the best portrait of him in the world. I gave . . . guineas, but would not take 10 times that sum for it. It is life size. . . .
Nearly 12 at night tired, and anxious for a smoke and read before going to bed.
Ever yours,
T. WOOLNER.

In 1876 Woolner exhibited at the Royal Academy the marble bearded bust of Tennyson, which he had modelled in 1873. It is the greatest bust of the Sculptor, a majestic

[1] Flaxman drawings.

X

and idealistic representation of the Poet Laureate. The
bust was purchased after the Sculptor's death, for the
National Art Gallery at Adelaide, and was unveiled by
King George V, when Duke of Cornwall and York, on
his world's tour in 1901.

Australia owns Woolner's finest marble bust and his
greatest bronze statue—that of Captain Cook at Sydney.

Many people wrote to the Sculptor after the portrait-
bust or medallion had been received home, to express their
pleasure and increasing pleasure in it, and that the more
they became acquainted with his work and the longer they
lived with it the more they rejoiced in its possession; as
an instance Mrs. Tyndall wrote in January, 1877 : " I cannot tell you what *delight* the medallion gives me; I feel
more pleasure in it every day, and my gratitude to you for
all the care and labour you have bestowed upon it grows
proportionately. Pray accept my most heartfelt thanks."

So, in judging of the permanent delight a portrait gives
and of its real excellence one must live with it for some
time, when if it truly reveals the person represented, each
day it becomes more admirable and more satisfying. That
is why, as a rule, photographic portraits fail so often to
please for any length of time—the reason probably being
partly that they are taken in an instant, and that instant
naturally only gives a passing expression or phase; whereas
a serious artist studying a face before him for many days
and for many hours at a time is enabled, if he tries, to
represent the real personality of the sitter.

And if with insight goes skill of execution, one has a
perfect portrait.

Among the distinguished men who sat this year for their
portraits were Sir John Simon, and Professor Huxley, who
gave Woolner sittings for the bust he modelled in June
of 1877.

In 1877 Woolner was elected Professor of Sculpture at
he Royal Academy—he resigned the position in 1879,
never having given any lectures. He used to say he was
the best professor there ever was, for he only professed
and never practised ! He wrote out two or three lectures
which were never delivered, but he could not give the time
to finish the series and compose the required number. Of

THE WATER LILY, 1884

[*To face page* 306.

the lectures he did write, one is called " Introduction," one is on " Conception " and one on " Finishing "; they were technical lectures suitable for students, it is to be regretted they were never given. Woolner taught in the Academy Schools; his visits were much appreciated by the students—and he enjoyed teaching them.

Woolner's half-lifesized statuette of Godiva was exhibited at the Royal Academy in 1878. Mr. F. G. Stephens, the art critic, writes of it as " the stately and beautiful statue in marble of Godiva disrobing, letting the last white garment of her sacrifice glide downwards to her feet," and describes her as so " gravely passionate and intensely pure—she thinks less of her nakedness than of her reward." Her face has that far-away look of unconsciousness which the face of such a woman bent on so great a deed of self-forgetfulness, would have.

William Allingham to T. Woolner

18, *Neville Street,*
Onslow Gardens, S.W.,
March 6, 1878.

My dear Woolner,
I am much gratified by your gift. Photography does specially well for bas-reliefs.[1] There is no modern sculpture work to compare with these, if I had to choose I should perhaps name " Achilles shouting " as my first favourite.
Always very truly yours,
W. Allingham.

William Allingham to Mrs. Woolner

Shere, Surrey,
June 25, 1878.

My dear Mrs. Woolner,
Your letter this morning interested me so much that first I grunted to think that *Fraser* was *just printed* for July, next I felt inspired (?) to write some lines and send them to the *Athenæum* journal. I did write some and why I send them now to you is to ask if they will do the work of art discredit, by blundering or otherwise. Tell me frankly how they strike you, and *is there* an " outstretched hand " ? (I forget and have nothing to refer to.) Also, is the word " mountain " at all allowable for the site,

---

[1] The three bas-reliefs around the Gladstone Bust at the Bodleian, Oxford.

say by a stretch? I don't like "headland" and "sea and land." And is it near Sydney?

If you think it *will do* please send it at once to post in the enclosed cover for both subject and artist have my full sympathy.

We have taken on our Cottage here till Sept. 1. Will you both come down to see us some Sunday?

In haste, always yours truly,

W. ALLINGHAM.

A STATUE FOR SYDNEY, NEW SOUTH WALES

Cook, mariner of Whitby, gave the chart
Another England in the great South Sea.
Lo, re-embodied now by Woolner's art,
The bold and honest Spirit! who once more
Will voyage to that Australasian shore,
The fog-bank show'd him, lifted suddenly:
Bearing a message, without tongue or pen,
As brief, as full, as English words could say.
There on his breezy column will he stand,
The bloodless conqueror, viewing sea and land.
An English city, in whose deep blue night
For Charles's Wain the Southern Cross hangs bright,
Ships from old England gliding up the bay,
    And signify with that uplifted hand,
(The gesture once of joy—astonished heart,)
  "Greeting to all my Brother Englishmen!"

W. ALLINGHAM.

June, 1878.

(Printed by kind permission of Mrs. Allingham.)

WILLIAM ALLINGHAM TO T. WOOLNER

Shere, Surrey,
August 10, 1878.

MY DEAR WOOLNER,

Best thanks for the letter to the Lion of Redhill, delivery delayed by Whooping cough, caught from my children, a tedious thing but which I hope to get rid of before all the corn is cut. Congratulations on your cottage and your love of cottage life. Live and prosper!

Yours always,

W. ALLINGHAM.

I put the Cook lines (full number) into last *Fraser.*
I have seen the statue with admiration.

CHAPTER XIX

Mr. W. Aldis Wright, the Cambridge scholar and the authority on Shakespeare, stayed with Woolner and his family at Cranesden in October, 1880—and while there he told the following anecdote among many others.

A literary young lady wished to write an epic poem on "The Fall of Man" and began thus—

"Man was made perfect, and he—"

but could get no further, and left her writing lying on the table. A young wag coming in finished it off with—

"Would have remained so, but She!"

In the beginning of the winter Woolner began to write his poem of "Pygmalion," which when completed his friend Aldis Wright criticised for him.

T. Woolner, R.A., to Vernon Lushington

29, *Welbeck Street, W.,*
February 27, 1879.

My dear Vernon,

Pray do not mention trouble, The young lady being a daughter of an English officer is enough and to spare, beside the fact of your being interested in her. Mrs. Wood has been singularly misinformed to think the Council of the R.A. regards the tenderness of youth or the totterings of age. The truth being that they know nothing whatever of either beyond what the work itself says. I sat on the Council for two years and saw Fathers, Brothers, Friends sit like imitations of Rhadamanthus while sons, daughters, brothers and dearest friends' works were remorselessly rejected. These worthies may be wrong in their judgments, but I think no body can mean to be more just than they are in the selection of works for Ex.

309

If Mrs. Wood sends a letter containing title of Picture, Name & address of Artist and price, I can send it on to the R.A. . .

Ever truly yours,
THOMAS WOOLNER.

W. ALDIS WRIGHT TO T. WOOLNER

Chapter Library,
Westminster, S.W.,
May 18, 1881.

MY DEAR WOOLNER,
Your letter has found me here working through the second week of revision with a cold caught in the service. I feel inclined to envy you in the quiet of Cranesden, but the term is so short that after this work is over I must stick to Cambridge till the end.

When " Pygmalion " comes I will do my best to leave no joint in your armour for the critical gnats to get in their stings.

Yours ever,
W. ALDIS WRIGHT.

CARDINAL NEWMAN TO T. WOOLNER

Birmingham,
December 21, 1881.

DEAR MR. WOOLNER,
Your very kind present [1] came to me yesterday. I began to read it directly with much interest. I doubt not that the more I read the more I shall be struck with its poetic beauty. It is indeed very beautiful, though not so severe perhaps as would suit the taste of the old classics.

Thank you very much and believe me to be
Most truly yours
JOHN H. CARD. NEWMAN.

T. WOOLNER TO RT. HON. W. E. GLADSTONE

Garrick Club,
December 20, 1881.

DEAR MR. GLADSTONE,
Mr. Frith told me a few days back, that you mentioned my poem of " My Beautiful Lady " to him, but that you had not heard of another of mine just published. I

---

[1] The poem of " Pygmalion."

have asked Messrs. Macmillan to send you a copy if you will kindly accept it. I thought you would before now have forgotten the existence of my former poem or should have sent this before.

The subject, " Pygmalion," has not been understood as an artist understands it, and I hope I have succeeded in making the story intelligible.

Please do not reply for you must be overwhelmed with letters that must have a reply.

Believe me,
Very truly yours,
Thos. Woolner.

Rt. Hon. W. E. Gladstone to T. Woolner

Hawarden Castle,
Chester,
December 22, 1881.

Dear Mr. Woolner,

I am extremely obliged to Mr. Frith if as you say he made the suggestion which has procured for me an early sight of your (to my mind) very beautiful Poem,[1] which I am reading with much enjoyment.

It shows how close you sit to the centre of your art, and how you have drunk in its soul.

This making of Hebe is full of interest for me: as I believe myself to have done one and only one good thing in my life for Art, *i.e.* to have been the first to teach and preach that the secret of excellence in the Art of Greece, lay in the anthropomorphism, or, as I commonly call it, theanthropism, of the Olympian religion.

Do I understand you to have the City Commission for a bust of me? If so, I shall be sincerely glad, and ready to hear from you at any time about your preparations & plans.

Always faithfully yours,
W. E. Gladstone.

T. Woolner to Rt. Hon. W. E. Gladstone

29, Welbeck Street, W.,
December 26, 1881.

Dear Mr. Gladstone,

It pleases me to know how aptly my translation of the maid Ianthe into the Goddess Hebe helps to

<hr>

[1] " Pygmalion."

illustrate your doctrine of the human nature in the great Olympian Gods. I think, if I may venture to say so, that you are not fair towards yourself in thinking this the only good you have done for art. I speak from impression and not distinctly from memory but I think you were the first person in power to recognize the importance of our Water Colour School. Water Colour Drawing is one of the most perfect arts of the world and in its highest development belongs exclusively to us, and when you honoured Sir J. Gilbert as President of the Chief Institution, you gave that public sanction which placed it level with the other great arts. Your letter was a great gratification to me; and I have received similar ones in the kindliness of their expression from the Master of Trinity, Cambridge, Mr. Munro, the Editor of " Lucretius," and from Cardinal Newman, so that I am tempted to the belief I have not wholly wasted my time in writing Pygmalion's story. I have the commission to do your bust, for Guildhall whenever you can give me the sittings and will begin whenever it will suit your convenience. I was half engaged to go to Athens this winter, but put it off chiefly on account of doing this Bust; and considered it too important a matter to trifle with.

Believe me,
Very truly yours,
Thos : Woolner.

[April 22, 1882.] Woolner was invited by the committee of the Urban Club, a literary Club which numbered many members, to give them a speech on Shakespeare on their annual Shakespeare Night and after much consideration he consented. Having touched on his doubt of being able to interest them he began his speech by referring to the criticisms of the learned which attacked Shakespeare for borrowing many of the wise axioms of the great Classic writers, and then continued :—

" Can it in any way modify or diminish the proportions of greatness that greatness uses an inheritance common to the human race ? The wisdom handed down to us by our forefathers; as they have handed down to us knowledge of how to grow, grind and bake corn for our food; the use of the loom for our textures; the handling

SIR STAMFORD RAFFLES
Colossal statue for Singapore, 1887

of arms for our defence. We all know, gentlemen, it is not the material, but use of the material, that marks the difference. There shall be two men, one a dauber, and the other a gifted artist. They shall both buy their canvasses, their brushes, their pigments of the same colourman. With materials absolutely similar, the one by his utmost efforts shall produce a result most distressing to behold, whereas the other transforms his colours into lures that catch sunbeams; these by magic he fixes in lovely shapes upon his canvass; concentrates them to a glory whose radiance shall illumine a remote posterity. . . .

" In the genius of our mighty one (Shakespeare) imagination rose to its zenith and sheds its glory on us all. . . . Many years ago I was elected into a literary club similar to yours, gentlemen, but on a smaller scale. It was founded by Charles Dickens, Douglas Jerrold, Jessel, Hawkins, Serjeant Parry and others, most of them gone into the mystic past, or have become so famous they can spare no time now for the little Club. Being indulgent and complimentary to a new member the committee asked me to take the chair on their next Shakespeare Night; but Chairmanship being as far from my habits as making watches or silk stockings I reluctantly declined. Some weeks after this, enjoying myself with the other members after dinner, with no preliminaries, although I had refused, with a splendid audacity characteristic of him up rose Mr. Hepworth Dixon and proposed I should take the chair at the next Shakespeare Dinner. This was seconded and carried with such cordial unanimity that I had not the heart to refuse.

" Well, said I, but what am I to say of Shakespeare? To talk of him is like talking of nature in general; how is one to begin? ' Give us a discourse on the illustrations of Shakespeare.' . . .

" I thought the subject over and came to the conclusion that the most significant illustration of a man's works and a man's life was in a man's own countenance; where every passion, every thought, every act, and every impulse to act or refrain was written in unerring lines and touches on an infallible index. We may err in the reading, but the soul never errs in the writing. It is a hard book to read; and if scanned too closely adds not to our comfort. It was because he knew one, . . . made Shelley pen the famous sonnet—

> ' Lift not the painted veil which those who live
> Call Life. Tho' unreal shapes be painted there
> And it but mimic all we would believe
> In colours idly spread.'

" Thomas Carlyle had told me that Sir F. Chantrey expressed an opinion the Stratford Bust was taken from a cast after death; but as he gave no proofs in support of his belief I was no wiser, and felt a great desire to examine the work myself. I had long wished to see the Stratford country, and went with a literary friend. We wanted to see where our poet had first seen the light and where it last closed from him. The streams and the woodlands, the green fields and hedgerows; the pleasant spaces by the river where he gathered those flowers he took with him to refresh and delight old London so many generations past. Flowers that have not dried, or become faded. Flowers that cease not breathing their ethereal sweetness whose cups are yet filled with immortal light !

" We know in simple description of nature, our poet to be unapproachable, but I think the fullness of his love for country scenes is more indicated in touches that illustrate some purpose in the great structure of the drama; as for instance when Henry IV reprimanding Prince Hal warns him by Richard's example in making himself too common with the populace when

> ' He was but as the cuckoo is in June,
> Heard, not regarded.'

We went into the church between morning and afternoon services and had the good fortune to find the sexton, whom I asked to get a ladder to enable me to mount and examine the bust. . . . Whether to punish me for faults already committed, or whether by pain and tribulation to fit me for a better world I know not, but it does chance, I believe, that I have done more likenesses from casts after death than any other alive, and I hope for their former happiness more than any persons before; and therefore in this experience of reading a cast from death over my fellow creatures I occupy what may be justly called a sad pre-eminence. I found the form of the skull, so far back as I could trace it, good. The forehead, temples, brow; the space between the eyebrows and partly down the nose were also good. The cheekbones were true to nature, and the spaces between the cheekbones and the nose tenderly rendered. The cheeks were fairly good to the junctions of the double chin, where were genuine touches of truth. The eyes were dead eyes, with but little knowledge of form or attempt at expression; the lids above and below being merely conventional lines of weak ovals. The lower half of the nose was poor with no breath of life in the nostrils. The length of the upper lip exceedingly long; and the mouth if not altogether without form was certainly void. The chin could not be seen for scratchy lines intended for what we now call an imperial. The hair was utterly bad, and could be known as the symbol of hair only by its position on each side of the head. These, gentlemen, were the facts; and they told me the Bust was done from a cast taken after death by a rude sculptor; but by one who conscientiously did the best he could according to the knowledge he possessed.

" Now I will endeavour in the best way I can to offer you the proofs. The skull, forehead, temples, brow, space between the brows, and in part down the nose, the cheek-bones; spaces between them and the rise of the nose; cheeks and double chin were good because these are the parts least affected by death, and the plaster or wax used in taking the cast after death. The eyes were bad because the cast could not help the sculptor there. The lower portions of the nose and nostrils would have sunk in death because they are of cartilage and flesh, and the sculptor could not compensate the defects by knowledge of form. The upper lip was so long because the nostrils had shrunk upwards and the lips had dropped; chap-fallen is the old

phrase of the time, and the sculptor knew not how to lift
them into the smile of life, and left them perforce void of
animation but not void of meaning, for we see in it the lack
of all expression, a pathetic proof of the sculptor's incom-
petency.   The hair on the chin and sides of the head being
plastered down for the purpose of taking the cast, gave no
aid save as to position, hence their inadequate rendering.
All the features that could be faithfully copied, allowing
for the rudeness of art in both cases, correspond with the
Droeshort portrait, which, you know has the sanction of
Ben Jonson's authority; and between the two, with the
aid of a little imagination and observation of nature, we
may fairly construct a credible similitude.   If, gentlemen,
you have followed closely what I have told you, which in
reading casts after death, is the expressed experience of
my life, you now know the Stratford-on-Avon Bust as well
as I know it myself, . . . I know of no illustrations till
Al. Boydell made his great attempt at the end of the last
century; the first volume being published 1803.

"But the Masters of Music were not idle.   They did their
duty; and transcended duty, winging beat for beat with
our poet to his highest flight.   When we think of Purcell,
Bishop, Arne. . . . we can but feel those divine Masters
heard spheral music, and have given us strains of that ante-
natal song our poet, during his earthly life remembered in
faint catches, and in his own fair language strove dimly
to hint : for melodies of such ineffable sweetness must
surely be more the breathing of Immortals, than notes
touched from instruments made by human hands."

Woolner then, before proposing the toast of the evening
asked permission of his hearers to bring to their recollection
the Poet's treatment of flowers.

" Perdita at the Shepherds' Feast distributed flowers with
every charm of quality specified—

> ' Daffodils
> That come before the Swallow dares and take
> The winds of March with beauty, violets dim,
> But sweeter than the lids of Juno's eyes,
> Or Cythera's breath.'

And Ophelia when giving flowers—

> ' There's rosemary, that's for remembrance,
> And there is pansies, that's for thoughts.'

But there is one little flower she offers without epithet or circumstance. It is the first to delight our baby-hood; an enjoyment throughout our lives; and when even flowers can no longer gladden, brightens the grass upon our graves. She offers it merely saying ' There's a daisy.'

. . . . . .

" I now ask you, gentlemen all, to drink to the memory of William Shakespeare."

The little club (" Our Club ") alluded to was a small literary club made up more or less of men of note. Besides the names mentioned in this speech, it numbered among its members the great Sanscrit scholar, Dr. Ginsburg, a great friend of Woolner's, and a great admirer too. Dr. Benjamin Richardson, the famous advocate of teetotalism, was another member; Walter White, the secretary of the Royal Society, another; and Dr. Diamond, a delightful personality and most hospitable host, whose dining-room at Twickenham House was lined, one might say, with teapots : teapots of all sizes, shapes and ware— a fascinating and unusual collection. Dr. Diamond was a picturesque figure with his pink face, thick, snowy hair, and bluest of eyes; he had many a queer and interesting tale to tell, and gossip of the Palace at Kew and of its inmates in the days of the Georges, when, owing to financial reasons or for economy the fireplaces were filled with fennel in the summer and with holly in the winter ! Dr. Diamond was one of the first really good amateur photographers, and his prints are uncommonly full of detail, and would hold their own with any portraits done by amateurs now, his photograph of Douglas Jerrold being exceptionally good.

" Our Club " met once a week between October and May and dined together. It was a most friendly, cosy club, and Woolner went there very often. His chief club

was the " Athenæum," to which he was elected an honorary member in 1869. The " Cosmopolitan " was one he
attended oftenest in earlier years, and about 1861 he went
there continually, meeting a very varied and distinguished
company. Although very fond of his home and home life
he went to his clubs pretty constantly, and after dinner
would often drop in for a pipe and chat. He was a member
of the " Savile," the " Savage," and a life member of the
" Garrick " since 1865, and at the latter he would entertain at dinner his special friends. It is impossible to name
all the friends Woolner made during his life; many of the
club friends were very interesting men and genial companions—actors, writers, lawyers, newspaper writers and
business men. He was a member of several other clubs,
and for a time belonged to the Reform Club, from which
he resigned in 1871.

He belonged to several societies : to the Society for the
Promotion of Hellenic Studies, and for some years he
belonged to the Burlington Fine Arts Club and to the
Statistical Society; he was a member of the Rabelais
Club, of which the well-known novelist Walter Besant
was secretary. Woolner was a great raconteur, and had
a store of amusing anecdotes and interesting facts which
he related with much vivacity.

During a dinner at a country house where Woolner was
staying, a man of science present was arguing with a
neighbour about the theory of spontaneous combustion
and explaining its horrors, and discussing the possibility
of the danger to a person, sodden with spirits, smoking or
going near to a candle or any open light, for fear of ignition.[1]
When the butler left the room the host turned to his
scientific guest and said : " You have done a very good
deed talking about spontaneous combustion : I noticed
O'C. turn pale—he is an excellent servant but he is too
fond of drink, this will be a good warning to him." Very
soon afterwards the butler returned with a Bible which he
took to the clergyman present saying : " Swear me, Sir,

[1] See Charles Dickens's *Bleak House*, 1st ed., 1853, p. 320.

swear me—I want to be sworn this minute." "But not now — afterwards." "No, Sir, now," and placing his hand on the Bible he said solemnly : "I, Patrick O'C. swear *never*, *never*, *never to*—blow out a candle again " !

The following story was another Woolner was fond of telling.

Years ago a Viceroy of Ireland, a merry soul, and his equerry were out on a frolic one night and went to a little inn famous for the excellent punch brewed by the landlord ; after spending a cheery evening his Excellency called for a last bowl of punch, which mine host made especially tasty. So delighted was the Viceroy he called to his friend with him for his sword and telling the landlord to kneel tapped him on the shoulder saying " Arise, Sir Peter." The next morning the equerry talked over with his superior last night's escapade and they agreed they must hush it up. " Go and offer him a hundred pounds to forget his knighthood," said the Viceroy. The messenger went and represented the case and urged the old fellow to forget the whole affair as nonsense, offering him at the same time the hundred pounds. He answered *He* didn't care for the title, he'd much rather have the hundred pounds, " but," he added regretfully : " Her ladyship's uncommon proud ! "

CHAPTER XX

T. Woolner to Rt. Hon. W. E. Gladstone

29, *Welbeck Street, W.,*
May 22, 1882.

Dear Mr. Gladstone,

You will remember that Sir Henry Parkes ordered a replica of your Bust that I am doing for the City of London to be placed in the new Executive Buildings at Sydney. Since ordering your Bust he has thought of giving me a commission for the four other Prime Ministers of England since the introduction of responsible government in the Colonies :—

Earl Russell	Earl of Derby
Lord Palmerston	Earl of Beaconsfield

Sir Henry tho' satisfied himself would be glad of an opinion to justify him; therefore may I ask you to kindly let me know if you approve of his idea as that will entirely satisfy him.

Pray pardon my troubling you, but we could decide on no other opinion that would satisfy us both.

Believe me truly yours,
Thomas Woolner.

Rt. Hon. W. E. Gladstone to T. Woolner

10, *Downing Street, Whitehall,*
May 30, 1882.

Dear Mr. Woolner,

I am extremely pleased to find that your bust of me is so highly appreciated.

It is a very great compliment to us both that Sir H. Parkes should have desired a replica for New South Wales; but the greater half is yours.

I am a little embarrassed about the question of the four;[1]

---

[1] A series of busts of English Premiers Sir Henry Parkes had commissioned Woolner to execute for Sydney.

320

and I am not quite certain of the date from which responsible government in N. S. Wales should be reckoned. Lord Russell, however, the first on the list, was the first Minister I think who ever recognised responsible government for Colonies. When once acknowledged, it could not but spread. Without going minutely into particulars, I have no doubt that carrying this series of busts to Sydney would be a graceful and acceptable testimony to the good relations subsisting between these locally severed branches of our race, & would tend to confirm them.

Very faithfully yours,
W. E. GLADSTONE.

In July, 1882, Woolner suffered a great loss by the death of his younger son Geoffrey, a lovable boy with unusual charm of character, without guile, endowed with the gift of humour and showing at that early age a true appreciation of poetry. He died at Marlborough College of scarlet fever, aged fourteen and a half years, and was buried in Preshute Churchyard. Thus came the first break in the Sculptor's family of two sons and four daughters.

Extract from a letter of W. M. Rossetti to T. Woolner; after expressing his sympathy for the loss of his son Geoffrey he continues : " July 23, 1882—That drawing [1] of my brother will be *most precious* to me. I thank you very sincerely for thinking of me in connexion with it : it will remain one of my most valued possessions. Of course it will be a satisfaction to me on all accounts to include the portrait in the collection at the R.A."

Early.

RT. HON. W. E. GLADSTONE TO T. WOOLNER

10, Downing Street, Whitehall,
October 30, 1882.

DEAR MR. WOOLNER,
It was to my wife and me matter of the utmost satisfaction to see the bust which you have recently executed of me for the Guildhall. My eye and judgement are worth very little and therefore I will not trouble you with

---

[1] This is the portrait of D. G. Rossetti by W. Holman-Hunt, sent out to Australia to Woolner, with the others mentioned in the letter from Rossetti, April 16, 1853.

Y

dwelling on my own very warm admiration.   But my wife
is I think both ready and accurate, as I have often observed,
in the faculty of immediate appreciation, and her tribute is
rendered not less freely, not less abundantly, than my own.
. . . . You will I hope have a day of lively pleasure at the
Guildhall tomorrow, and I remain

Most faithfully yours,
W. E. GLADSTONE.

THOS : WOOLNER, ESQ., R.A.

Please to let my name be put down for five of the earliest
of the small guinea reproductions.[1]

T. WOOLNER TO RT. HON. W. E. GLADSTONE

29, Welbeck Street, W.,
October 31, 1882.

DEAR MR. GLADSTONE,

Accept my thanks for your most kind letter which
I showed to the Lord Mayor, who pronounced it a " valuable and interesting letter."

He and the City Lands Committee were enthusiastic
in their praises of the likeness, and said the severe classic
treatment[2] was most appropriate to your character, and
befitting your scholarly accomplishments.   In fact the
handsome eulogy of the Lord Mayor upon your career,
and position in the Empire and the way I had rendered
your countenance were all the most exacting could desire,
and I must add very comforting as showing that my close
labours have not been in vain.

Believe me truly yours,
THOMAS WOOLNER.

I shall not forget Plato on the 8th !

COVENTRY PATMORE TO T. WOOLNER

Hastings,
March 18, 1883.

MY DEAR WOOLNER,

My wife and I would be much pleased if you and
Mrs. Woolner could come on Saturday in Easter week and

---

[1] Messrs. Elkington reproduced the bust in several sizes.

[2] The block of marble for this bust was sent as a gift by the Greeks.
Woolner said it was the hardest marble he had ever carved.   It came
from the ancient quarries in the Island of Paros.

stay a few days with us. The weather is likely to be fine by then and I would drive you to some places well worth seeing, but which are wholly unknown because they are only forty or fifty miles from London.

I am glad that you think so well of Henry's verses. I have some of his MSS much finer than the *Athenæum* poem. He used to say in fun to his sisters that I should be known to future times as " The Father of Patmore." Had he lived I believe his jest would have come true. His little poems have a manliness and sweetness which reflect his character, and are in strange contrast with nearly all modern verse, the texture of which is either inorganic and gritty as rough-cast, or soft and flabby as the flesh of an unclean salmon.

Ever truly yours,
COVENTRY PATMORE.

T. WOOLNER TO COVENTRY PATMORE

29, *Welbeck Street, W.,*
January 29, 1884.

MY DEAR PATMORE,

Best thanks for proofs, your words are very.encouraging, and if you saw the first sheet you would see that I was profiting largely by your pencil marks. Your suggestion is good, and when I have gone thro' all the proofs and got " revise " I will make use of your kindness, run down and talk over improvements. The truth is I had the whole poem in my mind at once always (as I may say) and good workmanship unless it came naturally, I did not pay enough attention to. . . . Nothing like a " candid friend," for tho' the phrase is used as a joke I am convinced it is the best way of avoiding obscurity and slovenliness. . .

Truly yours,
THOMAS WOOLNER.

COVENTRY PATMORE TO T. WOOLNER

Hastings,
April 15, 1884.

MY DEAR WOOLNER,

Accept my best thanks for the lovely Flaxman, and the Turner, which is like a painted perfume. There are two spaces of wall in my study for which I had nothing good enough. Now these will be filled. I don't think you will regret the work you have put upon your poem.[1] . . .

Yours ever truly,

C. PATMORE.

In 1884 the Sculptor went for two delightful cruises, the first being in April, with Admiral Sir Anthony Hoskins on board H.M.S. *Hawk*, on a coastguard inspection tour around Ireland, beginning at Tory Island and going on to the Giants' Causeway, Belfast, Dundalk Bay, Dublin, Wicklow Bay, Waterford Harbour; and then by the Bristol Channel to England, having visited with the Admiral 109 stations within a month. He describes at Ardglass "the ruins of a castle, built in the reign of King John by De Courcy, who beat all the Irish Kings about here and at last threw off his own King John. On one side of the castle facing South, which is the warm side, there are such numerous patches of yellow wallflowers that the walls look to be almost plated with gold. They begin to bloom in March, continue in rich blossom throughout the summer and do not end till November. All the other sides are dark gray stone and look very gloomy."

The second cruise he went was on board the yacht *Zingara*, as the guest of Sir Donald Currie, starting from Dundee in July to see the midnight sun. They stopped at Stavanger, where on visiting the cemetery Woolner saw, which seemed to him a curious custom, little chairs placed near the graves. On her way to the North Cape the *Zingara* stopped at most of the important and famous towns on the coast, giving the travellers the opportunity of seeing Laps and Finns and taking drives now and again inland to see the country—on one occasion the party surprised a reindeer on the top of a rock they had climbed, and a note in Woolner's diary states " saw eagle chased by a gull." In September the Sculptor went up to Scotland to model portraits of Sir Donald and Lady Currie and one of the daughters.

" Silenus."

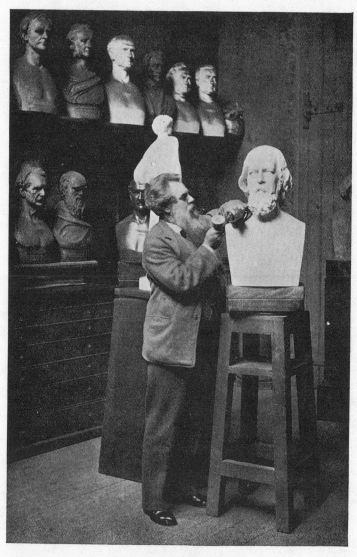

T. WOOLNER IN HIS STUDIO

Printed by permission of Messrs. Speaight.]

[*To face page* 325.

CARDINAL NEWMAN TO T. WOOLNER

July 24, 1884.

DEAR MR. WOOLNER,

I thank you for your new Poem.[1] You have the gift of writing what is *music*, and it is kind in you to send it to me. In some respects I am little fitted to be your critic : for (tho' I am not sure) you seem to me to have some deeper meaning than the smooth and calm tenor of your versification makes necessary, but what this is I cannot determine.

You illustrate by your subject what Gibbon, I think, calls the "elegant mythology" of Greece and Rome—but, as found in the great classic poets, it is severe as well as graceful, and, putting aside other considerations, I prefer, as a matter of critical rule, the severe school.

Excuse a short acknowledgement from an old man, whose brain and fingers move slower than they once did.

Very truly yours,
JOHN H. CARD. NEWMAN.

THOMAS WOOLNER, ESQ.

COVENTRY PATMORE TO T. WOOLNER

Hastings,
May 14, 1886.

MY DEAR WOOLNER,

I have just received a lovely little picture, which must have come from you, as it is in the case in which you received Bertha's drawing for the Academy. How shall I thank you enough ? But how shall I look over your proofs for the future, if, every time I do so, you send me some precious work of art—especially when, in other ways, you have more than cancelled such petty obligations ?

Yours ever truly,
C. PATMORE.

The Spring is in full glory now. Cannot you & Mrs. Woolner spare a day or two at once ?

_____

[1] "Silenus."

T. Woolner to Coventry Patmore

Charmouth House,
Charmouth,
June 18, 1886.

My dear Patmore,

I ought before to have thanked you for sending me
your book, which looks very compact and dainty without,
as befits its contents.

I have sent a copy to Sir Frederick Weld, Governor of
the Straits Settlements, and Lord of the Manor of Chideock
close by here.   He is fond of poetry, and I wanted to pay
him an elegant little compliment, and your book came in
just the thing.   He was a very intimate friend of dear old
Sir John Simeon.   I am much obliged for your having
written to *Spectator* and am not surprized you have received no reply, the fact is he is a queer creature and cannot
in any way be relied on except to do something funny.   It
seems to me, that the boycotting which has been established
against me for 24 years as regards sculpture, has now begun
in literary matters.   This is not to be wondered at and I
have often thought it curious that it has not begun before.
I have 3 girls down here who enjoy themselves amazingly.

Ever truly yours,
Thomas Woolner.

Sir Frederick Aloysius Weld gave Woolner the commission to execute the statue of Sir Stamford Raffles for
Singapore; the Sculptor said it was the most pleasing
public commission he had ever had—there was no committee.   The statue was colossal and of bronze.   The
unveiling ceremony was very imposing: the natives
expressed their admiration of the work, but regretted the
figure had no hat under the burning sun of the Straits
Settlements!

Coventry Patmore to T. Woolner

Hastings,
October 18, 1886.

My dear Woolner,

We have been hunting about for some one to do the
figure vignettes for the " Angel," and have actually been
consulting the only man who could do them—yourself.
The dignity, sweetness, and originality of your vignettes

to the " Golden Treasury Series " and one or two drawings I have seen of yours, shew that you and no other are capable of the thing wanted. I have mentioned it to Bell, who has asked me to write to you about it. Don't say " No " in a hurry. If the work is done, it will be done handsomely in all respects.

Yours ever truly,
C. PATMORE.

Did you see my letter on the Dartford speech in the *St. James's*, a day or two after it was delivered ? If not I think you would like it. I have received a pressing invitation from one of the biggest quarters to write political articles on the strength of it. Fancy my turning politician at this time of day !

T. WOOLNER TO COVENTRY PATMORE

29, *Welbeck Street, W.*,
October 24, 1886.

MY DEAR PATMORE,

. . . I must come down one Saturday and have a chat with you about the illustrations. Were I free and in the habit of sketching I know of nothing that would give me greater pleasure than making a series of poetic designs for your poems, as the quality of the workmanship is of a kind to inspire the finest pencil.

You will be shocked to know that I have purchased another estate in Sussex of about 132 acres near Horsham, which is scarcely more than an hour from London. . . . My land begins opposite Field Place, the birthplace of Shelley; from where I think of running up my cottage I can see Blackdown where Tennyson lives, so you see, I shall be in as it were a poetic atmosphere. I should like you to look the place over some day as your ideas would be good guidance for me. . . .

Truly yours,
THOMAS WOOLNER.

The little estate mentioned in the letter to Coventry Patmore was in Sussex, near the borders of Surrey—a small peasant's cottage stood in the midst of fields half a mile down a winding rough cart-road. Woolner built a good-sized house on to this little cottage and took the keenest interest in laying out the garden and pleasure grounds—for which occupation he had a gift, and the greater part of the last two years of his life were spent going down there to plant and to plan. He had a small farm which gave him about as much bother as pleasure. He got weary of the worries of the farm bailiffs and the expense, as he did with his other country house; and decided to sell the place and had given instructions to an estate agent to dispose of the little property a few months before he died in 1892.

COVENTRY PATMORE TO T. WOOLNER

Hastings,
October 25, 1886.

MY DEAR WOOLNER,

I cannot tell you how much I am pleased by the hope that you will undertake the figure pieces for the " Angel." So long as there was talk of any one else doing them, I did not feel a grain of interest in the project. . . . But it will be very different if you do it. . . .

Come down any Saturday you can, except Nov. 6, when I am going down to Cambridge for a day or two. . . .

Yours very truly,
C. PATMORE.

T. WOOLNER TO COVENTRY PATMORE

29, Welbeck Street, W.,
February 2, 1887.

MY DEAR PATMORE,

Your Sussex Farmer papers are simply excellent. . . . I have thought a great deal about your illustrations but with no effect. The truth is that when I am deeply occupied with one thing I cannot turn to another. I began reading the poem with the best intentions, and with a view to designs, but after a book or two I quite forgot the drawings and became absorbed in the poetry, and not until I had finished did I remember that I had been enjoying myself instead of working as I ought to have been. When out of practice designing is like anything else and gets rusty. . .

You must now begin to see signs of spring in crocuses and daffodils. Happy Man !

Truly yours,
THOMAS WOOLNER.

W. B. Scott to T. Woolner

Penkill,
Girvan, Ayrshire,
July 31, 1887.

My dear Woolner,

I have a pleasant task to perform in thanking you for the two little lyrical poems about Children. My wife is here just now, and we three had a holiday hour in her reading your little book aloud, which she did very well.

It is full of rich and beautiful touches of description of external nature and the aspects of the day. These it appears to me are what you have gone in for more than for anything else. Of beautiful human nature in children I have had few opportunities of judging—to my thinking little boys care for nothing that is not alive, nothing that they can't hurt and appropriate; and little girls nothing they can't appropriate for dress or decoration. What you say of the *Angel in the House* is Pro-di-gious. . . . I knew Patmore very well, that is to say we exchanged presentation copies w^h I still preserve, and I always spent an evening or more with him on my annual visits to town for two or three years. His poems are not the kind of poems uncultivated people w^d care for, are they ? . . .

My dear Woolner,
Ever yours,
William Bell Scott.

Coventry Patmore to T. Woolner

Hastings,
August 23, 1887.

My dear Woolner,

. . . Mrs. Patmore joins with me in hoping that you and Mrs. Woolner and your eldest daughter will be able to come and stay with us for a week, any time after that date [1] that may best suit you. It will be a real treat to all of us if you can come. We are going to spend the fortnight at Chillam—a most lovely old and apparently unknown village about six miles from Canterbury—every house a model of the old English cottage architecture, all the houses forming two sides of a little square " place "—a third side being occupied by the walls & gateway to a Tudor

---

[1] September 12.

Castle and the fourth by a fine old church. It is quite unlike anything else I have seen in England. . . .

Yours ever truly,

C. Patmore.

W. Aldis Wright to T. Woolner

Trinity College, Cambridge,
November 24, 1887.

My dear Woolner,

I was quite unprepared for the surprise you have arranged for me. You told me five years ago when you first proposed my sitting to Ouless that you intended my portrait at some time to come into the possession of the College, but I had no idea that it was coming so soon and I was absent from the Council Meeting at which your letter was read. The distinction you have conferred upon me is only shared by Professor Cayley, whose portrait is in the small Combination Room. All the other portraits are of the dead. I can assure you I esteem it a great honour and can only thank you for the friendly feeling which has prompted you to exaggerate my deserts.

Believe me,

Yours very sincerely,

W. Aldis Wright.

T. Woolner, Esq.

The Rev. Dr. Montagu Butler to T. Woolner

Trinity Lodge, Cambridge,
December 5, 1887.

Dear Mr. Woolner,

I was so sorry to miss you to-day. It has been a day of veritable slavery. It is well really that you were not able to accept my Luncheon proposal for 1.30, for our Council lasted from 11 till all but 2.30. . . .

After the Council followed innumerable letters & a Committee, lasting straight away till 8.15. . . . We must hope that, when we are able to celebrate the Commemoration you will come again among us. By that time the Council will probably have determined the final resting-place, at least for a time, of the Portrait.[1] It has been

---

[1] The portrait of W. Aldis Wright, by W. W. Ouless, R.A., given by Woolner, for whom it was painted, to Trinity College.

removed from the front Hall to the State Drawingroom upstairs.

Believe me to be
Most truly yours,
H. Montagu Butler.

Coventry Patmore to T. Woolner

Hastings,
December 17, 1889.

My dear Woolner,

Your letter is a great relief to me, for, as I get older I value more the very few friends whom death or the vitiating effects of fame have left me.

I bought all last Saturday's papers, to see what they would say about Browning. It was, as you say, a marvellous chaos of silliness. B. was a man of various and remarkable ability. But two things are essential to Poetry. It must be interiorly worthy and externally beautiful. Without a beautiful exterior, however worthy the interior, it is not poetry, any more than a dish of stewed apples is a pie. A pie must have a crust, and a good pie a good crust. Stewed apples with a lid of leather which defies the teeth are even less of an approach to a good pie than the stewed apples would be, if served in an open-dish, *i. e.* prose. In all Browning's 16 or 17 volumes I do not remember as many pages of poetry properly so-called. Herrick is a far better Poet than Browning, though intellectually an insect in comparison.

Yours ever truly,
Coventry Patmore.

W. Aldis Wright to T. Woolner

Beccles,
January 9, 1890.

My dear Woolner,

I have been aware for some time of a strange umbrella in my rooms and did not know to whom it belonged. When I come to town next I will bring it with me. . . .

My interpretation of Hamlet's soliloquy does not in the least interfere with the business of the play. His mind is filled with the idea of suicide as a ready release from his difficulties, and he meditates upon it in all its aspects, his meditation in this as in all other parts of his conduct leading to inaction. All that I dispute is that the first line, "To be, or not to be, that is the question," means "Shall I or shall I not put an end to my existence?" and that this question is repeated in another form in the two lines that follow. The dramatic fitness seems to me the same on either supposition.

I went yesterday in a south fog to Framlingham to see the old tombs of the Howards in the Church. This comes of writing notes on Henry 8. . . .

Yours ever,
W. ALDIS WRIGHT.

T. WOOLNER, ESQ.

COVENTRY PATMORE TO T. WOOLNER

Hastings,
November 24, 1890.

MY DEAR WOOLNER,

I am grieved and disgusted by all you tell me. Every day I live makes this rotten hole, the world, more hateful to me. Only let us try that it may be Purgatory, not Hell to us.

Yours ever,
COVENTRY PATMORE.

The Salters' Company, in May, 1891, conferred on the Sculptor the Honorary Freedom and Livery of their Guild. He was very pleased at this compliment, and much enjoyed the intercourse with his new friends.

In July, before the Banquet to inaugurate the new member, Woolner attended the court to receive the Freedom of the Guild on an illuminated roll presented to him in a silver-gilt casket.

After the feasting was over the Master, Mr. Coventry, proposed the heath of the new member; and Woolner, in acknowledging the honour, replied in an eloquent speech on art and artists.

In 1892 Woolner was working on " The Housemaid," a life-sized figure of a servant girl wringing out the cloth with which she washes the doorstep (a sight which may be seen any morning early in the London streets); it was a subject

THE HOUSEMAID, 1892
Life-size bronze statue.

[To face page 332

which the Sculptor had long wished to do—having noticed the graceful action—he used to say the servant girls in their plain print frocks and caps were the best dressed women in London on week-days, and the worst dressed on Sundays! He finished the clay model, and it had been cast and cleaned up by him a few weeks before his last illness. After his death the model was cast in bronze in time for the Royal Academy Exhibition in 1893, but it was placed in a poor position and could not be seen on all sides, so that Woolner's last work has really not been properly seen by the British public: the central place of honour that year was given to a mass of ferns and flowers.

In the autumn of 1892 Woolner underwent an operation from which he was believed to be recovering, but he died suddenly from a heart seizure on October 7, the day after the death of his old friend Lord Tennyson, the Poet Laureate.

On October 13 Woolner was buried in the churchyard of St. Mary's, Hendon, near a fine old ash-tree. The spot where he lies is marked by a coped tombstone, on which is carved a large thorny rose-stem, blossoming out into wild roses at the head. At the foot, carved in the triangular space, is a design within a circle, of his sculptor's hammer and chisels.

Towards the end of his life false insinuations and ignorant criticisms could not fail to embitter him, and although to his special friends and to his family he was genial, kind and responsive, to the outer world he appeared stern.

He found it difficult to forgive meanness and ingratitude. He was very generous himself, and loved giving presents —even his own works he would often give away, although, as a rule, men do not care to do this, as the great Dr. Johnson remarks.

He was a devoted husband and a kind and indulgent father—interested in his children's pursuits and amused at their opinions of men and politics fearlessly expressed. He was very fond of animals, and was a constant visitor to the Zoological Gardens, generally taking with him one or two children besides his wife. Many of the animals grew to know him, and one little monkey in particular, "Jimmy," would, on seeing him approach his cage, hurry to select from his store of delicacies hidden in hay, his best morsel, a date, and gently offer it to the sculptor, and remain for a long time clinging to his finger chattering his satisfaction.

Woolner had a fine and interesting collection of books, he was a great reader, and his reading aloud was a treat to his children; often after dinner they would assemble in the library to hear him read aloud Borrow's *Lavengro* and *Romany Rye*, or the poems of Crabbe; sometimes he would read them his own poems before they were published. Two of his favourite authors were Jane Austen and Samuel Richardson; Shakespeare was, to his mind, above every other writer, but this preference is almost universal with any great reader and thinker.

Mr. Callander Ross, a friend of later days, wrote this appreciation in the obituary notice of *The Times*—

" The dominant characteristic of Woolner's work, whether in sculpture or in poetry, is its entire conscientiousness and thoroughness. He spared no pains to get at the heart of his subject and to master every detail. . . . His workmanship was as thorough as his study. His time and labour were freely expended in the pursuit of perfection, without regard to the pecuniary considerations that too often take precedence of all else. There are no pot-boilers from his hand, and nothing in the long catalogue of his works that does not display truth of sentiment, purity of taste, and consummate executive ability. In life, as in art, he was the uncompromising foe of shams, of clap-trap, and of superficiality. To other men's work in all departments he applied no other standard than that by which he habitually tested his own, and while indulgent and even tender to honest effort, however imperfect its results, he was a severe critic of pretentious mediocrity. To those who won his confidence he was a firm and generous friend, and to many whose only claim was their misfortune he proved a liberal benefactor. His racy conversation, his pungent criticism, and his rich store of anecdote and reminiscence, drawn from a long and varied experience, will long dwell in the memory of those privileged to enjoy his friendship. Happy in his friends, yet more happy in his family, endowed with keen perceptions and abundant vitality, and blessed with simple, healthy tastes, which are the true sources of perennial enjoyment."

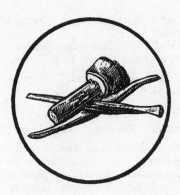

"LABORARE EST ORARE"

LIST OF WORKS

1843. " Eleanor sucking poison from wound of Prince
      Edward." Group, plaster.

1844. " Death of Boadicea." Life-size group, plaster.

1845. " Affection." Bas-relief, plaster.

1846. " Alastor." Bas-relief, plaster.

1847. Adolphus Ashford. Medallion, plaster.
      " Puck." (Exhibited British Institution.) Statuette,
      plaster.
      " Feeding the Hungry." (Boy and Chickens.) Figure,
      plaster.

1848. " Eros and Euphrosyne " (reproduced in black
      Wedgwood).
      " The Rainbow." Bas-relief, plaster.
      " Titania and the Indian Boy." Group, plaster.

1849? " Little Red Ridinghood." Figure (reproduced by
      Copeland).

1849. Coventry Patmore. Medallion, plaster.

1850. Mrs. Coventry Patmore. Medallion, plaster.

1851. Mrs. Orme. Medallion, plaster (not exhibited).
      Rosaline Orme. Medallion, bronze (not exhibited).
      Alfred Tennyson.[1] Medallion, plaster.
      Thomas Carlyle.[1] Medallion, plaster.
      William Wordsworth. Memorial tablet with medallion
      portrait. (Grasmere Church.) Marble.

1852. " England rewards agriculture." Design for medal.
      Design for Monument to William Wordsworth, consist-
      ing of seated figure of the Poet on a pedestal decorated
      with bas-relief " Peter Bell and his Ass," and two
      groups of two figures Father and Son, Mother and
      Daughter.

---

[1] With the medallions of Tennyson and Carlyle Woolner was dissatisfied,
and modelled others in 1855 and 1856.

1853 and 1854. THE AUSTRALIAN PORTRAITS.[1]

W. C. Wentworth. Medallion portrait.
Governor-General Sir Charles Fitzroy. Medallion portrait.
James Martin. Medallion portrait.
Governor Latrobe. Medallion portrait.
Captain Cole. Medallion portrait.
Octavius Browne. Medallion portrait.
John Pinney Bear. Medallion portrait.
Mrs. Bear. Medallion portrait.
Dr. Howitt. Medallion portrait.
Mrs. Howitt. Medallion portrait.
Miss Edith Howitt. Medallion portrait.
Charley Howitt (a child). Medallion portrait.
William Fanning. Medallion portrait.
Mrs. Fanning. Medallion portrait.
Admiral Philip Parker King. Medallion portrait.
Edward Hamilton. Medallion portrait.
Sir Charles Nicholson. Medallion portrait.
W. Macarthur. Medallion portrait.
George Macleay. Medallion portrait.
Mr. Reynolds. Medallion portrait.
James Macarthur. Medallion portrait.
Dr. Bland. Medallion portrait.
Thomas Barker. Medallion portrait.
Portrait of a Lady. Medallion.

1855. *Thomas Carlyle.* Medallion, bronze.

1856. "Love." Half-lifesized. Statuette, marble.
Mrs. Neville. Medallion.
Helen F. Orme. Medallion. (Exhibited at Royal Academy as " Portrait of a Lady.")
Robert Browning. Medallion.
Alfred Tennyson. Medallion.

1857. Lord Bacon. Statue, Caen stone. (New Museum, Oxford.)
Alfred Tennyson. Bust, marble. (In Library, Trinity College, Cambridge.)

1858. Models of Moses, David, St. John, St. Paul (for Pulpit of Llandaff Cathedral).

1859. *Mrs. Tennyson.* Medallion.
George Warde Norman. Medallion.

[1] All these medallions were cast in bronze, and some reduced to quarter size. Small specimens of Governor Latrobe and W. C. Wentworth are in the National Portrait Gallery, London.

Z

1859. *Rt. Hon. Stephen Lushington.* Medallion.
       Thomas Fairbairn. Medallion, bronze.
       Alexander A. Knox. Medallion, bronze.
       Rajah Brook of Sarawak. Bust, marble.
       Edward Henry Lushington. (A child's head.) Bust,
           marble.

1860. *Sir William Hooker.* (Linnean Society.) Bust, marble.
       Professor Sedgwick. (In Trinity College, Cambridge.)
           Bust, marble.
       Edward H. J. Crawford. Medallion.
       Design for Palmer Cross. Marble.

1861. *Sir Francis Palgrave.* Medallion.
       Rev. W. G. Clark. Medallion.
       Rev. F. D. Maurice. Bust, marble.
           Exhibited in Royal Academy 1863.
           Replica in Westminster Abbey.
           Replica in Trinity College, Cambridge.
           The original in Working Women's College.
       John Ashley Warre (Ramsgate). Tablet, marble.
       Professor Henslow. Bust, marble.
       Design for Cawnpore Memorial (not executed).

1862. *William Miller Christy.* Bust, marble.
       "Brother and Sister." (Constance and Arthur.) Life-
           size group, marble. (Exhibited at Great Interna-
           tional Exhibition, 1862.)
       William Fairbairn. Bust, marble. (Exhibited Inter-
           national Exhibition.)
       William Shaen. Bust, marble.

1863. *Archdeacon Hare.* Bust, marble.
       Arthur Hugh Clough. Bust, marble.

1864. The Prince Consort. Statue, Caen stone. (New Museum,
           Oxford.)
       Thomas Combe. Bust, marble.
       Gifford Palgrave. Medallion.
       William Spottiswoode. Bust, plaster.

1865. *John Robert Godley.* Statue, bronze.
           (Exhibited in South Kensington Museum. Erected
           in New Zealand, 1867.)
       Miss Emily Rhodes. Medallion, plaster.
       Professor Cockerell. Bust, plaster?
       Design for Spofforth Cross. Marble.
       Lord Ashburton. Bust, marble.

1865. *Richard Cobden.* Bust, marble. Three replicas were
carved of Cobden's bust: one is in Westminster
Abbey; one in National Portrait Gallery, London;
one went to Napoleon III, Emperor of the French.
David Sassoon. Bust, marble.

1866. *John M. Kemble*, Anglo-Saxon scholar. Bust.
John Fowler. Bust, marble.
Mr. Cox. Bust.
Sir William Hooker. Medallion.
Lord Macaulay. Statue, marble. (Seated figure in
Ante-Chapel, Trinity College, Cambridge.)
Dr. Symonds, of Clifton. Bust, marble.
" *Puck.*" Figure, bronze. (Exhibited Royal Academy.
Modelled in 1847.)

1867. *Dr. John Henry Newman.* (Afterwards Cardinal New-
man.) Bust, marble.
" *Heavenly Welcome.*" Marble monument, alto-relief.
(In memory of Mrs. Archibald Peel and Son, in
Wrexham Church, North Wales.)
Henry Christy. Bust, marble. (In British Museum.)
Henry Christy. Medallion, marble.
Prescott Memorial. Marble. (Recumbent figure and
bas-relief.)
Captain Fowke. Bust. (In Victoria and Albert Museum;
sent to the 1867 Paris Universal Exhibition.)
Mother and Child. Lifesize group, marble. (Called
the Trevelyan Group, executed for Sir Walter Tre-
velyan of Wallington. Exhibited South Kensington
Museum, 1867.)
Alfred Tennyson. Three-quarter medallion. (Modelled
in 1864. Exhibited Royal Academy, 1867.)

Designs modelled for Manchester Assize Courts—[1]

Figures of Alfred, Henry II, Edward I, Randolph de
Glanville, Judge Gascoigne, Sir Edward Coke, Sir
Thomas More, Sir Matthew Hale. Mercy. Justice.
Large statue of Moses.
Alto-relief Judgment of Solomon—figures Good Woman
and Drunken Woman.
Two Alto-reliefs of Historical Subjects.

1868. *Elaine.* Half-lifesize. Statuette, marble. (Three replicas
of this figure were carved.)

---

[1] These designs were modelled by Woolner between 1863 and 1867,
when they were finished. The figures are carved in stone.

1868. *William III.* Statue, marble. (Westminster Hall.)
    Dr. Robert Haines. Bust, marble. (Bombay.)
    Dr. William Hey. Bust, marble. (Leeds Infirmary.)
    Sir Mark Cubbon. Bust, marble. (India.)
    R. E. Ellis. Bust. (Trinity College, Cambridge.)
    W. E. Frere. Bust, marble.
    Thomas Carlyle. Bust, marble. (Modelled in 1865, exhibited Royal Academy, 1868, for Louisa Lady Ashburton.)
    Mrs. Hichens. Medallion.
    William Dobson. Bust, marble. (Cheltenham.)
    Three Bas-reliefs. Marble.
    Thetis coaxing Zeus.
    Achilles and Pallas Athena.
    Thetis and Achilles. (For Gladstone Memorial in Bodleian, Oxford.)
    Rt. Hon. W. E. Gladstone. Bust, marble.

1869. *Sir Bartle Frere.* Bust, marble.
    Joseph Pease. Bust, marble.
    Edward Wilson. Bust, marble. (Public Library, Melbourne.)
    " Ophelia." Half-lifesize. Statuette, marble. (Two or three replicas were carved of this work.)
    David Sassoon. Statue, marble. (Mechanics Institute, Bombay. Exhibited at South Kensington Museum.)
    Mrs. Hall. Medallion.
    Hatley Frere. Bust, marble.
    Design for Neave Memorial. Cross, marble.
    Mrs. Cleverly Alexander. Medallion, marble.
    Charles Darwin. Medallion. (Wedgwood.)
    Lord Palmerston. Statue, bronze. No. 1.

1870. " In Memoriam." (Four Children in Paradise.) Alto-relief, plaster.
    Charles Darwin. Bust, marble.
    Dobson Memorial Tablet. Marble. (Cheltenham College Chapel.)
    Design for Ogle Cross.
    Memorial medallion of Galt, novelist. (Greenock.)
    A. H. Novelli. Medallion.
    Dr. Rees. Bust, marble.

1871. *Sir J. Hope Grant.* Bust, marble.
    Bishop Temple. (Afterwards Archbishop of Canterbury.) Bust, marble.
    Bright. Memorial tablet.
    Dr. Bayer. Bust, marble.

1871. *Lord Lawrence.* Bust.
" Virgilia bewailing Banishment of Coriolanus." Alto-relief, marble.

1872. *Guinevere.* Half-lifesize. Statuette, marble. (Two replicas were carved of this figure.)
Four Bas-reliefs. Bronze.
Decoration of a Memorial Fountain at Wigton to Mrs. George Moore. (Exhibited Royal Academy.) Four *Acts of Mercy :* Feeding the Hungry; Clothing the Naked ; Visiting the Afflicted ; Teaching the Ignorant.
Charles Dickens. Bust, marble.
Mrs. Milnes-Gaskell. Bust, marble.
Sir Bartle Frere. Statue, marble. (Bombay.)
Mr. Tilleard. Bust, plaster.
Design for Lucas Medal for Royal Academy of Music (Mercury teaching a Shepherd Boy to sing).
Sir John Simeon. Bust, plaster.
" In Memoriam G. B." Alto-relief. (A boy in Paradise seated under a jessamine bough. Exhibited Royal Academy.)

1873. *Dr. Whewell.* Statue, marble. (Seated figure in Ante-Chapel, Trinity College, Cambridge.)
John Keble. Bust, marble. (Westminster Abbey.)
Professor De Morgan. Bust, marble.
Dr. Henry Bence Jones. Bust, marble. (Royal In-stitution.)
W. W. Pearce. Bust, marble.
Design for Simeon Cross. (Isle of Wight.)
Memorial Tablet to John W. S. Wyllie.
Professor De Morgan. Medallion. (Design for medal.)
Mr. Knowles. Bust, marble.

1874. *John Hunter.* Colossal bust, marble. (Leicester Square, London.)
Mrs. Alfred Morrison. Bust, marble.
" Ophelia." Bust, marble.
Alfred Tennyson. Bust draped, plaster.
James Milnes-Gaskell. Bust, marble.
" The Listening Boy." (Sketch for imaginary memorial to a deaf child.) Plaster. (*About this date.*)

1875. *Bishop Patteson* Memorial. Marble. (Merton College, Oxford.)
Ransom Memorial Vase. Marble.
Monument bas-relief. *Mrs. James Anthony Froude*, in St. Lawrence Church, Ramsgate. Marble.

1875.　*Sir William Fairbairn*. Memorial Tablet. (Manchester.)
　　　Meynell-Ingram Monument. Marble. (Laughton, Lincs.)
　　　Bluecoat Boy Group. (Lamb. Middleton. Coleridge.)
　　　　Bronze. (Christ's Hospital.)
　　　Winterbotham Medallion.
　　　Lord Lawrence. Statue, bronze. (Calcutta.)

1876.　*Daniel Hanbury*. Medallion, marble. (La Mortola,
　　　　Mentone.)
　　　Alfred Tennyson. Bust, marble. (The bearded bust,
　　　　in National Gallery, Adelaide. Modelled in 1873.)
　　　Lord Palmerston. Statue, bronze. (The second statue,
　　　　the first being found too small when in position in
　　　　Parliament Square.)
　　　"The Crucifixion." Reredos, marble. (St. John the
　　　　Evangelist, Liverpool.)
　　　Lord Sandon. Bust, marble.
　　　Charles Kingsley. Bust, marble. (Westminster Abbey.)
　　　Professor T. H. Key. Bust, marble. (University College,
　　　　Gower Street.)
　　　T. M. Talbot. Bust, plaster.
　　　Professor John Tyndall. Medallion.
　　　Sir Cowasjee Jehanghir Readimoney. Statue, marble.
　　　　(Bombay.)
　　　Sir Cowasjee Jehanghir Readimoney. Relief, marble.
　　　　(University of Edinburgh.)

1877.　*Edwin Field*. Statue, marble. New Law Courts,
　　　　London.
　　　William Fuller-Maitland. Bust, marble.
　　　Edmund Law Lushington. Bust, marble. There was
　　　　a replica. (University of Glasgow.)
　　　Cockerell Medallion.

1878.　*Sir Thomas White*. Statue heroic, marble. (Merchant
　　　　Taylors Company.)
　　　"*Godiva*." Half-lifesize. Statuette, marble.
　　　Sir John Simon. Bust, marble. (Royal College of
　　　　Surgeons.)
　　　John Owen. Medallion, marble. (Owens College,
　　　　Manchester.)

1879.　*Cookson*. Bust, marble. (Peterhouse, Cambridge.)
　　　Professor Huxley. Bust, marble.
　　　John Stuart Mill. Statue, bronze. (Seated figure.
　　　　Thames Embankment.)
　　　Captain Cook. Colossal statue, bronze. (For Sydney,
　　　　N.S.W. Exhibited in Waterloo Place, London, June,
　　　　1878; unveiled in Sydney, February, 1879.)

1879. *W. M. Torr.* Bust, marble.
  James Aikin, J.P. Bust, marble. (Liverpool.)
  Judge Quain. Bust, marble.

1880. *Sir Redmond Barry.* Bust, marble. (Melbourne Free
   Library.)
  W. G. Clark. Bust, marble. (Cambridge.)
  Joseph Chamberlain. Medallion, marble.
  Dr. Percival (afterwards Bishop of Hereford). Bust,
   marble. (Clifton College.)
  Memorial Headstone to *Sir Francis Grant, P.R.A.*
  Judge Keogh. Bust, marble.
  Hon. H. Dudley Ryder. Bust, marble.
  Lord Chief Justice Whiteside. Statue, marble. (Hall
   of the Four Courts, Dublin.)
  W. G. Clark Tablet.
  Sir William Gull. Bust, marble.
  Mr. Cammell. Bust, marble.

1881. *Lord Lawrence.* Bust, marble. (With Star of India.
   Westminster Abbey.)
  "*Enid.*" Half-lifesize. Statuette, marble.
  Design for tomb—Dr. Percy's wife.
  Hepworth Dixon. Three-quarter memorial Medallion.
   (Kensal Green.)
  Colossal Head of Bunyan. Alto-relief, stone.
  Colossal Head of Cromwell. Alto-relief, stone.
  Shakespeare. Alto-relief.
  T. Carlyle. Alto-relief. (Birmingham.)

1882. Design for Science Research Medal. (University College,
   Gower Street.)
  James Spedding. Medallion, marble. (Ante-Chapel,
   Trinity College, Cambridge.)
  E. M. Barry, R.A. Bust, marble.
  Sir Edwin Landseer. Monument, marble. (In Crypt
   of St. Paul's.)
  Design for Percival Cross. (Holywell, Oxford.)
  Earl of Clanwilliam (father of Admiral Earl of Clan-
   william.) Bust, marble.
  George Dawson. Statue, marble.

1883. *Queen Victoria.* Statue, marble. (Exhibited Royal
   Academy, 1883; sent to Birmingham, 1884.)
  Rt. Hon. W. E. Gladstone. Bust, marble. (For Cor-
   poration of City of London in Guildhall. Exhibited
   Royal Academy.)
  Sir William Erle. Bust, marble. (Temple Library.)

1883. *Dorothy.*[1] Medallion, marble.
   Miss Hankey. Bust, plaster.
   Alice Gertrude Woolner. Medallion.
   Clare Woolner. Medallion.
   Phyllis Woolner. Medallion.
   Lord Lawrence. Medallion. (Design for gold medal.)
   Walcott Leigh Browne. Medallion, marble.

1884. *Gleadhall* Tablet. (Foundling Hospital.)
   Earl of Beaconsfield. Bust, bronze.
   Earl Russell. Bust, bronze. (Sydney, N.S.W.)
   "*The Water Lily.*" Alto-relief, bronze.

1885. *Lord Frederick Cavendish.* Recumbent statue, marble.
      (Monument in Cartmel Priory Church. Exhibited
      Royal Academy, 1885.)
   Richard Quain, anatomist. Bust, marble.
   Mrs. Mirrielees. Medallion, marble. (Exhibited Royal
      Academy, 1885.)
   Sir Donald Currie. Bust, marble. (Exhibited Royal
      Academy, 1885.)
   James Barclay, M.P. Medallion, bronze.
   Mrs. Barclay. Medallion, bronze.
   Lord Palmerston. Bust, bronze.
   Earl of Derby. Bust, bronze. (Sydney, N.S.W.)

1886. *Lady Currie.* Bust, marble. (Not exhibited.)
   Miss Currie. Three-quarter medallion, marble. (Not
      exhibited.)
   Professor Munro. Bust, marble. (Trinity College,
      Cambridge.)
   Sir Henry Parkes. Bust, plaster.

1887. *Bishop Jackson.* Bishop of London. Recumbent
      statue, marble. (Monument in St. Paul's.)
   Andrew Knowles. Bust, marble.
   Design for the Brook Cross.
   Sir Stamford Raffles. Colossal statue, bronze. (Singa-
      pore.)

1888. *Bishop Fraser.* Colossal statue, bronze. (Albert Square,
      Manchester.) (Three reliefs on the pedestal of statue
      in bronze.)

1889. *Rev. Coutts Trotter.* Bust, marble. (Trinity College,
      Cambridge.)

   [1] Dorothy, daughter of T. Woolner, R.A., married, in 1900, George
Henry Stephens, C.M.G., who was then in charge of the construction of
the Assiout Barrage, Egypt.

1889. *Sir Joseph Whitworth.* Medallion, marble. (Owens College, Manchester.)
Principal Harrison. Bust, marble. (Muir College, Allahabad.)

1890. *Sir Thomas Elder.* Bust, marble. (University of Adelaide, South Australia.)
The Marquis of Salisbury. Bust, bronze. (Sydney, N.S.W.)

1891. *Sir Robert Rawlinson.* Bust, marble.

1893. " *The Housemaid.*" Life-size figure, bronze. (Exhibited in 1893 at Royal Academy. The model was finished in Autumn of 1892. The sculptor's last work.)

As a rule the dates of works in this list represent the date of exhibition, not when the work was finished. The date on a marble bust means when it was finished. As examples, the bust of Sir William Hooker was finished in 1859, and has that date on the base; but it was exhibited in 1860, which constitutes the date of copyright. The bust of the Rev. F. D. Maurice was finished in 1858, and not exhibited till 1861.

LIST OF WRITINGS

"My Beautiful Lady"[1]: a Poem. 1863. Second edition 1864; third edition 1866. With frontispiece by Arthur Hughes. Published by Macmillan.

"Pygmalion": a Poem. 1881. Published by Macmillan.

"Silenus": a Poem. 1884. Published by Macmillan.

"Tiresias": a Poem. 1886. Published by George Bell.

"Nelly Dale" and "Children."[2] Poems. 1887. Published by George Bell.

"William Mulready": an Essay. 1886.

"William Collins": an Essay. 1886.

"James Chambers, the Beggar Poet." Article in *Nineteenth Century* magazine. 1887.

"A Sea Story." Tale in *The Argosy* magazine. 1888.

"*The Wife*": a Poem.

Woolner designed and drew three frontispieces for books: the most admired and well known being "The Piping Shepherd" for Palgrave's *Golden Treasury*. Next in interest is the frontispiece for Patmore's *The Children's Garland*, and King David for the *Book of Praise;* all these three designs being finely engraved by Jeens.

An engraving after Woolner's Statue of Bacon adorns *Bacon's Essays* ("Golden Treasury Series"), and an engraving after his statue of "Guinevere" forms the frontispiece of the "Idylls of the King," by special request of Lord Tennyson, Poet Laureate.

[1] In 1887 Woolner gave his poems "My Beautiful Lady" and "Nelly Dale" to Messrs. Cassell for their National Library.

[2] The poem of "Children" was written long before its publication with "Nelly Dale."

INDEX

Academy, Royal, 4, 13, 53, 55, 57, 59, 65, 114, 131, 158, 168, 175 (*note*), 189 (*note*), 190, 191, 192, 238, 289, 300, 303, 306, 307, 310, 321, 333
  Schools, 3, 307
Acland, Dr., 123 (*note*), 269
Adelaide (National Art Gallery), 306
" Alastor " (bas-relief), 4
Allingham, William, 9, 55, 71, 118, 154, 184, 199, 234–5, 243–4; 271 (his views on Ireland); 273–4, 275, 276, 297, 307–9
  Mrs. W., ix
Amberley, Lady, 279
Argyll, Duke of, 216
Arnold, Matthew, 145
Art Treasures Exhibition (Manchester), 135
Arts, Society of, 3
Ashburton, Lousia, Lady, 4, 258, 261, 279 (*note*)
  Lord, 203
Athenæum, The, 55, 118, 124, 276, 280, 308, 323

Bacon (statue of), 115, 123, 134
Bailey (sculptor), 64
Barnes, William (poet), 176
Barrett, Mr., 133
Bateman, Edward Latrobe, 14, 17, 18, 31, 35, 47, 50, 51, 54, 56, 57, 60, 63, 69
Behnes, William (sculptor), 2, 3; (painter), 2
Bell, Rev. George C., 299
Bellows, Dr. (of Boston), 143
Besant, Sir Walter, 315 (*note*)
Bland-Sutton, Sir John, 4
Bodleian Library, the, 237, 270, 307 (*note*)
Bonham-Carter, Miss, 129 (*note*), 266

Bourke, Sir Richard, 64
British Institute, 4, 5, 58, 69
British Museum, the, 256
Brodie, 107 (*note*), 165
Brooke, Sir James, Rajah of Sarawak, 148, 152, 153, 155, 158, 159, 160, 165, 167, 168, 171, 197
Brookfield, Mrs. and Mr., 123, 134
Brown, Ford Madox, 14, 46, 54, 69, 71, 186
Browning, Robert, 5, 6, 115, 118, 120–1, 122, 124, 125, 126, 127, 151, 159, 165, 195–6, 215, 216, 244–5, 259, 331
  Mrs. E. B., 103, 116, 123, 124, 125, 127, 133, 151
Butler, Rev. H. Montagu, D.D., 173, 178, 200, 226–7
Buxton, Charles, M.P., 180, 205
Byron, Lady Noel, 193

Cambridge (*see* also Trinity College), 146, 173, 182, 187–8
Cameron (family), 132, 139, 147, 181, 196
Carlyle, Jane, 103, 125, 133, 134, 146, 148–9, 150, 153, 176, 183, 197, 201–2, 203, 216, 226, 232, 254–5, 264
Carlyle, Thomas, 11, 12, 56, 65, 116, 124, 132, 134, 136, 144, 145, 147, 150, 153, 154, 156, 164–5, 175, 197, 216, 228; 232 (with Dickens); 247–8, 249–50, 251–2, 258, 259, 262, 264, 265, 275, 295, 315
Cayley, Professor, 330
Chantrey Bequest, 303
  Sir F., 315
Chapman & Hall, 133, 196
Christie's (sale at), 168, 294 and *note*

347

Churchyard (painter), 287
Clark, W. G. (of Trinity), 146, 182,
    187, 189, 196
Clough, Mrs., 274
Clubs: "Our Club," Athenæum,
    Cosmopolitan, Savile, Savage,
    Garrick, Reform, Burlington
    Fine Arts, Rabelais, 314–15
    (notes); Urban, 313
Cobden, Richard (busts of), 262 and
    note
Cockerell, Frederick (architect), 291
Coleridge Memorial (at Christ's
    Hospital), 299
Coliseum, Regent's Park, 3
College, Working Men's, 155, 157
Collins, 54
Collinson, J., 4, 54
Combe, Thomas (of Clarendon
    Press), 184–5, 194, 236, 240,
    246 (note), 268, 269
    Mrs., 184, 235, 246, 271, 278
Commons, House of, Rossetti on
    frescoes at, 49
Cook, Captain, 295–7 (statue of, for
    Sydney); 306; 308 (poem on)
Cornhill, 274
Cox, David, 135
    Frank R., 160
Critic, The, 55
Currie, Sir Donald and Lady, 324

Darwin, Charles, 197, 283, 284, 288
    W. E., 283
Davy, Dr., 12, 13
Deverell, Walter, 54, 59, 67, 68, 69
Diamond, Dr., 314 (note)
Dickens, Charles, 135, 232; 289
    (bust of); 290, 314, 319
Dilberoglue, Stauros, 300
Dixon, Hepworth, 315

Edinburgh, 119
Elkington, Messrs., 322 (note)
Emerson, R. W., 118, 143, 165
"Eros and Euphrosyne" ("Lanky
    Nan"), 5
Exhibitor, The, 53

Fairbairn children, the, 135, 137,
    138; 140 (and parents); 141,
    149, 171, 186, 205, 215, 216
Fairbairn family, the, 140; (T.) 148;
    152, 153, 154, 160, 162, 165,
    167, 168, 169, 171, 188;

    195 (William); 205, 216, 227,
    228
Fanning, William, 103
Fechter, 290
Fitzgerald, Edward, 277–8, 287
Flaxman (drawings), 305, 323
Fletcher, Mrs., 11
Foley, 168, 297
Fowler, John, 273
Franklin, Lady, 123
Fraser's Magazine, 241, 274, 307, 309
Frere, Sir Bartle, 289
Frith, Mr., 311, 312
Froude, J. A., 128, 129, 147, 161,
    202, 204, 206, 229, 233, 239,
    253, 293 and note, 303–4
    Mrs., 249, 293

Gaunt, Miss, 265, 266
George V., King, 306
Germ, The, 9, 244
Gibson, 135
Gilbert, Sir J., 313
Ginsburg, Dr., 314 (note)
Gladstone, Henry N., 237, 246
    Herbert, 237
    Right Hon. W. E., 178, 229, 236,
    237, 251, 262, 263, 270, 271,
    275, 320–1, 321–2
    Mrs. W. E., 237, 238, 239
"Godiva" (statue), 307
Godley, John Robert (statue), 230,
    241, 247, 280
Grant, Sir Alexander, 161, 162, 163
    Sir Francis, P.R.A., 296
Granville, Lord, 178
"Guinivere" (statuette), 290
Gull, Sir William, 242

Haehnel, Julius, 63, 229, 241, 242
Hallé, Sir Charles, 174
Hannay, 47, 54, 55, 56, 71
Harcourt, Vernon, 161
Hare, Archdeacon, 200, 205; (and
    Mrs.) 227
Helps, Sir Arthur, 129 (note)
    Miss Alice, 129 (note)
Henning, Mr., 3
Henslow, Professor, 205
Hervey, Lord Francis, 292
Hilliard, Mrs., 162
Hogarth Club, 157 (note), 164
Hollis, F., 128
Hooker, Dr. Joseph, 154, 155, 169–
    70, 171, 190, 192, 280–1

Hooker, Mrs., 190–1, 192
Sir William, 155, 171, 172, 175, 186, 188, 189 (*note*)
Lady, 171, 191
Hoskins, Admiral Sir Anthony, 324
" Housemaid, The," 332–3
Howitt, Charles, 60, 103
Edward (son), 20
Godfrey, Dr., 18, 19, 34, 36, 59, 60, 63
Mr., 20, 26, 48, 53
Mrs., 17, 48, 51, 53, 60
Miss, 51, 53, 54, 69, 103
Hughes, Arthur (painter), 54, 253, 254, 264, 267
Hunt, W. Holman, 4, 6, 9, 10, 45, 46, 50, 51, 52, 53, 58, 59, 62 (*note*), 63, 64, 70, 72, 105, 114, 128, 133, 135, 139, 154, 159 (*note*), 180, 184, 185 (*note*), 192, 193, 196, 197, 227, 256, 275, 299
Mrs. (Fanny Waugh), 261, 275
Cyril, 284
Huxley, Professor, 306

Ingres, 6, 294

Jenner, Sir William, 129
Charles, 129, 180, 267
Jermyn, Arch., 240
Jerrold, Douglas, 314 and *note*
Jewsburys, the, 141
Joachim, Dr. J., 174
Jowett, 157, 188, 259

Keats, 275
King, Lady Annabella, 129
Kinglake, 135
Kingsleys, the, 181, 204, 304 (bust of Charles); 305
Knox, Mr., 167, 171, 182

Latrobe (Governor of Victoria) and wife, 14, 18, 34, 53, 63, 103
Lawrence, Lord (busts and statue of), 289
Sir Henry, 137
Lay, Mr., 228, 229
Lear, Edward, 58, 134, 154, 162, 185–6, 196–7, 250, 284–5
Legros, Alphonse, 300
Lewis, John Frederick, R.A., 165, 293, 294 (*note*), 297, 299, 300, 302–3

Lewis, Mrs., 305
Liddon, Canon, 304 (*note*)
Linton (the engraver), 132, 133
Little Holland House, 168
Lloyd, Watkiss, 262
Lonsdale, Mrs., 34
Luchesi, 110, 111
Ludlow, 152, 155
Lushington, Edmund Law, 175
Dr., 122
Edward Henry, 134, 175, 177
F., 196
Stephen, Rt. Hon., 120 (*note*)
Vernon, 120, 122, 123, 131, 133, 140, 173, 177, 180, 292

Macaulay (statue), 195, 217, 218, 241
McCracken (of Belfast), 52, 59, 71
Macmillan & Co., 74, 174, 204, 206, 243
Mr., 146
Macready, 6
Mann, Dr. and Mrs., 122–3
Marochetti, 135, 183, 195
Martineau, Robert, 186
Mrs., 196
Massey, Gerald, 141
Masson, 161, 206
Maurice, Frederick Denison and Mrs., 132, 138, 152, 155, 157, 159, 160, 161, 162, 181, 200
Millais, J. E., 4, 46, 50, 53, 54, 55, 58, 59, 65, 69, 71, 105, 112; 114 (his " Blind Girl "); 121, 130, 192
William, 46
Miller, Mr. (picture collector), 141
Milnes-Gaskell, Miss Cecil, 228 (*note*)
Monteagle, Lord, 139
Moore, Mrs. George (Memorial Fountain to), 290
Morris, William, 143, 284
Moxon, 71, 108, 109, 111, 121, 122
Mulready, W., 135, 165, 281
Munro, 54, 69, 119, 135
Professor, 313
Murray, John, 216

Naftal, Paul, 253
Napoleon, Louis, 144, 183, 262
National Portrait Gallery, 132
Newman, Cardinal, 184 (*note*), 271, 272, 311, 325
Nicholson, Sir Charles, 65
Norman, George Warde, 169

Novelli, A. H., 148, 152, 153, 167, 169, 190, 192, 203, 289

Orme family, the, 22, 35, 39–40, 42, 47, 51, 71
Osborn, Captain Sherard, 228, 229, 239
O'Shea (stonemason), 213
Ouless, W. W., R.A., 330 (and *note*)
Overstone, Lord, 197
Owen, Richard, Professor, 165, 261

Palgrave, Frank T., 149, 154, 157, 162, 180, 181, 192, 198, 199, 203, 205, 206, 207, 213, 227, 236, 253, 256, 263, 264, 265, 266, 267, 272, 278, 279, 280, 305
Gifford, 245, 265, 272, 277
Palmerston, Lord (statue), 280
Paris, 6, 137, 294
Parker, J., 145, 147, 161
Parkes, Sir Henry, 320
Patmore, Coventry, 5, 6, 7, 9, 11, 55, 103, 107, 116, 137, 145, 147, 176, 193, 206, 233, 234, 241, 267, 292, 322–4, 325, 326, 327, 328, 329, 331, 332
Mrs. (" The Angel "), 103, 104, 118, 137, 176, 193, 206
George, 58
Mrs. George, 225
Peel, Archibald, 242 and *note*, 279
Pinchin (the brothers J. and H.), 21, 24, 25, 26, 27, 29, 32, 33, 34, 37, 60
Pre-Raphaelite Brotherhood, 4, 5, 9, 10, 14, 17, 50, 53, 62, 64, 65
Prescotts, the, 139, 197, 273
Prinseps, the, 135, 138, 149, 165, 169, 174
" Puck " (bronze), 4, 6, 7, 65, 283 (*note*)
Punch, ix, 179 (*note*)
" Pygmalion " (poem), 311, 312

Raffles, Sir Stamford (statue of), 326
Read (poet), 123
Record Office, the, 249
" Red Riding Hood," 53
Rhodes, Emily, 264–5
Rice, Spring, Mr., 136, 139
Richardson, Dr. Benjamin, 314
Richmond, Sir William, 200, 203

Rolleston (Rowlson), 178
Ross, J. Callander, 334
Rossetti, Christina, 47, 51, 53
D. G., 4, 5, 6, 10, 19, 44–57, 58, 59, 62, 64, 66–72, 103, 105, 108, 116, 120, 121, 128, 131, 132–3, 321 (*note*)
Maria, 53, 68
W. M., 4, 6, 8, 9, 46, 47, 51, 53, 55, 59, 62, 68, 73, 103, 135, 183, 321
Ruskin, 12, 52, 53, 71, 86–8, 114, 130–6, 138, 144, 183, 203
Ruxton, Mr., 143

Sadler's Wells Theatre, 6
Scott, William Bell, 57, 69; 103 (and wife); 124–5, 126–7, 131, 141, 142–3, 150–1, 229, 329
Seddon, Thomas, 128
Sedgwick, Professor Adam, 182, 186, 187, 188, 189, 202, 203; 204 (bust of); 217–81
Shaen, William, 205
Shelley, Percy Bysshe, 8, 275, 315, 327
Simeon, Sir John, 117, 118, 123, 125, 132, 152, 169, 181, 185, 186, 206, 228, 230–1, 247, 267, 306, 326
Simon, Sir John, 306
Smith, Alexander (of Glasgow), 55
Bernhard, 14, 17, 18, 21, 27, 31, 34, 47, 48, 50, 51, 54, 56, 57, 60, 71
Spectator, The, 65, 124, 326
Stephens, F. G., 4, 10, 45, 54, 57–9, 69, 70, 71, 307
Stone, Frank, 182
Stothard, 161, 162, 163
Stowe, Mrs. Beecher, 55
Swinburne, Sir John, 119
Miss, 119
Symonds, Dr., 262, 263

Tait, 150, 201
Taylor, Bayard, 135
Temple, Dr., 225
Tennyson, Alfred (Lord), 5, 10, 11, 12, 13, 65, 105, 107, 109, 111, 114, 116, 117, 121 (*note*), 135, 145, 147, 159, 169; 179 (poem on his bust); 189, 190, 202, 208, 213, 216, 218, 229, 244, 251, 257, 262, 279, 306, 333

Tennyson, Emily (for Letters see "Contents"), 102 (*note*), 103, 150, 157, 185, 218, 258, 262
  Hallam (Lord), 102 (*note*), 106, 109, 110, 111, 114, 147, 148, 163, 180, 291
  Lionel, 106, 110, 127, 133, 148, 258, 291
Tewsbury, Frank, 135
Thackeray, W. M., 135, 139, 165, 169
Thompson, Professor, 134. 146
Times, The, 182
Trench, Dean, 197
Trevelyan, Sir Walter and Lady, 118, 119, 125, 126, 127 (*note*), 137, 138, 142, 154, 155, 156, 159, 194, 199, 240, 262
Trinity College, Cambridge, 145, 146, 172, 177, 180, 200, 204, 227, 330 (*note*)
Turner, 87, 119, 135, 169, 261, 294, 323

Venables, 176, 197

Ward, Lord, 140
Warre, John Ashley, 202
Waterhouse, Alfred, 233
Watts, G. F., 49, 135, 165, 166
  H. E., 135, 165, 166, 167 (*note*)
Waugh, Alexander, 250
  Alice Gertrude (*see* also Mrs. Woolner), 248, 249, 250
  Fanny (Mrs. Holman Hunt), 159, 261, 275
  George, 248
  Mary, 248
Wedgwood, 5, 283
Weld, Mr. and Mrs., 109, 131
  Sir Frederick Aloysius, 326
Wellington, Duke of, 13, 52, 73
Wentworth, W. C. (statue of), 64, 65, 66, 72, 73, 103, 104, 134–5
Westminster Abbey, 180, 289, 304
  Hall, 3
Whewell, Dr., 178, 179, 180, 200
White, Walter, 314 (*note*)
Wilson, Edward, 185, 195, 196, 249, 256
Wright, W. Aldis, 310, 311, 330, 331, 332
Wood, Mrs., 311
Woodington (the sculptor), 260, 261

Woodward, Benjamin, 156, 205
Woolner, Thomas, R.A., birthplace and origin of name, 1; education, 2; enters R.A. Schools, 3; early exhibits, 3–5; methods of work, vii.; anecdotes, 1–3; association with P.R.B., 4–5; Stanhope Street Studio, 5; visits Paris, 6; at Great Marlow, 7; contributes to *The Germ*, 9; visits Tennyson at Coniston, 11; Carlyle sits for portrait medallion, 11–12; Wordsworth medallion for Grasmere Church, etc., 13–14; sails to Australia in *Windsor*, 15; account of voyage, 15–17; Melbourne, 18–20; life in country and in gold-fields, 20–34, 36–44; Sydney, 44; letters to father from Melbourne and Sydney, 60–6, 72–3; his sea story, 74–82; log on homeward voyage on *Queen of the South*, 82–96, 98–102; correspondence with Mrs. Tennyson from London, 104–16; Browning and Tennyson on medallions, 115; visits the Trevelyans, 118; the Bacon Statue, 123; to Manchester, 135; Tennyson bust for Trinity College, 173; to Cambridge, 182; to Oxford, 194; tour in Devon and Cornwall with Tennyson and Palgrave, 198; Sedgwick bust, and Ramsgate Tablet, 204; buys house in Welbeck Street, 205; his "Fisherman's Story," for Tennyson, 208; Browning on "Fairbairn Group," 216; "The Sermon" (for "Aylmer's Field"), 219; the Godley statue for Sydney, 230; to Hawarden for Gladstone's bust, 237; Diploma work for R.A., 238; Haehnel's "Wild Boar," 242; "Moses" statue for Manchester, 245; engagement to Miss A. J. Waugh, 248; marriage, 253; his studio workmen (with Turner story), 260; Peel Monument and Cobden busts, 262; birth of first child, 264;

"Virgilia," 279; Palmerston statue, 280; as picture collector, 281; elected A.R.A., 289; his country house at Cranesfield, 291–2; the Cook statue for Sydney, 295–7; his portrait by Legros, 300; Continental tour, 300; elected R.A., 302; Professor of Sculpture, 306; his finest marble bust, 306; speech on Shakespeare, 313 *et seq.*; as clubman, 314–15 (*notes*); membership of learned societies, 315; as raconteur, 319; correspondence with Gladstone *re* busts of English Premiers for Sydney, 320–2; death of son Geoffrey, 312; takes two cruises, 324; buys estate near Horsham, 327; becomes Hon. Freeman of Salters' Co., 332; his home life, 333; appreciation of, 334–5. (For Letters *see Contents.*)

Woolner, Geoffrey, 321

Helen (sister), 19, 62

Henry (brother), 70

Mrs. (see Waugh, A. G.), 253, 254, 258, 264, 270, 278, 284, 285, 286, 292, 307

Thomas (father), 15, 59–62,63–4, 70, 72–3, 97

"Woolnerian tip," the, 283, 288

Wordsworth (medallion), 12, 13; 14 (memorial design)